How Race
Is Lived in
America

Correspondents of The New York Times

How Race Is Lived in America

Pulling Together, Pulling Apart

Introduction by Joseph Lelyveld

Times Books
Henry Holt and Company, New York

Times Books
Henry Holt and Company, LLC
Publishers since 1866
115 West 18th Street
New York, New York 10011

Henry Holt® is a registered trademark of Henry Holt and Company, LLC.

Copyright © 2001 by The New York Times
Introduction copyright © 2001 by Joseph Lelyveld
All rights reserved.
Published in Canada by Fitzhenry & Whiteside Ltd.,
195 Allstate Parkway, Markham, Ontario L3R 4T8.

Library of Congress Cataloging-in-Publication Data

How race is lived in America : pulling together, pulling apart / correspondents
of the New York times ; introduction by Joseph Lelyveld. — 1st ed.
    p. cm.
    Originally published as a fifteen-week series in the New York times.
    ISBN 0-8050-6740-X
    1. United States—Race relations—Anecdotes. 2. Ethnicity—United
States—Anecdotes. 3. United States—Biography—Anecdotes. I. New York
times.
E184.A1 H665 2001
305.8'00973—dc21   00-053648

Henry Holt books are available for special promotions and premiums.
For details contact: Director, Special Markets.

First Edition 2001
DESIGNED BY FRITZ METSCH
Printed in the United States of America
2 4 6 8 10 9 7 5 3 1

CONTENTS

INTRODUCTION

When it was over, when we had finally gone to press with the last long article in a lengthy series of articles that strained the very definition of what a newspaper series could hope to be, we tried to pinpoint the moment when our impulse to explore America's shifting racial frontiers had originally sprouted. Some *Times* editors thought it had been around the time of the verdict in the O. J. Simpson trial, in 1995, when the preponderance of whites and blacks reached starkly different conclusions about what it was that was most obvious about this latest "trial of the century." Others thought it might have come even earlier, in the aftermath of the case of Tawana Brawley, the black teenager from the Hudson valley whose frightful tale of having been gang-raped by whites in 1987 ultimately came to be discounted as a negative image of the weirdest and most ancient of white racial fantasies. At a minimum, *Times* editors had had this itch, this wish to do something ambitious on the theme of race in America, for five years before we finally hit on a way into the story that promised to be something other than the usual mosaic of dreary census, school, and income statistics, studded with pious quotations from the civil rights era of blessed memory or from academics and clergymen speaking earnestly.

It's not easy to recall now whether the reasons we had this itch were ever fully articulated in the early phases of the project, but the reasons are obvious enough. There was a sense that the country had long since grown tired of the fact and the rhetoric of racial protest; that blacks and whites who thought of themselves as well meaning, who revered the memory of the civil rights movement, were giving up on each other and the rituals of their fading aspirations. There was a sense as well that racial issues were receding on the political agenda in an age when successful politicians had sought to remove race from the public discourse by promising to "end welfare as we know it" (thereby appealing to working whites with stagnating incomes) while simultaneously celebrating "diversity" as a cardinal American value and source of strength. In boom times, poverty issues were reinterpreted. They were issues not of race or social welfare but of law enforcement and education: 100,000 new cops on the streets, 100,000 new teachers in our classrooms — round numbers slung as slogans, replacing worn-out doctrines of social engineering. And yet, we knew, if this was still America, there had to be *news* about race.

It's almost embarrassing to declare what it finally took to get us mobilized and rolling. We went back to the basics — not, at first, of race relations, but of the news business; that is, we thought of asking questions to which we did not know the answers, in the hope of finding stories that would be surprising, not predictable, stories that in a larger sense might count as news. And, most important, we thought of asking such questions in the private sphere and not, this time, in the public sphere, where the old news was welfare reform and the retreat from affirmative action, signaled by various judicial decisions and the passage of Proposition 209 by California voters. With the welfare rolls, unemployment and crime rates way down and the rate of poverty declining, the white majority seemed unusually placid on issues connected to race. Virtually the only noticeable activity in the public sphere was an exceedingly cautious — yet oversold — effort by a president who, fresh from capturing the welfare program of his opponents, now sought to promote "reconciliation" via "a great and unprecedented conversation about race." ("Dialogue kits" were prepared by a presidential commission and distributed to scores of communities. By most accounts, many monologues by blacks and whites ensued.)

Mere talk about race, we realized, was unlikely to be surprising, was unlikely to be news, at this — also oversold — millennial juncture. But staying with the idea of asking questions to which we did not know the answers, we fastened on the very words *race relations:* What were they actually like now, anyhow, and where did they occur? In the workplace more than anywhere else, given the continuing white flight to remoter, whiter suburbs, we surmised, but also in schools and perhaps churches. For the first time in our history, it was not uncommon for whites to be supervised by persons of color. Where besides the armed forces did that happen? Where besides the sports world and entertainment industry were blacks gaining wealth? What was it like to be the single black corporate executive in a room full of white peers? When a city was racially polarized, how did a multiracial police squad cope? What was the racial story of competitive sports teams? The questions spilled out, and suddenly we were in a realm where the answers were no longer obvious, where the reporting opportunities seemed rich rather than dutiful. We would simply find real stories of real people—maybe no more than two or three in each narrative—whose lives and circumstances spanned this great and enduring fault line in American life.

Simply? It turned out not to be simple at all. Except perhaps on afternoon television, real people don't normally speak in sound bites or partake in media events. Their stories unfold over time in all their complexity, the patterns emerging only gradually to the beholding of a patient onlooker who has won their confidence and therefore the opportunity to serve as a sympathetic witness. And if this is true in general, it is exponentially truer when the subject under discussion is race, in particular on the white side, where, we were to discover, much seems repressed and open conversation about race is considered unnecessary and risky, if not taboo in decent company.

Getting from the generic to the particular—from the initial idea of zeroing in on a black entertainer with white collaborators, or from the thought of camping out in the executive suite of a high corporate official of color—was in many cases the most difficult part of the assignments we gave our fifteen reporters, once the team was assembled. Janny Scott initially hoped to persuade Chris Rock, the black comedian, and his white writers to allow her to see how his jokes with a racial edge evolved. She was turned down, but after many twists and turns, her inspiration bore fruit when she found Charles S. Dutton and the filming of a television movie, *The Corner*, that had few laughs. Amy Harmon ran through a roster of black executives in Fortune 500 companies, eventually persuading the CEO of Monsanto that hers was a worthwhile project, only to run into the killer conditions laid down by his public relations advisers, who wanted what amounted to veto power over all her interviews. Along the way, though, she heard of Tim Cobb, a young black entrepreneur who had made it big with an original idea for the Internet, where color is supposed to have no bearing.

In each case, prospecting for an article's protagonists was an adventure in itself, but even where that process took months, it was only the beginning. The interaction among the subjects was, after all, the actual story, and in nearly every case that actual story had yet to unfold. Michael Winerip could not know, after gaining access to a police narcotics squad in Harlem in the autumn of 1999, that the dramatic climax of his story would come months later, in February, when the jury in the case of Amadou Diallo acquitted the four police officers who had fired forty-one rounds at the young African as he was reaching for his wallet, it turned out, not a gun, in his Bronx entryway. The two women portrayed in Ginger Thompson's piece about the legacy of slavery on an old plantation called Magnolia in central Louisiana — one a proud descendant of the white owners and the other a determined black park ranger — had never met when she began her reporting. Steve Holmes had followed almost two complete eight-week basic training cycles at Fort Knox before his story crystallized.

Looking back, it is clear we had set a nearly impossible standard for a daily newspaper: that we would find original and compelling stories that portrayed race relations today and that we would stay with those stories until we truly understood the backgrounds, motivations and values of our protagonists, the key characters we were writing about. Our shorthand was to say we wanted to "go deep" and "hang in there." If we had known in the beginning what that would really and truly mean — how much time and effort it would take, how many return trips would have to be made — we might well have been daunted. Once we did know, we were too fascinated by what we were discovering to even think of turning back or curtailing the project, which turned out to require the largest commitment of time and talent the *New York Times* had ever made to a single series of articles — larger than even the Pentagon Papers.

There was another promise we made to ourselves at the very beginning: a promise not to be glib in a way that journalists normally consider to be mandatory, not to force all the articles into a thematic grid of our own devising, but rather to tell the stories we found as honestly and directly as we knew how and then leave it to our readers to reach their own conclusions on what our narratives actually meant. In the jargon of the newsroom, we made this revolutionary and humbling promise to ourselves by stipulating from the start that there would be no "nut grafs" in the series. A nut graf is the paragraph that comes high up in a newspaper article and points as clearly and succinctly as possible to the themes that give the article its essential meaning and point. According to our normal standards and practices, running long articles about the real situations of real people without the aid and comfort of nut grafs is an invitation to confusion, even anarchy. What it amounts to, we persuade ourselves with a self-importance that can easily sound patronizing, is asking our readers to set off on an expedition into uncharted territory without a map, compass or declared destination. Here, for once, all our instincts told us to trust our readers to find their own way—or, rather, individual ways into the worlds we hoped to portray.

This was done out of respect for our readers and respect for what you might call the architecture of the series. If our basic concept was valid, the meaning of the articles would not be found simply in each narrative as the reader went along but in the resonance among all the narratives—in their overlay, each one on top of all those that came before, striking a richer chord because of the progression from one situation or sphere to the next. If our basic concept was valid, the meanings would not need to be declared: they would emerge forcefully.

Plainly, this was asking a great deal of newspaper readers used to dispensing with their newspaper at the breakfast table or the end of a commuter ride. Fourteen articles of unusual length were to appear in the newspaper over a period of only six weeks. A final article—the narrative of the personal odyssey of one of our reporters, Don Terry, reflecting on the experience of growing up in America both black *and* white—was to appear in a special issue of the *New York Times Magazine*. And all of these articles were to be amplified on our Web site with personal narratives by the reporters and photographers engaged in the project, with video and other supporting material and with wide-open, unrestrained interactivity in which our readers in the thousands—a self-designating encounter group—could talk about the meanings they individually found.

That was our design. Without intending to sound grandiose, I think it's reasonable to declare that this journalistic venture had some of the ambitions of literature or theater, in that it looked for dramatic situations that conveyed deeper meanings and that it placed the burden of discovering those meanings in large measure on its audience. Such ambitions, let's face it, are more conveniently encompassed in a book than in the pages of a large daily newspaper; hence this volume, which makes it possible to draw some conclusions about the usefulness and value of this yearlong reporting exercise.

It's unseemly, and in any case too late, for a *Times* editor to draw such conclusions. But reading the articles consecutively from start to finish in a way I was never able to do when I was busy helping to put them in the newspaper tempts me, after all, now that it's over and done, into a wary discussion of meanings. It's possible to find evidence of progress on race in these articles — in the surprising experience of an integrated Pentecostal church in the shadow of Stone Mountain outside Atlanta, where, as Kevin Sack writes, blacks and whites are discovering "the common threads of their middle-class lives"; or in unconventional black success stories like that of Tim Cobb, the Internet millionaire Amy Harmon portrays; or in the story of Ron Sims, the would-be governor of Washington, whose approach to politics in an overwhelmingly white state is contrasted by Tim Egan with that of the nation's first Chinese-American governor, Gary Locke. And it is possible to find a dearth of progress — in the color-coded apartheid at the North Carolina slaughterhouse where Charlie LeDuff, one of our reporters, worked on the cutting line; or in the Americanization of Joel Ruiz, a black Cuban immigrant who was drawn into a segregated pattern of living during his first years on our shores.

But scorekeeping aside (are we as a nation ahead or behind?), it's impossible to read any one of these tales, let alone the whole collection, without encountering, freshly and memorably, the undeniable sting of the slights, hurts and self-doubt that are casually visited, still, on black Americans in their daily lives. It's impossible not to wince at the pain, be it the pain a successful black professional feels when he is praised for having "transcended race," fearing he might put everything at risk if he allows himself to appear to be an "angry black" for even a moment; or the pain of a black worker at a slaughterhouse who returns home from numbing labor to confront his exclusion in the drumbeat of a television stock market report.

It's impossible to read these stories, too, without encountering a parade of whites who want to believe that the time has finally come to lay this ages-old matter of race in America to rest; that is, for blacks to get over their morbid preoccupation with *it* and give *it* — and the rest of us — a rest.

The white elder of the multiracial church outside Atlanta grows restless and actually thinks of moving to a new congregation when the preacher returns too frequently to the issue that grips the black worshipers to whom the whites have allowed themselves to draw close. "With this race deal, once a year is adequate," says the elder, Howard

Pugh, who is conscious of having moved far in his own racial attitudes. His wife, Janice, is similarly put off by the preoccupations of her new black friends. "If I were in their shoes," she says, "I would take the attitude that the past is past. You have to go on, and the blacks now, this is the time for them."

So it goes. Achmed Valdés, the white immigrant in Mirta Ojito's revealing look at the fate of two Cubans who had come to America, wonders why Joel Ruiz, his old Havana buddy, has gotten himself mired in Miami's black community. "If I were him," he says, "I would get out of there and forget about everyone else's problems and begin my own life." Betty Hertzog, whom we meet in Ginger Thompson's account of the struggle to reclaim a plantation's history, thinks it's time for blacks to "stop complaining about the past and go out and do something." Bob Dyer is a white columnist for the *Akron Beacon Journal* who imagined for a time, as Dana Canedy shows, that he had earned the right to speak frankly on race after playing a leading role in the newspaper's proudest achievement, a prize-winning series on racial attitudes in the community. "Don't take it personally," he advises blacks in his column. Whites also encounter rudeness, he writes; they also get "hammered."

That blacks are oversensitive, that race is something that needs to be purged from their consciousness, that the problem of race is now mainly in their heads, is a leitmotif of white conversation captured in these articles—the first response of whites who, knowing themselves to be well meaning and guiltless by definition, find no connection between the persistence of race as a fundamental category in American life and their own individual lives. In simplest terms, race and issues of race make no obvious demand on them.

But, thanks to the persistence of our reporters over time, the reader of the series also hears what most of the white protagonists in the articles typically neither hear nor even sense: the candid reflections and voiced emotions of the blacks with whom their lives are temporarily interwoven. Whites can walk away from race: it's over when they go home. With blacks, it's seldom so easy.

In reading these stories, in being exposed to the raw reactions and forthright statements on both sides of the racial divide, there is an experience of voyeurism, a sense that one is getting both an overview and insights that the people portrayed could not have quite imagined before sitting down to read the articles themselves. How little in the end we really know about one another (and not just blacks and whites, when you come to think of it, but humans in general). Sergeant Harry Feyer, a white who tries to think of himself as the "battle buddy" of Sergeant Earnest Williams, who is black, could have had little inkling of where he stood in the other man's eyes until he read this harsh judgment in Steve Holmes's narrative of life among the noncoms at Fort Knox: "The reason he doesn't fall on his face now is because I don't let him." Tim Cobb never tells Jeff Levy, his Internet partner and friend, that he caught a whiff of racial condescension when Jeff, referring to a younger black entrepreneur, said, "He doesn't have your polish." Billy Harwood, the convict laborer at the slaughterhouse, doesn't exactly mean to let his words travel when he confides to Charlie LeDuff, "At least I ain't a nigger." The white descendant and the black park ranger who have of necessity become polar opposites on Magnolia Plantation, discover each other's thoughts in our pages after circling each other at a distance for more than a year. A black reporter on the Akron paper tells Dana Canedy that Bob Dyer is one of those "crybaby white boys," a remark our reporter, needless to say, hears before he does.

Such cutting conversational shards give us reason to squirm, not because they come as revelations but because they are so carefully hidden away in the daily lives of those who speak them and yet so near the surface, so ready to be excavated. Whites trying to understand the constraints under which many blacks must live in a white world have only to step into the shoes of Marcus Jacoby, the white quarterback Ira Berkow describes, who's so hungry to play that he takes the field for Southern University, a black school. His teammates and the student body suspect that he has benefited from some kind of racial privilege. In fact, he learns what it is to try to get along as an unwelcome, if not scorned, member of a minority, an experience seldom visited on whites there in Louisiana or elsewhere. Eventually, after several seasons, he transfers to the predominantly white campus of Louisiana State University on the other side of Baton Rouge, where, heaving a great sigh of relief, he can admit to liking country music without feeling that he's embarrassing himself. Even Upski, the avid white apostle of black music and culture, acknowledges to our reporter, Sonny Kleinfield, that after years of associating mainly with blacks and Hispanics, after making his living as an advocate for what he perceives to be their values, he's now content to find himself drifting back into the easier life of the majority from which he'd fled as a teenager. In such moments of emotional nakedness, we are compelled to recognize what it really means to give race a rest. It means giving up on having lives that reach across the divide in any significant way.

That would be fine, so they seem to be saying, with the three businessmen—a white builder, a Latino with his own engineering firm and a black architect—who have formed a working alliance to steer their way through the shoals of Houston's complex racial politics to lucrative public projects. Their alliance, as portrayed by Mia Navarro, is cordial enough but coolly impersonal; none of the three seems at all curious about the others' lives, at all eager to step into their separate cultural spheres. In one sense, their enlightened self-interest stands as a model, but it is not, finally, a model of openness or harmony. "We treat each other civilly. We send each other work," says Richard W. Lewis, the builder. "How close are we supposed to be?"

Perhaps no one feels this undertow, this drift to separation, more than the three Maplewood, New Jersey, teenagers who confided in Tamar Lewin in the course of their first year in high school. They had always been a threesome, but now suddenly the fierce tugs and expectations of cultural identity were pulling them apart, irresistibly, it seems, even in a middle-class community self-consciously striving to achieve integration. Aqeelah Mateen, a black girl, has been friends since kindergarten with Johanna Perez-Fox, who is half Puerto Rican and half Jewish and able to "go both ways." The third friend is Kelly Regan, a white girl who senses that she is seen as "ghetto" by other whites. Each of the three feels a pressure to act according to the expectations of a group, but this cruel pressure of adolescent identity politics is heaviest on Aqeelah. "I'm too white to be black and I'm too black to be white," she says in a moment of exasperation. What one Maplewood student shrewdly describes as "stupid stereotypical stuff" finally prevails, but not without leaving a residue of nostalgia, even regret, that sometimes surfaces as an aspiration to re-create the closeness, if not the innocence, that came before race consciousness. The undertow pulls Aqeelah away from her friends, but none of them seems really reconciled to that outcome. In their sense of loss, there is a kind of hope.

It is obvious that *How Race Is Lived in America* is neither a demographic survey (with its protagonists duly weighted by race, ethnicity, class and geographic location and therefore perfectly representative of the nation) nor a cultural forecast of America's racial future. We set out to find stories across a broad swath of American life and took it as a given, we have to admit, that the central conundrum of American democracy can still be found in the legacy of human slavery and the relationship between blacks and whites. But, of course, that equation is being changed by the rise of other groups with their own issues, their own perspectives on race in America, just as Johanna Perez-Fox has her own perspective on race in her Maplewood high school. In our reports from Miami and Houston, from Tar Heel, North Carolina, and Washington state, the reader gets a sense of these new issues and perspectives involving Hispanics and Asian-Americans—a sense also that while their road is not easy, it is neither as rough nor as twisting as that of blacks.

Mercedes Fernandez, from Tehucán, Mexico, in her second year on the slaughterhouse cutting floor, already knows how it is with blacks here. "Blacks have a problem," she says. "They live in the past. They are angry about slavery, so they steal from us." Achmed Valdés, the white Cuban immigrant, has learned much the same lesson in his short time in America. "As far as blacks," he says, "I only trust those I know because I know they are not delinquent."

And for white Americans also, it seems, people of color are easier to accept if their background is not African-American. Latinos are less "hardheaded" than blacks, says Richard Lewis, the Houston builder. The voters of Washington seem pleased with themselves for having elected the nation's first Asian-American governor, but Ron Sims, the black aspirant, feels his race "like a huge anchor" around his neck. "Whether people want to admit it or not," says Norm Rice, the black politician whom Gary Locke defeated in a primary, "there is a hierarchy of race." He means a hierarchy in which blacks usually remain lowest.

I do not mean to sound defensive about what can be regarded as the failure of this series to go as deeply as it might have into all the intergroup relationships that will increasingly be woven into our unfolding racial narrative. The Census Bureau is experiencing new difficulties defining the categories of race, and so will the country. Clearly we did not find all the stories there are to tell. We found the stories we were able to find, and while we made a large commitment of time and reportorial talent, the stories in this volume are only samples refined from the ore of a vast reality that no platoon of fifteen reporters could possibly encompass or exhaust—samples that tell us, in simplest terms, that race *is* still very much lived in America, that the story of our struggle to become one nation is far from over, that the challenge has not receded.

But the series is more than a reminder of what we all should have known. Taken altogether, we believe, it is a compelling picture of our present reality. I cannot end without expressing my abiding admiration and gratitude to the writers who toiled on this project, to the photographers who worked with them, and to the editors backstage who delivered it into the pages of our newspaper. In particular, I want to pay tribute to the three editors who provided the day-to-day inspiration, leadership and passion that were necessary to bring the project home. Gerald M. Boyd and Soma Golden Behr were there at the inception and there at the end, always challenging our own conclusions and easy deductions, always committed to making sure that we had gone as deep as we could go. And Michael Winerip, a master of sustained reporting on large themes refracted through the prism of individual lives, not only reported and wrote one of these articles but worked with all the other reporters from the point they started searching for their subjects and defining their stories to the point they filed their last drafts. Among the writers, Dana Canedy and Steve Holmes also functioned as editors. Paul Fishleder, Bill McDonald, Mary Jo Murphy, Savannah Walker, Nancy Weinstock, Corinne Myller, Meredith Artley and David Shipley also played essential roles in shaping and producing the series, which is truly worthy of being preserved, I believe, between the covers of this book.

Joseph Lelyveld

Part I

The Stories

The Pugh and Burch families at the Assembly of God Tabernacle, Decatur, Georgia. From left: William Pugh, Janice Pugh, Howard Pugh, Ruben Burch, Vanessa Burch, and Jessica Burch. In front: Gabrielle Burch. James Estrin/The New York Times

Shared Prayers, Mixed Blessings

KEVIN SACK

DECATUR, GEORGIA

Howard Pugh, head usher, is on patrol. May the good Lord have mercy on any child, or adult for that matter, who dares to tread across the lobby of the Assembly of God Tabernacle with so much as an open Coca-Cola in his hand. Because first he will get the look, the alert glare of a hunting dog catching its first scent of game. Then he will get the wag, the slightly palsied shake of the left index finger. And then the voice, serious as a heart attack and dripping with Pensacola pine-sap: "Son, this is the Lord's house. And they just shampooed that carpet last week."

It goes without saying that Howard Pugh knows what is going on in his lobby. So when Pugh, a white man with a bulbous pink nose, spots eighty-one-year-old Roy Denson slipping out of the sanctuary, he doesn't even have to ask. He just knows. He knows because he has seen Denson flee the 10:30 service time and again, and it is always when one of the choir's black soloists moves to center stage.

This time it is Robert Lawson, a soulful tenor with a fondness for canary-yellow suits. As he begins to sing, the Pentecostal faithful grad-ually rise. First a few black members clap and sway. Then more join in. Finally, the white members are moved to stand, and before long the two thousand–seat sanctuary is washed over with harmony. Stretch-ing their arms toward the heavens, the congregants weave a tapestry of pinks and tans and browns.

But to Denson's ears, Lawson's improvisational riffs sound like so much screeching and hollering. And so he sits there seething, thinking about how he joined this church fifty-six years ago, how he followed it from downtown Atlanta to the suburbs, how he hung the Sheetrock with his own hands, and how the blacks are taking over and the whites are just letting it happen.

He gets angrier and angrier, listening to these boisterous black folks desecrate his music, until he simply cannot bear it. "I ain't sitting there and listening to that," he mutters on his way out. "They're not going to take over my church."

And there waiting for him is Howard Pugh, at sixty-five another white man of his generation, always with the same smart-alecky question. Never mind that Pugh and his wife, Janice, have themselves become uneasy about the direction of their church, that they have been quietly contemplating a walk of their own. "Now, Roy," Howard Pugh begins, stroking his seafarer's beard, "what are you going to do when you get to heaven? Walk out of there, too?"

Back inside, the ecstatic singing has ended, the speaking in tongues has melted into a chorus of hypnotic whispers and the members of the Tabernacle have been invited to roam the sea-foam carpet, welcoming visitors and greeting one another.

They embrace, the white people and the black people, with long, earnest hugs. Eletia Frasier, a Guyanese immigrant, kisses all who come her way, whether she knows them or not. Brad Jackson wraps his thick white arms around Eugene Glenn, a slender black man, and jerks him cleanly off the ground.

Ruben Burch, a six-foot-seven black man whose blue usher's blazer is a tad short in the sleeves, saunters down the aisle with an irrepressible grin. During the Sunday fellowship, Burch makes a point of approaching older whites to gauge acceptance. Will they offer hugs, or merely handshakes? Will they linger, or recoil?

Halfway down the aisle, he encounters Madge Mayo, the spry eighty-five-year-old widow of a pastor from the Tabernacle's segregated days. She stands four-foot-nine and keeps her luminescent white hair in a tight bun.

There was a time when Mayo could never have imagined hugging a black man, and even now she is not sure she approves of the integration of her church. But she has been touched by the bigheartedness of the Tabernacle's black members. And like so many of the whites who have stayed, she reasons that all believers are going to the same heaven, so they might as well get used to one another right here on earth.

Mayo sees Burch heading her way and trots a few steps toward him in her shiny black pumps. They smile fondly, and he bends at the waist to embrace her. She pats Burch on the back and presses her cheek against his, passing his test.

It is a moment that would probably chafe some of his relatives, who feel that he and his wife, Vanessa, are compromising their blackness by attending "the white church." But the Burches feel blessed by the blendedness of the Tabernacle.

"Man," Ruben Burch reflects later, "thirty or forty years ago I would have been hung for just touching this lady."

Praying Side by Side

Sixteen miles east of downtown Atlanta, a vast granite monolith known as Stone Mountain looms over DeKalb County. Up on that mountain in 1915, the twentieth-century Ku Klux Klan was born. And virtually in its shadow, the Tabernacle, all brick and glass and sharp angles, sits along Interstate 285 in the thick of the Atlanta sprawl.

Nearly fifty years after the Reverend Dr. Martin Luther King Jr. scolded Christians for making 11 A.M. Sunday the most segregated hour of the week, the Tabernacle is the rarest of religious institutions: a truly integrated church in a nation where 90 percent of all congregations are at least 80 percent one race. It is, to many of its eight hundred members, a slice of heaven on earth, a church whose spirituality is magnified by its multiracial character. What better evidence of God's presence, they reason, than the sight of whites and blacks praying side by side?

And yet, the Tabernacle is not some liberal church like the one nearby that took down its white stained-glass Jesus and replaced him with a black one. It is deeply conservative, socially and theologically. What draws the Pughs and the Burches and so many others is the intensity of their Pentecostal faith, which teaches that the Holy Spirit can move in the lives of all believers, regardless of background.

Pastor Roger W. Brumbalow's mission statement, displayed prominently in the lobby, challenges the congregation "to be a multiracial, multicultural maturing body of believers," and, indeed, the church is blended in almost every way. Fifty-five percent of the members are white, 43 percent are black and the rest are Asian or racially mixed. Perhaps a third of the blacks are foreign born, and the church flies thirty-six flags to honor their homelands.

The Tabernacle has had trouble integrating its eight-member pastoral staff, a legacy of the Assemblies of God's history as a white denomination. Its first black associate pastor resigned in the fall of 1999 after two years. In the following twelve months, Brumbalow, who is white, filled two openings with white associate pastors before finally hiring a black youth pastor. The board of deacons, by contrast, has been integrated since 1994 and became majority black after elections in March 2000.

The choir is thoroughly mixed, and its praise-and-worship-style music falls comfortably between the traditional country hymns of white Pentecostalism and the thumping gospel funk of the modern black church. Pastor Gary Smith, the music minister, jokes that his choir would be faultless "if we could just get the whites to clap on time and just get the blacks to be on time."

The congregation does not mix only in the pews. Blacks and whites visit each other in the hospital, share motel rooms at retreats and attend potluck dinners at one another's homes. They come together in kitchens and living rooms, forming circles of prayer around an ailing old man or a hopeful young couple, then laying hands on the supplicants' foreheads and shoulders. Visiting one another's suburban homes, with their manicured lawns and large-screen TVs, these accountants and teachers, nurses and software consultants discover the common threads of their middle-class lives.

Yet for all the utopian imagery, for all the hope and faith that the congregation has moved beyond race, the life of the church is still driven by race in countless ways.

Most everyone has made accommodations of some kind. The whites, mostly native Southerners, have been forced to confront their racial assumptions and cede some control over church governance and liturgy. The blacks have ventured from the safe harbor of the African-American church and, in many cases, have suppressed lifetimes of racial resentment and distrust.

The little compromises can be detected any Sunday. They show in the frustration of some black members with the regimentation of the morning service, which opens with exactly thirty minutes of singing and usually lasts precisely two hours.

"There are times when we're praising God and then they just cut it off," complains Robert Lawson. "You can't do that. You can't put God in a box."

Some whites, meanwhile, dart glances at black churchgoers who they feel may be worshiping too exuberantly. They search for delicate words to explain.

"In a lot of cases, the blacks are really more committed," says John F. Kellerman, a former deacon.

"More outgoing," agrees his wife, Grace.

"Where the whites are more reserved, you know," he says.

Behind such concerns, though, is the question at the heart of the Tabernacle's future: Is the church simply enjoying a fleeting moment of integration on the way to becoming predominantly black? With the church growing rapidly and blacks joining at twice the rate of whites, the Tabernacle could tip, like those neighborhoods where blacks move in and whites eventually flee.

The Tabernacle is a work in progress. But how far is it willing to go? And how much are the Burches, the Pughs and the others willing to concede in order to realize St. Paul's declaration that "you are all one in Christ Jesus"?

Making "Colored" Friends

On a chilly Saturday afternoon in January 2000, a racially mixed crowd gathers at Howard and Janice Pugh's house for a catfish feast. They segregate quickly, of course. The men decamp to the garage, handicapping the Super Bowl and admiring Howard Pugh's skill with the deep-fat fryer. The women settle in the sun room, swapping tales about the cold snap and the flu bug.

When the group comes together for dinner, everyone laughs knowingly at Eugene Glenn's stories about his sixteen-year-old daughter's interest in buying a car and lack of interest in finding a job. Before long, the joshing turns to the male love affair with the channel changer and, eventually, to Howard Pugh's vigilance in the church lobby. The guests tease their host about how he was spotted letting the youth pastor's wife cross the carpet with an open can of soda.

"You're slipping, Howard," taunts William Turner, a black deacon.

"Yeah," he chuckles, "I'm getting soft."

As much as anyone, the Pughs have been transformed by the church's integration. Having lived most of their lives with little exposure to blacks, and little interest in gaining any, they now count blacks from the church among their closest friends.

"My feeling before I got to know them was that there really wasn't that many good blacks out there," Howard Pugh explains. "After being around them and working with them, shoot, I don't even think about them as colored anymore."

Of course, Howard Pugh's "colored" friends would prefer he use a synonym. But in his mind, his choice of words marks some progress. "Hey, I've come a long way," he says. "I don't say 'nigger' anymore."

"That's right," his wife chimes in, "they should see where you've come from."

Where they both came from were country churches in the piney woods of northwest Florida. When Howard was an infant, his mother would slide him under the bench so he wouldn't get trampled while they danced in the spirit. Janice was abandoned by her parents and raised by a grandmother who enforced a strict Pentecostal code: no smoking, no drinking, no dancing, no makeup, no short pants.

They found each other twenty-one years ago via CB radio and began courting over a cup of truck-stop coffee. Pugh, a widower, could be gruff as an Alabama trooper. But he was also giving and good-hearted and a fine provider. She was pretty and sweet and recently divorced. She kept a Christian household and had no problem letting her husband be head of it. Even today, she cooks and cleans and lays out his clothes.

"All he has to do is put them on," she says, rolling her eyes.

"Yeah," he grins, sunk into his recliner, his toy poodle, Pepe, in his lap, "all them guys at the church comes up to me and says, 'Boy, your wife dresses you nice.' "

After working for years in pulp mills, Howard Pugh brought his bride to Atlanta nineteen years ago and started a lucrative business pouring concrete in the ever-expanding suburbs. With its sizable black middle class and political structure, the city was a shock.

The Pughs had come up in a strictly segregated culture. Howard Pugh remembers having little childhood exposure to blacks, and during the civil rights movement he couldn't figure out what all the fuss was about. As far as he could tell, blacks had the same opportunities as he and other poor whites, even if they did have their own neighborhoods and schools.

"I just wanted to stay on my side of the fence and for them to stay on theirs," he says. "I never abused them. But they pretty much knew that I was white and they were niggers and we just ran our own way."

Janice Pugh, forty-six, says she was never taught prejudice but recalls her grandmother's warning to avoid the black side of town. Her view of black men, she says, came from movies that portrayed them "raping a white woman or something."

In Atlanta, she had to confront her fears. "You'd turn the TV on and it's a black mayor and a black city council," she says. "I'd say: 'Howard, where did you bring me? Are there any white people here?' "

When the Pughs joined in 1992, the Tabernacle was perhaps 10 percent black. They had never worshiped with blacks before. But the black folks tended to sit on the right side of the sanctuary, separated from the whites by a demilitarized zone of empty pews. "We came at a good time," Janice Pugh recalls. "There weren't so many of them that it was overwhelming. We could adjust."

The Burden of Blending In

In 1999, Ruben and Vanessa Burch moved into a new house with an orange-brick facade in a subdivision that is perhaps a third white. Determined to raise their two daughters in an integrated setting, the Burches had been impressed while house hunting that white neighbors had waved to them, a black couple, from their lawns.

A week after the Pughs' fish fry, many of the same couples gathered for a house-blessing dinner at the Burches'. To the strumming of a guitar, the crowd welcomed the Holy Spirit into the airy two-story home. "Come in today, come in to stay," they harmonized, "come into my house, Lord Jesus."

Vanessa Burch, tall, slender and poised, handed out cups of olive oil, and the blacks and whites anointed doorknobs, bedposts and televisions with slick smudges of oil. The ceremony ended when the Burch family—Ruben, Vanessa, twelve-year-old Jessica and seven-year-old Gabrielle—huddled in the center of the living room and surrendered to the prayers of their friends. The guests gave them a wall plaque, and little Gabby haltingly read, "May the Lord bless this home and keep you in the company of angels." Then spaghetti was served.

Like most black Southerners of their generation, the Burches have experienced their share of racism. Ruben Burch, forty-six, grew up in Albany, Georgia, a stronghold of resistance to the civil rights movement. His wife, forty, grew up in Blakely, a south Georgia town whose high school still has separate homecoming queens and class reunions.

Both remember "colored only" water fountains and parental warnings not to be caught on the white side of town after dark. Vanessa Burch still recalls the indignity of hearing white children call her mother by her first name. And then there was the day, perhaps fifteen years ago, when her white boss in a South Carolina bank informed her that the one thing he hated was an "uppity, educated nigger."

"It almost knocked me to my knees," says Vanessa Burch, then a teller at the bank. "I walked off and went into the rest room and cried because it hurt me so bad."

The Burches reacted to all this in different ways. Ruben Burch, happy-go-lucky and confident to a fault, says he never grew deeply bitter. His mother shielded him from the worst affronts, and when his high school integrated, he saw it as an opportunity to date white girls, discreetly. "You knew how far to take it," he says. "I mean, you wouldn't walk down Broadway holding somebody's hand."

Vanessa Burch was more defiant. When her school desegregated, her white classmates learned that anyone who tossed a racial epithet her way was liable to go home with bruises. At age twelve, she dressed down a white woman who had scolded her sick mother for sitting in the white section of a doctor's waiting room. "After that," she says, "Mama didn't take me too many times to the doctor's office."

Their experiences left both Burches, though, with a strong understanding that their world would be multiracial, and that schooling, diction and personality would be important tools in getting ahead. Those lessons were reinforced in the Navy, where Ruben Burch spent twenty-two years as a medic.

In 1996 they moved to Atlanta, where he found work inspecting commercial waste-water systems. They looked for an Assemblies of God church and found the Tabernacle, then about 30 percent black. Before long they were fully involved, he as an usher, she as a Sunday School teacher and both as scout leaders.

"I liked the diversity," says Vanessa Burch, an administrative assistant for a computer company. "I wanted my children to grow up with differences in a church so they could see that whenever they went to heaven it wasn't going to be all black and it wasn't going to be all white. It was going to be mixed."

A "Walk with the Lord"

When the Tabernacle was founded, in 1916, it was most definitely not mixed. And it remained that way through most of its history, moving twice to escape the migration of blacks into its neighborhood. In the 1940s it affiliated with the Assemblies of God, a historically segregationist Pentecostal denomination. But ultimately, the church could outrun neither the changing demographics of postsegregation Atlanta nor some stark fiscal realities.

Shortly before the Pughs arrived, an unmanageable mortgage put the congregation in debt. To dig out, the church called as its senior pastor Coy Barker, a onetime rodeo rider, and agreed to pay him 25 percent of tithes and offerings. With a financial incentive to fill the pews, Barker tapped the most readily available market—the middle-class blacks flocking into the area.

By 1984, when the church's current building was completed, the surrounding suburbs were in the midst of a stunning transformation. In 1970 there was one black among the 11,000 residents in the church's census tract. Twenty years later, two-thirds of the residents were black.

Barker, a typecast televangelist with silver hair, flashy jewelry and a black Lincoln Town Car, had a high-stepping style that mimicked the traditional black preacher. By the time he was forced out in 1993, in the throes of a messy divorce, the church was perhaps 20 percent black and on the road to financial recovery.

Predictably, some whites left. Susan Carithers, a member since birth, could never quite accept integration as God's will. Her husband grew agitated, she says, because "he just didn't want black boys sniffing up to his daughter." They left in 1996, shortly after a black man gave her a big hug during a Sunday service.

The Pughs could also have left, but they liked Brumbalow's preaching and their son's participation in the youth group. And as they got to know black members, they found they liked them, too. A lot.

The black churchgoers did not fit the Pughs' stereotypes. Howard Pugh noticed that they did not loll around or always have their hands out like the black men who smooth his concrete, the ones he calls "the boys."

Even today he draws distinctions between his black employees and his black church friends. Sometimes he cannot recall his workers' last names, though they have been with him for years.

He says that he occasionally has to bail one out of jail, and that if he drives around a corner fast enough he will catch some lounging.

But he admires the blacks at the Tabernacle. They work hard and dress well, often better than the whites, and live in two-story houses on well-tended lanes. "As I began to be around them a lot more," he says, "I saw that there was a lot more of them trying to benefit themselves."

The Pughs held cookouts and invited mixed crowds, disregarding, even slightly savoring, their white neighbors' stares. On Saturday mornings Howard would round up a crew of church men, white and black, to go paint a widow's house or serve soup to the homeless. One Easter the Pughs took their black friends Paul and Rudine Hardy to an all-white club for dinner.

"Oh, my God, it was so funny," Rudine Hardy says. "I said: 'Janice, Janice. These people are all just looking.' They had all this fancy food, and every time I chewed they was just looking."

Janice Pugh sometimes gets weepy talking about her deep kinship with Rudine Hardy and other black women from church. She feels connected to them spiritually and turns to them when she needs prayer.

As she has learned about the bigotry they face, she has come to empathize. It isn't guilt exactly. She doesn't feel she owes black people anything. After all, her life hasn't been so easy either. But she understands, and that is something new.

"When I moved to Atlanta," she says, "I had never had any occasion to know what these people were going through. I'd never had anyone come up to me and say, 'I was treated this way because I was black.' When you hear someone say that, with tears in their eyes, you know they just want to be loved. And I guess I connected with them because I was the same way when I was a little girl. All I wanted was to be loved."

As she sees it, God is using the Tabernacle's integration to test "whether you move on in your walk with the Lord."

Her husband's walk has been less steady. He remains capable of offending black friends even as he beckons them into his life. They recognize that he has come a long way, that he has a good heart. But they also suspect that he continues to use the word "colored," often to their faces, to make it clear that he, not they, will define the terms of their relationships.

"It's a control thing," Janice Pugh says. "He wants people to know that he still knows the difference."

In August 1999, one of Howard Pugh's black friends decided to confront him, fearing newcomers might be put off by his ways as head usher. But the man later backed down. Don't major in minor, his wife had advised him. "I do value my friendship with Howard and Janice," the man reasoned, "and if it's my friendship with them versus this, it's really very insignificant."

Ruben Burch reacted much the same way at a retreat that year, when Howard Pugh told him a joke, the one about the black guy who moved next door to the white guy:

The white man was leaning over his fence as his new neighbor mowed the yard. With each pass, the black neighbor taunted the white man, "I'm better than you are, I'm better than you are." Exasperated, the white man finally asked, "What makes you so much better than me?" And the black man replied, "I don't have a nigger living next to me."

"Old Ruben just about fell out," Pugh remembers. "He didn't have a problem with it." And, in fact, Burch says he didn't have much of a problem with it, though he was surprised Pugh felt comfortable enough to tell him the joke. "That's just Howard," he told himself. He let the moment pass, thinking that Pugh was like an old car, sputtering down the highway: "You just say, 'Well, this is just an old car smoking and we'll go ahead and pass it and one day it'll give out and be gone.' "

What the Relatives Say

The Burches may want to make sure, as Vanessa Burch puts it, that their girls don't grow up "in an all-one-race anything." But when it comes to their choice of church, they have been wounded by second-guessing from their relatives, particularly Ruben Burch's sister Jacalyn Ray. It has become personal, and at times ugly.

"It's a wannabe thing," says Ray, who attends a black church. Her sister-in-law, she thinks, is too eager to make white friends and entertain them in her home. "Some people don't know who they are and have to go somewhere to validate themselves. She doesn't feel comfortable being black."

Vanessa Burch cannot figure out what she did to provoke Ray, other than marry her brother. But other family members, while more tactful, do not fully reject Ray's assessment. Ruben Burch's half brother Frederick Caldwell has long noticed that Burch feels most comfortable in interracial settings.

"I think of Rick as my white brother," he laughs, using a nickname. "He has Caucasian features. Not facial features, but he has a white body type. He can't dance. He'll wear plaid pants. He played on the tennis team in school. He's a Newt Gingrich fan. I wouldn't necessarily say he wants to be white, but he has opinions not normally associated with a black man in the United States."

The relatives say they are also concerned that the Burches may be sending their daughters mixed signals. "I do know with Jessica there's kind of a working out of who she is," Caldwell says. "My concern for Gabrielle and Jessica is that they have a healthy respect for who they are."

Ruben Burch concedes some concern that his daughters may be too color-blind, that a life without overt discrimination has left them with little racial identity. Someday, he fears, an act of bigotry will shatter their naïveté.

Still, he resents the suggestion that he and his family prefer integration because they want to be white. He is comfortable with who he is. "I enjoy me," he says. "And I feel if you don't know me you're missing out." As for his sister, he says: "She's not in touch with reality. I mean, how do we want to be white? Because we want different things, want to live in different neighborhoods? No, she's totally wrong. I think it's a chemical imbalance."

Jessica, tall and outgoing like her parents and engagingly mature for her age, acknowledges inner conflict over racial identity. But it is not that she rejects her blackness or wants to be white. Rather, it is that she feels torn between her parents' insistence on living an integrated life and her black peers' suspicion of anyone who does.

Her parents insist that she and her sister speak "proper English" and scold them gently if they slip into black slang. But her classmates tease her relentlessly for her speech and for having white friends, and sometimes she cannot resist the pressure.

"I do talk improper English, or ebonics, with black friends," she admits. "Maybe I think they'll pick on me if I don't."

Two years ago, she decided to drop her white friends to placate the black ones. But she felt distracted, her grades suffered and she concluded that God was not pleased.

"I finally told myself that it doesn't matter what they think about me, it doesn't matter what color I hang out with," she says. "I have too much respect for who I am."

Not surprisingly, Vanessa Burch is annoyed by her daughter's problems and her in-laws' carping. But it has all made her think.

"I think long and hard about it to see, you know, could this really be true," she says. "And then I go and ask other people, 'Do you think I try to be white?' And they're like: 'What? No. You couldn't be if you wanted to.' It used to really weigh on me and I used to pray about it. 'Lord, what is it? Show me. If I'm doing something to make people see me like this, show me.' "

It hasn't come. People just don't understand, she says, that she is motivated by pragmatism, not racial treason. The reality is that her daughter will face a white world, with certain rules for getting ahead.

"I know that being black is one strike against us," she says, "and in the business world, where she's going to have to compete, being a woman is two against her. So I want her to have enough education that they can't resist her. I want her, when she gets up to speak, that they're like, 'Wow, who is that?' And believe me, voice and articulation get attention."

She is trying, she says, to help her daughters realize that there are no limits, that the restraints and prejudices of her own youth have been lifted. They can do anything, live anywhere, even someplace more extravagant than their new three-bedroom house.

"You want to live in that house on the hill over there," she challenges them, "you can live there. You have the same rights as the next person before you, beside you, behind you, around you. All of you can do the same thing. Once upon a time we couldn't. But now we can."

A Color-blindness Test

There was little chance that the Burches and Pughs would miss the wedding of Dorothea Lemon and Curtis Lockridge in June 1999. It was to be the Tabernacle's first big interracial ceremony, and as Madge Mayo explained it, "Something is about to happen that we haven't all fully digested."

The bride, forty-three and black, and the groom, fifty-eight and white, had both recently been widowed. The two couples had been friendly at church, and Lockridge and Lemon comforted each other through their grief. Before long, they were holding hands through the Sunday service and scribbling notes on the church bulletin.

"I luv you, Curtis," she would write.

"I'm glad," he would respond.

It raised some eyebrows when Pastor Brumbalow announced their engagement. One elderly white lady asked if Scripture permitted mixed marriages, and he told her there was no prohibition. Blacks and whites asked if it was wrong to want their children to marry within their races. He said it wasn't, and made a point of telling the men's group that he was not encouraging interracial dating.

The afternoon of the wedding, Vanessa Burch slid into a pew toward the back. "What are these people thinking?" she remembered wondering. "How many are going to be in an uproar, and how many aren't going to be back?"

Howard Pugh recognized that the couple were grownups and could do as they pleased. But interracial relationships just went against his upbringing.

"Oh, Lord," he thought as the bride walked down the aisle. But by the end of the afternoon, Pugh could not help smiling. The couple looked awfully cute, and very much in love. The ceremony had been elegant, the reception lavish. "I'll tell you the truth," he said. "I haven't seen many white folks' weddings put on like that."

Still, some remained uneasy. "The thing that worries me most," said Madge Mayo, "is that this is going to turn things loose for the young people and it's going to get, I shouldn't say entangled, but I'd just say more mixed."

Sense and Sensitivity

What Janice Pugh cannot understand, despite her newfound empathy, is why black folks remain obsessed with race, why they can't just let it all go. She and Rudine Hardy talk about it from time to time, sitting on a green leather couch outside the sanctuary. Hardy will wonder why the pastoral staff is so white, and Janice Pugh will bristle.

"You need to stop being so sensitive about all this," she will say.

"You don't understand," Hardy will respond. "You're not black."

"I'm not black, and I never will be black," she will answer. "I just think there are other issues out there that you have to be concerned about that have nothing to do with race."

She thinks about it often. The church should be about love, and love should know no color. "If I were in their shoes," she says, "I would take the attitude that the past is past. You have to go on, and the blacks now, this is the time for them. They're more accepted now."

Because the Tabernacle is an island, and a refuge, it is often hard to accept that racial tensions lie just beneath the surface, vulnerable to exposure from the slightest scratch. But the island is in the world, and in the world there is no refuge.

Kathy Watson, a children's pastor, learned that lesson when she was rebuked by a black parent for referring affectionately to her toddlers as "monkeys." Another youth pastor got an earful about a Bible lesson that equated the color black with sin.

But those flare-ups do not rival what happened in the summer of 1999 with the Homebuilders, a Sunday School class for couples. Until 1998 it was led by a white couple, and attendance was predominantly white. Then Enefiok Umana, a deacon from Nigeria, and his wife, Eno, assumed the leadership, and the class became overwhelmingly black.

Many blacks concluded that whites were simply unwilling to submit to black leadership. And their suspicions were stoked one August morning when two associate pastors interrupted class to introduce a white couple as leaders of a Bible study being started for younger couples. One pastor, Ray Martin, added that the Homebuilders would come under the new class's "umbrella."

After church, the blacks huddled in the parking lot and burned up the phone lines. Some wrote in protest. The implication was clear, they felt. The church was starting a white class for those unwilling to attend the black-led class. And the bit about the umbrella really set them off.

"It was like a kick in the behind to me," said Hardy.

Brumbalow ate lunch at William and Lula Turner's house that day. And as they told him of the discontent many blacks were feeling, the pastor started to weep and vowed that the Enemy—meaning the Devil—would not divide his flock. But he had to leave town the next day, and the flames raged on.

The associate pastors were flabbergasted by the reaction and wounded that the blacks could think there was racial intent. "I really thought they were a little further down the healing curve," Martin said. "It let me know that we're dealing with people that still have some wounds."

In conversations with class members, Martin acknowledged that the word "umbrella" had left the wrong impression. What he had meant, he said, was simply that the two classes would be parallel ministries that would occasionally come together for functions.

When Brumbalow returned, he took charge of damage control,

delaying the new class to let emotions calm. The next night, though exhausted from his trip, he made a point of attending a Homebuilders potluck dinner.

Still, when the new class finally began, it was attended mostly by whites. And when the new group held a retreat, only one Homebuilders couple chose to attend.

When to Preach on Race

Two Sundays after the Homebuilders incident, Brumbalow did something he had hardly ever done. He preached about race. "I don't normally get this blunt," he began, slapping his hands for punctuation, "but I will get this blunt this morning.

"I want to say to you of color and you that are white" — he was screeching like the brakes on a train — "that if you look at a person based on the color of their skin and you evaluate them right then and there, then, my friend, you have missed the purpose of the love of God."

Sometimes, he said, it takes a while to catch on — to comprehend that God is working a miracle at the Tabernacle so people might have a glimpse of heaven. "When I look across this congregation," he said, "I understand what God is doing. I understand the eternal kingdom."

Brumbalow recognizes that not everyone was brought up that way. In fact, he wasn't brought up that way. Growing up near Atlanta, he didn't really know any blacks, and he wasn't particularly godly. It was only after some wild days as a rock guitarist with a band called Completely Souled Out that he found God and his future wife, Becky, at a Pentecostal revival. He left shortly for Vietnam, where he won decorations for heroism.

His previous pulpit, in suburban New Orleans, had few blacks. And yet, at fifty, he has managed and accelerated the Tabernacle's integration with considerable skill. Both races trust him like a parent and admire his evenhandedness, political instincts and common touch.

"He'll drink out of the same glass," Ruben Burch says. "That's the kind of feeling I get from him, you know, that I'm not higher than you."

He is a gifted preacher, fashioning sermons that are neither inaccessibly erudite nor insultingly shallow. But he prefers, he says, not to preach about race. He would rather lead by example, embracing each in his flock with the same tenderness, blessing each with the same prayers, accepting dinner invitations from all.

"I think the pitfall of having a blended church is when you make race the issue," he says. "What we're doing here as a church is not about race, and if we make that the emphasis then we miss the bigger picture. Our main goal is to reconcile people to God."

He would never say it, and maybe doesn't even let himself think it, but there is another reason not to make race the issue. To preserve the Tabernacle's fragile balance, he must reach out to newcomers without alienating old-timers like the Pughs.

The blacks at the Tabernacle were jubilant about the pastor's race sermon. And the Pughs, like many of the whites, had no real problem with its content. But that he delivered the sermon at all rubbed them the wrong way. He was playing to the crowd, they felt, or at least to part of it.

From time to time, the Pughs had discussed looking at other churches. The Tabernacle was a long drive from home. Now they shared this gnawing sense that race was beginning to supplant God's love as its driving force.

"What would cause me to leave," Janice Pugh said, "is for them to constantly have a platform on the black issue, to always talk about race, and not let the Holy Spirit lead us."

Sometimes, though, Brumbalow says, God just lays a message on his heart and he can't shake it loose. It happened again the following February, when, voice quavering, he read King's "I Have a Dream" speech and prophesied that the Tabernacle would become a beacon for others.

"God is saying, 'I am going to prepare you to be a light, to be an example to the city of Atlanta and to the state of Georgia,'" he said. "I want to tell you, God has a dream and his dream is being fulfilled in this house this morning in the name of the Lord. Hallelujah!"

The Pughs would have preferred a different topic. "He keeps bringing it up and bringing it up," Howard Pugh said. "With this race deal, once a year is adequate, not every other Sunday."

Several weeks later the Pughs visited another church.

A Delicate Balance

If the Burches and other black leaders at the Tabernacle have a complaint, it is with the level of diversity in the staff. They do not always protest publicly, fearing they might break the spell of racial goodwill.

But they are always watching and counting. All you have to do, they say, is look at the 1999 Christmas card photograph of "the Tabernacle team," nineteen red-sweatered staff members, every last one of them white.

And yet when positions have opened, black deacons have chosen not to lobby Brumbalow to fill them with blacks. They recognize, they say, that the task is not easy. The Assemblies of God is still virtually all white, with fewer than 400 blacks among its 32,000 licensed ministers. And because Brumbalow holds a statewide leadership position with the Assemblies, it might be considered bad form to hire from outside the denomination.

Even before he was successful, he had searched assiduously for black prospects, knowing that "it would certainly speak volumes that I pretty much practice what I preach." In several instances he let the congregation know that he had offered jobs to black prospects, only to be rebuffed. That seemed to satisfy his black constituents.

"He interviewed black people and they turned it down, so what can you do?" Ruben Burch said after one such search.

In general, black members suspect that it may not take much to upset the racial equilibrium of the church. Ultimately, they assume, it will come down to power. If black numbers increase to where whites feel disenfranchised, whites will leave, they predict.

For the moment, the pastors feel they must move incrementally. That was never clearer than in the planning of the 1999 Christmas pageant.

Like other blacks, Ruben Burch had long noticed that blacks had never been cast as Joseph, Mary or Jesus. The whites, he assumed, would have a fit. "Boy, if they figure out there was a black Jesus they probably wouldn't want to go to heaven," he joked.

Smith, the music minister, badly wanted to break that color barrier. He knew that Scripture was largely silent about Jesus' appearance and that various cultures portrayed him in their own images. But he, too, was unsure if the older whites were ready for an ebony Jesus.

So he devised a scheme to soft-pedal the racial transformation of Christ. He selected for the lead roles Stephen and Sobrina Smith, a light-skinned multiracial couple who happened to have a newborn son, Joshua. Sobrina Smith, born in Trinidad, is part African, Chinese, East Indian, Hispanic and South American Indian. Her husband, a New Yorker, is part Italian, Polish, black, Jewish and Native American.

The pastor theorized that if he could sell the Smiths, he could cast darker-skinned blacks in future years. "The first time it shouldn't be such a shock," he said. "They're not as dark. They're sort of a medium."

The pageant went off without a hitch, down to the triumphant finale, when an adult Christ figure, adorned with a crown and scarlet cloak, rode into the sanctuary on a stocky white horse. Sobrina Smith was fetching as Mary, dressed in a blue satin robe and a white shawl, cradling Joshua as her husband knelt nearby. Ruben Burch, playing a wise man, watched on bended knee.

Smith could not have been more pleased. He received lots of compliments and not a single comment about the racial makeup of the cast, which was how he wanted it. Most white members, if they noticed at all, reacted about the way the Pughs did, with a shrug.

"I think the white people have been shocked so many times that it doesn't make any difference anymore," Janice Pugh said. "They just say, 'Well, that's the way it is now.' "

Even the Smiths, told later that they had been selected for their complexion, said they didn't mind too much, so long as it helped move the church forward. And yet the whole experience made them wonder.

"If we are an integrated church, as we claim to be," Sobrina Smith asked, "why do we still have to go through hoops and loops to make a point and get a message across and pacify certain people and keep waves from starting? If we're still playing around with this, then maybe we're not really who we say we are."

The Tabernacle has continued to grow, adding members of both races. In the fall of 2000, to handle the expansion, the church opened a new building with classrooms and a chapel. The new black youth pastor, the second African-American ever to join the staff, began work that summer. Brumbalow also hired a Korean minister, the church's first, to help draw in Asian parishioners, and began searching for a Hispanic minister as well.

The Pugh and Burch families have remained active in the church. In September 2000, Howard Pugh was diagnosed with bladder cancer, and had two major operations. During his lengthy hospitalization, he received numerous visitors from the church, both white and black, and they prayed for him at his bedside.

Joel Ruiz (left) and Achmed Valdés (right), both of whom separately fled Cuba by boat, looking at snapshots in Miami, Florida. Librada Romero/The New York Times

2

Best of Friends, Worlds Apart

MIRTA OJITO

MIAMI, FLORIDA

Havana, sometime before 1994: As dusk descends on the quaint seaside village of Guanabo, two young men kick a soccer ball back and forth and back and forth across the sand. The tall one, Joel Ruiz, is black. The short, wiry one, Achmed Valdés, is white.

They are the best of friends.

Miami, January 2000: Valdés is playing soccer, as he does every Saturday, with a group of light-skinned Latinos in a park near his apartment. Ruiz surprises him with a visit, and Valdés, flushed and sweating, runs to greet him. They shake hands warmly.

But when Valdés darts back to the game, Ruiz stands off to the side, arms crossed, looking on as his childhood friend plays the game that was once their shared joy. Ruiz no longer plays soccer. He prefers basketball with black Latinos and African-Americans from his neighborhood.

The two men live only four miles apart, not even fifteen minutes by car. Yet they are separated by a far greater distance, one they say they never envisioned back in Cuba.

In ways that are obvious to the black man but far less so to the white one, they have grown apart in the United States because of race. For the first time, they inhabit a place where the color of their skin defines the outlines of their lives—where they live, the friends they make, how they speak, what they wear, even what they eat.

"It's like I am here and he is over there," Ruiz said. "And we can't cross over to the other's world."

It is not that, growing up in Cuba's mix of black and white, they were unaware of their difference in color. Fidel Castro may have decreed an end to racism in Cuba, but that does not mean racism has simply gone away. Still, color was not what defined them. Nationality, they had been taught, meant far more than race. They felt, above all, Cuban.

Here in America, Ruiz still feels Cuban. But above all he feels black. His world is a black world, and to live there is to be constantly conscious of race. He works in a black-owned bar, dates black women, goes to an African-American barber. White barbers, he says, "don't understand black hair." He generally avoids white neighborhoods, and when his world and the white world intersect, he feels always watched, and he is always watchful.

Valdés, who is twenty-nine, a year younger than his childhood friend, is simply, comfortably Cuban, an upwardly mobile citizen of the Miami mainstream. He lives in an all-white neighborhood, hangs out with white Cuban friends and goes to black neighborhoods only when his job, as a deliveryman for Restonic mattresses, forces him to. When he thinks about race, which is not very often, it is in terms learned from other white Cubans: American blacks, he now believes, are to be avoided because they are delinquent and dangerous and resentful of whites. The only blacks he trusts, he says, are those he knows from Cuba.

Since leaving Havana on separate rafts in 1994, the two friends have seen each other just a handful of times in Miami—at a funeral, a baby shower, a birthday party and that soccer game, a meeting arranged for a newspaper photographer. They have visited each other's homes only once.

They say they remain as good friends as ever, yet they both know there is little that binds them anymore but their memories. Had they not become best friends in another country, in another time, they would not be friends at all today.

Two Boys on a Bus

They met on a bus, No. 262, the one that took Joel from his home in the racially mixed neighborhood of Penas Altas to middle school, thirty-five minutes away. Achmed got on in Guanabo, and they sat together talking, as boys do, about everything and nothing.

Both grew up in orderly homes, with hard-working parents who supported the Castro government. Their fathers worked for the state oil

company. Their mothers—Joel's was a nurse, Achmed's an adminis-
trator in stores for tourists—knew each other and sometimes met for
coffee.

The boys' friendship was cemented through school and sport. They
stood up for each other against troublemakers. "Just to know we were
there for each other was good," Ruiz recalls. When Joel's girlfriend got
pregnant in high school, Achmed was the first person he told. They
played soccer and baseball and ran track. Joel often stayed for dinner
at Achmed's, where there was a color television and an antenna powerful enough to pick up American channels.

Because of her job, Achmed's mother had access to some of Havana's best restaurants. Every year she would take him out for a birthday dinner, and every year he would invite his best friend, Joel. "I
couldn't think of anybody I would rather spend my time with," Valdés
recalled.

But as they grew older, each became restless with the limitations of
life in Cuba.

Achmed was in sixth grade when an aunt who had fled to Venezuela
gave him a pair of white sneakers. He loved them so, he immediately
wore them to school. Almost as immediately, the principal visited him
at home to warn him about the troubling political implications of those
foreign sneakers. At the university, too, his professors wondered why
he wore foreign clothes and rode a nice bicycle. He wondered right
back why he could not wear and ride whatever he wanted. When he
was expelled for failing two classes, he saw it as punishment for being
politically incorrect.

Before long, he found work at sea, trapping lobsters and selling them
for $4 each. In a country where most people earn less than $10 a
month, it was a living, though not a life. When the government allowed thousands of Cubans to leave in small boats and rafts in 1994,
he was ready.

His friend Joel was ready, too, though it had taken him far longer
to make up his mind. Indeed, given Cuba's racial history, it is hardly
surprising that black Cubans have generally been far less eager than
whites to flee to America. After all, in prerevolutionary Cuba, blacks
and whites had lived largely segregated, separated by huge disparities
in economic and social standing. But two months after he seized power
in 1959, Fidel Castro ordered whites to look upon blacks as equals and
began leveling the economic and educational playing fields.

When Joel was very small, his family lived crammed into one room of an old carved-up mansion. Soon, the government gave them a three-bedroom apartment in a development that Joel's father had helped build. Before the revolution, Joel's mother had made a living cleaning white people's homes. It was Fidel, she told him over and over, who had given her the chance to become a nurse. And so Joel came to believe that it was no big deal, being black in Cuba.

As for America, he had seen the images on government television: guards beating black prisoners, the police loosing dogs or training hoses on civil rights marchers.

But as Cuba's economy fell apart in the 1990s, he began to see things differently. He left military school for a cooking program, hoping for a well-paying job at a tourist hotel. Once he graduated, the only job available was washing windows. Look around, co-workers told him, look who's getting the good jobs. The answer was whites.

He noticed, too, when he watched the American channels at Achmed's house, that some blacks seemed to live well in America. He saw black lawyers, politicians, wealthy athletes. It made him think: "It's not so bad over there. Blacks are all right."

On August 21, 1994, he climbed onto a raft and made for Florida. Like his friend before him, he was intercepted by the United States Coast Guard and sent to the American base at Guantánamo. The next year, they were freed—first Achmed Valdés, then Joel Ruiz—and headed straight to Miami.

A Shock of Identity

In Miami, Ruiz discovered a world that neither American television nor Communist propaganda had prepared him for. Dogs did not growl at him and police officers did not hose him. But he felt the stares of security guards when he entered a store in a white neighborhood and the subtle recoiling of white women when he walked by.

Miami is deeply segregated, and when Ruiz arrived, he settled into one of the black urban sections, Liberty City. He had family there. His uncle Jorge Aranguren had arrived in 1980 and married an African-American. Ruiz took a job at his uncle's liquor store and started learning English.

The first thing Ruiz noticed about his new world was the absence of whites. He had seen barrios in Havana with more blacks than others, but he had never lived in a place where everybody was black. Far from feeling comfortable, he yearned for the mixing he had known in Cuba.

In Cuba, he says, he had been taught to see skin color—in his case, the color of chocolate milk—as not much more important than, say, the color of his eyes. But this was not Cuba. This was Miami, and in Miami, as the roughly 7 percent of the area's Cubans who are black quickly learn, skin color easily trumps nationality.

Ruiz began to understand that in earnest on Valentine's Day 1996, three months after his arrival in Miami. He had gone to dinner with his uncle Ramón Suárez at Versailles, a popular restaurant in Little Havana, a bastion of white Cuban-Americans. They took three light-skinned girlfriends along. Ruiz wore one of his nicest outfits—black jeans and a red-and-green checked shirt. He was new to the country and unsure how to behave, but he felt comfortable at Versailles. After all, he remembers thinking, he was among Cubans. He knew the food, he could read the menu, and he could talk to the waiters.

The five sat in the back. Ruiz concentrated on the conversation and on his meal. More than four years later, he remembers what he ate: a breaded steak with rice and beans and fried plantains.

Shortly before midnight, the five left in a new red Nissan. One of the women drove. Suárez sat next to her, taking pictures of his nephew and the other women laughing in back. Twenty blocks from the restaurant, four police cars, lights flashing and sirens wailing, stopped them. The woman who was driving saw them first and yelled for Suárez to drop the camera.

The officers, with weapons drawn, ordered them out of the car. Terrified, Ruiz did as he was told, spreading his legs and leaning face-down on the car as the officers frisked him. It seemed like a very long time before they were allowed to go.

That was when one officer, a white Cuban-American, said something in Spanish that forever changed Ruiz's perspective on race. "I've been keeping an eye on you for a while," Ruiz recalls the officer saying. "Since you were in the restaurant. I saw you leave and I saw so many blacks in the car, I figured I would check you out."

Ruiz and his uncle stood speechless until an African-American officer approached them, apologized and sent them on their way. Afterward, his uncle said he was sure the police had been called by restaurant patrons uncomfortable with Ruiz's racially mixed group. His

English teacher, an African-American, told him that white police officers liked to single out blacks driving red cars. Ruiz is not sure what to believe, but the truth is not in the details.

"Up until that day, I thought all Cubans were the same," he says. "It took a while to sink in, but that incident made me start thinking in a different way."

All at once, he had to learn how a person with dark skin should behave in this country: if an officer is following your car, do not turn your head; the police don't like it. Do not stare at other drivers, especially if they are young and white and loud. He has even learned how to walk: fast in stores, to avoid security guards; slower in the streets, so as not to attract the attention of the police. On the street, he avoids any confrontation.

He pays bills in cash because of an incident at a bank two years ago. When he asked to buy a certificate of deposit with $6,000 in lottery winnings, the bank officer, a white Cuban woman, looked puzzled, he recalls, and told him: "This is different. Your kind likes to spend the money, not save it." Since then he has not had a checking account.

And, of course, he avoids Cuban restaurants in white neighborhoods.

"In Cuba, I walked as if I owned the streets," he says. "Here I have to figure out where, what, when, everything."

He often finds himself caught between two worlds. Whites see him simply as black. African-Americans dismiss him as Cuban. "They tell me I'm Hispanic. I tell them to look at my face, my hair, my skin," he says. "I am black, too. I may speak different, but we all come from the same place."

He has started to refer to himself as Afro-Cuban, integrating, indeed embracing, the ways of his black neighbors. He enjoys what he calls black food—fried chicken, collard greens, grits—though he still lusts for a Cuban steak and plantains. He listens to rhythm and blues at home and at work; in the car, though, he listens to a Cuban crooner whose romantic ballads he has memorized. He dresses "black," he says, showing off his white velvet Hush Puppies and silk shirts. When he speaks English, he mimics black Miamians, but his words carry an unmistakably Spanish inflection.

Some months after the Versailles incident, when Achmed Valdés first saw his old friend, he was puzzled. "Joel has changed," he said. "He is in another world now."

A Seamless Transition

Pretty much anywhere else in America, Valdés would fit nicely into the niche reserved for Hispanic immigrants. If the question of race came up, he would be called a light-skinned Hispanic. Here in Miami, such distinctions do not apply. Here he is not a member of any minority group. He is Cuban and he is white.

This, after all, is a city run by Cubans, white Cubans. Not only are the mayors of Miami and Dade County Cuban, so are seven of thirteen county commissioners and three of five city commissioners. Spanish is the dominant language heard in the streets.

Valdés's transition to this world has been seamless, so much so that he does not really think of himself as an immigrant at all. His self-image is of someone well along on a sure, quick path to the middle class, someone who would be right at home in a quiet neighborhood of well-kept houses and neatly mowed lawns. And that is where he lives, with his wife, Ivette Garcia, and his mother in a one-bedroom apartment off 17th Avenue in southwest Miami.

He drives the car he likes, a 1998 Nissan that he plans to trade in soon for a newer model, says whatever is on his mind and dreams of opening his own business selling mattresses in a strip mall.

He has had to learn about punctuality and paying bills on time, but being white and Cuban, he has not had to learn how to behave. His English is tentative, but that does not matter too much here. His childhood friend may wrestle with a new identity, but when Valdés is asked how he has adapted in a strange land, he looks dumbfounded and jokes: "What are you talking about? I was born in Hialeah Hospital." Hialeah is south Florida's most Cuban city, often the first stop for Cuban exiles.

Still, he struggles the immigrant struggle. He has held a dozen jobs, from delivering Chinese food for tips to cleaning monkey cages for $6.50 an hour. Each time, he has traded up a bit, to the point where today he makes $9.60 an hour, with paid vacations and frequent overtime, to drive an eighteen-wheel Restonic mattress truck all over the state.

On weekends, however, he looks refreshed and energized, positively glowing with the middle-class knowledge of having earned his weekly respite.

It is 2 P.M. one recent Saturday, and Valdés is home from his soccer game. Before he is out of the shower, the apartment fills up with his crowd — athletic white couples, all friends from Cuba. The men drive delivery trucks. The women, like his wife, work as medical or dental assistants.

The men plop themselves on the couch and watch soccer on television. The women cluster around the kitchen table, talking about the pill. They are all in their late twenties, all still childless, focused on the English classes or professional courses that will advance their careers. The pill is pharmaceutical insurance for their dreams: eventually having children, owning businesses, buying suburban homes. It is all planned.

With some pride, Valdés shows recent pictures of his house in Cuba. When he comes to one of his father with his new wife, his mother recoils at the sight of her ex-husband with his arm around a black woman. Valdés concentrates on the coconut trees he planted in the backyard years ago. "Look how tall they are," he says, as if surprised that his house, his father, his trees have gone on without him.

The talk drifts back to Cuba, as it so often does in Miami. Like much of Miami's Cuban community, Valdés is quite conservative politically. A favorite topic is how much he says he has learned about the Cuban government since arriving here — the political prisoners, the human-rights abuses.

He listens to Miami's Cuban exile radio every day, particularly enjoying a program in which the host regularly reads the names of the men and women who have died in prison or were killed trying to overthrow the Castro government. Like most Cubans in Miami — but unlike Ruiz and most Americans — he believes that Elián González, the six-year-old shipwreck survivor, should have stayed in this country rather than return to Cuba with his father.

Ninety miles and four and a half years later, Valdés has ended up back in Cuba — albeit a new and improved Cuba.

"The only thing I miss from Cuba is being able to see the ocean from my windows," he says. "Everything else I need and want is right here. This is exactly the country that I always imagined."

Confined in a Comfort Zone

"Qué bolá, acere?" ("What's up, brother?") Joel Ruiz asks a friend who has stopped to share neighborhood gossip. It is noon on a Tuesday, Ruiz's only day off.

The friend leans in the window of Ruiz's 1989 Buick, and they talk about a shoot-out in front of the friend's house the day before. Drugs, for sure. Both men know the shooters from the neighborhood, and his friend is worried that they may come back. His little daughter was in the front yard when the gunfire started.

Ruiz cuts him off politely and heads to the house of another friend, a middle-aged Cuban woman who, he says, loves him like a son. What she would really love today, though, is $30 for rice and meat. "I don't have any money in the house," she says, lighting a cigarette. "It's terrible."

Having just cashed his paycheck—$175 for six days of work at the bar—Ruiz has money in his pocket. He peels off two twenties, and as he drives away, the woman yells after him, "Come by tonight and I'll make you dinner." He waves her off. He is in a rush. As always on these days of rest, relaxation is in short supply.

Like Achmed Valdés, Ruiz is a man of middle-class ambitions. He is studying English and wants to be a physical therapist. With the help of his uncles, he bought a house in Allapatah—a neighborhood of dark-skinned Latinos and African-Americans—and rents out half of it for extra income. Sure, he would like to be spending his day off hanging out, having a beer, watching sports on TV. But this day, like all his days, is circumscribed by race and the responsibilities that come with being a black man in a poor place.

For the most part, blacks are outsiders in this racially charged city, the scene of some of America's worst race riots. Blacks, especially black Cubans, lack economic and political power and resent the white Cubans who have so much of both. Steadily, relentlessly, the problems of Miami's poor have become Ruiz's, too.

When his uncle was imprisoned for drug dealing, Ruiz was shamed and told almost no one. But the uncle had helped him get started in Miami, and so he stepped in to keep his bar going and help support his little girl. When another uncle was killed by a drunken driver and left his family with no insurance, Ruiz stepped in to help the widow and her three-year-old daughter. He also sends money to his eleven-year-old son in Cuba.

His entire routine, almost his entire life, is focused on a twenty-block area around his home. Occasionally he ventures to South Beach, the fashionable zone where race is not much of an issue. Once, he went to a park in Little Havana, where Cubans, mostly retirees, gather to play dominoes and reminisce.

"But I left right away," says Ruiz, whose politics, despite a dislike of the Castro government, are more moderate than Valdés's. "I couldn't be sitting around talking about Cuba and Fidel all day."

Indeed, if his life is confined, he also feels comfortable in this place where he can be black and Cuban, where he can belong. As he drives with the windows down, he waves at people he knows, black men and women, Cubans and non-Cubans alike.

He has ambitions for the evening — some basketball, a date with his girlfriend, a black Cuban, to see *Best Man*, a film about successful black professionals.

But 4 o'clock finds him at the bar, Annie Mae's, getting things ready for the night. He puts beer in the cooler, sweeps the floors, cleans the bathrooms, polishes the tables and waits for the women who are supposed to run the bar when he is off. He waits, goes out for a while, then waits some more. Still no relief. He turns on the TV and begins watching the news.

"Have you noticed there are no blacks on television?" he says suddenly.

He should have been playing basketball by now, but instead he begins to play video tennis, his eyes fixed on the ball's glowing path through the darkness of the bar.

Encountering the Unknown

When Valdés arrived in Miami, friends and relatives did not just give him the obligatory immigrant lessons on how to fill out forms and apply for jobs. They also sent him a clear message about race, one shared by many, though not all, white Cubans: blacks in America are different from Cuban blacks. Do not trust them and do not go to their neighborhoods.

Valdés has visited his old friend's home just once. In late 1995, when he heard that Ruiz had arrived in Miami, he went to see him in Liberty City. Following his friend's directions, Valdés found the place — a small wood house set back in a huge grassy lot. A chain-link fence surrounds it, and there is an air of abandonment about it, but it does not inspire fear.

Still, he felt uneasy, the only white man in a black neighborhood. The houses were ugly, he says; the few people on the streets stared at him.

"Maybe it's just because, for us, that world is the unknown, but we felt uncomfortable," says his wife, who is as talkative as her husband is reserved. "It's like this: in Cuba I ventured out into the ocean, swimming by myself, because I knew the water, the currents. Here, when I swim, I never stray far from shore because I don't know what's out there."

One of Valdés's early jobs was delivering Ritz soda. Twice, he says, his truck was broken into in black neighborhoods. He lost sixteen cases of soda and $2,000 in checks. "Everywhere else you leave the truck open and nothing happens," he says.

Those experiences have left him with no interest in the black world and not a kind word for African-Americans. "They basically have kids and go on welfare," he says. "What else is there to know?"

In Cuba, he says, he grew up with blacks. It was almost impossible not to, and so he never gave it much thought. His immediate neighbors were mostly white, and he never dated a black woman—"I just don't find them attractive," he explains—but he attended racially mixed schools, and several of his soccer buddies were black.

Here, his contacts with African-Americans are limited to chance encounters at work, his relationships with blacks to those he knows from Cuba. "As far as blacks," he says, "I only trust those I know, because I know they are not delinquents."

Valdés does not flinch when expressing his feelings about blacks. He is passionate and definitive, but he can also be generous and kindhearted, a man who shared his food with children in Guantánamo and regularly sends care packages to his friends, black and white, in Cuba.

Ruiz, he explains, is not his only black friend here. He is also friendly with Fernando Larduet, a man he knew marginally in Cuba but grew to like at Guantánamo. In a video of their time there that Valdés likes to watch to relive his daring escape from Cuba, there is an image of Valdés, who, for lack of a mirror, is gently shaving Larduet.

"It's not that I'm racist," Valdés says. "But even in Cuba, I had a vague sense blacks were different. That becomes more real here. In Cuba, everybody's the same, because everybody's poor. Not so here."

Soon after arriving in Miami, Valdés and his wife went to visit a friend at a hotel downtown. On their way, they made a wrong turn and ended up deep in black Miami.

"It was a cold night and it was really dark, even though it was early," his wife says, over dinner at a restaurant in Coral Gables, a fashionable and very white area of Miami. "People were walking around with sheets over their heads, and there was a fire in a trash can in every corner."

"And the houses were boarded up with pieces of wood to keep the cold away," her husband chimes in, barely lifting his eyes from his lasagna. "And people were smoking crack in the middle of the street."

She shudders. "We got out of there fast," she says.

In Cuba, the Limits of Equality

The soccer field where Joel and Achmed played back in Guanabo is still a busy place, a scrum of young men vying to put the ball into a goal strung together with scraps of fish netting. On a January day in 2000, the game is still an easy mix of blacks and whites.

A few miles away, in the main plaza of the University of Havana, about two hundred students of all colors form a circle around a troupe of dancers. They are not clustered by race. At one point they form a human chain and then they, too, begin to dance, a rainbow of Cuba's best and brightest bathed in sunlight.

At first blush, Cuba might seem to be some kind of racial utopia. Unlike the United States, where there is limited cultural fusion between blacks and whites, Cuban culture—from its music to its religion—is as African as it is Spanish. But despite the genuinely easy mixing, despite the government's rhetoric, there is still a profound and open cultural racism at play.

The same black students who were part of that dancing rainbow say it is common to call someone "un negro," or "black," for doing something inappropriate. "When a man insults a woman in the street, I will shout at him, 'You are not a man, you are black!'" said Meri Casadevalle Pérez, a law student who is herself black.

And a white mechanic named Armando Cortina explained that he would never want his daughters to marry a black. "Blacks are not attractive," he said.

Blacks, he added with conviction, commit the overwhelming majority of crimes in Cuba—a statement impossible to assess in a country that seldom publishes crime statistics. Even Cuba's racial breakdown is uncertain, with a black population thought to be as large as 60 percent.

What is clear is that while the revolution tore down most economic barriers between blacks and whites, there is inequality at the top. Blacks hold few important positions in government or tourism. They are underrepresented at the university and in the nicest neighborhoods. And the few blacks who have tried to organize around the issue of civil rights have been jailed or ostracized.

Bill Brent, a former Black Panther leader who lives in Cuba, said he had arrived full of hope that the government had found the "antidote to racism." Not only does racism persist, he lamented, but black Cubans lack the racial identity to do anything about it.

"The revolution convinced everyone that they are all Cuban and that their struggles were all the same, not separate or different because of their race," he said. "If a Cuban raises his voice to say, 'I am being discriminated against because I am black,' then he would be labeled a dissident."

Still, a voice of black identity can occasionally be heard.

In a sun-scorched neighborhood outside Havana, that voice resonates in the angry rap of Tupac Shakur. It blasts from a boom box at the feet of a group of young black men propped casually against a wall, dressed in a fair imitation of American hip-hop fashion: baggy jeans, oversize T-shirts, Nike sneakers and khaki caps with the brims turned down.

Relatives in Miami sent them the clothes and the rap tapes, they say. As they listen to the music now, it is clear they have not mastered the English lyrics and have only a sketchy sense of the song's meaning. But it does not seem to matter.

"It's about the lives of black people," says eighteen-year-old Ulysses Oliva. "It is for us. That is why we love it."

Two Men in Two Miamis

When Joel Ruiz told his mother that he, too, would be joining the migration to America, she fell to her knees and begged him to stay. Only when she realized she could not change his mind did she get up, dry her tears and cook him his favorite meal—sugar-coated ham with rice and black beans. Then she accompanied him to Guanabo and cried and cried and waved his wisp of a raft out toward the horizon.

Ruiz rarely talks about his mother; at the thought of her, his eyes seem to melt under a curtain of tears. But he says he does not for a minute regret leaving Cuba. It's not that he isn't acutely aware of the way his blackness has guided his story so far in America. He understands the bargain he has made. In Cuba, he says, he did not think about race, but he had no freedom and few options. Here he cannot forget about race, or his many responsibilities, and he has grown apart from his best friend. But instead of the limits, he focuses on the opportunities.

"To eat a good steak in Cuba, I had to steal it from the restaurant where I worked," he says. "Here, I may not want to go to Versailles because I feel uncomfortable, but I can go anywhere else I choose, and no one can stop me at the door because it is illegal and I know my rights."

Along with his identity as a black man, he has found refuge in a community that welcomes him. And he has acquired an American vocabulary to frame his Cuban past. Thinking back, he points to instances of racism that he once shrugged off.

Once, on a bus in Havana, he got into a scuffle with a man he felt had stolen his seat. Afterward, a white friend's mother told him he had behaved like a black man.

" '*Te portaste como un negro,*' that's what she told me," he says. "Now, what could she possibly have meant by that, and how come I didn't see it then?"

Another time, at one of those special birthday dinners with Valdés, the maître d'hôtel stopped him at the door and asked, "And who is this?"

"What he really meant was, 'Who's the nigger?' " Ruiz says. "If that happened to me now, I would know."

Ruiz insists he does not dislike whites. He cites his friendship with

Valdés as an example of his open-mindedness, just as Valdés uses their relationship to establish that he is not racist. And talking to the two men, watching them in one of their rare times together, it is impossible not to feel their fierce loyalty and genuine affection.

Yet both also know that theirs is now mostly a friendship of nostalgia. They are adults with ambitions and jobs and bills to pay, they point out, with little time to talk on the phone. When they do they seldom discuss anything beyond their families in Cuba or how busy they are with work.

When it comes to race, Ruiz will give his friend the benefit of the doubt. Ruiz is proud that when he turned thirty in February 2000, Valdés ventured to black Miami for the party at Annie Mae's. "I understand that it is more difficult for him to cross the line than it is for me," Ruiz says. "It's not his thing and I respect that."

Valdés seems uncharacteristically thoughtful when discussing his friend's life. His friend, he says, has chosen to live as a black man rather than as a Miami Cuban.

"If I were him, I would get out of there and forget about everybody else's problems and begin my own life," he says. "If he stays it is because he wants to."

Ruiz thinks his friend cannot possibly understand. Even after he moved in April to an apartment south of Miami to escape the pressures of his needy relatives, Ruiz could not cast his family or his blackness aside. He spends most of his time back in Allapatah, near the bar and the neighbors who have embraced him.

"I know he would do anything for me if I ask him to, but the one thing he can never do is to walk in my shoes," Ruiz says of his old friend. "Achmed does not know what it means to be black."

Valdés and Ruiz have never talked about race. When told of his friend's opinion of blacks, Ruiz shifts uncomfortably in his seat.

"He said that?" Ruiz asks, lifting his eyebrows. "I don't know why he would think that blacks are delinquents. I know he doesn't think that of me, and I'm black. I've always been black." A pause. He thinks some more. "He grew up with blacks," he says. "I don't understand it. Maybe something bad happened to him. I am sure he is talking about American blacks."

Valdés has never told him about his experiences in Miami's black neighborhoods, just as Ruiz has never told him about the police outside the Versailles.

Yet Ruiz says he understands his friend's fear of crime in black neighborhoods. There are parts of Liberty City even he avoids. What he is wariest of, though, are white neighborhoods. Thinking back on that encounter outside the Versailles, he says: "Now I know enough to be grateful we weren't killed that night. The police could have thought Ramón's camera was a gun."

In Ruiz's new world, whites, even white Cubans, have become a race apart, and while they are not necessarily to be avoided, they must be watched and hardly ever trusted. He can no longer see himself in a serious relationship with a white woman. "Not for marriage," he says. "Not for life."

When he is working in the bar, the only man running a place where money, alcohol and loud music flow into the early hours of morning, the customers who catch his attention are the white men who sometimes wander in.

As he sat at a corner table right before Christmas, a black plastic Santa smiling down at him, Ruiz was relaxed, debating whether to leave for a quick basketball game or stay to help out.

Just then, two white men walked in. It was easy to tell they were Cuban. They walked as Ruiz does, that chest-first Cuban walk. Ruiz perked up. He trailed the men with his eyes. They ordered beers, and as they walked over to the pool table they were momentarily blinded by the light reflecting from a hanging ball of mirrored glass. Averting their eyes, they looked toward the darkness. There they found Ruiz's cold stare. He stared them down until they left.

"You see," he said, relaxing again, "this is why I can't leave this place. You never know who is going to walk in."

Joel Ruiz's bad luck with red cars continued. On the night of June 27, 2000, he was stopped by the police while driving a red Buick that he had bought earlier in the year. He was handcuffed, searched, told to keep his face against the hood of the car. Unbeknownst to him, he said, he had been driving a stolen car. Ruiz spent the night in jail. He lost the car, the $1,800 down payment, even a bag of dirty laundry in the back seat.

The police quickly dropped the stolen car charge, but, while searching Ruiz, they found a four-inch knife. Absentmindedly, Ruiz said, he had walked out of the bar that night with the knife he used to slice lemons for the drinks. He was charged with possession of a concealed weapon, and after his lawyer advised him not to fight the charge, he was ordered to do ten hours of community service.

Without a car, Ruiz relied on friends to take him to work. He had to drop out of school, where he had been learning English, and seldom played basketball anymore. He had not visited his friend, Achmed Valdés, in a long time.

In July, Valdés traveled to Cuba to visit his family. Back in Miami, he got a new job, delivering cardboard boxes instead of mattresses. He spent fewer hours behind the wheel of his truck and never traveled outside Dade County. On weekends, he still played soccer in the park near his apartment.

Ruiz was there, too, but not to play football or see his old friend. To fulfill his ten hours of community service, he was at work, back bent, eyes on the ground, picking up garbage from the fields.

Drill Sergeants Harry Feyer (left) and Earnest Williams (right) with the 4th Platoon, Fort Knox, Kentucky, just after an inspection. Ozier Muhammad/The New York Times

3

Which Man's Army

STEVEN A. HOLMES

FORT KNOX, KENTUCKY

Staff Sgt. Harry Feyer was parking cars and looking glum when the four platoons of Bravo Company, including his own, came marching toward him up a long grassy hill on their way to the winter graduation.

They stepped smartly, 214 strong, their brass buttons gleaming on dress greens, their black shoes buffed to a high sheen. They displayed all the discipline and dash that Feyer, a leader of Fourth Platoon, had helped pound into them in nine weeks of basic training.

Striding beside them were his fellow drill sergeants, shoulders back, chests out, their full-dress uniforms a deep green backdrop for clusters of glinting medals and rainbows of ribbons, their brown Smokey Bear hats cocked aggressively low on their foreheads. Feyer, six feet tall and lanky, might have been among them.

Instead he stood apart in his mottled fatigues and dusty combat boots, directing traffic outside the dingy yellow gymnasium where the ceremony was to be held. It was a duty he had volunteered for. It was his one-man protest.

Feyer was angry that he had been denied an award given to the top-performing drill sergeant at the end of each basic-training cycle, an award he felt he deserved. True, it didn't look like much — just a cheap bronze-plated statue, a generic eight-inch-tall figure of a sergeant. But in the pressure cooker that is the United States Army, winning even a small award could help make the difference between promotion and stagnation, between a better life for his family and just scraping by.

And he knew why he had lost out, or believed he knew: because he is white. No white drill sergeant had won the award since the company was founded in April 1998. Of the five given out, three had gone to blacks and one to a Hispanic. The one time a white sergeant was selected, he gave the trophy back when a group of black sergeants kicked up a fuss, saying he didn't deserve it.

That Feyer had lost out this time came as no surprise in Bravo Company, particularly to the white sergeants. Everyone knew that in Bravo, a clique of black sergeants ran things.

Feyer said he didn't like to think that way. People make too much of race, he said. But there were times when it did matter to him. "When it's a matter of something that I deserve because of my position," he said, "if I outrank a person and he gets a job because of his color, then there's something wrong."

As Feyer stewed in the parking lot, Staff Sgt. Earnest Williams stood erect in front of Fourth Platoon, his square, muscled frame pushing at the seams of his uniform. Williams was part of that black coterie that ran the company, and ran it smoothly. The white sergeants might grumble, but they acknowledged that the blacks got things done. Yet Williams was not feeling particularly powerful this morning. This was his last day with the company. He was being transferred to another unit, away from his buddies, away from his position of influence.

It seemed unfair to him. He was a good soldier, a good leader. His superiors—his white superiors—had said there were too many drill sergeants in Bravo Company and not enough in others. He did not believe them. He was convinced he was being shipped out because he is black. As far as he could see, the powers that be didn't like it when the brothers were in control.

"We had it for a little while," said one of his black compatriots. "But then they said, 'Oh no, we can't let this be.' "

So on a chill December morning in 1999, two soldiers—one black, one white, both part of an institution portrayed as a model of race relations—stood only yards apart in the middle of this sprawling base, each believing himself the victim of racism.

Just then a gray Honda Accord glided into a parking space and out popped Sgt. First Class Henry Reed, resplendent in his dress greens. "Good morning!" he bellowed, a broad smile splitting his dark, soft-featured face. "It's a wonderful day!"

Reed was going to receive the award that Feyer saw as rightfully his; Reed would get the glory even though it was Feyer who had worked the late nights, who had pitched in to help other platoons when they were short-handed, who had made sure the washers and dryers got fixed.

Reed was limited by a back injury suffered in a car crash, and it had not escaped Feyer's notice that Reed had skipped the long days on the rifle range, that he hadn't humped a forty-pound rucksack up and down steep, chest-busting hills on fifteen-kilometer marches.

"We all know that Reed is broke," one white drill sergeant said. "He can't do the work anymore."

Reed was also nearing retirement; at thirty-nine he was the oldest drill sergeant in the company. This was probably his last chance to win the company's drill-sergeant award. So his fellow black sergeants had decided to select him, they said, on the basis of what he had done in the past.

As Feyer watched his colleague stride jauntily into the field house, he had another reason to fume. Reed had parked his car off by itself, leaving a devil-may-care gap in the row of vehicles that Feyer—who finds satisfaction in rote, mechanical tasks—had meticulously arranged.

"He ruined my parking," Feyer said. "Not only did he screw me out of my award, but he ruined my parking."

Ideal? Get Real

The Army is not supposed to harbor racial resentment anymore. Integrated since 1948, it is now marbled with blacks, Hispanics and other minority members of all ranks. It is one of the few institutions in America in which blacks routinely boss around whites, and to hear the Army brass tell it, no one gives it a second thought.

But that is an idealized image. The Pentagon itself discovered as much in 1999, when it found that two-thirds of the men and women in the armed forces had experienced a racially offensive encounter in the previous twelve months. Those findings more or less mirrored the view from Bravo Company, First Battalion, 46th Infantry, in the summer and fall of 1999. Racial tensions abounded, but seldom were they out in the open. Even less often did they rise to high drama. Race-related fights were rare; the angry spitting out of a slur was uncommon.

The sixteen sergeants in Bravo Company appeared to get along, too, eating together in the mess hall, joshing one another about cultural differences in food, music and sports. In part they were helping to fulfill the Army's goal of not so much changing racial attitudes as altering behavior; to some extent they were carrying out orders—to treat one another with respect regardless of race.

"It's like wearing seat belts," said Sgt. First Class Thomas Ballard, a white drill sergeant from Aberdeen, Mississippi. "When I was growing up I never wore a seat belt. But the Army says you've got to wear them."

On the surface, at least, Williams and Feyer seemed good candidates for getting beyond race. Both were thirty-four years old and married. Their children—Williams has three, Feyer two—are of similar ages. Both men had been in the Army twelve years and had been "on the trail," as drill-sergeant duty is called, since the company was formed. Both had spotty academic records and both had been worrying about their careers.

They were also partners—"battle buddies," in military parlance—in running Fourth Platoon, though Williams, as platoon sergeant, was technically Feyer's supervisor. Their metal desks sat three feet apart. They even lived on the same street, less than 200 yards from each other.

But neither had ever set foot in the other's house. Williams had a simple explanation: "We don't have anything in common. We're just different."

They were certainly different in background. Earnest Williams grew up poor in a fatherless household in Waco, Texas. Harry Feyer led a sheltered, stable life in tidy, middle-class, lily-white Sheboygan, Wisconsin.

They also came to be drill sergeants by very different military paths. On the wall next to Feyer's desk was a pen-and-ink drawing of a Cobra helicopter, a memento of his days as a copter mechanic.

Williams, by contrast, was pure infantryman. Hanging next to his desk was a framed pencil drawing of a soldier carrying a rucksack and an M-16. After he bought the sketch, in Hawaii, he had an artist erase the white soldier's face and draw one with black features. It kind of looked like him.

Of the two, Williams was far more comfortable with the racial structure of Bravo Company. Though a white captain and white lieutenant oversaw the unit, the four black drill sergeants were unofficially in charge. Alongside Williams, Staff Sgt. Otis Thomas ran the Third Platoon, Reed the Second and Staff Sgt. Robert Boler the First.

Then there was First Sgt. Anthony Boles, a black man who was in charge of day-to-day matters for the entire company. The four black sergeants held great sway with him—or so it appeared to some white and Hispanic drill sergeants.

"If I complained about something, I would get shot down quicker than Reed or Williams would," said Sgt. First Class Rogelio Gomez, a Hispanic drill sergeant who left Bravo Company in August 1999. "That was the first sergeant's fault, because he was more comfortable dealing with his homies."

Boles scoffed at the notion that he played favorites. But he and the other black sergeants, including Williams, acknowledged that having a company in which African-Americans were in control was a source of racial pride. They considered it unusual, and they feared it would not last.

To Climb, Compete

Race wasn't the whole story in Bravo Company. Career and financial pressures exist in Army life with or without racial tensions. When race does come into play, though, it only aggravates the stress.

While the Army proclaims itself to be about teamwork, its soldiers, including its sergeants, compete against one another. The sergeants push their troops to be named honor platoon, to win marching and marksmanship citations, to score the highest on the PT, or physical training, test. That means doing the most push-ups and sit-ups, and running the fastest two miles.

Winning is not just a matter of satisfying testosterone-fueled egos. Any award, any citation, goes into a soldier's personnel file and can help lift him or her to the next rank. Promotions are everything. The raises they bring may be small, but they are the only means of easing the financial strain.

Like other sergeants, Harry Feyer and Earnest Williams each made about $2,000 a month before taxes. With that they had to buy their own uniforms, knapsacks, sleeping bags, helmets and even the stripes they sewed on their sleeves. Meals in the company mess hall were charged to them.

Housing is free if soldiers live on the post. But that means families must make do with cramped row houses.

"I'd like to have more than five bucks in my back pocket or, sometimes, no dollars in my back pocket," Feyer said. "I want to be able to go to the ATM and not worry, 'Should I do this?' " He said he would love to move into one of those bigger, duplex houses with attached garages. But houses like that are set aside for sergeants first class, a rank above him.

In such an environment there can be gnawing suspicions about why you're not moving up, or not moving up faster. Maybe it's your short-comings. Maybe someone is holding you back. Or maybe, you think, you're not getting ahead because of your race. It's hard to tell.

It was hard to tell with Williams and Feyer. Williams confided that he thought little of Feyer as a soldier and even less of him as a leader. He felt his colleague let too many things fall through the cracks and didn't push the privates enough. As Boler said one day, using Williams's nickname, "In that platoon, Will's the daddy and Harry's the mommy." In the macho world of the Army, "mommy" is not a compliment.

There was a Monday in July 1999 when Williams returned from the weekend to find the barracks a mess. Feyer had had weekend duty. Williams was worried that the first sergeant would see the scuff marks on the floor and the scum in the showers and blame him, as platoon sergeant. That would have stained his record at a delicate time; his name was before the promotion board again.

Apparently unaware of Williams's disrespect, Feyer wondered aloud why his partner didn't share more responsibility with him, why he didn't trust him more. Why was it that Williams tended to confer with Reed, Thomas and Boler on matters involving Fourth Platoon?

"I'm his battle buddy," Feyer said. "I feel he should be discussing things with me."

Showing Who's Boss

Basic training had entered the hot, suffocating days of a Kentucky August, and Feyer was angry and hurt. Williams had undermined his authority, he said — again.

A few days before, as Bravo Company was finishing up on the hand-grenade range, the sergeants had put the recruits in formation for a "shakedown," frisking them to make sure they were not smuggling dummy grenades, a favorite souvenir, back to the barracks. Feyer called on Pvt. David Kellar, a tough-looking black recruit from Chicago, and got a scornful look in return.

Kellar had been a problem from the start. He was big and intimidating. He liked to bully the other privates. Once, he got into a fight and broke another recruit's jaw. He was rebellious. When given an order, he would often suck his teeth or cast a baleful gaze.

Kellar's behavior unnerved Feyer. "It wasn't like I was afraid of him," he said. "I'm sure I could take him if I had to. But it was like he wasn't giving me any respect." He had never seen the private treat Williams that way, he said.

So when Kellar gave him the look this time, the sergeant decided to show him who was boss. After patting him down, Feyer picked up the recruit's canteen and casually tossed it into an open field. "Go get the canteen, private," he told him.

But Kellar wasn't about to fetch anything. He turned to another recruit and gruffly ordered him to retrieve his canteen.

Feyer only got angrier. He and Staff Sgt. David Hanson, a white Californian, grabbed the rest of the recruit's gear—helmet, equipment belt, rucksack—and heaved it into the field as well. "Get your gear yourself," Feyer said.

Kellar obeyed this time but then complained that his helmet was missing an identification holder. It held not only his Army ID, he said, but also $50. He implied the loss was the sergeants' fault.

One black drill sergeant wasn't buying it. "Better check him," he said. But before anyone could touch him, Kellar patted his chest himself. Oh, he said, it had been around his neck the whole time.

Now Feyer wanted the private punished for lying. Back at the barracks, he typed out papers that could have led to a fine or an outright discharge. But to Williams that was overkill. A number of black drill sergeants thought the white sergeants were too harsh with black recruits, he said, and he agreed. He recalled his days in basic training when he was a tough-talking hardhead and black drill sergeants had cut him some slack. So Williams and the first sergeant pressed Feyer to withdraw the charges.

Feyer relented, but the episode did not sit well. He saw it as part of a pattern in which Williams would contradict him, criticize him, ridicule him or bypass him altogether. Sometimes when they were shooting the breeze, Williams would regale the others with a tale of the latest Feyer screwup. He said he knew this bothered Feyer but hoped it would prompt him to shape up.

"It's easy to make him feel insufficient or not good enough," Williams said. "I didn't enjoy it, but I did it to put pressure on him to do better."

Feyer would laugh at himself along with the rest. But inside, he said, he seethed. He hated the way his partner embarrassed him.

Steamroller from Waco

On a bright summer afternoon Williams was marching Fourth Platoon along one of Fort Knox's wooded back roads. Each drill sergeant has his favorite cadence—the rhythmic call-and-response chant used to keep the privates in step. Williams was calling out one of his.

"I'm a steamroller, baby," he sang in a strong tenor, "and I'm rolling all over you."

The words fit well, physically and temperamentally. At five feet ten inches and 210 pounds, Williams was a model of muscle and power. When he had free time, he was usually pumping iron in the company's weight room. He was careful with his diet and didn't smoke, though he did occasionally like a beer. His desk drawer rattled with bottles of pills labeled "Ripped Fuel—Metabolic Enhancer" and "Metaform."

He also had a bright, boyish smile that went well with his impish sense of humor. But in an institution that puts a premium on physical fitness, it was important to Williams to camouflage his charm with sternness and to impress the privates with prowess.

One evening they challenged him to do fifty push-ups in a minute. He accepted but, not wanting to embarrass himself, first retreated to his office to see if he could pull off such a feat. There he dropped to the floor and did fifty. Naturally the effort tired him. But he would not let himself show weakness, so he swaggered out into the sleeping bay, slapped a stopwatch into a private's hand and knocked out another quick fifty. The men were wide-eyed.

"In the Army you're either a stud or a slug," Williams said. "You can be really intelligent. But if you can't run three miles or hump a rucksack, then you're a slug."

Williams learned the necessity of toughness long before he got to Bravo. He grew up in the central Texas flatlands, bouncing among housing projects and running through the weeds around shacks in a neighborhood of drugs and poverty.

Earnest Williams was the sixth of fourteen children born to Shirley Ann Hunter. Abandoned by her first and second husbands, she had little choice other than welfare. But with so many mouths to feed, it was never enough. Clothes came from the Salvation Army. The family was constantly being evicted for failure to pay the rent.

Relatives offered to take in some of the children, but she refused. "The one thing our mother showed us was endurance," said another son, Robert Bell. "Because we had it so hard, we would have these

family group sessions. She would call all my brothers and sisters together and tell us that the only thing we had was each other, and the
only thing we could do was endure."

Not all the children did. The oldest brother, Greg, became a crack
addict, and a younger brother, James, was killed during a drug deal.
But Earnest stayed out of trouble, channeling into sports the determination his mother had taught him. In high school he became a
football and track star. Or, more precisely, he willed himself to become
a star; he could not abide the word "can't." One summer he watched
people in the deep end of a public pool. Not content at the shallow
end, he watched them and mimicked them until he had taught himself
to swim.

But he was never much of a student. "I went all the way through
high school and I don't think I cracked a book once," he said one day,
looking wistfully off in the distance from a bleacher seat at Fort Knox.

In some ways he is the perfect soldier: strong, driven and unques-
tioning.

After enlisting he was steered into the infantry, and with his physical
abilities he found it easy. "I felt like I'm at home here," he said. He
was considered a first-rate infantryman. Once, during the Persian Gulf
war, he walked point for an entire battalion of the 82nd Airborne Division as it moved to attack the Iraqis. That was as close as he came
to combat; the Iraqis surrendered at the Americans' approach.

But he never gave much thought to where his career was going. He
dutifully took the elite infantry jobs his superiors recommended — par-
atrooper, Ranger — and succeeded at whatever was asked of him, to the
extent that he got his sergeant's stripes. He was a natural leader as a
drill sergeant, fast-talking, quick-moving and impatient with those who
were not.

Yet his career hit a wall after the Gulf War. He was promoted to
staff sergeant in 1992. Seven years later, he had yet to make it to the
next level, sergeant first class. Four times his name went before promotion boards, and four times he was rejected.

He and his wife, Ruth, a Puerto Rican whom he met in 1987, suspected that his academic deficiencies were behind his stagnation. He
had never taken any college courses in the Army, even though he had
had the opportunity. During a stint at Fort Benning, Georgia, for example, he had enough time on his hands to become a part-time security guard.

"He talks about going back to school lots of times," Ruth Williams said one afternoon in their living room, between running one child to dance and another to basketball. "A big obstacle for him is being afraid to go back. He feels he was never really prepared in high school to do college work."

But as they watched other sergeants move up—mainly white ones, whose credentials were no better than his—the Williamses also began to suspect race.

"It makes you wonder," she said. "Is he being passed over because he's a black male?"

Williams was getting older and going nowhere. He decided that if he didn't get a promotion by this summer, he would quit. His two years as a drill sergeant were up in April. His wife was already typing out his application to the Secret Service. He toyed with the idea of running an ROTC program at a black college somewhere and taking courses at the same time. He even considered volunteering to serve a year in Korea, figuring that if he put in twelve months there, he had a chance for an ROTC slot when he rotated back to the States.

But Korea is considered a war zone, meaning soldiers cannot take their families with them, and his wife made it clear that she would not stand for that. "It would not be good for my kids not to see their father for a year, especially my son," she said. "So that's not going to happen."

Tinkerer from Sheboygan

Feyer liked to show off Bravo's cavernous classroom. He had spent hours refurbishing it, pasting blue sisal halfway up the white walls to relieve the drabness and deaden the echoes. He had even designed the floor, using royal blue tiles against white to make a large "146," Bravo's battalion and brigade.

It was his kind of work. "I've always loved working with my hands," he said. "I guess I got that from my dad."

His father, Gerrit, was a Dutch immigrant, a wood-carver who helped make molds for machine parts. Harry was the youngest of seven children whom Gerrit and Cornelia Feyer reared in Sheboygan, a manufacturing town on Lake Michigan north of Milwaukee and south of Green Bay.

The Feyers had moved there for the work and for their faith. Sheboygan offered a school run by the Christian Reformed Church, an offshoot of the Dutch Reformed Church, and the Feyers wanted their children educated in the Reform tradition. Sheboygan was a safe setting in which to raise children, but it was isolated.

"Because he was going to a Christian school and hung around with Dutch people, he was kind of sheltered," his father said.

There were hardly any blacks in Sheboygan. A local joke has it that if you see a black man on the street, he must play for the Packers. Sergeant Feyer remembers knowing one black family. The father was a police officer. The son was a thief.

While Earnest Williams was a football hero in high school, Harry Feyer faded into the crowd at his school. He didn't play sports, he didn't participate in extracurricular activities, he didn't do well in his studies.

"He was kind of a laid-back kid, not a natural leader," recalled Art DeJong, his high school English teacher. "I wouldn't say Harry was the most highly disciplined guy I've ever met. He was friendly and likable, the type of kid who sometimes gets lost."

Where he usually got lost was under the hood of a car. He would spend hours in a neighbor's garage, breaking down and rebuilding engines. Mechanical tasks absorbed him, just as they would in the Army, to the point where they distracted from the rest of his life.

After finishing school, he married his high school sweetheart, Laurel Cluk, a strong-willed, outspoken woman. He got a job in a plant that made wall paneling and shortly concluded that it was a dead end. That was when he decided to enlist.

In the Army he gained recognition as a first-rate mechanic and was given the job maintaining Cobras. He wound up doing little more than that; it took him almost eight years to become a sergeant. In part he blames a supervisor, in part himself.

It was 1991, and the Army was phasing out the Cobra, so promotions for people who worked on it were becoming rare. He was supposed to be notified of a special program permitting Cobra mechanics to switch to other specialties. But he was a good mechanic and his supervisor didn't want to lose him, so, the sergeant said, the supervisor hid the notification papers.

Feyer learned of the ruse the next year, but by then it was too late for the retraining. "I should have gone straight to the IG, the inspector general, and said this guy just screwed me," he said. But the supervisor "was somewhat of a friend of mine," he said, "and I didn't want to get him in trouble.

"So I didn't say anything."

He does say something when his assertiveness is questioned, however. He'll smile, bob his head and, like some goofy cartoon character, sing, "Doh-dee-doh-dee-doh."

That sort of passivity drives his wife crazy. At dinner one night at home, he was complaining about being cheated out of the top drill sergeant award that went to Reed. Without missing a beat he began describing the work he was going to do during the break between cycles to improve the company's classroom.

But why put yourself to all that trouble after what has happened? he was asked.

"Because he's stupid," Laurel Feyer interjected.

Feyer smiled sheepishly. "Doh-dee-doh-dee-doh," he sang.

Promotion Blues

The promotion board was meeting during the summer and Feyer was eager for a shot at platoon sergeant. But he wondered what chance he had when all the platoon sergeant slots in Bravo Company were held by blacks.

Feyer had been in an almost identical situation in South Korea. There a white sergeant, a talented helicopter mechanic, was bypassed for platoon sergeant because all the platoon sergeants were black and a black first sergeant looked out for them. Or so most people, especially whites, suspected. As far as Feyer knew, no one bothered to find out the truth.

Now he saw history repeating itself. "I hated thinking like that," he said. "But I just didn't want to get screwed."

Not again. Besides, he saw himself as a new man now.

His transformation began, he said, the day in 1994 when the Army told him that it was kicking him out. It had been three years since his supervisor had sandbagged him into remaining a Cobra mechanic, and he still had not made sergeant. The Army was pruning itself of dead wood, and he, stuck at corporal, was on the list.

Laurel Feyer was pregnant at the time, and the couple had a five-year-old son; they needed the Army's medical benefits. One night Feyer lay awake, his chest so constricted he could hardly breathe. "I was really scared," he said. "I didn't know what I was going to do."

Fear galvanized him. He pleaded with the Army not to discharge him and volunteered to work in nuclear, biological and chemical warfare. Not many soldiers choose that specialty. Most are scared off by it, imagining themselves in stifling chemical-warfare suits, never mind the poisons. Promotion possibilities there are wide open.

"I took it because I didn't want to throw away eight years of being in the Army," Feyer said.

He made sergeant a few months later.

The promotion brought another surprise. Attending mandatory classes for noncommissioned officers, he graduated with honors. Buoyed by his success, he signed up for courses at a community college in Colorado Springs, where the family was living. He got As, Bs and an associate's degree. He was stunned.

"I went all through high school thinking I'm a failure, that I'm nothing but a D-minus student," he said.

In short order he became staff sergeant, then drill sergeant, finishing near the top of his class. Now, at Fort Knox, he had a chance for platoon sergeant, and he wasn't going to be denied by a group of blacks just because he wasn't one of them.

He talked over the situation with the company's executive officer, Lt. Paul Bergson, a chubby, college-educated white officer with a mordant sense of humor. Bergson warned him that before raising a stink he should determine whether the blacks promoted to platoon sergeant had more seniority. He checked, and they had.

But the black sergeants got wind that whites were questioning the platoon leadership's racial makeup and resented it.

"They never want to see a black man get ahead," Reed said as he sat with a group of black sergeants in the mess hall one night. Williams agreed. As soon as whites feel even a little threatened, he said, "they all stick together."

A Truce, or Maybe Not

By the autumn of 1999 Williams and Feyer had reached a kind of accommodation. It might have had something to do with Williams's promotion; in September he received word that on his fifth try he was being made sergeant first class. The pressure, for the moment, was off. His wife could put away the application for the Secret Service.

A few days before the fall graduation, Feyer gingerly approached Williams and mentioned that his parents would be visiting from Sheboygan and that they had never seen their son at work. Williams picked up on the hint and gave Feyer his place at the ceremony marching in front of Fourth Platoon.

"This stuff don't mean nothing to me, anyway," Williams said.

For his part, Feyer began trying to work more effectively with Williams. He tried to anticipate what was wanted of him. He felt Williams tried to talk with him more. "We're clicking now," he said. "We don't even have to say anything. We each know what to do."

Williams had a different view: his partner still wasn't pulling his weight. "He wants his own platoon," Williams said. "I feel he should get it and then fall on his face. The reason he doesn't fall on his face now is because I don't let him."

But Williams soon had something else on his mind. Near the end of the fall cycle he was told that he was being transferred to Echo Company, across the parade ground.

The orders outraged him. He had achieved a position of power in Bravo Company. The transfer would mean he would have to start over again. And it messed up his plans. Bravo was not participating in basic training for the January cycle, meaning that its drill sergeants would essentially have nine weeks off. Williams had enrolled in a college course for the break. Now he would have to withdraw and work another basic training cycle with Echo.

Why the transfer? Williams saw the reason, again, as racial. To him and his black colleagues, the battalion's white hierarchy could not tolerate one of its four companies being run by black sergeants. One of the sergeants had to go.

Williams and the other black sergeants say they had a premonition of this during a ceremony in November 1999 to replace the company commander. As the battalion commander and the battalion command sergeant major looked out on the parade ground and saw a black sergeant standing in front of each platoon and a black first sergeant in front of the entire company, you could see the shock in the officers' eyes, the sergeants said.

Not so, said Col. Mark Armstrong, the battalion commander, and Sgt. Maj. Franklin Ashe. They had barely taken notice of the company's racial makeup, they said.

"This blows me away that they would have these perceptions, because the thought never crossed my mind," Ashe said.

Two days before the December graduation, Feyer and Williams sat brooding in their office along with Sgt. First Class Mike Martin, the replacement, who is white. Williams was angry about his impending transfer. Feyer was still upset about having been denied the drill sergeant's award. He was speculating about who might or might not have voted for him. Williams, who had voted against his partner, sat in silence.

"It's Too Late"

The winter graduation, minus Feyer, was over. Friends and relatives were mingling in the barracks, congratulating the recruits. Several parents dropped by Williams's office to shake his hand for molding their strapping young men into soldiers. But as the minutes ticked by, Williams grew impatient. He wanted to hurry up and move his things into Echo. He was supposed to meet Boler and Reed for beers. Feyer was going golfing with Hanson.

Walking outside the barracks, Williams mentioned an overture he had received that morning. "Harry said to me at breakfast: 'You live only 200 yards away, and you've never been over my house and I've never been over your house. Why don't we try to get together?' "

He said he would consider it. "But I kind of feel like, what's the point? It's too late.

"It's like, 'Let's patch things up.' But there's really nothing to patch up."

He enlisted a number of privates to help him take his gear over to Echo. They loaded up a truck, drove it across the parade ground and lugged the stuff up two flights of stairs. Williams hung his fatigues in a locker and tossed some equipment onto an unmade bunk.

From down the hall he could hear music drifting out of the office he would share with his new partner. It was gospel music, the sound of a choir. Williams didn't care for gospel; he was a rhythm-and-blues man. But it didn't seem to bother him. He had met his new battle buddy, Mordecial Hale, who was thirty-five, six feet five and black.

So will it be better, Williams was asked, having a brother as a partner?

"Without a doubt," he replied. "Without a doubt."

David Mills, Charles S. Dutton, and David Simon (left to right) on the Baltimore, Maryland, set of the HBO series The Corner. Andrea Mohin/The New York Times

4

Who Gets to Tell a Black Story?

JANNY SCOTT

BALTIMORE, MARYLAND

David Simon was white but he knew he could write black people.
Maybe not all black people but the ones he had known in Baltimore,
where he had been a crime reporter for fourteen years. He had spent
a year on a Baltimore drug corner and written a book that had done
something almost unheard-of: It had shown black inner-city drug addicts as complex and startlingly human.

So Simon was not thinking much about his whiteness when he
walked into the Los Angeles offices of HBO in January 1998 and set
about trying to interest three white programming executives in the
improbable idea of making the book into a television series.

No one talked about race at that meeting. At least, not directly. No
one remarked upon the fact that Simon was white and that nearly
everyone in his book was black. Nor did anyone mention that HBO
was not about to make a series about black drug addicts created by, as
one HBO executive put it later, "a bunch of white guys."

Instead, the executives asked Simon a lot of questions. How did
black people in Baltimore react when his book, *The Corner: A Year in
the Life of an Inner-City Neighborhood,* came out? What did the mayor,
who was black, say? What would happen if HBO were to make the
series, and shoot it in Baltimore, and protests broke out?

Then they asked him to suggest a writing partner. He offered two
names. One was James Yoshimura, an Asian-American playwright and
television writer he had worked with on *Homicide: Life on the Street,*
the NBC series based on Simon's first book. The other was David
Mills, an African-American writer and friend of Simon's since college,
who had recently been nominated for two Emmys for episodes of
NYPD Blue.

Simon suggested Yoshimura and Mills for the same reason, he said later: He liked working with them. He did not feel he needed a black writer to help him tell a black story. He had spent his career as a white reporter in a mostly black town. He had a good ear and had paid attention in a way he knew most white people did not.

He was not unaware, however, that Mills might have special appeal for HBO. It was apparent from the line of questioning that a black writer was high on HBO's priority list. And, as Simon put it, as soon as the bait was dangled in the water, the fish leapt onto the hook.

At the mention of Mills, a look shot between two of the executives, Kary Antholis and Anne Thomopoulos. Antholis had been following Mills's career. He had even mentioned him to Thomopoulos—as a smart writer who had worked at the highest levels of television, and who also happened to be black.

Do you know David Mills? one of them asked Simon.

Yes.

Could you get him to work on this project?

Sure.

Within minutes, Simon had a deal, HBO had a miniseries and Mills had a new job as Simon's writing partner and fellow executive producer.

The Risk and the Buzz

A miniseries about drug addicts was risky television. But it appealed to Chris Albrecht, the president for original programming at HBO, because HBO defined itself by doing what broadcast networks would not. That approach had earned HBO the admiration of critics, lots of Emmys and an expanding audience of subscribers, a fifth to a quarter of them black.

The Corner would not need a mass audience on HBO, because HBO did not make its money off commercials. What HBO wanted was attention and buzz. If the series could be shot quickly in the summer and fall of 1999 and put on the air the following April, it would be in Emmy voters' minds when they voted in June.

But no matter how good *The Corner* might be, Albrecht said later, there would be black people who would want to know why HBO was doing it at all. They would forget *Introducing Dorothy Dandridge, Lau-*

rel Avenue, The Tuskegee Airmen, Miss Evers' Boys. The question would be, Why are you portraying black people that way?

HBO needed African-Americans involved for two reasons, Albrecht said: for creative reasons and for public relations.

"I really still wanted to find somebody who would be my . . ." Albrecht recalled later in his office in midtown Manhattan, choosing his words, "who would be an additional, uh . . ." He paused, then used a vulgar expression for a person capable of detecting pretentious nonsense. "You know?"

He wanted Charles S. Dutton to direct *The Corner.*

If anyone knew Baltimore's corners, it was Dutton. He had grown up in the city and spent his early years on its streets, where rock fighting—snowball fighting, except with rocks—earned him the lifelong nickname Roc. His only sister was a recovering cocaine addict. His only brother, who died of AIDS in 1993 at age forty-four, had been a heroin addict for nearly twenty-five years.

What had saved Charles Dutton was prison. He dropped out of school at twelve and pleaded guilty to manslaughter at seventeen, after stabbing a black man who had pulled a knife on him in a fight. He served two years. Then he was sent back for weapons possession, fought with a white guard, and ended up serving another seven and a half.

The tale of his redemption is well known. He grabbed an anthology of plays by black playwrights on his way into solitary confinement one day. By the light under the cell door, he read *Day of Absence,* a social satire by Douglas Turner Ward. He was so taken with it, he organized a production, starred in it and discovered what he had been put on earth to do.

He formed a drama group that performed Shakespeare and Arthur Miller. He got his high school equivalency certificate and a junior college degree in prison, went to Towson State University in Maryland and Yale Drama School while on parole, and won his first Tony nomination for his performance in the August Wilson play *Ma Rainey's Black Bottom* on Broadway in 1984.

After a performance of *The Piano Lesson* by Wilson in 1990, Albrecht introduced himself to Dutton. He then lured him to Los Angeles to star in his own television program, *Roc.* The sitcom, in which Dutton played a garbage man, Roc Emerson, appeared on Fox for three tumultuous seasons starting in 1991.

Dutton was not overjoyed with Hollywood. On stage, he said, he had felt he could change the world. He had found the closest thing he knew to a utopian, race-neutral place. But he arrived in Hollywood suspicious of half-hour television and determined, as he put it, that no one would make a monkey out of him in prime time.

To accomplish that, he spent much of his three years "stomping, kicking and being a despot," he recalled. Then he moved on to movies, everything from *Cry, the Beloved Country* and *Alien 3* to *Cookie's Fortune* and Spike Lee's *Get on the Bus*. And he became an outspoken critic of racism in Hollywood.

"There isn't a single black person in Hollywood with any power," he said in the fall of 1999. "This isn't paranoia. Because if I stood in a room with every major black star, just talking, then I would hear the same things out of their mouths that are coming out of mine. Multimillionaires. The main thing you'll hear is, 'Whenever I take a project, I can't get it done unless I have a white partner.'

"In other words, if Denzel Washington, Danny Glover, Morgan Freeman, Wesley Snipes, Laurence Fishburne, if they went to a studio and said, 'I want to do the movie of Hannibal.' They'll say, 'Yeah, well, we have to call in Al Pacino or the latest young Italian actor to play Scipio,' the guy who defeated Hannibal many years after all his conquests. And, damn it, that's who the story will center around."

In the world beyond Hollywood, Dutton, forty-nine, was widely admired. A striking figure with a stocky build, shaved head and eloquent face, he often traveled the country, speaking at small black colleges and in prisons. He was respected by working-class and upper-middle-class blacks alike, and by many whites.

HBO sent the scripts to Dutton and no one else.

At first he said no. He had directed just one movie, an HBO film called *First-Time Felon*. But he was not interested in another urban drama, especially one about drugs. "I had a certain bitterness and anger with family members who allowed themselves to be destroyed that way," he recalled. "I had to ask myself, do I want to take this emotional journey through this world?"

Yet the scripts intrigued him. What he admired about the story was that it was told from the addicts' perspective, not some glamorized dealer's. It made clear what he had long seen as the hypocrisy of the war on drugs. And it could serve, he said, as a raw reminder of an element of society that Americans chose to forget.

HBO offered him two episodes. Then four. Then all six. The shooting schedule would be a killer, but doing all six might give him a degree of control that television directors rarely had. He would take a bath financially, he said later, because he made his real money as an actor. But he wanted to prove he had the stamina and the concentration to pull it off.

In what he would later call a momentary lapse of sanity, he said yes. He had come to respect Simon and Mills, he said shortly after accepting the job. But, as he also said, there would not be one moment when he would forget that "it's a white writer and a white producer and it's HBO and a black director."

And no matter how many supportive black people HBO would line up, the job of defending the miniseries would fall to him. "I'm going to have to be the person saying, 'Hey, y'all, it's cool,' " he once said, chuckling at his impersonation of himself. " 'Ain't no sense in gettin' upset. This is a *gooooood* movie. Go watch it. Order HBO!' "

The Crew Is Too White

On July 22, 1999, Dutton laid eyes on his crew for the first time.

They were gathered at the intersection of Montford Avenue and Oliver Street, a broken-down place with a bar, a corner store, a boarded-up deli and little else. Three weeks before they were to start shooting, the heads of the various departments, newly hired by the producers, had come with the producers and several HBO executives to scout their principal location.

Dutton arrived separately. He slid out of his car and focused on the stream of men and women emerging from a couple of vans.

They weren't all white. But almost.

It was not as if the producers hadn't known that he wanted a racially mixed crew. He had brought up the subject with the unit production manager, Nina Kostroff Noble, on his first day in Baltimore: I'm not going into the ghettos of Baltimore city for a whole damn summer with an all-white crew, he would remember saying. And if you guys were smart, you wouldn't either.

What makes you think it's going to be all white? she had responded.

It was always the same, Dutton said later. The business was "full of nepotism and cliquism." Italians hired Italians, Asians hired Asians. "So why is it a problem when it's a black project?

Every black project that I've worked on, with the exception of the

Spike Lee movies, you've got to go through this every time. You've got to say, 'Why can't we have some more black folks on the crew?' "

Not that Dutton wanted an all-black crew. Having healthy black representation was a matter of pride and fairness, but he also believed it was more fun when a crew was truly diverse. For a series about black addicts, filmed in East Baltimore, he thought the right percentage of African-Americans was their percentage in the city, roughly 65 percent.

Affecting an earnest white voice, he mocked the response he got in Hollywood whenever he complained: Are you saying the studios are *deliberately* not hiring black people? No, he said, they didn't go into a room and say: "You know, we ain't hiring no damn black people. Everyone agreed? And here's the story if we get questioned about it."

It just came naturally, without thinking. And if you confronted them, they would say: "Hey, my next-door neighbor is black. My best friend is black." You could throw racism two inches in front of white peoples' faces and they still wouldn't see it, Dutton said. Or they'd deny it and say you were the one causing the problems.

"There isn't a black actor in Hollywood, on the star level or the lowest level, who doesn't in private vehemently rail against the industry," he said. "The biggest stars. The hugest stars. Because somewhere along the line they are still reminded, 'You know something? You're a big star but you're just another nigger.'

"And so either you succumb to it and you roll over and you grin and you bear it and you shuck and you jive and you laugh when it ain't funny and you scratch when it ain't itching. And you go about being a good little boy and you're patted on the head and they give you the next little movie. And you look around and there ain't no black folks on that one, either."

He paused, then added: "But those that do that will probably rot in hell somewhere."

At Montford and Oliver, he could hear the first assistant director starting to introduce him: "This is the director, Charles Dutton." Instead of walking over and shaking hands, he turned his back on them all and crossed the street.

It would have been phony, he said later, to shake hands and grin and act as if everything were all right. So, flanked by his black bodyguard and his black driver, he went to work studying the location. He figured everybody got the message: I'm not doing this with a white crew. Sorry. Nothing personal.

Nina Noble, the unit production manager, was upset. She recognized the problem immediately. But Dutton was not behaving like the captain of the ship, she said later. Some of the black crew members felt like tokens; some whites felt slapped in the face, she said. They told her so.

Noble was white, but she prided herself on being color-blind in her work. In the case of *The Corner,* she had intended to go further than usual to hire a racially mixed crew. She and David Simon and the other producers had discussed it at length. None of them wanted anyone in the community, cast or crew feeling exploited or degraded.

But there were not many black technicians in the business, especially in Baltimore, Noble said later. And it was expensive to bring them in from other cities and house them. When she had asked one of the unions if it had a minority roster, she had been warned against trying to violate seniority rules.

Even so, the crew she had begun putting together already included a number of African-Americans. Unfortunately, some of them were not there that day, because they were not department heads. And one of those who were there might have been mistaken for white. "OK," Noble said later. "It's not enough that we have people who are black. We have to hire people with dark skin."

She had been hoping that Dutton, after several weeks on the job, had begun to deal with everyone on what she called "more a personal level and less on a racial level."

"I guess I was wrong about that," she said.

Later that day, Dutton spoke with one of the visiting HBO executives, who then spoke with Noble and Robert F. Colesberry, the third executive producer. Along with Simon, they all agreed they had to try even harder to hire more African-Americans on to the crew.

In the following weeks, they hired a black script supervisor, hairdresser, director's assistant and production assistant, all of them from out of town. The Teamsters came up with three black drivers. By the end of production, the shooting crew consisted of forty-one white people and thirty-three black people, by Noble's count.

Many crew members said it was the most racially mixed crew they had ever seen. It was a source of satisfaction for many people, including Simon, who believed that the white people had learned from the experience. He said later: "If Charles wanted us to be 65 percent, and if inertia would have made us 10 or 15 percent, somewhere in between is where we ended up. And I don't know what perfect is."

Dutton thought he did. And where they had ended up was not perfect.

That day would remain a defining moment for him. "I didn't see anything but white people, white people, white people," he said later. " 'Hey, we're making a movie about these black people and *we're* the experts.' Absolutely, I felt like, well, hold it. The way to impress me with your liberalism or your humanity or your honesty or your integrity where the black community is concerned is to share the damn pot."

Something lingered after that day, Simon remarked many months later. A few people told him they felt that whiteness was a liability on the set, he said. If they got their feelings hurt, it could be a hard shoot. But he believed the wrong move at that moment was to get offended. It solved nothing.

"There are white people for whom that moment of having somebody be standoffish or curt or unpleasant, or even the veiled suggestion that race is a barrier, that ends it," Simon said. If there was one thing that being a white reporter in a mostly black city had taught him, it was what could be gained by not walking away.

A Long Way from Silver Spring

David Simon grew up in a mostly white world, the youngest of three children in a liberal Democratic household in Silver Spring, Maryland, in which books and newspapers were revered and argument was sport. He went to suburban public schools that were heavily white. He recalls as a child having heard a racial epithet used only twice, but having known enough to be indignant.

Race was rarely discussed at home, but equality was a given. Simon's father was the director of public relations and a speechwriter for B'nai B'rith. His mother worked for several years for a group called the Negro Student Fund, which helped underachieving public school students move to independent schools.

Simon learned about race in Baltimore. The *Sun* hired him out of the University of Maryland in 1983. Race was out in the open in Baltimore in a way he had never seen before. It was no big deal, he said, to walk into a bar in Highlandtown and hear white people talking about black folks, or to meet a black person and be told everything that was wrong with white people, no offense.

Race seemed to permeate everything in Baltimore: housing, education, politics, criminal justice. It was as if the city had swallowed whole every other trend but had choked on race, he said. The biggest crime story was drugs, and intravenous drug use in Baltimore occurred predominantly among African-Americans. To be a decent reporter, he had to learn to listen to black people.

In 1988, Simon spent a year with the Baltimore Police Department's homicide unit, doing the reporting for what became his 1991 book, *Homicide: A Year on the Killing Streets.* Waiting around at crime scenes and in people's houses, he ended up shooting the breeze for hours upon hours with people the police encountered on cases.

"So then the trick becomes: can I just be patient enough not to ask every question at once, to laugh only at the jokes that they tell when they're funny, and not to laugh at the ones that, if you laugh at them, they know you're full up with it, and to venture your own joke about something," Simon recalled.

At the *Sun*, he made a specialty of turning obscure murders into full-blown dramatic narratives. Gregarious, voluble and funny, he believed he could talk to anybody. And every time someone rendered himself or herself human, he said, "it was an argument against whatever racial simplicities you've constructed in your mind."

In 1993, he took a leave of absence and went to work on *The Corner* with a former police detective named Edward Burns, also white, who believed that the drug war had led the police badly astray, and who shared with Simon the impulse to demonstrate to the credit-card-carrying world that the people the drug war had demonized had lives and sensibilities and deserved understanding.

Simon and Burns picked the intersection of Fayette and Monroe Streets, one of a hundred open-air drug markets in a city said to have the highest rate of heroin use of any in the country. They went every day. They talked, joked, hung around, listened, eventually winning the confidence of dozens of people whose stories would become the soul of the book.

When *The Corner* came out in 1997, the *New York Times* chose it as one of the notable books of the year. The Reverend Frank Reid, pastor of the largest African-American church in Baltimore, based sermons on it and held a party to celebrate it. Five hundred people showed up.

Simon had leapt a chasm few white people cross, David Mills, his friend and writing partner, believed. He had written about black addicts not through a microscope but by sitting next to them. He had learned the language, sensibility and sense of humor of the ghetto, a sensibility Mills knew from his childhood. And he had gotten more intimately involved with his subjects than Mills could imagine doing himself.

Simon's newspaper articles, meanwhile, looked less and less like what normally turns up in a newspaper. They began with paragraphs like " 'You don't look so good,' says the cop, smiling. 'You look like death.' " Then an editor at the *Sun* accused him of ennobling criminals. Disgusted, he left in 1995. He went to work as a writer and producer on *Homicide*.

That the subjects of his journalism were often black was not what drew Simon to them, he insisted. Race had simply made the territory seem less accessible, so their voices had not been heard. There were things he missed because he was white, he said. But there were other things a black writer from that world might have missed because he or she was too close.

Occasionally, he found himself accused of exploitation.

"I'm losing patience with the idea of it being exploitive," he said. "Except to acknowledge that in one sense all journalism is exploitive. Janet Malcolm was right. We're all selling used cars. And any journalist who tries to say we're not is lying through his teeth.

"The only ethic that I can find that you can hang your hat on says: Now that I have the material, how do I treat my subjects? Do I accord them all the humanity they deserve, or do I write a crude and simplistic exposé?"

Faces from the Old Days

The shooting schedule in Baltimore was relentless: twelve- and thirteen-hour days, five days a week, no end in sight. By early October 1999, Charles Dutton had not slept eight hours straight for two months. The production was on time and under budget. But at times the film was being written, cast, shot and edited almost simultaneously.

It was emotionally grueling, too. Day in and day out, they were shooting in the depths of the world they were depicting, in the decaying row-house neighborhoods that in Baltimore seem to stagger on forever, with the drug corners, tumbledown bars, boarded-up windows, rumble of demolition trucks, shriek of sirens. Everywhere, there were children.

Every day people would turn up to watch, a shifting collection of neighborhood residents, acquaintances of Dutton, survivors from his prison drama group, aspiring actors and hangers-on — more than a few of whom found their way into small parts in the series, blurring the boundary between the film and the street.

For Dutton, being back in the old neighborhood was not necessarily fun — the handshaking, embracing, hearing sob stories, shelling out money, seeing people he had once idolized who had gone nowhere. He kept waiting for someone, he said, just someone, to arrive by car, not on foot, and get out with kids and a wife and everyone looking healthy.

Simon was around, too, along with many of the people from his book. Of those who had not died, some were clean and turning their lives around. Simon had remained close to them. Now he found joy in helping them get small roles, for which those in speaking parts could rake in the princely Screen Actors Guild rate of $596 a day.

Mills visited the set rarely. What he loved was the solitary process of writing, so he passed his days in the office, writing and fine-tuning scripts. Simon let him try anything, and relied on him. But there was a well-defined hierarchy, Mills observed without resentment. *The Corner* was Simon's project; he was there to serve Simon's vision.

They had first worked together on the University of Maryland student paper and Mills, like Simon, had gone into journalism. They had written their first television script together, for *Homicide*, in 1992, winning an award from the Writers Guild of America. Mills had then quit his job at the *Washington Post* to become a television writer. Their friendship, they both said, had long ago moved well beyond race. And that appeared to be the truth.

For the first few weeks of production, Simon was on the set every day, often in the background, watching or talking with Colesberry and Noble, and occasionally Dutton. Then, after a few weeks, he began coming less often. At the time, he said he had pulled back because he was confident that all was in good hands. But later, he said he had also begun to sense that Dutton responded better to Colesberry than to him. Dutton seemed distant, more curt. Simon said he figured Dutton was feeling the pressure, like everyone.

In fact, Dutton had come to distrust Simon.

"As good as some of this material is, I'm wondering where his real heart is in this," he said in October. "Is this really and truly an effort to do something about this?" No matter how sincere Simon was, he was "taking somebody else's misery and making a dollar off of it. Which can't be denied, whether he's the most sincere goddamn white man in the world."

Where the distrust had started, Dutton could not say for sure.

Early on, he had gotten the impression through HBO that Simon and Mills had doubts about having him direct all six episodes. Then, the initial encounter with the crew had badly soured his enthusiasm. He blamed Simon, in part; if his niche was going to be writing about black people in Baltimore, then he should have made sure there were more behind the camera.

From the first days of the shoot, Dutton said, Simon was getting on his nerves. Dutton was not accustomed to having a writer on set, and he was not interested in hearing how Simon had envisioned particular scenes. There always seemed to be people, like Simon and Noble, whispering in corners.

He hated to say he felt unappreciated. But he did feel monitored, judged and second-guessed. The only reason he had not cussed somebody out was because he had to get through the shoot. If he had gotten angry, it would have been intimidating and disruptive. To keep the peace, he let things go.

He was suspicious of white writers, he said at the time. Every aspect of black life had been distorted by white people, he said, and the series was about an element of society that he knew white people detested. He would have felt more comfortable, he said, if the writer had been black. As for Mills, Dutton felt he knew little about him; when they had first met, he had not even realized that the light-skinned Mills was African-American.

"I know that David Simon can visit and sit with as many black folks in this city as he wants to," Dutton said one day in late September, standing on a crumbling stretch of sidewalk in the rain. "They can pay the families to get the stories. They can listen and walk around with dope fiends. They can write about murders, and they still won't know a damn thing about black people. Not this, you know. Not this."

He added: "I know the pulse of *this*. I know what people think the minute they walk out them doors. I know what mothers feel when their sons and daughters walk out of the house to go to school. I know what it feels like to kill somebody. I know what it feels like to get shot. I know what it feels like that people be looking to kill me. I don't have to show up as a crime journalist after the fact."

A Painful Scene

The scene on the schedule for Columbus Day was especially difficult. Simon had watched firsthand the event it was based on, back in 1993. Two addicts he had been following had emerged from a courtroom, accompanied by their mothers. Suddenly, one of the mothers had exploded at the other, raving and hurling obscenities in the crowded corridor.

Simon had considered leaving the scene out; it had been painful to witness and painful for the mother on the receiving end. But it had seemed essential, showing the way the corner world kept intruding on people's attempts to lead ordinary lives. Simon and Mills had ended up including it, but toned down the language.

The performance could not be cartoonish, the producers had agreed; it could not be an eye-popping, head-rolling, sitcom stereotype. But the actors who had auditioned for the part had leaned in that direction. So the producers had gone to the expense of importing a New York actor to play the part of the angry mother.

Privately, Dutton found the scene embarrassing. "There was something about it that was so ghetto, so stereotypical ghetto," he said later. Not that he doubted that it had happened. But there would be black viewers who would ask, Why did you have to show that? And there would be white people who would think, Oh, yeah, that is just how they are.

When HBO had first approached him, he had had reservations about exposing the world of the corner. Not just those aspects that were embarrassing but those that felt intimate and precious, he said later. Now, he said, he sometimes felt he was giving Simon more than he could have imagined. He felt he was giving away secrets.

He remembered a performance of *The Piano Lesson* on Broadway. Dionne Warwick had been in the audience and had walked out during the second act. Months later, she told him why. "She said she couldn't take it anymore," Dutton remembered. "Because we were letting white folks in on all of our sacred little things. It was almost like that's all we had, or have."

On Columbus Day Simon was on set, a courthouse in East Baltimore. He was standing near the corridor where Dutton, intense and absorbed, was having the actors repeatedly rehearse the scene. The corridor was crowded with extras hired for the day to mill around in the background.

Simon was watching the extras. They kept failing to react to the commotion between the mothers. A couple of women looked so oblivious and white-bread, it was funny. A man playing one of the bailiffs kept going to great lengths to make sure he would be in the shot. Simon, who knew him, would remember later that he had shared a laugh with the man about that.

Meanwhile, the actor playing the raving mother was dead on. It was the moment Simon had witnessed in another courthouse corridor six years earlier, reinvented by a television production crew, transformed by artifice. He was elated. He laughed again.

Out of the corner of his eye, at one point, Dutton caught sight of Simon laughing. It made him furious.

He shot Simon an angry look. Simon seemed to turn away.

Maybe he had misinterpreted that laugh, Dutton said later. But he didn't think so. One of the actors had noticed it, too. "Why has he got to be laughing at *this* scene?" Dutton would remember the actor asking.

Dutton never mentioned the moment to Simon. But he said privately that a black writer would never have laughed. Not even a snicker. "Because they would have even felt a little bit of shame in it. It boils down to nobody wants to look in the mirror and see ugliness. Nobody wants to look in the mirror and see ignorance."

Months later, Simon would remember an angry look. He said he had assumed Dutton thought he was meddling, because he had asked one of the assistant directors to get the extras in the background to react.

Maybe he should have been more sensitive, he said. But how could he have been? The moment between the mothers had been painful to witness, but its power was attenuated six years later. If it had not been that moment, it could have been ten others. He had laughed at ten other things that were not funny in reality but were funny in the process of representing them.

"I know what I wasn't laughing at," Simon said later. "I wasn't laughing at somebody who was black and poor and uncouth making a spectacle of themself in a hallway. That's the one thing that wouldn't have been funny to me, and wasn't when it happened."

One Connection

If there was one thing Simon and Dutton could talk about, it was Baltimore street lore. Simon loved the crime history of Baltimore the way other writers loved stories about the mob. Baltimore's organized crime was its black drug trade. The most enjoyable conversations Simon and Dutton had were about that world.

For years, Simon had believed there was a great story to be told about the period in the early 1960s in Baltimore when men who had made their money as hustlers and gamblers moved into drugs. It was a moment of reckoning, he thought. That story, perhaps wed to the War of the Roses, as in Shakespeare's history plays, had the makings of a classic black gangster film.

At its center might be the character of Melvin Williams, who was said to have risen from the pool halls of Pennsylvania Avenue in Baltimore to lay the groundwork for the heroin industry that then engulfed the city. Simon had written a five-part series about Williams's drug empire for the *Sun* in 1987. Dutton, it turned out, had known Williams since childhood.

Looking back, Dutton would marvel that Simon had first mentioned the idea to him not long after they met. And it had come up again and again in the following months. Just in passing, Simon said. But Dutton believed he knew what Simon was getting at. In late October 1999, he mentioned to Simon that he liked the idea of the project, too.

So, four days before the end of the *Corner* shoot, Simon made his way over to Dutton during a break. He gave him a copy of the newspaper series and laid out his idea in detail. On the sidewalk outside the fast-food restaurant where they were shooting, they fell deep into conversation, then continued inside, squashed side by side in undersized plastic chairs.

Simon believed he would have a hard time selling the idea to a studio without Dutton, he said later, and an easier time persuading Williams to cooperate if Dutton's name were attached. Dutton knew that world, had the draw to get the project made and would even be great in the role of a police lieutenant colonel who was key to the story.

Similarly, Dutton believed that Simon would have the screenwriting reputation needed to win over a studio, he said later. Simon had the passion needed to get the project off the ground. He would have access to older police officials. And, Dutton said, he might be the only person Williams and others would open up to.

"I'm going to be the first one to admit, the idea is very, very, very clever," he said later, referring to Simon's choice of the War of the Roses as a frame for the story. "If more writers would think of those kinds of clever devices, a lot of those so-called black films in that genre would be a lot more interesting."

By early November, the editors had pieced together the first episodes of *The Corner*. Seeing those rough assemblages, Dutton thought he and Simon and Mills were on the same page about many things after all. He was struck by how distinct and memorable each character was. Watching a scene in which an addict was stabbed to death, he had found himself weeping.

Maybe he had not given Simon enough credit, he had begun to think. "All the credit from the literary point of it, but from the humanity point of it, I was a little guarded," he said. On the other hand, it was a two-way street, he insisted; he remained convinced that Simon had had doubts about him, too.

In the final days of shooting, Dutton said, he took a step back and watched Simon with some of the "real people" from the book. Dutton was impressed by the emotional bond between them, and by Simon's commitment to remain involved. "If he has the patience for it," Dutton said, "I envy him."

Simon was truly fascinated by the world of the corner, Dutton believed. "There are times when he's been around the real people in this, I would look at him from afar and he'd be totally enraptured," he observed one day. And Dutton would be sure that the person Simon was listening to was full of it. Without hearing a word, he said, he could tell.

"So, in that regard, I have a soft spot for David," he said, adding: "Sometimes I shake my head and I say, 'Poor boy, if he's going for that.' But then other times I'm wary. Because, wait a minute, is this guy as nonchalant as he seems?"

Editing by Committee

When the shoot ended, Simon, Mills and Robert Colesberry moved to Manhattan and set up shop in an editing studio in TriBeCa to work on their cuts. Dutton kept his distance, often working on his own cuts in a midtown hotel. His creative juices flowed better there, he said. But it also felt awkward in TriBeCa, "those guys tiptoeing around me."

Under the rules of television, the producers had the power to overrule Dutton on cutting the series. He submitted his director's cut of each episode, then they took it and made theirs. Dutton disliked many of the flashbacks that had been shot: "I'd say 3 percent work. The other 97 percent don't," he said one day. He took some out—and the producers put some back.

He also chose particular takes of certain scenes, only to have the producers replace them with selections of their own. They were eviscerating one of the characters, Dutton complained privately. He hated their musical choices, too. Using blues music for the title theme was, to him, "the typical white-boy idea of what black life is like."

Still, he kept his complaints to himself. The producers had the right to do what they were doing. So why bother objecting?

By late December he was not sure he would be showing up in Pasadena in mid-January to help promote the series at a semiannual meeting of television critics. "I could say, 'I wish you guys well, but I'm unavailable,'" he said. "I could be shooting a picture in London." Or, he said, he could be on his farm in Maryland, shoveling manure.

But on January 19, 2000, there he was in Pasadena. Minutes before the preview, he stalked into the room at the Ritz-Carlton where the HBO contingent was waiting. He seemed barely able to bring himself to say hello to Simon, Colesberry and Mills. "I didn't know why Charles was so mad," Simon said later. "I thought it was the cuts."

Simon resolved not to let the day end without inviting Dutton to have a drink and talk things over. Dutton had plans but took Simon's cell phone number, just in case. It felt as though the ice was cracking, Simon said later. Then Dutton never called. When they bumped into each other the next morning, Dutton explained cheerfully that he had been out late.

Back on the east coast, HBO asked Dutton at the last minute to film a personal preamble to the series, describing his reasons for making it. The idea worried Simon and Mills; they did not want HBO apologizing for the series in advance. They shipped a draft script to Dutton. But he sent back a message saying he would write the preamble himself.

Then, two days before it was to be shot in Baltimore, an HBO executive informed Simon, Mills and Colesberry that Dutton did not want them there. They were stung but complied. So, on a cold Saturday in early March, Dutton returned one more time to Montford and Oliver and filmed his ninety-second introduction, alone.

"I didn't need two cents from anybody," Dutton said later. "I didn't want five opinions on how we should shoot it or any genius ideas for rewriting. I don't even know why anybody wanted to be there. If they wanted to be there because they were worried about what Charles Dutton was going to do, then that's indicative of the entire shoot."

The Corner had its premiere at 10 P.M. on Sunday, April 16, 2000. Apart from a few lukewarm notices, one in the *New York Times*, the reviews were unanimous in their admiration: "ferociously written," "superbly directed," "spectacularly acted," "unblinkingly honest." In the *Washington Post*, Tom Shales called the series "an act of enlightenment, raw and shattering and strangely, inexplicably, beautiful."

Week after week, the ratings were unusually high for HBO in that time slot, especially in African-American households. There was none of the black backlash everyone had feared. Sales of Simon and Burns's book surged. People seemed stunned by the series' realism. Watching it at home, Dutton found himself struck again by the writing.

"I have to say the writing is absolutely brilliant," he said, looking back on what Simon had accomplished. "Without a doubt, he captured the hell out of those lives. Whatever painstaking efforts he had to go through, to sit and live for a year on those corners, it is totally a credit to him to have put it down on paper in the noncompromising way that he did.

"That's what makes the piece as beautiful and strong as it is. That he didn't take any weak shortcuts to appease a certain element of society, that he presented it just as it was told to him and just the way he observed it and just the way he analyzed it. In a nutshell, it's absolutely remarkable what he did."

With distance, Dutton believed he had let the strains of the production cloud his judgment. He had failed to see that Simon had been as nervous about the project as anyone, maybe more so, he said. Simon was probably worried about career, life, limb, everything, if it had come out badly.

Simon, meanwhile, continued to raise the Pennsylvania Avenue idea with Dutton when they saw each other. He had been rereading Shakespeare's history plays and had begun trying to contact Melvin

Williams in prison. He was planning to write an outline and send it to Dutton. It had begun to seem possible that they might eventually work together again.

"I can't express to you how minimal whatever problems Charles and I had were compared to how I felt when I went onto that corner in 1993," Simon said. "People were a lot more direct about not wanting us there on that corner than Charles was when I was on set. The trick was coming back every day. Most people's opinions changed. To an extent, I had sixty days with Charles. I think by the sixtieth day his impressions might have been different. If not, I would suggest sixty more might help. Or one hundred twenty.

"Now, racially, in this country, you don't usually get that kind of prolonged experience. Either people bend over backwards to get along or they don't and they steer clear. But I've sort of been trained—and you could call it crassly manipulative, because I want the book or I want the movie to be better—to stay put.

"If he thinks I was a bastard to work with, I don't think he was so easy to work with, either," he said a couple of days later. "But I would still do it a second time, based on the quality of the work that occurred. I know this: This time directing for him, he has directed something that's better because I wrote it, and I've written something that's better because he directed it.

"If we come out of it the second time and we've managed not to acquire some degree of understanding of our own foibles and insensitivities and misunderstandings, if we wind up in this exact same moment, then we're idiots. We ought to be able to learn."

In September 2000, The Corner won the Emmy award for best miniseries. Charles Dutton won the award for best director of a miniseries or television movie, and David Simon and David Mills were honored for the best writing in a miniseries, movie or special.

Dutton found himself suddenly in demand as a director, weighing a half-dozen film-directing offers while continuing to act and accept speaking engagements around the country. Simon spent the summer and early fall writing a pilot for a possible police drama for HBO. Mills wrote a pilot for HBO, then began work on one for CBS about a white professional athlete who becomes mayor of a mostly black city. He and Simon also spent two weeks in South Africa conducting a workshop on writing and producing television dramas.

When they were in Los Angeles for the Emmy awards ceremony, Simon and Dutton again discussed the possibility of working together on a project set in the world of black gangsters in Baltimore in the early 1960s. Simon said he intended to begin setting up interviews with survivors of that era in order to explore the idea further.

Timothy Cobb (left) and Jeff Levy (right), Atlanta-based cofounders of RelevantKnowledge, an Internet research company that merged with a rival in 1999.
Richard Perry/The New York Times

5

A Limited Partnership

AMY HARMON

It was shortly before midnight on the eve of 2000, and Timothy Fitz-gerald Stevenson Cobb was savoring the moment. Debonair as always in a white dinner jacket, sipping from a glass of the 1990 Krug Champagne he had selected for the party, he was in Miami Beach, surrounded by the friends and relatives he was putting up for the weekend, waiting for the fireworks to start.

He had much to celebrate. Like the dashing hero in *The Thomas Crown Affair*, a recent Hollywood remake that had quickly entered his movie pantheon, Cobb had pulled off something of a coup.

Over two sleep-deprived years, he and his partner, Jeff Levy, had built an Internet research company in Atlanta that ultimately captured half of a fast-growing market. Then came a merger with their only rival and the payoff: a public stock offering. By the end of trading on May 7, 1999, each man's net worth had swelled by about $25 million.

In the booming Internet economy, their windfall was by no means the most spectacular. But it conferred an uncommon distinction on Cobb: he became one of the country's few black Internet millionaires, joining an elite group of blacks in the upper reaches of American industry.

It also happened to be Cobb's thirty-fifth birthday that balmy night at the Art Deco–style National Hotel in South Beach, and when the clock struck twelve, there were hugs all around. Cobb remembers in particular a warm embrace with Levy. It reminded him, he recalled later, of how strong their bond had been. They had shared a single-minded drive to succeed, often reading each other's thoughts and finishing each other's sentences. To Cobb, Jeff Levy, thirty-seven—one of the few white people in the room on New Year's Eve—understood his satisfaction in a way that probably no one else could.

Yet Cobb also recalled a creeping uneasiness that weekend. It showed in his oversleeping the day before, a rare lapse for someone who took pride in never having to set an alarm. And it showed in what he described as one of his worst rounds of golf ever.

One reason for his distraction was his shifting fortunes. Shortly after the merger, Levy and Cobb went off to start separate Internet ventures. Levy's was doing fine. Not so Cobb's.

Another reason was the racial mantle Cobb bore: the black success story in a white world. He calls it both a source of pride and an enduring burden. For all he and Levy lived through together, in this he was alone.

The racial backdrop to Cobb's accomplishments went largely unmentioned by the people he did business with, but he seemed never to forget it. When things were good, being black made them better; when things were not so good, it made them worse.

Not that he dwelled on it, he insisted. To wonder how race might have made his success harder or its aftermath rockier would be counterproductive. Besides, he said, it would be unseemly for him to complain. He had a new Porsche, a new Range Rover and trust funds for his sons, ages four and ten months. He was well invested in other Internet companies. He was preparing to move into a luxurious new house.

Moreover, he said, in his business world overt discrimination had been alleviated by legal protections, changing notions of acceptable behavior and an actual improvement in racial attitudes. And the new high-tech economy provided a better semblance of equal opportunity. It was one reason he had risked becoming a Web entrepreneur.

Still, he said, he had no illusions. He knew how race could tip the scales. How skin color could trump money and status when it came to forging business ties. How self-imposed pressures to succeed, particularly as a black man, could take a toll on every part of life. Certainly, he acknowledged, race was in his thoughts as he churned over his game plan that weekend. As he often reminded his wife, Madelyn Adams Cobb, he was nearly alone as a black Web entrepreneur in Atlanta. If he failed, he believed, others would not get the chance. He was a role model.

"Failure is not an option for me," Cobb said. "I can't accept it. I won't accept it. I won't let it happen. There are other folks coming down the path who will all do much cooler things than I've done, and I want to be sure I'm not blocking their way."

Simply not failing didn't cut it for him, either. When he was growing up in Durham, North Carolina, he recalled, his parents told him that he would have to work twice as hard as white people to achieve as much.

Perhaps that was why he took care to be the best-prepared and best-dressed for every business meeting. And why he is so driven to excel. "Michael Jordan is not a role model," he said. "I compete with him."

In one way that statement was a measure of his brashness; it was also a half-joking nod to his freshman year at the University of North Carolina, spent warming the bench while Jordan dominated the basketball court. But what he really meant, he said, was that to be black and successful in business you had to be more than good; you had to be a superstar.

That was how some friends at the Miami Beach party said they saw him. But Cobb said he knew that in this moment of glory he had to admit to a more recent defeat: he was spending half a million dollars a month on an idea he had lost faith in. He remembers thinking he would have to work harder than ever on a new venture. And he said he put out of his mind the question of whether his marriage, already frayed, would survive the strain.

Friends and Rivals

Close partners and good friends, Tim Cobb and Jeff Levy were also friendly rivals. On the golf course Levy was the superior player, but Cobb challenged him all the same, a trait that impressed Levy when they were getting to know each other.

"Most African-Americans I know are in some way intimidated or uncomfortable with the white man's world," Levy said. "They never learned how to play golf, so you take them to a golf course and they're terrible, so they don't want to play. Well, Tim never learned to play golf, and he was terrible, and he didn't care."

Cobb eventually sought Tiger Woods's coach for tutoring. But if he took some ribbing on the fairways, he dished it back elsewhere, rating Levy's fashion sense a lukewarm "improving" and urging him to forget his grandfather's maxim, "Dress British, think Yiddish."

"Not so preppy," advised Cobb, who favored Italian suits.

As they went their separate ways, the former partners kept tabs on each other's business exploits. Each invested in the other's company, each sat on the other's board. Each also noticed who had the bigger office and how much cash the other was burning.

They were, it seemed, equally well-equipped to steer a new enterprise in an industry that claims to be the ultimate meritocracy. In Silicon Valley, the mantra goes, the business is evolving so quickly that the only color that matters is green. In Atlanta, a budding technology hub in an area with a much larger black population, the refrain is much the same.

"I can't imagine that race would be an obstacle," said a white industry executive on the board of Cobb's new company. "If somebody has a good business plan in the Internet space, that's all that matters."

For whatever reason, though, by the start of 2000 Levy had clearly pulled ahead of Cobb. He had raised an additional $11 million to finance his venture, eHatchery, which helps companies start up in exchange for a sizable ownership stake. The company's offices, in a renovated ice-cream factory, were filling up with dot-com fledglings. And good press was plentiful.

But Levy, a consummate schmoozer who counts compulsive efficiency as one of his greatest virtues, was coping with pressures of his own. He was determined, for instance, to measure up to his great-great-grandfather, Julius Rosenwald, an early chairman of Sears Roebuck & Company who had given millions of dollars to build more than five thousand schools for blacks in the South. Levy had dabbled in civic causes and thought about philanthropy, but he first wanted to build an even larger fortune, and to do that he was counting on eHatchery.

That meant he was always drumming up interest in eHatchery's investments and calculating how and when to cash in. At the same time, he said, he had to be careful not to stretch himself too thin. He and his wife agreed a few months earlier that he needed to be "present" when he was home and to be home more often. What was the point of the money, she wanted to know, if she and his sons, ages four and two, never saw him?

Still, in a life Levy described as a multilevel chess game, the racial plane was one he did not have to play on. As a Jew, he said, he often felt like an outsider himself. But he also knew that his blond hair, blue eyes and white skin shielded him from the kind of scrutiny Cobb faced.

"Tim has to take things over a hurdle that I don't have," Levy said. Though sensitive to race, Levy prides himself on looking beyond it. He and Cobb rarely talked about it. "I never saw Tim as black," Levy said. What mattered, he said, was that they thought alike.

But they didn't always. There was a moment in the fall of 1999 when the two were discussing a young black man pitching an idea. "He's smart, but he doesn't have your polish," Cobb recalled Levy's saying. The comparison to an aspiring entrepreneur with no experience rankled, Cobb said, but he let the remark roll off. He knew Levy did not mean to offend, he said.

On another occasion Levy told Cobb that he thought being black could be an advantage in business when diversity was increasingly viewed as a plus. Cobb considered. Then, as a way of gently informing his friend that in his experience the drawbacks outweighed any benefits, he broke into a mock-gospel chorus: "Nobody knows the trouble I've seen."

But Cobb's black friends did know. They included David Crichlow, who in March 2000 became the first black partner at the 132-year-old Wall Street law firm Winthrop, Stimson, Putnam & Roberts; Ed Dandridge, who had recently left ABC, where he was one of two black senior executives; and Henry Moniz, who was Democratic counsel to the House Judiciary Committee during the Clinton impeachment hearings.

Each could attest to the power of race. They told stories of being too eagerly sought by co-op boards needing a respectable black face; of being told too often by well-meaning whites that they "transcended race"; of not hailing taxis to avoid being passed by. There was a risk of falling into the "angry black man syndrome," as one of Cobb's friends put it: show too much anger and people will write you off.

These were the subtle ways race played out. Other moments weren't so subtle. Crichlow said he would not easily forget the time he stood in a law office lobby, wearing his customary suit and tie and waiting to meet an opposing counsel, who is white. When the lawyer appeared, he mistook the only other person there, a white man, for Crichlow. The man wore green work pants and a short-sleeve shirt and was standing next to his delivery of Poland Spring water.

Moniz remembered appearing in court to handle a drunken-driving case as a favor to the defendant's father, an important corporate client. When Moniz started to speak on behalf of the accused — a young white man in a goatee — the judge, also white, interrupted, apparently assuming that the black man had to be the defendant. "You have a competent attorney," the judge told Moniz.

Dandridge said that when he went out on weekends in casual clothes near his home on the Upper West Side of Manhattan, he was invisible to the ABC colleagues he might pass on the street, even though they were neighbors. To him, the truth about the daily lives of Cobb and his high-powered black friends is captured in a monologue by the black comedian Chris Rock. "There ain't no white man in this room that will change places with me — and I'm rich!" the routine goes. "That's how good it is to be white. There's a one-legged busboy in here right now that's going: 'I don't want to change. I'm gonna ride this white thing out and see where it takes me.'"

The joke had struck Cobb, too. Told that a white executive at Levy's company had described him as a "black James Bond," Cobb knew it was meant as a nod to his fondness for gadgets and risk. But "why a 'black' James Bond?" he had wanted to know, supplying his own answer: "Black is the identifier that goes before you, always. It raises the odds that you will get a real reminder that you are an outsider every time they meet you."

Yet to Cobb there is a joy in being black. There is the pleasure in the color of his own skin, he said. There is the bond among his black friends, based in part on their being outsiders. There is the trash-talking in basketball that he and his friends have transposed to the golf course. And there is something about being black and successful in a white world without compromise that can make him break into his wide, easy grin. "I love being black," he said.

He remembered telling his mother he would not have had the same success if he were not black. If he were white, he told her, maybe he would have believed more in his chances of making partner at his old law firms. Maybe as a junior executive at Turner Broadcasting he would have had mentors and so would not have left. In some ways, he said, the doors that seemed less open directed him down the entrepreneurial path where he was happiest.

Still, Cobb called the idea that race was not a factor in the technology industry "laughable," if only because of who has more access to capital. Like most Internet entrepreneurs, he and Levy had raised their first million from friends and family—and most of it had come from Levy's friends and family.

"It's one thing to have people who can write checks for $1,000," Cobb said. "It's another thing if they can write checks for $100,000."

But he would not blame race for the disparity between his and Levy's recent fortunes. That would be too easy. They had started different businesses; the market moved in unpredictable ways. And he harbored no resentment toward his former partner. Levy remained one of the few people he could talk to about what really mattered: business.

"Dude, what's your burn rate right now?" Levy demanded recently, speaking into his ever-present cell phone. "How much of the company are you giving away?" On the other end, Cobb, in his faint drawl, said something that made Levy laugh.

Only One Could Be CEO

The first time the Levys and the Cobbs met as couples was in early 1994 at an Atlanta cafe. Valerie Hartman Levy had wanted them to get together since Cobb, a lawyer, joined Turner, where she held a senior position in the legal department.

Struck by his sense of humor, she remembered telling Cobb in his job interview that he reminded her of her husband. Later, Cobb told his wife that Hartman Levy, strong-willed and forthright, reminded him of her.

The couples soon discovered they had a lot more in common. Two years earlier, both men left coveted jobs at fancy New York law firms to follow the women, whose careers had taken them to Atlanta. And both men soon chafed at their new jobs, Levy's with another law firm.

By the time dinner was over, the women had become friends and the men had begun plotting their entrepreneurial escape. Their rapport was immediate.

It was a rare thing, both men said, the way they could let their guard down and talk so freely. When the Levys' first son was born, Tim Cobb became his godfather.

The men soon became convinced that the Web was their generation's cable television. Then the idea struck. "You know," Cobb recalls saying, "I don't think there's a Nielsen's of the Internet." His idea was to create an audience measurement system for Web sites that Internet companies would use, much the way the television networks rely on Nielsen ratings. He thought of a name, too: RelevantKnowledge.

By then Levy had joined Turner's legal department and Cobb had moved on to its business development unit. They began meeting for coffee at 6:30 every morning, calculating and debating their chances of success.

Finally, during the opening ceremonies at the 1996 Olympic Games, Cobb turned to Levy. "If Billy Payne can bring the Olympics to Atlanta," Cobb said, referring to the lawyer who had done so, "we can start this company."

As Levy saw it, Cobb had more to lose, having less of a financial safety net. But at the same time Cobb felt that at thirty-two he had hit a glass ceiling. Of the several hundred vice presidents at Turner, only seven were African-American, he recalled.

Levy remembers taking courage from Cobb's resolve. In the fall of 1996 they quit their jobs. RelevantKnowledge was born.

At first, the two were 50-50 partners in everything: finances, decision making, titles. But when they began raising money, the venture capitalists told them that a company led by co-CEOs would not fly. Investors would be comfortable only if there was one chief, someone to hold accountable for making a profit.

The decision about who would be chief executive was made in one of the nearly wordless exchanges they often had in those early days. Both knew that Cobb was more qualified, they later acknowledged. He had more business experience than Levy, whose specialty was libel law. And the company was his idea. But both also believed it would be easier to raise money with a white chief executive than a black one. They did not think people would refuse to invest simply because Cobb was black. Not exactly. They just thought a black CEO would make the company look more unusual, Levy said. And as much as Cobb cared about being a positive role model, risking the company over racial pride could be self-defeating.

Anyway, did it really matter? That was the question they kept asking.

They were grateful just to have found each other, two ambitious young men—one the descendant of a sharecropper, the other of a millionaire.

The eldest of three children, Levy grew up in Lawrenceville, New Jersey, in a modest home that reflected the family's conscious effort not to show off its wealth. Levy's father, Paul, was a judge, who as a lawyer in the 1970s had represented the National Urban League. His mother, Linda Levy—an heiress to the Rosenwald fortune—was a humor columnist and cookbook author.

For Levy, the family heritage always loomed large. Things came easily to him: childhood summers on Martha's Vineyard; family golf vacations in Scotland; early admission to Harvard, where he was captain of the fencing team; a first job with a good law firm in Manhattan. Taking risk, too, came easier with family money to fall back on. But for Levy the family money was also what made him so determined to prove that he didn't need it.

Tim Cobb was born in Burlington, North Carolina, where his father, Harold, was a Baptist minister and his mother, Armadia, a teacher. Race was the main topic of conversation at the dinner table. Once, Tim's father came home drenched. He had been marching for civil rights and hoses had been turned on him. Cobb's mother still lowers her voice when she says "white," an indication, he said, of her perception of how the world was divided, which side had power.

When the family moved to Durham, Tim excelled in class and on the basketball court. In the eleventh grade, he was accepted to Andover, the elite Massachusetts prep school, and persuaded his parents to let him go. His father had suspicions, though. "They said, 'We need a black kid,' and Tim had good grades and spoke nice," Harold Cobb said.

When Tim Cobb decided to attend law school at the University of Pennsylvania, an uncle warned that corporate law firms would not hire blacks. But for Cobb, law school was an epiphany.

"That was the beginning of seeing firsthand dozens of people like me who had similar ambitions, similar talents and similar skills and résumés, all getting job offers and getting hired," he said. "That was a confirmation in my mind that there are times when individuals can limit themselves by not trying, and so I vowed never to say I'm not going to try that because I don't see any black people doing it."

And yet, about a decade later, the issue before him was whether he and Jeff Levy would dare try a path that few had taken—naming a black man chief executive.

Levy remembers as painful their conversation about the CEO question. They were taking a huge risk with their careers. They would be investing their money and that of friends and family. In the end, Levy recalls, they sort of said it without saying it. Cobb picked up the phone afterward and left Levy a message: "If you want to be CEO, that's fine with me."

The Payoff, Then the Parting

If their bow to pragmatism was troubling, it is hard to argue that it did not pay off. A friend of Levy's from Harvard put them in touch with J. H. Whitney & Company, the venture capital firm that eventually put up several million dollars after dozens of others had turned them down.

Cobb and Levy knew they were really co-CEOs, Levy said. "It wasn't like I would ever say, 'I'm CEO, so that's what we're doing.' " Friends remember that he always took care to refer to Cobb as his partner and co-founder, and Cobb, who took the title of president, attended every meeting with potential investors.

Neither man recalls overtly racist incidents during their partnership, although they remember that an associate of Cobb's once told Levy that he had been "jewed" out of something, and Cobb called to demand an apology.

Cobb had a joking explanation for the paucity of racist remarks. "I think they were afraid I was going to beat them up," he said. Lowering his voice, he mimicked what a venture capitalist might say about him: "He could be angry."

"The angry Jewish man just doesn't command the same fear in the heart," Levy said.

But there were times when racism may have operated below the surface, they said. For instance, an investor who seemed ready to give them money abruptly changed his mind after meeting them. Billions of dollars had been flowing into Internet companies, and the venture capitalists at J. H. Whitney had told the partners that getting financing from that investor should be "a layup."

"From my perspective it was the most bizarre thing," Cobb recalled.

"It could have been for some other reason. But I chalked that one up to his just being uncomfortable with me."

Levy is reluctant to link any difficulty in their raising money to Cobb's race. But he remembers noticing how people sometimes looked to him in a meeting as if he, not Cobb, would have the answers.

"It wasn't like, 'Hey, he's the better business person.' It was, 'Hey, he's the white guy,' " Levy said.

Yet he also said he thought Cobb was able to use race to his advantage, drawing a comparison to a woman who might use sexual attraction to gain an edge. He could "play the angry black man" when he felt like it, Levy said, and people reacted.

"All's fair in love and business," he said. "You play to win."

By the beginning of 1998, much of the Internet industry was relying on RelevantKnowledge to measure Web-site popularity. And because he carried the top title, Levy was becoming more closely identified with the company's success. He was the one quoted in the media; he was the one who networked with other Internet moguls.

That March, Levy spoke in Tucson at PC Forum, an annual gathering of technology executives. At the next year's forum he met Bill Gross, an Internet entrepreneur who became a mentor and, later, the biggest investor in eHatchery other than Levy.

Whether it was because Cobb always seemed to be one of only three black people at conferences or because he was too impatient to mingle without purpose, he was glad to leave that duty to Levy. So what if his name wasn't in the paper?

But Cobb's taking the lesser title and a quieter role appears to have had a price. Levy was reminded of it at the next year's PC Forum. On Cobb's behalf, he approached the sponsor of another conference, which Cobb wanted to attend.

"You remember my partner, Tim Cobb?" Levy asked.

"No, never heard of him," came the reply.

"To the world, I was CEO," Levy said, "and I think certainly that had an impact."

If Cobb regretted taking the No. 2 job, the closest he would come to saying so was to comment: "I don't make the rules. I have to play by them, and I have to win by them."

Still, once the partners decided to merge with their major rival, Media Metrix, Cobb did not stick around long. He knew that only one of them would be able to participate in taking the company public, he said. Levy wanted that job, and as the public face of Relevant-Knowledge, he seemed like the logical choice for it.

Instead, Cobb invited Levy to help him start a Web site aimed at teenagers, an untapped demographic niche, according to the information they had gathered at RelevantKnowledge. This time Cobb would be chief executive, and this time they would take the company public themselves.

Levy declined. The idea of a lifestyle site for teenagers did not grab him, he said. And he couldn't imagine not being chief executive. He, too, wanted to take his own company public, and he tried to persuade Cobb to be his No. 2 at eHatchery. This time, Cobb declined.

One Succeeds, One Struggles

HipO.com, Cobb's new company, let teenagers buy clothing and accessories through its Web site with "HipCards" and attracted some major sponsors and investors. But by late fall 1999, Cobb was stumbling. Deal after deal with potential partners had fallen through. By the following January, visitors to the site were seeing an animation bidding them farewell.

Adams Cobb, now a vice president for employee development at the *Atlanta Journal-Constitution*, believed that her husband might have had an easier time with HipO had he not ceded the top job at RelevantKnowledge. Little slights gnawed at her. Sitting in the audience at the Atlanta Convention Center in October 1999 as Cobb and Levy were introduced on a panel of local technology executives, she bristled as Cobb was introduced last, even though he was not sitting at the end of the dais. The moderator introduced Levy as the "former chief executive of RelevantKnowledge" and described eHatchery. When he got to Cobb, he said simply, "This is Tim Cobb, who helped found RelevantKnowledge." Helped found?

"It was almost like an aside," Adams Cobb said. "I know how hard he worked, and he didn't get the credit."

Cobb had a different theory.

"I often feel on panels like this that the moderators don't know what to say to me," he said. "Maybe they're afraid they're going to say something offensive, so they don't say anything. I don't know."

In college, when a member of a fraternity known for flying the Confederate flag called him "nigger" one drunken night, the response was clear: a punch. Now, in a more sophisticated world, he was often left with nothing to do but shoulder the weight of shadowy perceptions.

Did the demise of HipO have anything to do with race? He did not think so, he said. Even in the midst of the current Internet frenzy, the majority of start-ups fail. But he could not know for sure. How had he performed at dinner when the Time Warner executives talked about wine and people they knew in common? What impression had he made on the National Football League executives when he had tried to recruit the NFL as a sponsor? Anyone might go through such a self-evaluation after an important business meeting, but for Cobb each question came with an unspoken qualifier: how did he perform, what impression did he make, as a black man?

Asha Appel, his lieutenant at HipO's New York office, said she often thought that potential partners wanted to work with Cobb because joining a successful black man would make them look good. Appel, who is white, said she had been conscious of feeling that way herself and had not been proud of it; it is a reaction to racism that is racist itself, she said.

"In meetings they all look to him, and that look doesn't come from just wanting to see his reaction," Appel said. "It comes from, 'We want you to know we're respecting you.' "

Her white boss in a previous job never got those looks, she said. "Now they will speak to me and look to Tim for approval," she said. "And it's not about business. It's personal. Tim is a touchstone. His color is a touchstone."

Reactions like those by white associates only make it harder for him to establish the rapport that is often necessary to make business deals, Cobb said. "Ultimately it comes down to relationships," he said. "I've got to be able to connect with the person, and it's harder for people to connect with me as a black man.

"I'm never going to remind somebody of their little brother or their cousin or their next-door neighbor. I might remind them of someone in business school who they thought was smart and wish they'd gotten to know better."

Levy had no such concerns, of course. He was busy leveraging his reputation from RelevantKnowledge to attract investors and draw attention to eHatchery. A spread in *U.S. News & World Report* and an appearance on CNN followed the first article about the company in August 1999 in the *Atlanta Journal-Constitution.* "Jeff Levy is an Internet success story," it began.

By contrast, HipO received scant press attention in its early days. In January 2000, the *Atlanta Business Chronicle* ran an account of the demise of Cobb's HipO.com under the headline "Not Hip Enough? Web Site Dumps Pursuit of Teens."

But if Levy's public profile is higher than Cobb's, in part owing to his position and exposure at RelevantKnowledge, he also made an effort to raise it. He joined the board of Atlanta's science museum, helped the Democratic Senatorial Campaign Committee and was invited to Washington for a dinner with President Clinton. Occasionally he answered his cell phone and found a senator on the line. He got a kick out of that. And his "Thursday Nights at the Hatch" cocktail parties attracted a crowd of Atlanta movers and shakers.

He was also spending more time with his sons as his wife became more involved in causes like the Million Mom March.

"Jeff is a poster boy for the new economy in Atlanta," said a prominent lawyer in a toast one evening in the spring of 2000.

Cobb, meanwhile, was traveling more and working longer hours. He was determined to make sure his investors did not lose their money and was working furiously to transform HipO's assets into a new Internet business. His wife remembers his coming home exhausted, with little energy for anything but watching ESPN.

He was also too overextended to think about community involvement, he said. Besides, he had never shared Levy's enthusiasm for it. Although he joined a panel of black entrepreneurs in a program for black students at the Wharton Business School, Cobb turned down requests to join political campaigns and civic groups and passed on a chance to work with Magic Johnson on a Web venture aimed at blacks.

In his view the struggle for blacks now was mainly economic. He could do more good, he said, by ensuring his own success, by supporting other black professionals and by offering himself as a model. And he had a hard time with peers who chose not to, like the black man working out at his gym who turned out to be the chief executive of a public Internet company. The man told him he kept a low profile, Cobb recalled, because he thought it would be better for the company's stock performance if people did not know he was black. "I told him that was messed up," Cobb said.

Soon, Cobb insisted, there would be more like himself. To ensure that, he paid special attention to black entrepreneurs who asked him to invest, and recently put $200,000 into an Internet start-up run by young African-Americans. If they did well, they in turn would finance others, Cobb said. "That's how you get the momentum."

But sometimes, he said, he grew frustrated with how slowly the ranks of black entrepreneurs were growing. He wished he could page the entire listening audience of the Les Brown show, a radio call-in program aimed at blacks, and tell them: "Here, do this. I did it, you can do it. I didn't do it dunking a basketball or singing a song, not that there's anything wrong with that. So have all my close friends, they've done it too. But we need other people, other success stories."

Tolls and Prospects

In April 2000 Cobb and Levy dined together at an Atlanta restaurant. They ordered a bottle of cabernet. They talked about business.

Levy was preparing to raise more money. He wanted to set up another eHatchery office, perhaps in Washington, DC. Soon, he hoped, an eHatchery investment would be ready to take public or be sold.

Prospects had also brightened for Cobb. He had transformed what was left of HipO into a new company, Edaflow, which was using the Internet to connect clothing manufacturers and retailers.

They also talked about their personal lives. Levy's four-year-old son, Cobb's godson, had been admitted to a private preschool where he would start learning Spanish. As for Cobb, shortly after they returned from Miami, he and his wife separated. He moved into a new house while his wife remained with the boys a few blocks away. But he spent more time with his sons, three nights a week.

Adams Cobb said some combination of the missed family dinners and the constant feeling that her husband had blinders on had worn her down. Cobb acknowledged that his approach to work had burdened the relationship: "When I'm in a foxhole I divorce all emotion from what I'm doing and just do it," he said. "Madelyn doesn't like me when I'm like that."

Their marital troubles were similar to those of many entrepreneurs battling the odds. But some of Tim Cobb's friends suggested that because the sense of going into daily battle was heightened for black men in business, so were frictions at home.

"The toll," Cobb said, "is probably higher than I realized."

Meanwhile, Cobb's oldest son, a few months older than Levy's, had begun to explore the meaning of race in his young life. Cobb had started what he knew would be a continuing conversation with him about what it means to be black in America, and why a white boy in a similar situation might have an easier time. In lectures that echo those of his own parents, Cobb said, he tells his son that he must not allow his race to hold him back.

"I tell him it's important to work hard, it's important to succeed. Absolutely, I'm burdening him with all that early on. He'll be like, 'I hear this stuff in my head, I don't know where that comes from.' "

Yet Cobb said he was confident that his sons' racial experiences would be better than his, partly because of social progress and partly because of his effort to provide for them. It will never occur to them that they should not have access to something because of their race, he said.

When he was growing up, he remembers, there was a country club he knew his family could not belong to. Now his sons play in the pool with Levy's at the exclusive Ansley country club and never question whether they should be there. Still, they were becoming aware of a difference.

"Dad," Cobb recalled his older son's observing one morning, "I'm the only brown boy in my class."

"I told him not to worry so much about color of skin," Cobb said. "I told him to look at his friends, and if they're nice people, to make his determination based on that. And I told him I was the only brown kid in my class too, and it's OK."

By the fall of 2000, Tim Cobb's divorce was almost final. His older son, Avery, was becoming a karate star, and TJ, almost two, had started talking nonstop. Because Cobb's new Internet company, Edaflow, had taken aim at the business market, it remained somewhat sheltered from the loss of investor confidence that had laid low many consumer-oriented dot-coms.

Jeff Levy's company, eHatchery, was not so fortunate. Over the summer of 2000, two of the start-ups that eHatchery was nurturing folded, several of its top executives left, and several employees were laid off. In November, Levy was facing a hard sell as he tried to raise funds to support his previous investments. But he was confident that the pen-

dulum of the market would eventually swing back his way. He and his wife were discussing having a third child.

Because their wives are close friends, Levy said, he and Cobb had not spoken much lately about their personal lives, but they continued to discuss working together on another business venture.

Workers on the kill floor of the Smithfield Packing Company, Tar Heel, North Carolina. Edward Keating/The New York Times

6

At a Slaughterhouse, Some Things Never Die

CHARLIE LEDUFF

TAR HEEL, NORTH CAROLINA

It must have been 1 o'clock. That's when the white man usually comes out of his glass office and stands on the scaffolding above the factory floor. He stood with his palms on the rails, his elbows out. He looked like a tower guard up there or a border patrol agent. He stood with his head cocked.

One o'clock means it is getting near the end of the workday. Quota has to be met and the workload doubles. The conveyor belt always overflows with meat around 1 o'clock. So the workers double their pace, hacking pork from shoulder bones with a driven single-mindedness. They stare blankly, like mules in wooden blinders, as the butchered slabs pass by.

It is called the picnic line: eighteen workers lined up on both sides of a belt, carving meat from bone. Up to 16 million shoulders a year come down that line here at the Smithfield Packing Company, the largest pork production plant in the world. That works out to about 32,000 a shift, sixty-three a minute, one every seventeen seconds for each worker for eight and a half hours a day. The first time you stare down at that belt you know your body is going to give in way before the machine ever will.

On this day the boss saw something he didn't like. He climbed down and approached the picnic line from behind. He leaned into the ear of a broad-shouldered black man. He had been riding him all day, and the day before. The boss bawled him out good this time, but no one heard what was said. The roar of the machinery was too ferocious for that. Still, everyone knew what was expected. They worked harder.

The white man stood and watched for the next two hours as the blacks worked in their groups and the Mexicans in theirs. He stood there with his head cocked.

At shift change the black man walked away, hosed himself down and turned in his knives. Then he let go. He threatened to murder the boss. He promised to quit. He said he was losing his mind, which made for good comedy since he was standing near a conveyor chain of severed hogs' heads, their mouths yoked open.

"Who that cracker think he is?" the black man wanted to know. There were enough hogs, he said, "not to worry about no fleck of meat being left on the bone. Keep treating me like a Mexican and I'll beat him."

The boss walked by just then and the black man lowered his head.

Who Gets the Dirty Jobs

The first thing you learn in the hog plant is the value of a sharp knife. The second thing you learn is that you don't want to work with a knife. Finally you learn that not everyone has to work with a knife. Whites, blacks, American Indians, and Mexicans, they all have their separate stations.

The few whites on the payroll tend to be mechanics or supervisors. As for the Indians, a handful are supervisors; others tend to get clean menial jobs like warehouse work. With few exceptions, that leaves the blacks and Mexicans with the dirty jobs at the factory, one of the only places within a fifty-mile radius in this muddy corner of North Carolina where a person might make more than $8 an hour.

While Smithfield's profits nearly doubled in the past year, wages have remained flat. So a lot of Americans here have quit and a lot of Mexicans have been hired to take their places. But more than management, the workers see one another as the problem, and they see the competition in skin tones.

The locker rooms are self-segregated and so is the cafeteria. The enmity spills out into the towns. The races generally keep to themselves. Along Interstate 95 there are four tumbledown bars, one for each color: white, black, red and brown.

Language is also a divider. There are English and Spanish lines at the Social Security office and in the waiting rooms of the county health clinics. This means different groups don't really understand one another and tend to be suspicious of what they do know.

You begin to understand these things the minute you apply for the job.

Blood and Burnout

"Treat the meat like you going to eat it yourself," the hiring manager told the thirty applicants, most of them down on their luck and hungry for work. The Smithfield plant will take just about any man or woman with a pulse and a sparkling urine sample, with few questions asked. This reporter was hired using his own name and acknowledged that he was currently employed, but was not asked where and did not say.

Slaughtering swine is repetitive, brutish work, so grueling that three weeks on the factory floor leave no doubt in your mind about why the turnover is 100 percent. Five thousand quit and five thousand are hired every year. You hear people say, They don't kill pigs in the plant, they kill people. So desperate is the company for workers, its recruiters comb the streets of New York's immigrant communities, personnel staff members say, and word of mouth has reached Mexico and beyond.

The company even procures criminals. Several at the morning orientation were inmates on work release in green uniforms, bused in from the county prison.

The new workers were given a safety speech and tax papers, shown a promotional video and informed that there was enough methane, ammonia and chlorine at the plant to kill every living thing here in Bladen County. Of the thirty new employees, the black women were assigned to the chitterlings room, where they would scrape feces and worms from intestines. The black men were sent to the butchering floor. Two free white men and the Indian were given jobs making boxes. This reporter declined a box job and ended up with most of the Mexicans, doing knife work, cutting sides of pork into smaller and smaller products.

Standing in the hiring hall that morning, two women chatted in Spanish about their pregnancies. A young black man had heard enough. His small town the next county over was crowded with Mexicans. They just started showing up three years ago—drawn to rural Robeson County by the plant—and never left. They stood in groups on the street corners, and the young black man never knew what they were saying. They took the jobs and did them for less. Some had houses in Mexico, while he lived in a trailer with his mother.

Now here he was, trying for the only job around, and he had to listen to Spanish, had to compete with peasants. The world was going to hell.

"This is America and I want to start hearing some English, now!" he screamed.

One of the women told him where to stick his head and listen for the echo. "Then you'll hear some English," she said.

An old white man with a face as pinched and lined as a pot roast complained, "The tacos are worse than the niggers," and the Indian leaned against the wall and laughed. In the doorway, the prisoners shifted from foot to foot, watching the spectacle unfold from behind a cloud of cigarette smoke.

The hiring manager came out of his office and broke it up just before things degenerated into a brawl. Then he handed out the employment stubs. "I don't want no problems," he warned. He told them to report to the plant on Monday morning to collect their carving knives.

$7.70 an Hour, Pain All Day

Monday. The mist rose from the swamps and by 4:45 A.M. thousands of headlamps snaked along the old country roads. Cars carried people from the backwoods, from the single and double-wide trailers, from the cinder-block houses and wooden shacks: whites from Lumberton and Elizabethtown; blacks from Fairmont and Fayetteville; Indians from Pembroke; the Mexicans from Red Springs and St. Pauls.

They converge at the Smithfield plant, a 973,000-square-foot leviathan of pipe and steel near the Cape Fear River. The factory towers over the tobacco and cotton fields, surrounded by pine trees and a few of the old whitewashed plantation houses. Built seven years ago, it is by far the biggest employer in this region, seventy-five miles west of the Atlantic and ninety miles south of the booming Research Triangle around Chapel Hill.

The workers filed in, their faces stiffened by sleep and the cold, like saucers of milk gone hard. They punched the clock at 5 A.M., waiting for the knives to be handed out, the chlorine freshly applied by the cleaning crew burning their eyes and throats. Nobody spoke.

The hallway was a river of brown-skinned Mexicans. The six prisoners who were starting that day looked confused.

"What the hell's going on?" the only white inmate, Billy Harwood, asked an older black worker named Wade Baker.

"Oh," Baker said, seeing that the prisoner was talking about the Mexicans. "I see you been away for a while."

Billy Harwood had been away—nearly seven years, for writing phony payroll checks from the family pizza business to buy crack. He was Rip Van Winkle standing there. Everywhere he looked there were Mexicans. What he didn't know was that one out of three newborns at the nearby Robeson County health clinic was a Latino; that the county's Roman Catholic church had a special Sunday Mass for Mexicans said by a Honduran priest; that the schools needed Spanish speakers to teach English.

With less than a month to go on his sentence, Harwood took the pork job to save a few dollars. The word in jail was that the job was a cakewalk for a white man.

But this wasn't looking like any cakewalk. He wasn't going to get a boxing job like a lot of other whites. Apparently inmates were on the bottom rung, just like Mexicans.

Billy Harwood and the other prisoners were put on the picnic line. Knife work pays $7.70 an hour to start. It is money unimaginable in Mexico, where the average wage is $4 a day. But the American money comes at a price. The work burns your muscles and dulls your mind. Staring down into the meat for hours strains your neck. After thousands of cuts a day your fingers no longer open freely. Standing in the damp 42-degree air causes your knees to lock, your nose to run, your teeth to throb.

The whistle blows at three, you get home by four, pour peroxide on your nicks by five. You take pills for your pains and stand in a hot shower trying to wash it all away. You hurt. And by eight o'clock you're in bed, exhausted, thinking of work.

The convict said he felt cheated. He wasn't supposed to be doing Mexican work. After his second day he was already talking of quitting. "Man, this can't be for real," he said, rubbing his wrists as if they'd been in handcuffs. "This job's for an ass. They treat you like an animal."

He just might have quit after the third day had it not been for Mercedes Fernández, a Mexican. He took a place next to her by the conveyor belt. She smiled at him, showed him how to make incisions. That was the extent of his on-the-job training. He was peep-eyed, missing a tooth and squat from the starchy prison food, but he acted as if this tiny woman had taken a fancy to him. In truth, she was more fascinated than infatuated, she later confided. In her year at the plant, he was the first white person she had ever worked with.

The other workers noticed her helping the white man, so unusual was it for a Mexican and a white to work shoulder to shoulder, to try to talk or even to make eye contact.

As for blacks, she avoided them. She was scared of them. "Blacks don't want to work," Fernández said when the new batch of prisoners came to work on the line. "They're lazy."

Everything about the factory cuts people off from one another. If it's not the language barrier, it's the noise—the hammering of compressors, the screeching of pulleys, the grinding of the lines. You can hardly make your voice heard. To get another's attention on the cut line, you bang the butt of your knife on the steel railings, or you lob a chunk of meat. Fernández would sometimes throw a piece of shoulder at a friend across the conveyor and wave good morning.

The Kill Floor

The kill floor sets the pace of the work, and for those jobs they pick strong men and pay a top wage, as high as $12 an hour. If the men fail to make quota, plenty of others are willing to try. It is mostly the blacks who work the kill floor, the stone-hearted jobs that pay more and appear out of bounds for all but a few Mexicans. Plant workers gave various reasons for this: the Mexicans are too small; they don't like blood; they don't like heavy lifting; or just plain "We built this country and we ain't going to hand them everything," as one black man put it.

Kill-floor work is hot, quick and bloody. The hog is herded in from the stockyard, then stunned with an electric gun. It is lifted onto a conveyor belt, dazed but not dead, and passed to a waiting group of men wearing bloodstained smocks and blank faces. They slit the neck, shackle the hind legs and watch a machine lift the carcass into the air, letting its life flow out in a purple gush, into a steaming collection trough.

The carcass is run through a scalding bath, trolleyed over the factory floor and then dumped onto a table with all the force of a quarter-ton water balloon. In the misty-red room, men slit along its hind tendons and skewer the beast with hooks. It is again lifted and shot across the room on a pulley and bar, where it hangs with hundreds of others as if in some kind of horrific dry-cleaning shop. It is then pulled through a wall of flames and met on the other side by more black men who, stripped to the waist beneath their smocks, scrape away any straggling bristles.

The place reeks of sweat and scared animal, steam and blood. Nothing is wasted from these beasts, not the plasma, not the glands, not the bones. Everything is used, and the kill men, repeating slaughterhouse lore, say that even the squeal is sold.

The carcasses sit in the freezer overnight and are then rolled out to the cut floor. The cut floor is opposite to the kill floor in nearly every way. The workers are mostly brown—Mexicans—not black; the lighting yellow, not red. The vapor comes from cold breath, not hot water. It is here that the hog is quartered. The pieces are parceled out and sent along the disassembly lines to be cut into ribs, hams, bellies, loins and chops.

People on the cut lines work with a mindless fury. There is tremendous pressure to keep the conveyor belts moving, to pack orders, to put bacon and ham and sausage on the public's breakfast table. There is no clock, no window, no fragment of the world outside. Everything is pork. If the line fails to keep pace, the kill men must slow down, backing up the slaughter. The boxing line will have little to do, costing the company payroll hours. The blacks who kill will become angry with the Mexicans who cut, who in turn will become angry with the white superintendents who push them.

10,000 Unwelcome Mexicans

The Mexicans never push back. They cannot. Some have legitimate work papers, but more, like Mercedes Fernández, do not.

Even worse, Fernández was several thousand dollars in debt to the smugglers who had sneaked her and her family into the United States and owed a thousand more for the authentic-looking birth certificate and Social Security card that are needed to get hired. She and her husband, Armando, expected to be in debt for years. They had mouths to feed back home.

The Mexicans are so frightened about being singled out that they do not even tell one another their real names. They have their given names, their work-paper names and "Hey you," as their American supervisors call them. In the telling of their stories, Mercedes and Armando Fernandez insisted that their real names be used, to protect their identities. It was their work names they did not want used, names bought in a back alley in Barstow, Texas.

Rarely are the newcomers welcomed with open arms. Long before the Mexicans arrived, Robeson County, one of the poorest in North Carolina, was an uneasy racial mix. In the 1990 census, of the 100,000 people living in Robeson, nearly 40 percent were Lumbee Indian, 35 percent white and 25 percent black. Until a dozen years ago the county schools were de facto segregated, and no person of color held any meaningful county job from sheriff to court clerk to judge.

At one point in 1988, two armed Indian men occupied the local newspaper office, taking hostages and demanding that the sheriff's department be investigated for corruption and its treatment of minorities. A prominent Indian lawyer, Julian Pierce, was killed that same year, and the suspect turned up dead in a broom closet before he could be charged. The hierarchy of power was summed up on a plaque that hangs in the courthouse commemorating the dead of World War I. It lists the veterans by color: "white" on top, "Indian" in the middle and "colored" on the bottom.

That hierarchy mirrors the pecking order at the hog plant. The Lumbees—who have fought their way up in the county apparatus and have built their own construction businesses—are fond of saying they are too smart to work in the factory. And the few who do work there seem to end up with the cleaner jobs.

But as reds and blacks began to make progress in the 1990s—for the first time an Indian sheriff was elected, and a black man is now the public defender—the Latinos began arriving. The United States Census Bureau estimated that one thousand Latinos were living in Robeson County in 1999. People only laugh at that number.

"A thousand? Hell, there's more than that in the Wal-Mart on a Saturday afternoon," said Bill Smith, director of county health services. He and other officials guess that there are at least 10,000 Latinos in Robeson, most having arrived since 1997.

"When they built that factory in Bladen, they promised a trickle-down effect," Smith said. "But the money ain't trickling down this way. Bladen got the money and Robeson got the social problems."

In Robeson there is the strain on public resources. There is the substandard housing. There is the violence. In 1999 twenty-seven killings were committed in Robeson, mostly in the countryside, giving it a higher murder rate than Detroit or Newark. Three Mexicans were robbed and killed that fall. Latinos have also been the victims of highway stickups.

In the yellow-walled break room at the plant, Mexicans talked among themselves about their three slain men, about the midnight visitors with obscured faces and guns, men who knew that the illegal workers used mattresses rather than banks. Mercedes Fernández, like many Mexicans, would not venture out at night. "Blacks have a problem," she said. "They live in the past. They are angry about slavery, so instead of working, they steal from us."

She and her husband never lingered in the parking lot at shift change. That is when the anger of a long day comes seeping out. Cars get kicked and faces slapped over parking spots or fender benders. The traffic is a serpent. Cars jockey for a spot in line to make the quarter-mile crawl along the plant's one-lane exit road to the highway. Usually no one will let you in. A lot of the scuffling is between black and Mexican.

Black and Bleak

The meat was backing up on the conveyor and spilling onto the floor. The supervisor climbed down off the scaffolding and chewed out a group of black women. Something about skin being left on the meat. There was a new skinner on the job, and the cutting line was expected to take up his slack. The whole line groaned. First looks flew, then people began hurling slurs at one another in Spanish and English, words they could hardly hear over the factory's roar. The black women started waving their knives at the Mexicans. The Mexicans waved theirs back. The blades got close. One Mexican spit at the blacks and was fired.

After watching the knife scene, Wade Baker went home and sagged in his recliner. CNN played. Good news on Wall Street, the television said. Wages remained stable. "Since when is the fact that a man doesn't get paid good news?" he asked the TV. The TV told him that money was everywhere — everywhere but here.

Still lean at fifty-one, Baker has seen life improve since his youth in the Jim Crow South. You can say things. You can ride in a car with a white woman. You can stay in the motels, eat in the restaurants. The black man got off the white man's field.

"Socially, things are much better," Baker said wearily over the droning television. "But we're going backwards as black people economically. For every one of us doing better, there's two of us doing worse."

His town, Chad Bourne, is a dreary strip of peeling paint and warped porches and houses as run-down as rotting teeth. Young men drift from the cinder-block pool hall to the empty streets and back. In the center of town is a bank, a gas station, a chicken shack and a motel. As you drive out, the lights get dimmer and the homes older until eventually you're in a flat void of tobacco fields.

Wade Baker was standing on the main street with his grandson Monte watching the Christmas parade march by when a scruffy man approached. It was Baker's cousin, and he smelled of kerosene and had dust in his hair as if he lived in a vacant building and warmed himself with a portable heater. He asked for $2.

"It's ironic isn't it?" Baker said as his cousin walked away only eight bits richer. "He was asking me the same thing ten years ago."

A group of Mexicans stood across the street hanging around the gas station watching them.

"People around here always want to blame the system," he said. "And it is true that the system is antiblack and antipoor. It's true that things are run by the whites. But being angry only means you failed in life. Instead of complaining, you got to work twice as hard and make do."

He stood quietly with his hands in his pockets watching the parade go by. He watched the Mexicans across the street, laughing in their new clothes. Then he said, almost as an afterthought, "There's a day coming soon where the Mexicans are going to catch hell from the blacks, the way the blacks caught it from the whites."

Wade Baker used to work in the post office, until he lost his job over drugs. When he came out of his haze a few years ago, there wasn't much else for him but the plant. He took the job, he said, "because I don't have a 401 k." He took it because he had learned from his mother that you don't stand around with your head down and your hand out waiting for another man to drop you a dime.

Evelyn Baker, bent and gray now, grew up a sharecropper, the granddaughter of slaves. She was raised up in a tar-paper shack, picked cotton and hoed tobacco for a white family. She supported her three boys alone by cleaning white people's homes.

In the late sixties something good started happening. There was a labor shortage, just as there is now. The managers at the textile plants started giving machine jobs to black people.

Evelyn Baker was forty then. "I started at a dollar and sixty cents an hour, and honey, that was a lot of money then," she said.

The work was plentiful through the seventies and eighties, and she was able to save money and add on to her home. By the early nineties the textile factories started moving away, to Mexico. Robeson County has lost about a quarter of its jobs since that time.

Unemployment in Robeson hovers around 8 percent, twice the national average. In neighboring Columbus County it is 10.8 percent. In Bladen County it is 5 percent, and Bladen has the pork factory.

Still, Wade Baker believes that people who want to work can find work. As far as he's concerned, there are too many shiftless young men who ought to be working, even if it's in the pork plant. His son-in-law once worked there, quit and now hangs around the gas station where other young men sell dope.

The son-in-law came over one day last fall and threatened to cause trouble if the Bakers didn't let him borrow the car. This could have turned messy; the seventy-one-year-old Evelyn Baker keeps a .38 tucked in her bosom.

When Wade Baker got home from the plant and heard from his mother what had happened, he took up his pistol and went down to the corner, looking for his son-in-law. He chased a couple of the young men around the dark dusty lot, waving the gun. "Hold still so I can shoot one of you!" he recalled having bellowed. "That would make the world a better place!"

He scattered the men without firing. Later, sitting in his car with his pistol on the seat and his hands between his knees, he said, staring into the night: "There's got to be more than this. White people drive by and look at this and laugh."

Living It, Hating It

Billy Harwood had been working at the plant ten days when he was released from the Robeson County Correctional Facility. He stood at the prison gates in his work clothes with his belongings in a plastic bag, waiting. A friend dropped him at the Salvation Army shelter, but he decided it was too much like prison. Full of black people. No leaving after 10 P.M. No smoking indoors. "What you doing here, white boy?" they asked him.

He fumbled with a cigarette outside the shelter. He wanted to quit the plant. The work stinks, he said, "but at least I ain't a nigger. I'll find other work soon. I'm a white man." He had hopes of landing a roofing job through a friend. The way he saw it, white society looks out for itself.

On the cut line he worked slowly and allowed Mercedes Fernández and the others to pick up his slack. He would cut only the left shoulders; it was easier on his hands. Sometimes it would be three minutes before a left shoulder came down the line. When he did cut, he didn't clean the bone; he left chunks of meat on it.

Fernández was disappointed by her first experience with a white person. After a week she tried to avoid standing by Billy Harwood. She decided it wasn't just the blacks who were lazy, she said.

Even so, the supervisor came by one morning, took a look at one of Harwood's badly cut shoulders and threw it at Fernández, blaming her. He said obscene things about her family. She didn't understand exactly what he said, but it scared her. She couldn't wipe the tears from her eyes because her gloves were covered with greasy shreds of swine. The other cutters kept their heads down, embarrassed.

Her life was falling apart. She and her husband both worked the cut floor. They never saw their daughter. They were twenty-six but rarely made love anymore. All they wanted was to save enough money to put plumbing in their house in Mexico and start a business there. They come from the town of Tehuacán, in a rural area about 150 miles southeast of Mexico City. His mother owns a bar there and a home but gives nothing to them. Mother must look out for her old age.

"We came here to work so we have a chance to grow old in Mexico," Fernández said one evening while cooking pork and potatoes. Now they were into a smuggler for thousands. Her hands swelled into claws in the evenings and stung while she worked. She felt trapped. But she kept at it for the money, for the $9.60 an hour. The smuggler still had to be paid.

They explained their story this way: The coyote drove her and her family from Barstow a year ago and left them in Robeson. They knew no one. They did not even know they were in the state of North Carolina. They found shelter in a trailer park that had once been exclusively black but was rapidly filling with Mexicans. There was a lot of drug dealing there and a lot of tension. One evening, Armando Fernández said, he asked a black neighbor to move his business inside and the man pulled a pistol on him.

"I hate the blacks," he said in Spanish, sitting in the break room not ten feet from Wade Baker and his black friends. Billy Harwood was sitting two tables away with the whites and Indians.

After the gun incident, Armando Fernández packed up his family and moved out into the country, to a prefabricated number sitting on a brick foundation off in the woods alone. Their only contact with people is through the satellite dish. Except for the coyote. The coyote knows where they live and comes for his money every other month.

Their five-year-old daughter has no playmates in the back country and few at school. That is the way her parents want it. "We don't want her to be American," her mother said.

"We Need a Union"

The steel bars holding a row of hogs gave way as a woman stood below them. Hog after hog fell around her with a sickening thud, knocking her senseless, the connecting bars barely missing her face. As co-workers rushed to help the woman, the supervisor spun his hands in the air, a signal to keep working. Wade Baker saw this and shook his head in disgust. Nothing stops the disassembly lines.

"We need a union," he said later in the break room. It was payday and he stared at his check: $288. He spoke softly to the black workers sitting near him. Everyone is convinced that talk of a union will get you fired. After two years at the factory, Baker makes slightly more than $9 an hour toting meat away from the cut line, slightly less than $20,000 a year, 45 cents an hour less than Mercedes Fernández.

"I don't want to get racial about the Mexicans," he whispered to the black workers. "But they're dragging down the pay. It's pure economics. They say Americans don't want to do the job. That ain't exactly true. We don't want to do it for $8. Pay $15 and we'll do it."

These men knew that in the late seventies, when the meat-packing industry was centered in northern cities like Chicago and Omaha, people had a union getting them $18 an hour. But by the mid-eighties, to cut costs, many of the packing houses had moved to small towns where they could pay a lower, nonunion wage.

The black men sitting around the table also felt sure that the Mexicans pay almost nothing in income tax, claiming eight, nine, even ten exemptions. The men believed that the illegal workers should be rooted out of the factory. "It's all about money," Baker said.

His co-workers shook their heads. "A plantation with a roof on it," one said.

For their part, many of the Mexicans in Tar Heel fear that a union would place their illegal status under scrutiny and force them out. The United Food and Commercial Workers Union last tried organizing the plant in 1997, but the idea was voted down nearly two to one.

One reason Americans refused to vote for the union was because it refuses to take a stand on illegal laborers. Another reason was the intimidation. When workers arrived at the plant the morning of the vote, they were met by Bladen County deputy sheriffs in riot gear. "Nigger Lover" had been scrawled on the union trailer.

Five years ago the work force at the plant was 50 percent black, 20 percent white and Indian, and 30 percent Latino, according to union statistics. Company officials say those numbers are about the same today. But from inside the plant, the breakdown appears to be more like 60 percent Latino, 30 percent black, 10 percent white and red.

Sherri Buffkin, a white woman and the former director of purchasing who testified before the National Labor Relations Board in an unfair-labor-practice suit brought by the union in 1998, said in an interview that the company assigns workers by race. She also said that management had kept lists of union sympathizers during the '97 election, firing blacks and replacing them with Latinos. "I know because I fired at least fifteen of them myself," she said.

The company denies those accusations. Michael H. Cole, a lawyer for Smithfield who would respond to questions about the company's labor practices only in writing, said that jobs at the Tar Heel plant were awarded through a bidding process and not assigned by race. The company also denies ever having kept lists of union sympathizers or singled out blacks to be fired.

The hog business is important to North Carolina. It is a multibillion-dollar-a-year industry in the state, with nearly two pigs for every one of its 7.5 million people. And Smithfield Foods, a publicly traded company based in Smithfield, Virginia, has become the No. 1 producer and processor of pork in the world. It slaughters more than 20 percent of the nation's swine, more than 19 million animals a year.

The company, which has acquired a network of factory farms and slaughterhouses, worries federal agriculture officials and legislators, who see it siphoning business from smaller farmers. And environmentalists contend that Smithfield's operations contaminate local water supplies. (The Environmental Protection Agency fined the company $12.6 million in 1996 after its processing plants in Virginia discharged pollutants into the Pagan River.) The chairman and chief executive, Joseph W. Luter III, declined to be interviewed.

Smithfield's employment practices have not been so closely scrutinized. And so every year, more Mexicans get hired. "An illegal alien isn't going to complain all that much," said Ed Tomlinson, acting supervisor of the Immigration and Naturalization Service bureau in Charlotte.

But the company says it does not knowingly hire illegal aliens. Smithfield's lawyer, Cole, said all new employees must present papers showing that they can legally work in the United States. "If any employee's documentation appears to be genuine and to belong to the person presenting it," he said in his written response, "Smithfield is required by law to take it at face value."

The naturalization service—which has only eighteen agents in North Carolina—has not investigated Smithfield because no one has filed a complaint, Ed Tomlinson said. "There are more jobs than people," he said, "and a lot of Americans will do the dirty work for a while and then return to their couches and eat bonbons and watch Oprah."

Not Fit for a Convict

When Billy Harwood was in solitary confinement, he liked a book to get him through. A guard would come around with a cartful. But when the prisoner asked for a new book, the guard, before handing it to him, liked to tear out the last fifty pages. The guard was a real funny guy.

"I got good at making up my own endings," Harwood said during a break. "And *my* book don't end standing here. I ought to be on that roof any day now."

But a few days later, he found out that the white contractor he was counting on already had a full roofing crew. They were Mexicans who were working for less than he was making at the plant.

During his third week cutting hogs, he got a new supervisor — a black woman. Right away she didn't like his work ethic. He went too slow. He cut out to the bathroom too much.

"Got a bladder infection?" she asked, standing in his spot when he returned. She forbade him to use the toilet.

He boiled. Mercedes Fernández kept her head down. She was certain of it, she said: he was the laziest man she had ever met. She stood next to a black man now, a prisoner from the north. They called him K. T. and he was nice to her. He tried Spanish, and he worked hard.

When the paychecks were brought around at lunchtime on Friday, Harwood got paid for five hours less than everyone else, even though everyone punched out on the same clock. The supervisor had docked him.

The prisoners mocked him. "You might be white," K. T. said, "but you came in wearing prison greens and that makes you good as a nigger."

The ending wasn't turning out the way Harwood had written it: no place to live and a job not fit for a donkey. He quit and took the Greyhound back to his parents' trailer in the hills.

When Fernández came to work the next day, a Mexican guy going by the name of Alfredo was standing in Billy Harwood's spot.

In the summer of 2000, Wade Baker became a grandfather for the second time and was helping to raise the boy. He was still driving a pallet jack at the pork plant, and in August he got a raise, to $9.45 an hour.

Mercedes Fernández was still working the picnic line. Her hands were giving her problems, and she still earned 30 cents an hour less than the men. Billy Harwood was working as a laborer, laying electric and phone cables for $8 an hour.

At the end of 2000, the United Food and Commercial Workers Union was waiting for the National Labor Relations Board to rule on its unfair labor practices suit against Smithfield before deciding whether to organize in Tar Heel again.

*King County Executive Ron Sims, Governor Gary Locke and former Seattle Mayor
Norm Rice (left to right) in October 1996, when they held the top three positions
in Washington State.* © 1996 Ned Ahrens

7

When to Campaign with Color

TIMOTHY EGAN

The ferry from Seattle is ten minutes from landing as first light slips through the silvered mist of Puget Sound, and Ron Sims is still not sure what face he will present to the world today.

The look is fine. He is not dressed like a Northwest guy. No camouflage of plaid, hiking boots or fleece vest. He wears his politician's suit and suspenders, his silk tie and leather shoes with a shine — standard uniform for the leader of a county with a population greater than that of a half-dozen states.

Passengers recognize him: there are stares and smiles directed his way. But he is also attracting the kind of curious glances that might fall on a square-jawed, rock-shouldered black man sitting next to a sheriff's deputy as he arrives at a place where blacks are more abstractions than neighbors.

The boat glides past million-dollar homes, and the big engines growl in reverse. The whistle blows. Almost show time. Two school assemblies in this county, barely ten miles across the water but a world removed from the one he governs, will hear him. The question is which Ron Sims will take the stage.

He is known as an ebullient man, someone who hugs teachers and police officers with equal zest. And at a time when so much of politics is about conveying the authentic personal narrative, Sims is a natural storyteller with a compelling one to offer, a bootstrap tale about a journey from anger to open arms.

Yet his friends and advisers have long urged him to keep a large part of that story — race — bottled up, even if it is the one thing that deeply affects how people view him. It would do him no good to talk about it, they say. Especially if he personalizes it. The way to succeed is to be seen but not seen. Flesh without color. What people want to hear from the second-highest-ranking elected official in the state are his views on property taxes, traffic, growth.

On this January 2000 day, however, Sims has been asked to talk about race, and he is tempted, he says, to throw caution aside, to let them see it through his eyes. But do they really want to hear what it is like for a black politician to live in two worlds?

"Are you kidding?" he says, laughing. "I lead a dual life. I struggle with it every day. There is Ron Sims the person and Ron Sims the public official. And my greatest fear is that in order to govern, I will end up divesting myself from who I really am."

Washington does not look like a state where a nonwhite politician would have to anglomorph to succeed. The old boundaries of race and power appear to be fading. When he was sworn in as county executive three years ago, Sims became one of three nonwhites holding the top political jobs in the state. The others were Gary Locke, the nation's first and only Chinese-American governor, and Norm Rice, Seattle's mayor, who is black. Asian-Americans have been elected to high office in Washington State for twenty years, and black mayors have won not just in the heavily Democratic Puget Sound area but in the over-whelmingly white and Republican eastern part as well—all this in a state that is 89 percent white.

Many voters say that by putting a Chinese immigrant's son and two descendants of slaves atop the governing pyramid of the state, Washington has transcended race; in the new century, in the New West, the expressed hope is that politics has shed its color barriers, and even its color consciousness. Not long after electing Gary Locke in 1996, the voters threw out all laws allowing Washington to hire based on racial preference. No more affirmative action. Competence was all that mattered. End of subject.

"In some ways, people think we are beyond prejudice here," said Locke, who is fifty. "Certainly growing up in Seattle I never felt any overt racism. And I think that's because of our newness. We are a young state, open to change."

But if the old racial order—of whites always on top—has eroded, a more complex one has replaced it. Now the system rewards nonwhites who know how to make the largely white electorate see in them what the voters see in themselves.

Thus Locke, a popular Democrat seeking reelection this year, has played up his family story—an American immigrant tale about his rise from a hovel in China to a country where the Chinese had long been barred. Thus Sims has concluded that the best way to get people to listen to him in a state that is barely 3 percent black is to shatter assumptions about black politicians and become an expert in what the white majority cares about most.

More than ten years ago, when he was first elected to a county legislative post, Sims was taken aside by Sam Smith, who was a Seattle councilman and the dean of black politicians in the city.

"Don't you sit on no health and human services committee," Smith warned him, Sims recalled.

He followed his mentor's advice. "And if you look at what Gary Locke and Norm Rice have done, they took the same path," Sims said. "We all became budget chairmen—the opposite of the stereotype."

Sims, who is fifty-one, has since become a national expert on the life cycle of Pacific salmon, a Northwest icon now in decline. "One of my African-American political friends back East said to me, 'You mean you get up every morning and talk about fish? Fish!' "

Gary Locke knows stereotypes, too. It was not so long ago, in the mid-1980s, that a few former colleagues in the State Legislature were not sure if he was Japanese or Chinese and, in any case, assumed his family was no friend of America.

"They said: 'Your people disrupted my life. I had to go off and fight because of your people,' " Locke recalled. His people—actually, his father—also fought, also in an American uniform, against the Nazis.

Even so, the Chinese-American governor has not heard or seen what the African-American county executive has—the kind of thing usually transmitted in a code that has become ever more sophisticated.

"People will call me an 'inner-city politician' whenever they want to remind someone of my race," Sims said. No matter that he grew up in the less populated, nearly all-white eastern part of the state and now spends most of his time talking about suburban concerns. By contrast, Locke lived in public housing as a boy in a racially mixed part of Seattle; he is by far the more "inner city" political leader. But that label has never been pinned on him.

Charting a course through the racial terrain of the post–civil rights era is tricky, Sims said. He saw what happened to his best friend, Norm

Rice, when as a black mayor he tried to step out of the urban political box by running for governor. And he has seen how Locke, who defeated Rice in a primary, has used a favorable public perception of Asian-Americans to advantage.

But Sims cannot change his skin color, and if he expects to follow Locke to the governor's mansion in four years, as he may try to, he has to find a way on his own, he said.

"You don't deny your race," he said at one point. "But it's there. It's always there. It's like a huge anchor around your neck, even though nobody ever asks about it."

Black politicians have learned certain approaches, he said: "One thing we do is called the get-over technique. You know how the world sees you. But in order for them to get over it, you speak their language."

Some of the best minds in American politics have told him as much, saying that if he wants to be governor, he has to stay out of the race zone. Be a black who does not run as a black, in the words of Frank Greer, a political consultant who helped L. Douglas Wilder of Virginia become the only black ever elected governor in the United States. Keep it neutral, upbeat, informed, the way he talks about salmon.

Today will be different, though. Today Sims has been asked by his hosts to talk about something other than salmon or sewers. The person and the politician will be one. That, at least, is the plan.

History Lesson vs. Life Lesson

A sea of white faces awaits Sims at Woodward Middle School on Bainbridge Island. It is early, and the seventh and eighth graders gathered in the gym are sluggish. A murmur rolls through the assembly as the King County executive walks in.

On Bainbridge Island, an outpost of new wealth and settled rhythms, blacks are a novelty, but throughout this side of Puget Sound, racial troubles still surface. At a high school basketball game in the southern part of the county a few days earlier, some boys chanted "Go rob a liquor store!" at visiting black players from Tacoma.

They later apologized, and school administrators said it had been an isolated incident, not reflective of predominant student attitudes.

But it did not surprise Sims. Growing up in Spokane, where a slim 1 percent of the population of 175,000 was black, he felt the daily rub of racial humiliation, he said.

"There was a kid who used to run by our house every afternoon and shout, 'Nigger, nigger, nigger,' and then run off," Sims recalled one day. "Same routine every day. One day my twin brother and I caught up with him, and let's just say we had a very physical discussion. When my father came home, he was furious at us. He said, 'Don't you ever stoop to their level!' "

Now he strolls to the microphone in front of the bleachers. The applause is polite.

"How many of you know who Harriet Tubman is?"

The students are blank-faced. A boy with a voice yet to descend into the octaves of puberty raises his hand.

"Uh, wasn't she a slave?"

"Yes! What else?"

"She got the underground railroad going or something?"

"Very good. What's your name?"

"Zack."

"O.K., Zack. Stand up, please. Why did slaves have to be smuggled north?"

Zack turns red and stammers. "I don't know."

Another hand goes up. A girl rises. "Something to do with Abraham Lincoln?"

Sims shakes his head in mock horror, then smiles reassuringly. He tells the students about a Supreme Court decision. They grow fidgety. Where does he go with this?

"A slave was still a slave back then because the Supreme Court ruled that they were property. Not human beings. Property. So if slaves are property, what does that make Harriet Tubman?"

No hands go up.

"She was an outlaw!" he says. "A thief. If slaves are property, as the Supreme Court has ruled, Harriet Tubman was a thief. They should have arrested her, right?"

He is pacing, microphone in hand, trying, it seems, not to lose the audience. His aim is to bring the story around to Martin Luther King, a onetime outlaw. How to make it matter to the Pokémon generation?

Sims has never shied away from speaking out on issues important to blacks in the Seattle area—about police harassment, about job discrimination. But those are matters of the public realm. The occasion at the middle school seemed to require more, something from the heart.

Maybe a searing story about his own childhood. He considered telling one, he reflected later. A Tupperware party had been planned, but the only black family in his Spokane neighborhood had not been invited, and the white mothers left it up to one of their boys to tell the Sims children that their mother was not welcome.

He had told this story once to a different audience, and he wound up regretting it, he said. Too personal. So looking at the white students now assembled before him, he said, he decided in midstream not to take the risk. He recalled how it had come out the first time, he said, how bitter he had sounded then, summing up the story in the bluntest of terms: "Let the two nigger kids go tell their nigger mom that she can't come."

Asian in the Governor's Mansion

To see the current occupants of the governor's mansion in Olympia is to realize how much this state has changed. A century ago Asians were considered such a threat to white employment that they were marched out of their homes at gunpoint and told never to return. And not quite sixty years ago, Asian-Americans were again uprooted, this time forced into internment camps.

Today, Governor Gary Locke lives amid Chippendale mirrors and windows fashioned after those at Monticello. For him, it is a return to public housing, albeit with twenty-seven rooms.

Afternoon sunlight pours into a cozy den; both the babies, Emily and Dylan, are asleep, allowing Locke's wife, Mona Lee Locke, who is also a child of Chinese immigrants, a chance to relax. A thirty-five-year-old former television reporter who still makes documentary films, she has the personality of young champagne and the kind of looks the camera loves. She is witty, fashionable, self-deprecating and still somewhat awed by the life the Lockes are leading as the crown couple of Asian-American politicians.

"I don't think either of us realized the scope of all this," she says. "People come up to Gary all the time and tell him what a role model he is, that they hope he runs for higher office. Even Republicans. And it's because of his race that they look up to him. They see in him the American Dream come true."

Locke sees himself in those terms as well. On becoming Washington's twenty-first governor, he noted in his inaugural address that his grandfather had worked as a houseboy less than a mile from the Capitol grounds.

"It took a hundred years to go one mile," he said. "But it's a journey that could only take place in America."

A fortune-teller in New York's Chinatown once told Jimmie Locke, the governor's eighty-three-year-old father, that one of his sons would be famous. Locke doubted him. "I said: 'Famous? What the heck. He's Chinese in America. What can you be famous for?' "

Now some Asian-Americans hope that Gary Locke will run for president one day. But even his father's wildest interpretation of the fortune-teller's prediction does not allow such a thought. "President is still the white people's position," he said.

Unlike Sims, the governor says he does not struggle to reconcile his public and private personas. He is shy, and if he is introspective he gives no hint of it. There are few lines on his face; with his paintbrush black hair, he looks two decades younger than his fifty years. His hobby is plumbing. His idea of a good time is cleaning out his father's garage.

Gary Locke says he knows in his heart that despite the model-minority tag, not every Asian is smart, and not every black gets a fair shake in the state he holds up as a beacon of the racial future. But he rarely uses the bully pulpit for social change.

He did make a public fuss, though, for an issue that touched his own life: affirmative action. Were it not for a race-conscious admissions policy, he said, he would not have to gone to Yale. "I was a three-fer," he said. "Asian. From the West. Public school." But though he spoke against a 1998 ballot measure rolling back affirmative action, the voters went their own way, removing racial preference from state hiring.

Voting was not an option when the Lockes came to America; most Chinese could not even own property. And until 1943, with few exceptions, the Exclusion Act made it against the law for a person from China to enter the United States as an immigrant. As a legacy of the law, the Locke family has shared a deep secret for three generations:

like a lot of Chinese-Americans, they had to lie to get into the country; the governor's paternal grandfather told the authorities that he had been born in America.

"Some members of my family are still very nervous about acknowledging what happened back then," Locke said.

Jimmie Locke came to America from southern China with his father in 1931, a boy of thirteen. Ten years later he was drafted into the Army and fought the Germans in France. After the war, he and his wife, Julie Locke, who was born in Hong Kong, had five children, Gary arriving second.

But unlike Sims, Locke says he lived a childhood virtually free of racial insults, living as he did in a melting pot. When pressed, however, he recalled several times when he was made to feel embarrassment about his heritage. His third-grade teacher once asked him what he had had for breakfast. When he replied that he had eaten a traditional Chinese meal of porridge and dried shrimp, the teacher struck him on the hand with a ruler, unhappy that he was not eating like an American.

"It was hard—doubting yourself, your culture, wondering if your parents did something wrong," he said.

Still, Locke called himself "a Seattle kid." He loved camping, Boy Scouts. What made him realize that he was thoroughly American, he said, was when his parents took him to Hong Kong at the age of ten to stay with his maternal grandparents and learn Chinese customs. He was appalled by what he saw.

"My grandmother lived in a room, eight feet by eight feet. Dirt floor. Cooked over an open fire. Scrounged around for kindling. There was raw sewage outside. It was essentially a refugee camp. The plan was to leave me with my maternal grandparents and be educated. I rebelled."

It was only when he left Seattle, at the height of the Vietnam War, that Locke began to understand how some people in his own country considered him foreign, if not the enemy. As he was leaving for Yale, he and his parents, waiting in the airport, were confronted by an American soldier, who cursed them and called them gooks.

At Yale, Locke was often complimented on his English and asked about his diet. "People would come up to me and say, 'Do you ever eat steak? Ever eat fried chicken?' They had these stereotypes: you only eat with chopsticks, you don't celebrate Thanksgiving, that sort of thing."

He also learned for the first time that he had grown up in a country whose official policy for sixty-one years had been to close the gates to the Chinese. His parents had never told him about the exclusion laws, or the internment of Japanese-Americans, and the subject had not come up in his textbooks.

"I was just very, very sad that this was part of the history of the United States," Locke said. "Very disappointed."

The Locke family was more vocal about young Gary's future. They hoped he would be an engineer or a businessman. Politics was unseemly. But Locke went his own way, winning a seat in the State Legislature in 1982, then rising swiftly to budget chairman. In 1993 he defeated an incumbent to become the King County executive.

His rise excited the pan-Asian community, an unusual alliance of Japanese, Chinese, Filipinos, Vietnamese and Pacific Islanders who make up about 6 percent of Washington's population. But Locke's heritage was rarely mentioned, in press accounts or by opponents, during any of his seven campaigns. His public life followed the unspoken rule for nonwhites in American politics: to be successful, be race neutral.

"If you were to ask people for adjectives to describe Gary Locke, you would get way down the list before the word Chinese would come up," said Brian Ebersole, Locke's friend from their legislative days together and now mayor of Tacoma.

Locke was the picture of a policy wonk, the last person to turn out the lights in the House of Representatives. One newspaper headline called him "The Man Who Mistook His Life for the Legislature."

He was also a lonely guy. Though he had been briefly married while attending Boston University Law School, he had spent most of his adult life searching for a perfect mate. Then, in middle age, alone and believing he had reached a political plateau, the world opened up for Gary Locke. The fortune-teller in New York had had it right.

The "Angry" Black Man

Fifteen minutes into his speech, Ron Sims drops the talk of slavery and summons the image of Bainbridge Island, 1942.

"The Japanese have just bombed Pearl Harbor," Sims tells the students. "The United States Army came to Bainbridge Island to round up the citizens who were of Japanese ancestry. You live here, and these people are your neighbors. What are you going to do?"

"Tell them to go to Canada," one boy says.

"Canada?" Sims lets the answer sink in. "OK. But most of these people are United States citizens. They don't want to go to Canada. They are your neighbors, remember? So what do you do?"

The children look at one another.

"The executive order says Japanese-Americans have to leave their homes. It is the law. Are any of you going to break the law to help them?" Two dozen students rise.

Sims himself was something of a militant once. In the turbulent sixties he was one of a handful of black students who pushed for change at Central Washington University, challenging teachers and administrators on curriculum and admissions policies. He wore a dashiki, grew an Afro and quoted Malcolm X.

He questioned not only authority but his own core beliefs. At one point he wrote a term paper on how Christianity had justified slavery. He spent months researching the paper, growing increasingly bitter about his faith, then took his work home to Spokane to show his father.

"My father said, 'Brilliant.' And then he told me, 'This is not the God I know.' "

Over several months, as Sims considered what his father had said, his thinking changed. He ultimately chose the God of his father, he said, coming to believe that most people were capable of looking beyond their baser instincts.

Only rarely does the old indignation seep out now. At a public hearing on land use in the new suburbs east of Seattle in 1998, a man stood up and shouted, "Ron Sims, you are nothing but bought and sold to special interests!"

Sims shot back: "There hasn't been a member of the Sims family bought and sold since my great-grandfather was a slave. And this member of the Sims family isn't for sale today."

When a reporter describes Sims as angry in a public debate, he will challenge the characterization. "That's code," he said. "A black man who is angry is a lethal label in politics."

The middle-school principal nods approvingly at the end of Sims's exercise on World War II internment. The students applaud those who stood and said they would help their neighbors. Having retreated

from the talk about slavery, Sims is back on comfortable middle
ground.

Running on the Record, Not Race

When Ron Sims is unsure of himself, he turns to the friend who served
as best man at his wedding, Norm Rice, now fifty-eight. In many ways
Rice set the standard for how a nonwhite politician could govern in
the Pacific Northwest.

In the late 1980s, when Rice held a meeting at his house to solicit
advice on whether he should run for mayor of Seattle, it was Sims
who made the comment that no one wanted to hear. He said a black
candidate could not be elected mayor.

But Rice proved his younger friend wrong. He served two terms,
becoming one of Seattle's most successful mayors. Under Rice, the
city rebuilt its downtown and improved its schools, the job and housing
markets boomed, crime plummeted and tax revenue rolled into city
coffers.

Going from popular leader of the state's biggest city to governor
seemed a logical next step for the mayor in 1996. But he faced a
formidable primary opponent in Gary Locke, then the King County
executive. A big question mark was race. Neither man had mentioned
the subject in earlier campaigns. But this would largely be a contest
between an Asian-American and an African-American. How much attention should be drawn to a candidate's race?

Rice's supporters were divided. Some wanted him to tell his story
about overcoming bigotry as a middle-class black in Denver. It was a
personal history with indelible moments, like his first day of college at
the University of Colorado in Boulder. As Rice remembers it: "I was
waiting to meet my roommate. His parents came in, took one look at
me and said, 'Good-bye,'" taking their son with them.

But Rice wanted to run on his record at the helm of the good ship
Seattle.

"I said to Norm, 'You've got to get past what you did for Seattle;
they won't elect you governor for that,'" said Sue Tupper, one of his
strategists. "People want to know you, the person," she told him.

Rice was unswayed. His response was that when race was brought
up directly, even in the context of defeating bigotry, it could backfire,

because then people would be asked to vote for a black man instead of a mayor who happened to be black.

"Sue, I won't go there," he told Tupper.

"Why not?" she asked. "You've got a great story."

"Yes," he replied. "I have a great story about how my family came to America. As good as Gary's. We just happened to have different travel agents."

Letting Race Play a Role

A different strategy emerged in the Locke camp. Locke was sitting on a gold mine of personal narrative, an immigrant tale echoing those of millions of white Americans. And no one was advising him that a Chinese-American could not be elected.

"The consensus was that because Gary Locke was so good at what he does, the voters would overlook race," said Lori Matsukawa, an anchor at KING-TV, who had introduced him to Mona Lee.

Locke married Mona Lee in 1994, and she changed his life, he says. He opened up, reached out, joked more easily. Even his wedding proposal was out of character. He hired a plane to trail a banner reading: "Mona, I love you. Will you love me?"

By 1996 she was not just a wife with star quality but a close adviser. Though a novice in the nuances of politics, she knew how to use television to tell a story. And rather than play down his Chinese background, she advised her husband, he should use it.

For Locke, it was a logical decision, part of his political evolution as he reached beyond his base of support to a statewide electorate less familiar with him. "You can't hide your race," he said. "My hair, my eyes, my skin color: people look at me and know I'm Asian."

The Gary Locke who was introduced to voters in 1996 was married, visibly happy and even openly affectionate with his new wife. And suddenly, for the first time in a campaign, he was calling himself "a person of color."

Whether speaking to apple farmers in Yakima, Rotarians in Spokane or suburban moms in Bellevue, he had a simple refrain when he brought up his family history: "I am Chinese, but I am thoroughly American."

His self-description went to the heart of old white fears about the Chinese in America: that their true allegiance was to the ancient nation across the Pacific. He emphasized his biography the entire campaign, first for the Democratic nomination, when Rice, a black mayor, was his main opponent, and then in the general election, when he faced Ellen Craswell, a white Republican and Christian conservative of the far right. Locke crushed Rice in the primary. The Seattle mayor won only two small counties, far away from Seattle. And in a state that leans Democratic and favors efficiency over ideology in its lawmakers, Locke beat Craswell by nearly 20 percentage points.

His campaign strategy, Locke said, had nothing to do with the race of any of his opponents but was a way to sell his biography. And both the governor and the first lady said that his talking about his heritage had been difficult at first.

"We never wanted to use race," Mona Lee Locke said. "Washington is mostly Caucasian, so there's no point. Gary's not comfortable. With a Chinese heritage, you're raised not to talk about it. But once we started talking about it, he felt more comfortable, because people responded to his story."

The story they told was couched in terms familiar to most Americans. "We helped to build this country with our blood, our sweat and our tears," Locke would say in his speeches. "Now it's time for us to share in governing it."

It bothers many Americans of Asian descent to be described, as a group, as clever, diligent or shrewd. Those very words were long used to keep Asians out of the country or to cast suspicion on them. But by the late 1990s, Asian-Americans, at least those on the West Coast, were finding they could use ethnic pride as Gary Locke had, as something that would appeal to whites.

Blacks, however, could not.

"I think it's tougher for a black than an Asian," said Ebersole, the mayor of Tacoma, who is white. "If there are stereotypes about race, the present stereotypes about Asians are positive."

Yet for Locke the old negative ones can resurface. When a campaign-finance scandal enveloped a handful of Asian-American contributors to the 1996 Democratic presidential race, he publicly questioned whether Jews or Irish-Americans would have been subjected to the same suspicions as the Asian-Americans. Conservative pundits and Republicans attacked him.

"They said I was playing the race card," Locke said.

It was a fresh variation on the lesson that Norm Rice and Ron Sims had been taught time and again. "You can't be too black, or too Chinese," as Ebersole put it.

Legacies and Latitudes

Gary Locke's first year as governor was euphoric. President Clinton singled him out in the audience during a State of the Union speech. The governor and his wife went to China, where they were mobbed, attracting more attention than Mel Gibson, who was making a movie there.

They journeyed to Jilong, the Locke ancestral village in Guangdong Province.

"I sat in the room where my dad was born, where my grandfather was born—a shed almost, with no electricity—and the whole experience was overwhelming," Locke said. He wept as he left the village, people who were with him said. It was the first time anyone could remember seeing him cry.

While Locke was gathering high approval ratings as governor, Ron Sims was learning the job that Locke had given up, touring the housing developments and strip malls of a fast-growing King County. As for Norm Rice, he left politics after his second term as mayor, at the end of 1997.

Today, Rice is the director of the Federal Home Loan Bank in Seattle. When he talks about the governor's race, he attributes his loss to no one but himself; he just ran a weak campaign, he says.

Yet when asked what the campaign had taught him about racial politics today, this normally gregarious man struck a different, more cautious note. "I think that if people have a choice between an African-American and an Asian-American, they will probably choose the latter," he said. "Whether people want to admit it or not, there is a hierarchy of race."

When Locke was asked about that notion, he looked puzzled. "Racial hierarchy?" he said. "You know, I've never really thought about it."

A Politician Gets Personal

The clock is winding down on Ron Sims's hour with the Bainbridge students. He has taken them through discussions of slavery and internment and brought some students forward to reenact a scene from the life of Dr. King. It is hard to tell if he has reached them. He seems about to take questions, but does not. Instead he walks to the edge of the crowd.

"I want to tell you a story about myself," he says. Once he starts, there is no hesitation. "I'm a little boy, four years old. We are driving across the country. In North Dakota, I fall out of the car, while it's going slow. I fall to the pavement. Blood everywhere. I'm lying there on the highway thinking, Please don't leave me in North Dakota."

He is seriously hurt, the back of his scalp peeled away, he says. His family panics and races to the nearest hospital, in a small town. As he speaks, the gym is as quiet as it has been all morning.

"What do you think happened to me?" Sims asks. "I was a black kid in a white state, and blood was pouring out of my head. What do you think they were thinking about our family? We went from one town to the next. We . . . were . . . turned . . . away . . . six times. Six times! Nobody would treat me.

"Finally, a nun at a Catholic hospital took me in. I needed two hundred stitches to put my scalp back together."

He walks back to the center of the room. "I got to be King County executive," he says, "because one person made a decision to treat me. One person made a difference."

Spontaneous applause. A standing ovation. The white principal, Clayton Mork, takes the microphone for routine announcements, then stops. He begins to weep. He tries to compose himself. "I know, as a middle-aged school principal, that, that there are not a lot of things I can say that carry a lot of weight with you kids, but this—" Again he is overcome.

Sims walks forward and gives the principal a bear hug. Afterward, a stream of awkward adolescents approaches Sims for hugs or high-fives.

"That was great, Mr. Sims!"

"Awesome!"

He leaves the gym beaming. The next stop is a much bigger audience, more than a thousand students at Bainbridge Island High School.

There he tells a story not about his family's past but about the present, and perhaps about the future. He is married to a woman from the Philippines, he tells them, and what an eye-opener that has proved to be.

"When I told my friends I was in love, they said, 'You know those Filipino women carry knives in their purses.' And when we married, boy, did we get it from all sides—her family and my family. We were outcasts."

He has now been able to see America from an immigrant's point of view, he says, and his wife, Cayan Topacio, has come to understand how a native-born black sometimes has to strain for respect. Their twelve-year-old son looks more black than Asian, and in watching how people react to him, Topacio says, she has learned something about the attitudes of her adopted country. Blacks are treated different from Asians, she says, "in little everyday ways."

Sims ends his second talk with a request. "You kids are told all the time to be tolerant," he says. "Well, don't be tolerant of me because I'm African-American. That really bugs me. Either include me or exclude me."

Afterward he is again engulfed by students, parents, teachers—all white. In the stands, one teacher turns to another and says, "Hard to believe that guy's a politician."

On the ferry ride home, Sims sits with the sheriff's deputy, his bodyguard, and watches the city come into view. He appears drained. Both speeches seemed to have worked, but those were impressionable children, not toughened adults. In four years he may run for governor. There is no way to know how voters would react. If he told his racial story, would he win as Gary Locke had? If he went the race-neutral route, would he lose as Norm Rice had?

The boat pulls into Seattle. Several people approach Sims. He is King County executive again. He straightens his tie. A woman asks him about his habitat-preservation program for kokanee salmon. He gives a very long, very detailed answer.

On November 7, 2000, Gary Locke was reelected by a large margin as governor of Washington. Locke defeated John Carlson, a Republican talk-radio host who had been instrumental in the successful 1998 campaign to dismantle affirmative action at all levels of government in the state. Race never came up—overtly—during the gubernatorial campaign, and Locke rarely dwelled on his Chinese-American heritage. The main issue was traffic congestion.

Ron Sims completed work on a salmon recovery program for King County. He continued to speak out about race in a year when the police shooting of an African-American became the subject of heated debate in Seattle. And he told friends that he would like to run for governor in 2004.

Carla Cowles, National Park Service interpreter, in one of the restored slave cabins at Magnolia Plantation, Natchitoches, Louisiana. Fred R. Conrad/The New York Times

Betty Hertzog, last remaining family member from Magnolia Plantation, who sold the plantation's slave quarters and other buildings to the National Park Service.
Fred R. Conrad/The New York Times

8

Reaping What Was Sown on the Old Plantation

GINGER THOMPSON

NATCHITOCHES, LOUISIANA

At the south edge of Magnolia Plantation, eight simple cabins stood in a field of clover. Generations of whitewash were peeling from the mud-brick walls. All but one front porch had rotted away, and there were gaping holes where doors and windows used to be.

Hidden from the main house by rows of live oaks, the cabins had been forgotten by many and ignored by most. There was almost nothing left—except the stories of the slaves who once lived in them.

Betty Hertzog hadn't been thinking about slavery when she agreed to go along with her rich friends' plans to turn part of her beloved Magnolia into a national park. She had been thinking about her family's land, and her struggle to hold on to it.

Hertzog's ancestors settled that fertile land at the south end of Cane River more than two hundred years ago, and she had lived in the big house at Magnolia nearly all her life. She had too little money to keep it going, no children to pass it on to. Sometimes when she talked about her devotion to the land, it sounded almost like religion. "If you had land," she would say, "you were raised that it is very important, and that if you had it, you had to keep it."

To listen to Hertzog is to feel the abiding power of Old South symbols. Slight but still sturdy at seventy, she is reserved to the point of reclusiveness, happiest walking the plantation grounds alone. But she had come to believe that the new national park, with its droves of tourists, offered a way to hold on to the land—to preserve her family's stories and teach future generations about the agricultural practices that made Magnolia the Goliath of Cane River when cotton was king.

Bobby DeBlieux hadn't been thinking about slavery, either, when he began his campaign to turn Magnolia's work buildings into a national park. He had just been trying to rescue his town.

He had been trying since he was mayor in the mid-1970s, and Natchitoches was drying up: farms were dying, working families were fleeing, much of downtown was boarded shut.

"I knew that history was the key to turning the whole town around," said DeBlieux, sixty-seven, who owns the Tante Huppe Bed & Breakfast on Jefferson Street. "First people would want to come here to visit, and if they did, they would want to stay."

DeBlieux doesn't look like an economic-development visionary. With his shock of cottony-white hair, his shirttails hanging over sagging jeans, he generally seems to have just rolled out of bed. But he was right. Before long, that ugly downtown had become a National Historic Landmark, a mile-long quarter of French Colonial buildings converted into antiques shops, restaurants and souvenir emporiums. The tourists came, and they stayed, often in the thirty-two B & B's — as people here will tell you, the most in the state.

Still, when DeBlieux and his preservationist friends thought about Natchitoches's larger possibilities, they tended to look down Cane River to Magnolia and its sister plantation, Oakland. The old places had gone to seed some, but with a little help and money from the National Park Service, they could make Natchitoches the Colonial Williamsburg of Louisiana.

In 1994, with some deftly applied pressure from Louisiana's senior senator at the time, J. Bennett Johnston — Hertzog's cousin by marriage — Congress created the Cane River Creole National Historical Park. As for how slavery would fit in, Hertzog hoped the Park Service wouldn't dwell on it too much.

"A lot of people around here have put slavery behind them," she said. "It is a part of the history here, and no one wants to ignore it. But I don't want them to talk about slavery and get stuck on that."

By the spring of 1999, though, she started to feel uneasy about the Park Service's plans. A new ranger, a black woman named Carla Cowles, had begun scratching around the old slave cabins.

Slavery was pretty much all Cowles was thinking about when she came to Cane River. A heavyset woman of forty with a booming laugh laid over an edgy determination, she had started her career at Colonial Williamsburg. But she came away with a very different ambition than DeBlieux's: to provide a face and a voice to the often-ignored stories of African slaves.

For a decade, in reenactment and song, she had shown the violent fate of captured runaways and the pain of families torn apart, had explained how people treated as property had held on to humanity and hope. Magnolia's slave cabins, she thought, would be the perfect stage for her work.

"I'm here to tell the whole story," she said. "Some people might call it revisionist history, but I think what's been going on around here is a lot of revisionist history."

Stories, of course, have consequences. And from the beginning, what hardly anyone really counted on was how a new park, on a plantation that once had 260 slaves, might stir things up in a place where people had agreed long ago that the last thing they wanted to talk about was race.

When the Park Service held hearings about what kind of programs people wanted at the park, there was a lot of enthusiasm about restoring the old buildings. When slavery came up, there was silence.

"Speaking about slavery proved difficult for whites and blacks, and promised complications for park interpretation," the Park Service reported. "Blacks and whites treated slavery as a delicate, nearly taboo subject for public discussion."

The Role of a Lifetime

Hertzog had spent weeks getting the big house ready for the Natchitoches Fall Pilgrimage of Historic Homes, and on opening day in October 1999, it looked like a movie set. Sunlight cascaded over the portrait of Magnolia's patriarch, Ambrose LeComte 2nd, striking a dandy pose in his ascot and Colonial jacket. The Baccarat chandelier bought years ago in New Orleans was up in the grand foyer once again. The air was suffused with the history of Hertzog's ancestors—it hung from every wall, filled every shelf—and she wondered if she was doing her family proud.

"Daddy wouldn't have liked these tours, because he didn't like strangers roaming through his house," she said. "But you can't make a living from farming anymore. The tourists help pay to keep up this old place."

As an only child, she had always known she would someday take over Magnolia. But she had expected to live a little of her own life first. She was just out of college and heading to Houston to look for work when the call came. Her father had had a heart attack. Someone had to manage the harvest. "It was panic, pure panic," she said. "I really wasn't sure I could manage it the way Daddy did, but I had to try, or else we might lose it all."

So at twenty-three, she traded her big-city dreams for a job at a local bank, and began her turn as caretaker of the land. No one asked her to stay. No one had to. Magnolia was simply not going to go the way of the other Cane River plantations, into strangers' hands.

But it has been more than ten years since Hertzog oversaw a harvest. In the late 1980s, when the bottom fell out of cotton, she rented her fields to corporate growers. Soon, she began the house tours. And then, in the early 1990s, her rich preservationist friends began talking about turning Magnolia's work buildings — the slave cabins and hospital, the blacksmith shop and cotton gin — into a national park.

On opening day of the fall festival, though, she talked about Magnolia's good times, not her own struggle. Dressed in a pink satin Civil War–era gown, she showed tourists the wooden clock rescued from the original big house, burned down by Union troops; the 1851 trophy won by the family's prize racer, an auburn thoroughbred named Flying Dutchman; and the chapel fashioned from an old workroom at the back of the manor.

Of the seven hundred tourists, all but ten or so were white. One black visitor, fifty-five-year-old Sam Dugar, had come looking for his own history. Dugar's father and grandfather had been sharecroppers at Magnolia, but till now he had avoided the place. As the tour ended, he said he felt cheated.

"All I kept thinking was that they accumulated all this wealth because of the blacks who worked here," he said. "But there was nothing on the tour about black people. It's as if their place in history was erased."

Betty Hertzog insists she is not trying to erase history. "We are showing this house," she explained. "I try to talk about what's here, and the history that I am aware of. The slaves didn't have a lot of records, and so you don't know who was here and where they all were on the place." If visitors are interested, she tells them the slave cabins are out there, on the Park Service's portion of the land.

Besides, she says, talk of slavery can offend. Her cousin Ambrose recalled a black visitor who demanded back her $5 admission after learning that the house was still owned by the original slaveholding family. "She was yelling so loud, I could hear her from my house," said Ambrose

Hertzog, who lives next door. "I was wondering, what does that woman know about Betty? The days of owning slaves was long ago."

Certainly, Betty Hertzog says, it was not right for humans to be held as property. But she feels no shame. "The government has given them every opportunity in the world," she said, "so stop complaining about the past and go out and do something."

She has a low opinion of the idea, embraced by some black intellectuals and politicians, of reparations for slaves' descendants. "I think they should be grateful they got their freedom back then," she said. "I think they ought to be glad they are Americans, living in a free country. The more of that stuff that gets stirred up, the more hate there will be on both sides."

From the little she has learned, Hertzog says, her family did not mistreat its slaves. A Northwestern State University historian has found no evidence of abuse or neglect, though a set of ankle stocks was evidence of punishment. A Park Service archaeologist also told her that the two-family brick cabins were larger and more comfortable than the log dwellings on other plantations. And inventories show that Magnolia's slaves had more balanced diets than others in the area.

Strolling among the cabins one evening, Hertzog said that in her mind, slavery looked a lot like the lives of the sharecroppers — slaves' descendants she remembered from childhood, who worked the land for part of the crop. To this day, that is the only way she has known blacks. Even after the last families left the cabins in 1968, she continued to employ a few black workers.

"That's just the way things have always been," she said. "Each group had different networks, I guess."

Some black old-timers, she says, have told her that their years at Magnolia were the best of their lives. While segregation governed life in town, she says, on Magnolia blacks and whites raced horses together and played on the plantation baseball team, the Black Magnolias. She knew that black children would not have the same opportunities as whites. "But for them," she said, "that's the way life was and they accepted it."

As for Magnolia's slaves, she knew some of their stories would be told at the new park. But she wanted those stories to reflect her family's hardships and kindnesses as well. Which was why she was getting so worried about the Park Service's plans.

Hertzog almost never talked directly about Carla Cowles. And for more than a year after Cowles arrived, Hertzog never met with her. "I guess I have just been too busy," she said.

But she complained a lot about the Park Service, and said she had heard Cowles and her boss were giving tours and talking about slaves who had never even lived on Cane River. She had been led to believe the park would be devoted to agriculture, she said, but increasingly it seemed the emphasis would be on slavery, on portrayals bound to vilify her family. She felt betrayed.

"That's the way people from other places feel about the South anyway," she said, "so I don't doubt it a bit."

An Outlet for the Anger

"When we learn about history, we are often told about kinder, gentler times," Cowles was telling a tour group at the cabins. (Though the park wouldn't open officially for a few years, she had begun giving tours of the work buildings and cabins.) "We are taught to think about the lives of the rich and glamorous, not about the common, everyday people — people like you and you and you."

"How many children do you have, sir?" she went on, turning to a man in the crowd.

He held up two fingers.

"If you lived here, with your two kids, would work be all that you did in your life?" she asked.

"No, I would have to take care of my kids."

"Well, the people who lived here couldn't even do that. Their children could be taken from them at any time and sold away."

This is the kind of simple exchange that Cowles uses to pull her audience into the lives of the mothers and fathers, cooks and carpenters who lived in bondage. The history of slavery is so painful and mind-bending, she says, that teaching anything meaningful in an hour seems impossible. So she makes it personal, makes the tourists become slaves, if only for one mental moment.

It was just such a moment that set her on the road to Cane River. In 1989, she answered an ad for a job at Colonial Williamsburg: "Talk about black history and get paid," it said. It sounded promising — except for having to portray slaves.

Growing up in Williamsburg, the daughter of a millworker and a teacher's aide, she had revered America's civil rights leaders. She had watched her mother, who never graduated from junior high, fight to get her children into Advanced Placement classes. And while attending college courses, which she remembers as "a sea of whites," Cowles organized sit-ins to demand more minority professors.

She saw no spirit of rebellion in slavery. "I was like a lot of people who think slaves were weak, and I didn't want to portray weakness," she said.

Her bosses at Colonial Williamsburg persuaded her to try. She started off in secondary roles, singing songs that showed "the lighter side of slavery." Later, in a burlap costume, she portrayed a slave named Secundia, who had just learned that her mother had died on another plantation.

"I was singing to my dead mother," she recalled, "saying how we were so busy working in the fields that I never had time to tell her I loved her."

The experience, Cowles says, was transforming. Suddenly, the slaves she had studied in documents came to life and had her face. Their history became her cause. And her portrayal of Secundia got her a job at the Jefferson National Expansion Memorial in St. Louis, organizing programs about the Dred Scott Decision, which barred slaves and their descendants from citizenship.

In the spring of 1999 Cowles was assigned to develop the Cane River historical and community outreach programs. She imagines the old cabins as a "living, breathing slave community," complete with people in costume portraying slaves.

She expected some resistance. She had read the reports from all the public hearings. Early on, she turned to Frankie Ray Jackson, a black former school-board member, for help in navigating people's sensitivities. As for Bobby DeBlieux and his friends, she had little to do with them; at one meeting she did attend, she asked why she was the only black person there. And she never knocked on Betty Hertzog's door. She just hadn't had the time, she said.

It's not that Cowles doesn't often deal with whites in Natchitoches. She speaks warmly of her boss, Laura Soulliere, who has encouraged her pursuit of slave history. She gets along well with the park volunteers, most of whom are white. And she deals comfortably with white tourists, putting them at ease when they make clumsy comments about slavery.

"We can't heal old wounds until we look at the way life was and all its problems," she often says.

Yet for all the healing power of history, it has increasingly channeled her racial anger. When she talks about that anger, she casts back in her mind—to the St. Louis landlord who at first refused her an apartment because she was black; to the man who called her a "pickaninny" as she guided him through Colonial Williamsburg in her slave costume; to the grade-school teacher who tried to fail her for refusing to pick a hero from a list of white American leaders.

Today, away from work, she leads an essentially black life. She dates a black man who calls himself a separatist. And though she says she does not share those views, she has had only two white friends. She tries not to wallow in anger, but the more she learns about slavery, the more she regards the old plantation elite with suspicion and reproach.

"It is almost impossible, living as a black person in America, and as a person who has studied so much about slavery, not to be angry about the injustices done to black people," she said.

She avoids talking directly about Betty Hertzog, just as Hertzog will not talk directly about her. She speaks of no one in particular when expressing resentment at the "furniture and antiques" tours popular around town. And while she is offended at the wealth that plantation owners accumulated on the backs of slaves, she is disturbed more, she says, by whites who ignore the less noble truths of their families' pasts.

"They don't have to say, 'I'm sorry,'" she said. "But if you remain silent about it, then you have blood on your hands, too."

A Social Contract of Silence

In the fall of 1999, for the first time, a black man ran for mayor of Natchitoches. He was a vice president at the local university and a six-term councilman. Many whites quietly talked of supporting him; polls predicted record black turnout. Then the candidate, John Winston, started talking about race, with the slogan, "Let's make history! Let's elect the first black mayor."

That didn't go over too well. White callers to the "Talk Back Natchitoches" radio show worried that Winston would not serve all equally. Some criticized him for making race an issue. White support faded.

In the end Winston lost, by sixty-three votes, to a white anesthesiologist named Wayne McCullen. More than 95 percent of Winston's supporters were black; more than 95 percent of McCullen's were white. Both men agreed there had been a backlash over the race issue, and Winston has had second thoughts about his slogan.

"When it comes to race, the truth gets twisted to mean a lot of different things," he said. "And so most people just prefer not to talk about it."

Public discussion of race is never easy, anywhere. But in this town of 17,000 in central Louisiana, not talking about race is at the heart of a social contract, rooted in the slave-owning past, that governs all sorts of black-white relationships — or nonrelationships. Whatever the inner tensions, Natchitoches has tended to get along.

Black and white Natchitoches are separate worlds of roughly equal size. (The black half generally includes the mixed-race Creoles, though socially and politically they float in between.) Whites live east of Fifth Street, blacks west. Natchitoches Junior High is mostly black; the junior high at St. Mary's Catholic School is mostly white. On Sundays, blacks fill the all-you-can-eat buffet near the Wal-Mart; whites crowd restaurants on the historic waterfront.

Though there are a handful of influential blacks, economic and political power rests in white hands. Indeed, even if John Winston had won, he would have had less power than the three well-endowed, and virtually all-white, private committees that turned Natchitoches into a tourist town. Whites own all the new businesses in the landmark district. In this place where so much revolves around history, the history it tends to revolve around is white Colonial history.

"The thing is, blacks think this historic district is white elite," Bobby DeBlieux said. "Well it is. But it's not because we designed it that way. It's sad, but black people here segregate themselves."

Blacks do not dispute those facts. They just give them a different spin. "It's true that blacks have not gotten involved in the historic things," said Clifford Blake, who owns a po' boy shop. "I had a chance to open up a place on the waterfront, but I didn't do it because it seemed like it was too white-dominated, and I didn't believe they really wanted blacks involved."

To local preservationists, the racial climate reflects Natchitoches's history as a "cultural island" in the South. From its founding by French traders in 1714, they maintain, its colonists were more accepting of other races than the British were, and generally kinder to slaves. Natchitoches, they say, is the best place to tell "a side to slavery most people have never seen."

"People here have always gotten along and respected one another,"

DeBlieux said, adding, "Maybe there's no social closeness now, but there's no tensions."

Even through the turmoil of the civil rights movement, Natchitoches was calm; there were no protests, and a single brief boycott. But silence, Winston and other blacks say, has been less a matter of contentment than ingrained reticence. They recall the one time Natchitoches did come close to open confrontation.

Back in 1927, a white plantation owner had given the city a bronze statue of a slave tipping his hat and bowing his head in greeting. A plaque said the statue had been erected "in grateful recognition of the arduous and faithful service of the good darkies of Louisiana," and whites saw it as a symbol of their enlightened view of slavery.

For forty years the Good Darkey stood on Front Street. But in 1968, as civil rights protests gripped the South, young blacks vowed to bomb it, calling it an abominable symbol of servitude. In the end, after a meeting with the mayor, blacks stood down and the Good Darkey went gently, removed by officials late one September night.

There was a sense of victory among blacks, and integration came peacefully. But that progress, many blacks say, has gone only so far. They remain in their separate world, profoundly wary of whites.

Across Cane River from the new park is St. Paul Missionary Baptist Church, organized 133 years ago by freed slaves. Even today, says the pastor, the Reverend Leo Walker, many in his congregation are struggling to overcome generations of distrust.

"A lot of them harbor deep anger about things that happened to them or their ancestors in the past," he said, "and they honestly believe that no whites can go to heaven."

A Son of "the Quarters"

Leslie Vercher winced whenever he heard people call Magnolia's brick cabins "slave quarters." They had once been his home.

His father was born and raised in the cabins, and his family did not move off Magnolia until the late 1960s. Those people were not slaves, he pointed out. They were the Hertzogs' employees, and they called their homes "the quarters."

But when pressed to think about any ancestors who lived there as slaves, this fireplug of a man looked as if he might become physically ill. He refused to watch movies like *Roots* or *Amistad*, and rejected the term "African-American" because he had never known any relatives from Africa. Certainly some black people on Cane River were interested in seeing slave stories, however painful, resurrected at the new park. But Vercher saw slavery only as a shameful part of the past, and tried to wipe it from his mind.

"I don't want to hear about my people being beaten and raped," he said, with his Cajun twang and willful scowl. "Let it go."

But in a twist of fate—he sometimes saw it as a divine trick played by his late father—Vercher, thirty-five, was now working for the Park Service, restoring the cabins. For a black man, especially one with a ninth-grade education, it was one of the best jobs on Cane River, with decent pay and benefits for his common-law wife and two sons.

His father, Ellis, had been happy that the cabins were going to become part of a new national park. The son was still coming to terms with the idea.

Ellis Vercher was one of Betty Hertzog's father's chief hands, and the family—there were twelve children—lived in the cabin at the end, the one with the porch still on the front. Ellis Vercher was always proud to say he was reared on a plantation, as if it gave more meaning to the five-bedroom house he built when the family moved away. And he tried to instill that feeling in his children.

"I don't mind being out here," Leslie Vercher said, "because I feel my daddy when I'm here."

Asked what he thought life was like for slaves, he frowned and said, "Hell, what you think?" But then he thought again about his father. There were indeed hard times, when they would work all season and not make a cent. But there were also good times—cookouts, horse races and dances at the company store—and good friends.

"I found a marble the other day and it felt funny in my hand," Vercher said. "I thought to myself, 'I bet my daddy played with this marble.'"

Bringing Up Slavery

A wintry chill hung over Cane River the November 1999 evening Carla Cowles brought slavery back to Magnolia Plantation.

For the opening of an exhibit called "Free at Last," Cowles had invited two black historical interpreters from Arkansas to perform skits showing slave life through fables and song. "We are going to be talking about things that are uncomfortable," she told the audience gathered at the cabins. "We are going to show you how people endured the institution called slavery."

Discomfort had been swirling through town ever since a notice appeared in the *Natchitoches Times* the week before. Cowles had enlisted her boss to deliver Betty Hertzog's invitation — "I have had very little contact with Miss Betty," she explained — and Hertzog seemed leery about the whole thing. "You can never tell," she said. "It might just be a bunch of stereotypes."

Leslie Vercher was also worrying about stereotypes. "It's easy for Carla to talk about slavery because she don't come from here," he said. "I don't think it would be so easy for her to tell those stories if she was talking about her own people."

Cowles had invited all fifteen schools in the area. But while teachers at three schools accepted, the rest did not respond.

She shrugged it off at first. With such short notice, there probably hadn't been time to arrange transportation. Then she heard that Samuel Jackson, a black man who is principal of Natchitoches Junior High, was worried the performance might ignite racial tensions. She went to see him, to explain that everything would be handled with great sensitivity. But he stood firm.

Jackson said he had worked hard to keep the peace at his school, where more than 70 percent of the students are black and almost all the whites are bused in by court order. Just a few weeks earlier, he said, a white student had shown up wearing a T-shirt with a drawing of Ku Klux Klansmen and the words, "We were the original Boys in the Hood." A black student had come to school upset that a local white fraternity was planning a mock slave auction. Exposing students to slave reenactments, Jackson said, would be like throwing a match into gasoline.

"I am afraid you would have white students making fun of the way black people talked, and then blacks might respond in a combative way," he said. "It could fester into a big problem."

In the end, about seventy people — black and white — showed up that evening. Leslie Vercher, anxieties and all, stood in back, pacing and puffing hard on a cigarette. Betty Hertzog came, too. If the story of slavery was going to be told, she said, she was going to make sure it was accurate.

The two performers, Curtis Tate and Daryl Minefee, leapt into the spotlight. They wore tattered pants, bright shirts and oversize shoes. Their stage was a bench. Tate stood on top, joking like a country bumpkin. Minefee, wearing that same foolish grin, sat playing an African drum.

First, Tate told several fables set in Africa. Then he transported the audience to America, and told a story about a slave beaten by an overseer for bringing her baby along to the cotton fields.

"The overseer was full of the master's whiskey," Tate growled, flailing one arm as if cracking a whip, "and when he saw that baby he started whippin' that girl, and whippin' that girl until she and the baby started to bleed."

But instead of returning to the fields, the woman ran to a wise elder who began chanting an African incantation, and all the slaves flew happily away.

For the finale, Tate portrayed a slave named Luther and his master, James McVicar. Luther had learned to read and write, but kept it secret for fear of punishment. The year was 1849, and one day he blurted out something from the morning paper about a gold rush in California.

A disturbed McVicar forced a Bible into Luther's hands and ordered him to read his favorite passage.

Luther trembled and said: "Naw suh, Massa McVicar. I can't read." McVicar insisted.

Luther opened the Bible and read in a quavering voice, "Moses said unto Pharaoh, 'Let my people go.' "

The audience held its breath as Luther slumped over in fear.

Then McVicar grinned and jumped with excitement. "I'll be darned, Luther, you can read! Can you write, too?"

Luther, paralyzed by confusion, forced his head to nod.

"This is great," his master shouted. "You can help me keep my books; you can help me with my ledgers."

For a moment, the audience seemed as stunned as Luther. But soon people were laughing and applauding in relief.

Betty Hertzog joined the standing ovation, then headed home, elated. "I liked it," she said. "I thought they did a real professional job. It was especially good for children."

Students and teachers from Simpson Junior High, a white group who had seen the show earlier that day, said they had learned important lessons about blacks.

"It makes us understand what they had to go through," said Jenna White, thirteen. "It opens our eyes and makes us respect them more."

Leslie Vercher, though, was pacing and dragging harder on his cigarette. With their silly grins and floppy hats, he said, the actors had given no dignity to the memory of slaves. It was as if the Good Darkey statue had come to life, not the strong, resilient people who were his ancestors. Slaves could not fly from the fields, he said, and if a master learned that a slave could read, he would reach for a rope.

"What kind of historians are they," he asked, "if they make up things instead of telling it like it was?"

When to Water Things Down

Carla Cowles was not stunned at all by the show. It went exactly as she had planned.

The week before, she had called Curtis Tate with a warning about the anxieties around Cane River. She told him that blacks had been feeling uncomfortable about slave reenactments, and that Principal Jackson was concerned. She also told him that the direct descendants of Magnolia's original family would be in the audience, along with some of the town's powerful preservationists. She went over the details of Tate's stories, and did not ask him to change the content in any way. But be sure, she cautioned him, that none of the stories appear to reflect the lives of Cane River slaves.

"There was a lot that went unsaid," Tate recalled. "But I got the clear impression that she was feeling pressure."

After the morning performance, over lunch at Lasyone's, a local meat-pie diner, they discussed the surprise ending to the Luther story. It did not, they acknowledged, reflect the reality of life for most slaves, who were beaten or separated from their families for seeking education.

But the story was not a complete lie. The truth is that there is no one truth to slavery. It was different from state to state, plantation to plantation. Tate had documents about a slave whose masters had taught him to read and write, and others about a slave beaten by whites when discovered reading a newspaper. In using that first slave as raw material for the Luther story, Tate said, he was concerned more with whites like Betty Hertzog than blacks like Leslie Vercher.

"They are the ones who can't handle the truth," Tate said, crouching over his plate and lowering his voice. "Isn't it the same for all black people, that we have to be careful to make white people comfortable?"

As they struggled to reconcile the Luther story with their strident commitment to teaching what they saw as the holocaust of slavery, it became clear that more pragmatic issues were at play, too. At historical sites across the country, a new generation of interpreters had begun to pull stories of slavery from the dust of history. And often, as Cowles and Tate kept hearing, they ran into turbulence.

"It all comes down to economics," Tate said. "Whites still control most museums and historical parks. Unless black people start putting more money into these places, then we will never really be able to have control."

Cowles added, "If you make them uncomfortable, they'll shut you down."

She had seen that kind of power right here in Natchitoches. Just weeks before, another Park Service official had come under attack from local preservationists. The official, John Robbins, headed up a prestigious federally financed center that develops and teaches preservation technologies. Robbins had supported a Congressional proposal that would have allowed the center to be moved. But after a few well-placed calls to Washington, the bill was killed, and Robbins was transferred to Washington.

"These people around here may come from the country," Cowles said, "but they are very smart and well connected, and if you cross them you're out of here."

A few days after the performance, Cowles stood in the doorway of a cabin and reflected on all that had happened. "I did not want to make the message too hard the first time," she said, "especially with me being an outsider and a black woman."

So she began to settle in for the long haul. Early in 2000, she turned down an assignment on the East Coast and began looking for land where she could build a house. It might take years, she realized, for the truth of slavery to be told on Cane River.

"If they felt good after that performance, they'll come to the next one and the next one," she said. "And I'll be able to present something a little bit stronger each time."

Bobby DeBlieux says he understands that slavery will be one of the park's main themes, and he thinks that, too, will ultimately be good for business. There is an untapped well of black tourists out there, he says, who might spend money on a plantation tour that incorporates slave history.

Over at the big house, Betty Hertzog sounds as if she is ready to move on. The twenty-seven-room house has become more showplace than home. Almost all her personal belongings are crammed into two bedrooms; the rest of the house stays dark unless tourists come by. Her relatives don't come too often, either, and so her most consistent companions are her two dozen cats.

Not long after the performance, she decided she was not going to worry about the new national park anymore. She asked Senator Johnston's daughter, Mary Catallo, to look out for the family's interests, and in April, Catallo met with Carla Cowles and offered herself as the family liaison.

Catallo, who is thirty-seven and is an executive of an engineering firm, is from the ninth generation of the family that built Magnolia, and her feelings about how its history should be portrayed seem to mark a clear shift from those of the woman she calls Aunt Betty.

"It is not a comfortable thing for me to come out and say that my relatives owned slaves," she said, "but it is important that we all openly acknowledge where we came from so we can start to work through the problems that were created in the past.

"Racism is a difficult thing to deal with because it runs so deep. To me this park offers a chance to at least help start a dialogue that doesn't exist right now."

Years ago, Betty Hertzog built herself a house near the river, thinking she would move there after her parents died. What with the responsibilities of holding on to Magnolia, she has yet to spend a night there.

"Every time I got ready to move, something else would happen and I needed to stay," she said. "But maybe the time has finally come. Used to be that it was hard to leave this old place. But now it's harder and harder to stay."

Slowly, more slave stories began to be told in Natchitoches. In October 2000, the local university decided, for the first time, to devote its next summer folk festival to African-American history. And black leaders in town received a $25,000 grant for an oral history project, an African-

American history of the Cane River region to be titled "The Elders' Utterances."

Carla Cowles continued to work at the new park and received a National Park Service grant for research on Cane River's black history. Betty Hertzog is still living in the big house, and in the fall of 2000 was preparing for another Christmas season of tours.

Ninth graders Aqeelah Mateen, Kelly Regan, and Johanna Perez-Fox (left to right), best friends in Maplewood, New Jersey. Suzanne DeChillo/The New York Times

9

Growing Up, Growing Apart

TAMAR LEWIN

MAPLEWOOD, NEW JERSEY

Back in eighth grade, Kelly Regan, Aqeelah Mateen and Johanna Perez-Fox spent New Year's Eve at Johanna's house, swing-dancing until they fell down laughing, banging pots and pans, watching the midnight fireworks beyond the trees in the park at the center of town.

They had been a tight threesome all through Maplewood Middle School — Kelly, a tall, coltish Irish-Catholic girl; Aqeelah, a small, earnest African-American Muslim girl; and Johanna, a light-coffee-colored girl who is half Jewish and half Puerto Rican and famous for knowing just about everyone.

It had been a great night, they agreed, a whole lot simpler than Johanna's birthday party three nights before. Johanna had invited all their friends, white and black. But the mixing did not go as she had wished.

"The black kids stayed down in the basement and danced, and the white kids went outside on the stoop and talked," Johanna said. "I went out and said, 'Why don't you guys come downstairs?' and they said they didn't want to, that they just wanted to talk out there. It was just split up, like two parties."

The same thing happened at Kelly's back-to-school party a few months earlier.

"It was so stressful," Kelly said. "There I was, the hostess, and I couldn't get everybody together."

"Oh, man, I was, like, trying to help her," Aqeelah said. "I went up and down and up and down. But it was boring outside, so finally I just gave up and went down and danced."

In the fall of 1999 the girls started high school, and what with the difficulty of mixing their black and white friends, none took on the challenge of a birthday party.

It happens everywhere, in the confusions of adolescence and the yearning for identity, when the most important thing in life is choosing a group and fitting in: Black children and white children come apart. They move into separate worlds. Friendships ebb and end.

It happens everywhere, but what is striking is that it happens even here. In a nation of increasingly segregated schools, the South Orange–Maplewood district is extraordinarily mixed. Not only is the student body about half black and half white, but in the last census, blacks had an economic edge. This is the kind of place where people — black and white — talk a lot about the virtues of diversity and worry about white flight, where hundreds will turn out to discuss the book *Why Are All the Black Kids Sitting Together in the Cafeteria?* People here care about race.

But even here, as if pulled by internal magnets, black and white children begin to separate at sixth grade. These are children who walked to school together, learned to read together, slept over at each other's houses. But despite all the personal history, all the community goodwill, race divides them as they grow up. As racial consciousness develops — and the practice of grouping students by perceived ability sends them on diverging academic paths — race becomes as much a fault line in their world as in the one their parents hoped to move beyond.

As they began high school, Kelly, Johanna and Aqeelah had so far managed to be exceptions. While the world around them had increasingly divided along racial lines, they had stuck together. But where their friendship would go was hard to say. And like a Greek chorus, the voices of other young people warned of tricky currents ahead.

Different but Inseparable

On her first day at Columbia High School, Kelly Regan took a seat in homeroom and introduced herself to the black boy at the next desk.

"I was trying to be friendly," she explained. "But he answered in like one word, and looked away. I think he just thought I was a normal white person, and that's all he saw."

She certainly looks like a normal white person, with her pale skin and straight brown hair. But in middle school, she trooped with Aqeelah and Johanna to Martin Luther King Association meetings; there were only a handful of white girls, but Kelly says she never felt out of place. "Some people say I'm ghetto," she said, shrugging. "I don't care."

She had always had a mixed group of friends, and since the middle of eighth grade had been dating a mixed-race classmate, Jared Watts. Even so, she expected that it would be harder to make black friends in the ninth grade. "It's not because of the person I am," she said, "it's just how it is."

Kelly's mother, Kathy Regan, is fascinated by her daughter's multi-racial world.

"It's so different from how I grew up," said Regan, a nurse who met Kelly's father, from whom she is divorced, at a virtually all-white Catholic school. "Sometimes, in front of the high school, I feel a little intimidated when I see all the black kids. But then so many of them know me, from my oldest daughter or now from Kelly, and they say such a nice, 'Hi, Mrs. Regan,' that the feeling goes away."

Johanna Perez-Fox is intensely sociable; her mane of long black curls can often be sighted at the center of a rushed gossip session in the last seconds before class. As she sees it, her mixed background gives her a choice of racial identity and access to everybody. "I like that I can go both ways," said Johanna, whose mother is a special-education teacher and whose father owns a car service.

Johanna has a certain otherness among her black friends. "If they say something about white people, they'll always say, 'Oh, sorry, Johanna,' " she said. "I think it's good. It makes them more aware of their stereotypes."

Still, she was put off when a new black friend asked what race she was.

"People are always asking, 'What are you?' and I don't really like it," she said. "I told him I'm half white and half Puerto Rican, and he said, 'But you act black.' I told him you can't act like a race. I hate that idea. He defended it, though. He said I would have a point if he'd said African-American, because that's a race, but black is a way of acting. I've thought about it, and I think he's right."

Aqeelah Mateen's parents are divorced, and she lives in a mostly black section of Maplewood with her mother, who works for AT&T. She also sees a lot of her father, a skycap at Newark Airport, and often goes with him to the Newark mosque where he is an imam.

Aqeelah is a girl of multiple enthusiasms, and in middle school her gutsy good cheer kept her close to black and white friends alike. But in high school, the issue of "acting black" was starting to become a persistent irritant.

After school one day, Aqeelah and two other black girls were running down the hall when one of them accidentally knocked a corkboard off the wall. Aqeelah told her to pick it up, but the girl kept going.

"What's the matter with you?" Aqeelah asked. "You knocked it over, you pick it up."

"Why do you have to be like a white person?" her friend retorted. "Just leave it there."

But Aqeelah picked it up.

"There's stuff like that all the time, and it gets on my nerves," she said later. "Like at track, in the locker room, there's people telling a Caucasian girl she has a big butt for a white person, and I'm like, 'Who cares, shut up.'"

On an Even Playground

Johanna and Aqeelah met in kindergarten and have been friends from Day 1; Kelly joined the group in fifth grade.

"Nobody cared about race when we were little," Johanna said. "No one thought about it."

On a winter afternoon at South Mountain Elementary School, that still seemed to be the case. There were white and black pockets, but mostly the playground was a picture postcard of racial harmony, white girls and black girls playing clapping games, black boys and white boys shooting space aliens. And when they were asked about race and friendships, there was no self-consciousness. They just said what they had to say.

"Making friends, it just depends on what you like to do, and who likes to do those things," said Carolyn Goldstein, a white third-grader.

"I've known Carolyn G. since kindergarten," said a black girl named Carolyn Morton. "She lives on my block. She's in my class. We even have the same name. We have so many things the same!"

As for how they might be different, Carolyn Goldstein groped for an answer: "Well, she has a mom at home and my mom works, and she has a sister, and I don't."

They know race matters in the world, they said, but not here.

"Some people in some places still feel prejudiced, so I guess it's still a kind of an issue, because Martin Luther King was trying to save the world from slaves and bad people and there still are bad people in jail," Carolyn Morton said, finishing up grandly. "I hope by the year 3000, the world will have peace, and the guys who watch the prisoners can finally go home and spend some time with their families."

A Shifting Sandbox

All through middle school, Johanna, Kelly and Aqeelah ate lunch together in a corner of the cafeteria where they could see everyone. The main axis of their friendship was changeable: In seventh grade, Johanna and Kelly were the closest. In eighth grade, as Kelly spent more time with Jared, Johanna and Aqeelah were the tightest.

But at the end of middle school, the three were nominated as class "best friends." And while they saw their classmates dividing along racial lines, they tried to ignore it. "In middle school, I didn't want to be aware of the separation," Kelly said. "I didn't see why it had to happen."

Most young people here seem to accept the racial split as inevitable. It's just how it is, they say. Or, it just happens. Or, it's just easier to be with your own kind.

When Sierre Monk, who is black, graduated from South Mountain, she had friends of all races. But since then, she has moved away from the whites and closer to the blacks. Now, in eighth grade, she referred to the shift, sometimes, as "my drift," as in, "After my drift, I began to notice more how the black kids talk differently from the white kids."

Sierre said her drift began after a sixth-grade argument.

"They said, 'You don't even act like you're black,' " she remembered. "I hadn't thought much about it until then, because I was too young. And I guess it was mean what they said, but it helped me. I found I wanted to behave differently after that."

Sierre had come from a mostly white private school in Brooklyn. She is the granddaughter of Thelonius Monk, the great jazz pianist, and more than most families, her parents—Thelonius, a drummer, and Gale, who manages her husband's career and father-in-law's estate—have an integrated social life.

For Gale Monk, it has come as something of a surprise to hear Sierre talk about her new distance from her white friends.

"What about the bat mitzvah this weekend?" Ms. Monk asked.

"Well, that's just because we used to be friends," Sierre said.

"What do you mean? She's in and out of this house all the time. I can't remember how many times she's slept over or been in my kitchen."

"That was last year, Mom. This year's different. Things have changed."

And Sierre's mother allows that some separation may be healthy.

"I don't have any problem with the black kids hanging together," she said. "I think you need to know your own group to feel proud of yourself."

There is a consensus that the split is mostly, though hardly exclusively, a matter of blacks' pulling away.

Marian Flaxman, a white girl in Sierre's homeroom, puts it this way: "You know, you come to a new school and you're all little and scared, and everybody's looking for a way to fit in, for people to like them. At that point, I think we were just white kids, blah, and they were just black kids, blah, and we were all just kids. And then a few black kids began thinking, 'Hey, we're *black* kids.' I think the black kids feel like they're black and the white kids feel like they're white because the black kids feel like they're black."

And Sierre does not really disagree: "Everybody gets along, but I think the white kids are more friendly toward black or interracial kids, and the black kids aren't as interested back, just because of stupid stereotypical stuff like music and style."

What they cannot quite articulate, though, is how much the divide owes to their growing awareness of the larger society, to negative messages about race and about things like violence and academic success. They may not connect the dots, but that sensitivity makes them intensely alert to slights from friends of another race, likely to pull away at even a hint of rejection.

Sometimes it is simply a misread cue, as when a black girl, sitting with other black girls, holds up a hand to greet a white friend, and the white girl thinks her greeting means, "I see you, but don't join us." Sometimes it is an obvious, if oblivious, offense: A black boy drops a white friend after discovering that the friend has told another white boy that the black family's food is weird.

And occasionally, the breach is startlingly painful: A white seventh-grader considers changing schools after her best friend tells her she can no longer afford white friends. Months later, the white girl talked uncomfortably about how unreachable her former friend seemed.

"I'm not going to go sit with her at the 'homey' table," she said, then flushed in intense embarrassment: "I'm not sure I'm supposed to say 'homey.' I'm not sure that's what they call themselves; maybe it sounds racist."

And indeed, the black girl believed that some of the things her former friend had said did fall between insensitive and racist.

For their part, both mothers, in identical tones, expressed anger and hurt about how badly their daughters had been treated. Each, again in identical tones, said her daughter had been blameless. But the mothers had never been friends, and like their daughters, never talked about what happened, never heard the other side.

Marian Flaxman went to a mostly black preschool, and several black friends from those days remain classmates. But, she said, it has been years since she visited a black friend's home.

"Sometimes I feel like I'm the only one who remembers that we used to be friends," she said. "Now we don't say hello in the halls, and the most we'd say in class is something like, 'Can I borrow your eraser?' "

Asked if she knew of any close and lasting cross-race friendships, she was stumped, paging through her yearbook and offering up a few tight friendships between white and mixed-race classmates.

Diane Hughes, a New York University psychology professor who lives in South Orange, has studied the changing friendships of children here. In the first year of middle school, she found, black children were only half as likely as they had been two years before to name a white child as a best friend. Whites had fewer black friends to start with, but their friendships changed less. But blacks and whites, on reaching middle school, were only half as likely as third graders to say they had invited a friend of a different race home recently.

By the end of middle school, the separation is profound.

At 10 P.M. on a Friday in October 1999, 153 revved-up thirteen-year-olds squealed and hugged their way into the South Orange Middle School cafeteria for the Eighth Grade Sleepover. At eleven they were grouped by birthday month, each group to write what they loved about school.

They loved Skittles at lunch . . . the Eighth Grade Sleepover . . . Ms. Wright, the health teacher / basketball coach / Martin Luther King Club adviser. And at the March table, a white boy wrote "interracial friendships."

But the moment the organized activities ended, the black and white eighth-graders separated. And at 2 A.M., when the girls' sleeping bags covered the library floor and the boys' the gym, they formed a map of racial boundaries. The borders were peaceful, but there was little commerce across territorial lines. After lights-out, some black girls stood and started a clapping chant.

"I can't," one girl called.

"Why not?" the group called back.

"I can't."

"Why not?"

"My back's hurting and my bra's too tight."

It grew louder as other black girls threaded their way through the darkness to join in.

"I can't."

"Why not?"

"I shake my booty from left to right."

Marian, in her green parrot slippers, was in a group of white girls up front, enjoying, listening, but quiet.

"It's cool, when they start stuff like that, or in the lunchroom when they start rumbling on the table and we all pick it up," she said. "It's just louder. One time in class this year, someone was acting up, and when the teacher said sit down, the boy said, 'It's because I'm black, isn't it?' I thought, no, it's not because you're black; that's stupid. It's because you're being really noisy and obnoxious. And it made me feel really white. And then I began thinking, well, maybe it is because he's black, because being noisy may be part of that culture, and then I didn't know what to think."

Jostling for Position

Aqeelah, Kelly and Johanna refuse to characterize behavior as black or white; they just hate it, they insist, when anyone categorizes them in racial terms.

"I think what makes Kelly and Johanna and me different is that we're what people don't expect," Aqeelah said. "I'm the only Muslim most people know, and one of two African-Americans on my softball team. There's Kelly, a white girl playing basketball, and Johanna, when people ask if she's white or Puerto Rican, saying, 'Both.' "

Most students are acutely aware of the signposts of Columbia High's coexisting cultures. The popular wisdom has it that the black kids dominate football and basketball, the white kids soccer, softball and lacrosse. Black kids throw big dancing parties in rented spaces; white parties are more often in people's homes, with a lot of drinking. Everyone wears jeans, but the white kids are more preppy, the black kids more hip-hop. Black kids listen to Hot 97, a hip-hop station, or WBLS, which plays rhythm and blues; white kids favor rock stations like Z100 or K-Rock.

"I know a lot of Caucasians listen to Hot 97, too," Aqeelah said, "but even if I had a list of two hundred Caucasians who listen to it, everyone still thinks it's an African-American thing."

Even though the two cultures are in constant, casual contact—and a few students cross back and forth easily—in the end, they are quite separate.

Jason Coleman, a black 1999 graduate who attends Howard University, remembers how the cultures diverged, separating him from the white boy with whom he once walked to school.

"The summer before high school, we just went different ways," he said. "We listened to different music, we played different sports, we got interested in different girls. And we didn't have much to say to each other anymore. That's the time you begin to develop your own style, and mine was a different style than his."

Jason's style included heavy gold chains, a diamond ear stud, baggy pants and hair in short twists. Asked to define that style, he hesitated, then said, "I guess what bothers me least is if you say that I follow hip-hop fashion."

At the start of high school, much of Jason's energy went toward straddling the divide between hip-hop kid and honors student. He was in frequent physical fights, though never with white students; that doesn't seem to happen. Although blacks are now a slight majority at the school, he, like many of the black students, felt an underlying jostling about who really owns the school. And he felt dismissed, intellectually and socially, by some teachers and classmates.

"African-Americans may be the majority, but I don't think they feel like the majority because they don't feel they get treated fairly," he said. "You see who gets suspended, and it's the African-American kids. I had one friend suspended for eating a bagel in homeroom because his teacher said he had an attitude. That just wouldn't happen to a Caucasian boy. It doesn't have to be a big thing to make you feel like it's not really your school. We can all hold hands and talk about how united we are, but if the next day you run into a girl from your classes at the mall with her mother and she doesn't say hello, what's that?"

To avoid these issues, Jason chose a predominantly black college, Howard, and he seemed relaxed there during his freshman year. The gold chains and diamond were gone, and he was studying hard to go to medical school, as his father and brother had.

White students at Columbia High have their own issues. Many feel intimidated by the awareness that they are becoming a minority at the school, that they tend not to share academic classes, or culturally much else, with a lot of the black students. It is striking that while there are usually a few black or multiracial children in the school's white groups, whites rarely enter the black groups. Many white students are reluctant to be quoted about the racial climate, lest they seem racist. But some recent graduates are more forthcoming.

"A lot of the black kids, it was like they had a really big chip on their shoulder, and they were mad at the world and mad at whites for running the world," said Jenn Caviness, a white graduate who attends Columbia University. "One time, in tenth grade, in the hall, this black kid shoved me and said, 'Get out of the way, white crack bitch.' I moved, because he was big, but I was thinking how if I said something racial back, I would have been attacked. It was very polarized sometimes."

She and others, however, say the cultural jockeying has an upside — a freedom from the rigid social hierarchy that plagues many affluent suburban high schools.

"If you're different here, it doesn't matter, because there's so many kinds of differences already," Johanna explained when asked to identify the cool kids, the in crowd. "There's no one best way to be."

In Johanna's commercial art class one day, there was a table of black boys, a table of white girls and a mixed table, where two black girls were humming as they worked. A white girl asked what the song was.

They told her, and she said, "It's really wack."

Yeah, one answered, "You don't know music like we know music."

"Yeah, and you don't know music like I know music."

"I know," the black girl said, smiling. "It's like two completely different tastes."

Acting Black, Acting White

Aqeelah, Kelly and Johanna did not have many classes together this year, but they had grown up in a shared academic world. While they are not superstars, they do their work and are mostly in honors classes. But if that common ground has so far helped keep them together, the system of academic tracking more often helps pull black and white children apart.

Whenever people talk about race and school, the elephant in the room — rarely mentioned, impossible to ignore — is the racial imbalance that appears when so-called ability grouping begins. Almost all American school districts begin tracking sometime before high school. And when they do, white students are far more likely than blacks to be placed in higher-level classes, based on test scores and teacher recommendations.

Nationwide, by any measure of academic performance, be it grades, tests or graduation rates, whites on average do better than blacks. To some extent, it is a matter of differences in parents' income and education. But the gap remains even when such things are factored out, even in places like this. Experts have no simple explanation, citing a tangle of parents' attitudes, low expectations of mostly white teaching staffs and some white classmates, and negative pressure from black students who believe that doing well isn't cool, that smart is white and street is black.

It can be a vicious circle — and a powerful influence on friendships.

Inevitably, as students notice that honors classes are mostly white and lower-level ones mostly black, they develop a corrosive sense that behaving like honors students is "acting white," while "acting black" demands they emulate lower-level students. Little wonder that sixth grade, when ability grouping starts here, is also when many interracial friendships begin to come apart.

"It sometimes bothers me to see how many of my African-American friends aren't in the higher-level classes, and how they try to be cool around their friends by acting up and trying to be silly and getting in fights," said Sierre, who this year moved up to honors in everything but math. "A lot of them just aren't trying. They're my friends, but I look at them and think, 'Why can't you just be cool and do your work?'"

The district does not release racial breakdowns of its classes. But at

Columbia High, which is 45 percent white, ninth-grade honors classes usually seem to be about two-thirds white, middle-level classes more than two-thirds black, and the lowest level — "basic skills" — almost entirely black. The imbalance is at least as great at Marian and Sierre's middle school.

Honors is where students mix most.

"You really see the difference when you're not in honors," said Kelly, who was in middle-level English this year. "In middle level, there aren't so many white kids, and whenever you break into groups, people stick with their own race."

The contrasts are stark. In Aqeelah's mostly white honors history class, the students argued passionately about the nature of man as they compared Hobbes, Locke, Voltaire and Rousseau. But the next period, when the all-black basic-skills class arrived, the students headed to the library to learn how to look up facts for a report on a foreign country.

"I'm still taken aback, shocked, each time I walk into a class and see the complexion," said LuElla Peniston, a black guidance counselor at the school. "It should be more balanced."

The issue has become especially delicate as the district has become progressively blacker, as more students have moved in from poorer neighboring towns with troubled schools, and as the ranking on state tests has slipped. Five years ago, a quarter of the district's children were black; now, with blacks a slight majority, many people worry that the district could tip too far. (Of course, black and white parents tend to have different ideas about how far is too far.)

The schools are still impressive. Columbia High always sends dozens of graduates, black and white, to top colleges. It produced Carla Peterman, a black Rhodes scholar, and Lauryn Hill, the hip-hop star, who still lives in town. This year Columbia had more National Achievement Scholarship semifinalists — an honor for top-scoring black seniors in the National Merit Scholarship Program — than any school in the state. And the previous year it had an 88 percent passing rate on the state high school proficiency test, three points above average.

Still, in a society that often associates racial minorities with stereotypes of poverty, the district has an image problem. Many parents — whites, but also some blacks — talk nervously about "those kids with the boom boxes out in front of school," and wonder if they should start checking out private schools or another district.

The district's administrators have been grappling with questions of racial balance and ability grouping for years. In middle school, for example, students can temporarily move up a level, to try more challenging work. But the program is used mostly by white families—to push a child or remove him or her from a mostly black classroom—so it has only increased the skew.

Many white parents, Peniston says, are adamant about not letting their children be anywhere below honors. "They either push very hard to get their children into the level where they want them, or they leave," she said.

It is not an issue only for whites. Many black parents worry that the schools somehow associate darker-skinned children with lower-level classes.

When Kelly's boyfriend, Jared Watts, transferred from South Orange Middle School to Maplewood Middle, he was placed in lower-level classes, something his parents discovered only on parents' night.

"There were all these African-American families, asking all these basic questions," said Jared's mother, Debby Watts. "I looked around and realized they'd put him in the wrong group. I was so upset I made my husband do the calling the next day. They moved him up right away. But you can't help but wonder if it would have happened if he'd been white."

Sierre Monk's parents are watching her grades, and thinking that unless she is put in honors classes in high school next year, they will move her to private school.

Sierre says she is comfortable with her white honors classmates, even if her best friends now are black.

"I feel friendly to a lot of the white kids, and still e-mail some of them," she said. As she sees it, she can be a good student without compromising her African-American credentials. Not everyone, she observes, has been so culturally dextrous.

"A lot of people think of the black kids in the top classes, the ones who don't hang out with a lot of African-Americans, as the 'white' black kids," she said. "I'd never say it to them, but in my head I call them the white black kids, too."

Still, she said, she was happiest in her middle-level math class, where every student but one was black.

"It's my favorite, because I can do well there without struggling," she said. "And I feel closest to that class, because I have so many friends there. Once I was waiting outside, alone, when I heard a group of white kids talking about, 'Oh, those kids in Level Three, they must be stupid.' I don't want to associate with people who think like that."

Fissures, Chasms, Islands

It was hard for Aqeelah, Kelly and Johanna to get together this year. They had different lunch periods, different study halls. Only Johanna and Kelly had any classes together. Johanna was on the varsity swim team, Kelly was on the ninth-grade basketball team and Aqeelah ran indoor track. The three could go weeks without getting together.

But they were still close. In the fall, when Johanna had big news to share about a boy she liked, she was on two phone lines simultaneously, telling Kelly and Aqeelah the latest.

When they finally met for dinner at Arturo's Pizza in November, their pleasure in being together was visible.

Aqeelah was a little late, so Kelly chose an orange soda for her. When she arrived, they were their usual frisky selves, waving to everyone who walked by and talking about the old friends they didn't see anymore and the new people they felt friendly with but would not yet ask to the movies.

They were still in giggle mode when Aqeelah said, "I get made fun of by everybody," and Johanna broke in, "Why, because you're short?" and they collapsed into laughter.

But a second later, Aqeelah was not laughing. She had her head down and her eyes covered, and when she looked up, a tear was leaking down her cheek.

"No, it's really confusing this year," she said. "I'm too white to be black, and I'm too black to be white. If I'm talking to a white boy, a black kid walks by and says, 'Oh, there's Aqeelah, she likes white boys.' And in class, these Caucasian boys I've been friends with for years say hi, and then the next thing they say is, 'Yo, Aqeelah, what up?' as if I won't understand them unless they use that kind of slang. Or they'll tell me they really like 'Back That Thing Up' by Juvenile. I don't care if they like a rapper, but it seems like they think that's the only connection they have with me.

"Last year this stuff didn't bother me, but now it does bother me, because some of the African-American kids, joking around, say I'm an Oreo."

Johanna and Kelly were surprised by her pain; they had not heard this before. But they did sense her increasing distance from them.

"It's like she got lost or something," Kelly said. "I never see her."

Aqeelah had always been the strongest student of the three, the only one in a special math class, one rung above honors. But by winter, she was getting disappointing grades, especially in history, and beginning to worry about being moved down a level. Math was not going so well either, and so she dropped track to focus on homework. She was hoping to make the softball team, and disappointed that neither of her friends was trying out. "I'll never see you," she complained.

All three, of course, have always had other friends, and they still did.

Much of Kelly's social life was with her racially mixed lunch group. She felt herself moving further from some of her white friends, the ones who hang out only with whites. "It seems like they have their whole clique," she said, and she was not terribly interested in them. Against the grain, she was still working to make friends with blacks, particularly with a basketball teammate.

Johanna found herself hanging out more with blacks, much as her older sister had—though not her brother, a college freshman whose high school friends were mostly white.

"In middle school, there were black and white tables in the cafeteria and everything, but people talked together in the hallways," Johanna said. "Now there's so many people, you don't even say hi to everybody, and sometimes it seems like the black and white people live in such different worlds that they wouldn't know how to have fun together anymore."

The three girls celebrated separately this New Year's Eve—Kelly with Jared, Johanna at a party with her family, Aqeelah at her father's mosque for Ramadan.

Kelly still tried to bring them together. One Friday night, she called Johanna and Aqeelah on the spur of the moment, and they came over in their pajamas. And at Kelly's last basketball game that year, Johanna and Aqeelah sat and joked with Jared, Kelly's mother, her grandmother and little brother.

The next day Kelly and Jared broke up. Kelly said she was sad and working hard to keep up her friendship with Jared, but that's about all she was saying.

And as spring arrived, Kelly, Johanna and Aqeelah acknowledged that, at least for the time, their threesome had pretty much become a twosome.

Johanna and Kelly were still very tight, and did something together almost every weekend. But these days Aqeelah talked most to a black girl, a longtime family friend. It was partly logistics: Aqeelah would run into her daily at sixth period and after school, at her locker.

"I don't know why I don't call Johanna or Kelly," she said. "They'll always have the place in my heart, but not so much physically in my life these days. It seems like I have no real friends this year. You know how you can have a lot of friends, but you have no one? Everyone seems to be settled in their cliques and I'm just searching. And the more I get to know some people, the more I want to withdraw. I'm spending a lot more time with my family this year."

It's not that Aqeelah was falling apart. She was still her solid self, with all her enthusiasms—for *Dawson's Creek*, movies, and the Friday noon service at the mosque. But increasingly, the gibes about being too white were getting to her. One day, walking to class with a black boy who is an old friend, she blew up when he told her she had "white people's hair."

"I just began screaming, 'What's wrong with these people in this school?' and everyone stared at me like I was crazy," she said. "Everyone, every single person, gets on my nerves."

Lessons and Legacies

The story of Aqeelah, Kelly and Johanna is still unfolding. But those who have gone before know something about where they may be headed.

Aqeelah's struggle is deeply familiar to Malika Oglesby, who arrived from a mostly white school in Virginia in fifth grade and quickly found white friends. Several black boys began to follow her around, taunting her. Lowering her eyes, she recited the chant that plagued her middle-school years: "Cotton candy, sweet as gold, Malika is an Oreo."

"I don't think I knew what it meant the first time, but I figured it out pretty fast," she said.

Jenn Caviness, one of her white friends from that time, clearly remembers Malika's pain.

"Malika was in tears every other day, they just tormented her," she said. "We all felt very protective, but we didn't know how to stop it." Malika felt powerless, too.

"I didn't tell my parents about it, I didn't tell my sister, but it was a hard time," she said. "If you'd asked me about it at the time, I would have said that there was absolutely no issue at all about my having chosen all those white friends. But that's not true. By the end of seventh grade, I was starting to be uncomfortable. Everybody was having little crushes on everybody among my friends, but of course nobody was having a crush on me. I began to feel like I was falling behind, I was just the standby."

The summer before high school, she eased into a black social group.

"I found a black boyfriend, and I kind of lost contact with everyone else," said Malika, who now attends Howard.

And yet, when Malika finished talking about her Oreo problem, when Jason recalled his fighting days, when others finished describing difficult racial experiences, a strange thing happened. They looked up, unprompted, and said how much they loved the racial mix here and the window it opened onto a different culture.

"Columbia High School was so important and useful to me," said Jenn, immediately after recounting how she had been pushed in the hall by a black boy. "It shaped a lot of parts of my personality."

She and the others remembered a newfound ease as high school was ending, when the racial divide began to fade.

"Senior year was wonderful, when the black kids and the white kids got to be friends again, and the graduation parties where everyone mixed," said Malika. "It was so much better."

Many parents say that is a common pattern.

"It is an ebb and flow," said Carol Barry-Austin, the biracial mother of three African-American children. "Middle-school kids need time to separate and feel comfortable in their racial identity, and then they can come back together. I remember when I wanted to give my oldest daughter a sweet-sixteen party, she said no, because she couldn't mix her black and white friends. But by the time she got to a graduation party, she could."

This year, among the seniors, there was a striking friendship between Jordan BarAm, the white student council president, and Ari Onugha, the black homecoming king.

They met in ninth grade when Jordan was running for class

president and knew he needed the black vote. Ari, he had heard, was the coolest kid in school, and he went to him in such a low-key and humorous way that Ari was happy to help out. From that unlikely start, a genuine friendship began when both were in Advanced Placement physics the next year.

Their senior year they had several Advanced Placement classes together, and they talked on the phone most nights, Jordan said, "about everything" — homework, girls, college. Ari was admitted to the University of Pennsylvania's Wharton School and Jordan to Harvard.

"No one looking at me would ever think I'm in Advanced Placement," said Ari, who wears baggy Gibaud pants, a pyramid ring and a big metal watch. "Most of the black kids in the honors classes identify with white culture. I'm more comfortable in black culture, with kids who dress like me and talk like me and listen to the same music I do."

Ari and Jordan have a real friendship, but one with limits. On weekends, Ari mostly hangs out with black friends from lower-level classes, Jordan with a mostly white group of top students. When Ari and his friends performed a wildly successful hip-hop dance routine at the Martin Luther King Association fashion show, Jordan, like most white students, did not go. And when Jordan and his friends put together a fund-raising dance for a classmate with multiple sclerosis, Ari did not show up.

"We've tried to get him to white parties, everyone wants him there, but he either doesn't come or doesn't stay long," Jordan said.

Jordan thinks a lot about race and has been active in school groups to promote better racial understanding — something he has tried unsuccessfully to draw Ari into.

And while Ari often visits Jordan's home, Jordan has only rarely, and briefly, been to Ari's.

Ari laughed. "Hey, dude, you could come."

As they began tenth grade in the fall of 2000, Aqeelah, Johanna and Kelly plunged into activities at Columbia High School. Johanna and Aqeelah became co-captains of the junior varsity volleyball team. Kelly was hoping to make the basketball team again.

Aqeelah began wearing the traditional Muslim headscarf to school each day. Of the three, she was still the one having the hardest time making her way in high school. "It's all getting worse," she said.

Over the summer, Kelly went to Puerto Rico with Johanna's family for two weeks. But back at school, the three girls moved further into separate circles of friends. Even so, said Kelly, on the rare occasions when they did get together as a threesome, "It's like, wow, we're together again, all three."

Reporter Carl Chancellor (left) and columnist Bob Dyer (right), who both worked on the Akron Beacon Journal's *Pulitzer Prize–winning report on race relations, in the paper's newsroom.* Stephen Crowley/The New York Times

10

The Hurt Between the Lines

DANA CANEDY

AKRON, OHIO

Swept up in the rush of New York City, Carl Chancellor and Bob Dyer looked like any other tourists that bright May weekend in 1994. There they were, snapping pictures at the Statue of Liberty, savoring Jamaican food at a trendy restaurant, clinking beer bottles and wineglasses in heady toasts back at their hotel.

But more than simply tourists, they were colleagues out on the town celebrating. In the long months that had led them to New York, Chancellor and Dyer were part of a team of reporters for the *Akron Beacon Journal* that had explored the racial attitudes of this city of 215,000 people. Their series earned the paper journalism's big award, the Pulitzer Prize. The two had gone to New York to bring the medal home.

Back in Akron, there were champagne showers and congratulatory speeches for a staff that had united behind the series and gloried in having been a healing force in the city, organizing and promoting projects to bring the races together. The *Beacon Journal* also tried to lead by example. Shortly after the series ended, the paper introduced a lineup of columnists reflecting "the perfect demographic," as Dyer put it. They included a black woman and a white woman as well as Chancellor, who is black, and Dyer, who is white.

The *Beacon Journal*, it seemed, had become a proud model of racial enlightenment, and the men were at the top of their careers. Which made it all the more startling when the jubilation began to fade.

The two columnists came to be viewed almost as counterpoints on race, starting with some explosive columns that divided many of their colleagues and angered readers. In an especially polarizing episode in 1999, the columnists fell out over a single word — *niggardly*.

Carl Chancellor, who is forty-seven, had been sipping coffee in his living room and channel-surfing through the morning news programs when a voice stopped him cold. Someone was defending a white District of Columbia official who had come under fire for using the word *niggardly* in a budget meeting with a black colleague. Chancellor said he felt his temperature rising when the white face looking back at him through the television screen suggested that any black person who took offense at the word obviously did not know what it meant. When he reached the newsroom that morning, Chancellor was still angry. So he pounded out a column telling readers that he understood why the debate over *niggardly* was generating national attention.

Years earlier, a *Beacon Journal* colleague had said at a union meeting that management was being niggardly with raises. Chancellor recalled thinking then that white people toss the word around too freely, knowing it means stingy but also that it reminds blacks of a far more hurtful word.

"In both cases, the incident in D.C. and my personal experience, the use of the word *niggardly* was calculated," he wrote. "It was a sophomoric, smart-alecky and cowardly way to deliver an insult through the back door."

Not a bad topic for readers to chew on, Chancellor thought. One of them was Bob Dyer, and he could not swallow what his friend was dishing out.

"I think the reaction I had to this column was, like, 'What? You've got to be kidding,' and it was very widespread among people of my color," said Dyer, forty-eight. "So part of me said, 'Let's get equal time here.' "

He did, in a rebuttal in the paper's Sunday magazine. "To defend the firing of a man who used a word that somebody misunderstood is to defend ignorance," Dyer wrote, noting that *niggardly* had an origin different from that of the word it was being compared with. "Today, apparently, if you say 'two plus two equals four' and somebody among the oppressed masses sincerely believes the answer is five, the person who said 'four' is wrong."

Dyer hit the send key on his computer and called Chancellor to let him know what was coming. He considered Chancellor a friend, after all.

As office acquaintances go, the men had gotten to know each other fairly well over the fifteen years they had worked together. Before there were lawns to tend and children to raise, they would meet after work on the basketball court, maybe share a beer.

"When we were covering baseball games and stuff, and just during lulls, we might talk about our families and our dreams and aspirations," Chancellor recalled. But he will not go so far as to say that he and Dyer were ever friends. "I guess we tried to stay away from some of the harder subjects or the more politically controversial subjects," he said.

But that unspoken agreement was fractured by the "niggardly" debate; at the height of it the men were barely speaking. And the rift extended beyond them.

"I guess the buzz was all around the newsroom that he was writing it," Chancellor said of Dyer, "and people would come by patting him on the back, massaging him, kind of reading over his shoulder and cheering him on.

"The black folks in the newsroom were upset, and so they called me at home and told me: 'Oh, you should see what is going on here. Everybody is cheering Bob Dyer on.'"

Carl Chancellor was not about to let Bob Dyer dismiss his view in print. So before Dyer's response was published, Chancellor read it, and in an unusual decision, his editors let him write a rebuttal to the rebuttal that went to press the same day.

"Well, I have been taken to the woodshed not only by my readers, who have called and written by the score, but also by some of my colleagues," Chancellor wrote in the later column.

"If I say that I'm offended by the word *niggardly* being used in my presence, my objection may make no sense to you, but I have a right to those feelings," he wrote.

"If, for example, you are standing on my toes, it is completely up to me to determine if my foot is hurting and to what extent."

The *Beacon Journal's* editor, Janet C. Leach, who is white, now says it was a mistake to let the columnists slug it out in print. "I don't recall getting involved with this until Carl wrote his rebuttal, and then I was like, 'Oh, why are we even bothering our readers with this?'"

Even so, she stands by her decision to let Chancellor throw the last punch. "Bob was attacking Carl's opinion," Leach said, "so Carl was allowed to defend his opinion. Although no more of this."

The columnists have since called a truce. "We were both hot at each other a little bit," Chancellor said, "but then it blew over."

Still, the men occasionally wonder whether confronting racially sensitive issues has hurt their careers. And many among the 157 people on the news staff—15 percent of whom are black and 4 percent other minorities—say that although the city's racial climate may have improved because of the series, seven years later the newspaper itself has shown less progress.

A few reporters who worked on the series still socialize, and some editors say it made them more attuned to potentially offensive articles, photographs and headlines.

"I was made more aware of some of the stresses and strains that affect black people and how what I might do or say could impact that," said David Hertz, a white editor.

Still, some of the staff seems resigned to the notion that though blacks and whites may act polite toward one another, they are still divided by mistrust and misunderstanding. Bonnie Bolden, the metro editor, who is white, summed up the sentiment: "I will never again say things are fine."

This is a place that just a few years ago was overcome with race religion. Troubled by the state of race relations, the *Beacon Journal* had gone further than most newspapers to investigate the gap between blacks and whites and to understand why it had not closed. It found mistrust and misperceptions, frustrations and tensions; it even looked inward, discovering much the same in its own newsroom. It had found, it seemed, a way to talk about race. And yet even here, in a place where men and women make a living seeking answers to questions and using words well, communication can break down. And race still seeps back in.

A Race Report Card

Walk into the third-floor newsroom and it is obvious that the race project, "A Question of Color," remains a source of great pride to the *Beacon Journal*, a scrappy member of the Knight Ridder chain with a daily circulation of 140,000. Against a wall the Pulitzer medal, for public service—the fourth Pulitzer in the paper's 162-year history—shines under a spotlight in a Plexiglas case surrounded by reproductions of the articles in the series.

For Carl Chancellor and Bob Dyer, the work reflected in that display is a reminder of more than the career-enhancing accolades and the New York weekend. They remember the months they sat behind a two-way mirror and listened to panels of citizens talk about race. White women admitted that they still crossed the street to avoid black men. Black fathers said they still did not want their daughters marrying white boys. When blacks and whites were thrown together, they mostly smiled politely and talked about the need to get along.

Chancellor and Dyer shaped those conversations into front-page articles that introduced the race series in February 1993 with what the paper described as "a separate, but equal, focus on our differences." Dyer's article appeared under the word *whites* in bold letters and Chancellor's under the word *blacks*.

When it comes to race, the *Beacon Journal* told readers: "Whites are tired of hearing about it. Blacks wish it would go away. All seem powerless to move it." But what was behind the divide, the paper was asking, and why did it persist?

Long before the newspaper sought the answers, those questions had nagged at David Hertz. It was 1992, and there was unrest in Los Angeles after the acquittal of four white police officers in the roadside beating of Rodney King, a black motorist. What troubled Hertz was that though many people had been disturbed by the incident, blacks had reacted more angrily than whites, and not just in Los Angeles but 2,000 miles away, in Akron.

So with his bosses' approval, Hertz, then an editor on the night metro desk, gathered a group of colleagues, Carl Chancellor among them, to discuss how race factored into their work and private lives. Hertz told how in middle school black children had pushed him around just for being white. A black reporter was in tears recalling the pain of realizing as a young girl that her skin color made her different from a beloved white playmate.

But where to go from there? Hertz, now the business editor, said it occurred to him that "we needed to do more than a reaction piece" to the unrest in Los Angeles.

His bosses agreed and conceived the race project, committing more than two dozen reporters, photographers, graphic artists and editors to a yearlong series of articles, thirty in all. The goal was to hold race up to the light and look at it from every angle — personal relations, housing, education, economics and crime among them. But as the work proceeded, and a troubling picture of race relations emerged, the editors decided on a more activist role for the paper.

It helped create multiracial partnerships among local community groups to foster unity and understanding. It also called on individuals to get involved. And they did:

More than 20,000 readers accepted a New Year's resolution challenge made by the paper to commit to racial healing and allowed their names to be published.

Hundreds joined in the first of what has become a yearly "Race/ Walk for Unity."

Through "town meetings" on race, organized by the paper, hundreds of others stepped out of the safety of their familiar circles and spoke up. Some who had never shared so much as a cup of tea or a beer with a person of another race even formed interracial friendships.

Churches began holding integrated services, which continue today. At one recent gathering, black congregants from one church and whites from another washed each other's feet in a ceremony that drew from the Last Supper.

And the newspaper started the "Coming Together Project," now a nonprofit agency that coordinates racial-unity programs in and around Akron, a recovering Rust Belt town that is 25 percent black. In June 2000, the Knight Foundation, which offers grants to educational and cultural programs and which is not affiliated with the newspaper chain, gave the project $350,000. The newspaper itself has given $300,000 to the project over the years.

The *Beacon Journal*'s effort to engage the city and its suburbs in a discussion of race was applauded by the Pulitzer judges at Columbia University. And so encouraging was the social progress attributed to the project that the White House selected Akron as the setting for President Clinton's first "town hall meeting" on race, in 1997.

But not only did the newspaper look at race in its own backyard; it also examined itself. For the final article, Bob Dyer wrote about race relations among his co-workers and their perceptions of how race affected the crime coverage. The article revealed that the journalists who had written Akron's racial report card were as confused and divided by race as the people whose words and images they had filtered into print.

"I think we all get along, but there are racists in the newsroom," a white journalist was quoted as saying. "I'm talking about people at parties who have a little too much to drink and suddenly start talking about 'niggers.' "

For Dyer, reporting on his colleagues made the race story almost personal. "I always thought, even well before that series, that people in the newsroom considered themselves enlightened, which was sort of debunked when we did the focus group," he said recently. "You know, we were like any other part of society. We didn't have a clue."

A Typical Newsroom

It was a slow February afternoon in the newsroom, and boredom had set in. Suddenly a rubber band whizzed by Reginald Fields, a black reporter. Laughter broke out behind a computer screen a few desks away. Moments later, a white editor, Mitch McKenney, joined in, firing off another rubber band. It was all in fun, a spontaneous show of camaraderie.

The previous year, when Melanie Payne, a black reporter, was stricken with a rare heart condition, a steady stream of colleagues, black and white, went to her bedside.

And in the fall of 1999, when the newspaper's art director, Terence Oliver, who is black, returned from a church missionary trip to Africa and told the editor, Janet Leach, how deeply the experience had moved him, she had him write about it for the cover of the local news section.

On any given day, the *Beacon Journal* newsroom hardly seems like a place where race would be an issue. Even when there is conflict, Chancellor said, "the real divisions in the newsroom aren't always race-based." Indeed, reporters and editors say that a recent wave of staff reassignments, budget cuts and defections to the rival *Plain Dealer*, in Cleveland, have done more to hurt morale than any racial tension.

"As a small newsroom, I think a lot of it is petty jealousy, just individual personality conflicts," Chancellor said. "And I guess it's the daily stress of working on deadline and people blowing up at each other because it's just the nature of the business."

Months can pass without Carl Chancellor's or Bob Dyer's writing about race. The subject is not often on the table when editors decide what to put on the front page. Nor is it a daily topic when co-workers meet over vending-machine coffee in the cafeteria.

In one respect, the *Beacon Journal* is even in the forefront of racial progress. It has a black publisher, John L. Dotson Jr., who, as part of a pioneering generation of black journalists, covered the Detroit race riots in the 1960s and worked for the *Philadelphia Inquirer* and *Newsweek*. Editors there, like those in most newsrooms, struggle earnestly with questions of racial sensitivity. They debated, for instance, whether they would publish a photograph of a black man washing a white man's feet during the church service, fearing it would be suggestive of black servitude. (The editors decided not to use such a picture and instead published one of a white man washing a black man's feet.)

Yet even in this environment, race still slips back into the room. It is there when reporters and editors, keeping score, immediately notice the color of a new employee's skin. It is there when a midlevel black editor perceives her demotion as racially motivated. It is there when a white reporter wonders whether political correctness instead of news judgment elevated one obituary, that of a local black civil rights leader, to the front page and relegated another, that of an internationally known white plastics-and-rubber industry inventor, to the cover of the local news section.

And it was there one day when the editor, Janet Leach, picked up an anonymous memo that had landed on her desk. "It made me sick," she said. The note criticized her hiring of a black journalist, calling the person incompetent, an affirmative-action mistake.

Color-coded scorecards and friendly rubber-band wars. Ask almost anyone on the *Beacon Journal* staff about the seemingly contradictory images of the place and they will say that the newsroom culture simply reflects the fragility of racial harmony in all segments of society.

"You go into a school and you'll see a bunch of black people sitting in a corner and a bunch of white people sitting in a corner," Bob Dyer said. "I mean, you've got to really make an effort to go out and reach across."

And you have to be even bolder to speak up about race at work. Is it worth the risk? Dyer has a mortgage to pay, a new swimming pool and two young daughters to put through college one day.

"You get to the newsroom," he said, "and you're thirty-two or thirty-four, and you've learned that if you're black and want to succeed or you're white and you want to succeed, you can say this but you probably shouldn't go there, and you ought to just back off."

Two Sons of Two Clevelands

Robert Bruce Dyer and Carl Clifton Chancellor were introduced to the world less than a year apart, wrapped in blankets in the same nursery at University Hospitals of Cleveland.

While they started out in the same place, Carl and Bob went home to different worlds in an era of whites-only country clubs and the first rumblings of black civil unrest.

Their early years influenced the men as journalists. "You have two educated men with two educated egos that see things very differently because they were raised very differently," said Sheila Williams, who has lived with Chancellor for thirteen years and is the mother of his youngest son.

Dyer, the son of an electrical engineer and an amateur figure skater, grew up in a suburban part of mostly rural Geauga County, outside Cleveland, where in pockets the Amish outnumbered the blacks. There he learned about doing unto others as you would have them do unto you; about doing a job right the first time, even if it was just washing your father's car. But race was not a frequent topic at the Dyer dinner table.

There were a few blacks at young Bob's school and some who worked at the country club, where he occasionally dined with his grandfather. But he remembers noticing the all-you-can-eat shrimp more than the help. Far away there were civil rights marches, boycotts, dogs turned on protesters — events he saw only out of the corner of his eye, on television.

But if the boy with the pale peach complexion saw race mainly in the media, the one with the apple-butter skin saw it in his own reflection. There was no ignoring race for young Carl Chancellor. It was in countless church sermons about better days ahead. It was at his grandmother's kitchen table, where civil rights leaders could count on a hot meal after a protest rally. And it was at a park in Florida, where he was turned away at the whites-only entrance to the glass-bottom-boat ride. (He recalled being one of only a handful of passengers on the blacks' boat, while whites crowded into a boat that looked full enough to capsize.)

Home for the Chancellors was Cedar Estates, a fancy name for a place that was anything but. Their apartment in that Cleveland public housing development was all they could afford while Carl's mother tended to her growing family and his father washed trucks at the electric company to pay his way through law school.

His father, Carl Eugene Chancellor, graduated less than a year after young Carl's birth, and the family was soon on a trajectory from penny-pinching to prosperity. Hired by the electric company's legal department, he promptly moved his family to a better neighborhood on the city's edge. The houses were modest, and every day, it seemed, a moving van rolled in to pack up another white family, but to the Chancellors it felt like sweet suburbia nonetheless.

The elder Mr. Chancellor taught by example, and in time it all made sense to Carl: the fine food, the parties with his father's accomplished black friends—a doctor, an architect, other lawyers—and even his father's insistence that Carl pass up a chance to attend a prestigious East Coast boarding school to remain in a public school where the principal and the teachers looked like him. Black did not mean inferior. That is what his father was trying to say.

So Carl did not find it nearly as interesting as some grownups that his father kept getting promoted and had a white secretary. And his only observation about his family's dining at the Four Seasons during vacations to New York was that "my father would always get mad at my little brother because no matter what restaurant we went to, he always ordered a hamburger."

In middle age, Carl Chancellor is content with the black man he has become. He is five foot ten, with a handsome, closely cropped beard and wavy salt-and-pepper hair. He favors tailored slacks, black turtlenecks and Italian leather shoes.

A soccer dad, Bob Dyer fits comfortably in his skin, too. He is six foot two with an easy smile, a thick mustache and a full head of dark brown hair. He prefers khakis, cotton sports shirts and loafers.

As different as they are, there is also a sameness about them. Both live in upper-middle-class suburban neighborhoods and say they are pleased that their children have a more racially diverse group of friends than they do. The women in their lives describe them in similar terms, as caring, but opinionated and "macho" too.

"I think we share a lot of values," Chancellor said. But factor in race, and they can be worlds apart.

"Carl can't understand what it is to be a white male in America any more than Bob can understand what it is to be a black male in America," his companion, Sheila Williams, said.

Once, Dyer was pulled over on a dark highway after edging in and out of his lane while trying to pass a truck. It struck him, he said, that he had experienced something comparable to racial profiling.

"I resented the fact that I was, you know, sort of randomly pulled over for no good reason," Dyer said. "I mean, it's not as if people like me never encounter situations where you go, 'What the hell is going on?'"

Another time, at a restaurant with his family, Dyer thought the service was terrible. When a black family a few tables away got the same treatment, he said, he wondered whether they would attribute it to discrimination and wrote in a 1990 column about seeing race where it may not be.

It is not that bigotry is a figment of the imagination, Dyer wrote. But, he added: "This white guy keeps getting hammered, too, day after day after day. So don't take it personally. There's plenty of rudeness and incompetence to go around."

For many of his readers and colleagues, though, that column was unremarkable compared to one he wrote in two parts in 1995 during Black History Month. He said it generated more response than anything he had written in twenty years. One call came from the publisher, who summoned Dyer to explain what he meant when he wrote this:

"I'll give you some black history: For the past fifteen years, a race that accounts for only 12 percent of this country's population has caused more than half its problems."

The column went on to say that "guilt-ridden white people have turned us all into contortionists, looking for new ways to twist the truth to make blacks look better." It described Afrocentrism as "the scholarly equivalent of flying saucers."

Explosive words, to be sure, but Dyer says he was misread. The column, he said, was meant as an uncensored expression of an internal debate with his conscience. It was meant to show the conflicted feelings that many whites have about blacks but are loath to express in a time of political correctness. Yes, he had exaggerated some points for the sake of argument. But Dyer was certain that even his critics would give him credit for asking, "If things are so equal, care to trade places with an African-American?" His well-meaning conscience also got the last say, reminding him that "things won't improve unless you pay more attention to me."

Dyer said he had assumed that coming in the wake of the race project and the goodwill it engendered, the column was timed just right. "I thought maybe now, since we seemed to be acknowledging that we have problems, and we can talk about problems, maybe it's time to push it harder," he said. But he had been wrong.

Whatever his intentions, his words drew little sympathy from some colleagues. "Bob is a racist without even knowing it," said Yuvonne Bruce, a black assistant features editor, who worked on the race series.

Dyer, who says he gets along with many of his black colleagues, contends that white people risk being slapped with ugly labels when they speak honestly about race.

Carl Chancellor says Dyer is not a racist, just naive about the pervasiveness and pain of bigotry. How could Bob Dyer know?

Unlike Chancellor, he has never had trouble trying to interview fans at Cleveland Indians games because stadium security thought his media credentials might be fake. Nor has he known the anger that boils up in black men who feel under siege.

Chancellor felt that anger when four white New York City police officers were acquitted in the shooting death of an unarmed African immigrant, Amadou Diallo. The verdict, in February 2000, was fresh in his memory a few days later when he noticed a white police officer driving behind him in a movie theater parking lot.

"I'm thinking, 'If he does say something to me, I think I will go off,' " Chancellor recalled. "I guess I just came to a decision: 'If he says anything about me, about anything, I'm just going to go off right then and there.' "

As it turned out, the officer was not trailing him but driving to meet an officer up ahead in a parked patrol car.

Chancellor laughs about the moment now. Life can be funny that way.

Just like the boy he once was, he still sees race all around him. Meanwhile, Bob Dyer still believes that people focus on it too much.

A Column Is Canceled

Carl Chancellor says he knows the double standards. A white man is confident, a black man is cocky. A white man has taste, a black man is flashy. And a white columnist can never write too white, Chancellor says, but if you are black, you learn quickly that your subjects and your sources had better not be too black too often.

So he found white people on welfare to write about. And if he found a reason to write about somebody who just happened to be black, he said, "I went overboard to not mention his race or downplay it because I was afraid that the readers would miss my point."

Some people in the newsroom suggest that his self-restraint did not go far enough for some editors. In the fall of 1999, Chancellor lost his column and was reassigned to a general news beat. He found himself covering Groundhog Day.

Janet Leach said the reassignment had had nothing to do with Chancellor's writing about race but rather with his productivity. She said he had been asked to do more reporting for his columns and contribute news articles as well. When he declined, the column was discontinued, she said.

Chancellor confirms Leach's account of what happened but has gone back and forth in his mind about whether the newspaper's demands were meant to force him to give up the column. Many of his black colleagues are far less willing to give the management the benefit of the doubt.

They say Carl Chancellor was no less productive than any other columnist and that his editors were simply punishing him for some of his views, a charge the editors deny. "I think that management did not like Carl's style," said Melanie Payne, a black features writer.

Yuvonne Bruce, the black assistant features editor, said she was shocked when she opened her newspaper and discovered that the column was gone. "I felt strongly that we were losing a strong black voice," she said.

In protest, she circulated a petition in support of Chancellor among only the black staff members. Charlene Nevada, a white editor on the metro desk, said she was not sure whether she would have signed or not. "But it would have been nice to be asked," she said.

The protest surprised Janet Leach because the journalists went over her head and took their "statement from the minorities," as Bruce described it, directly to her boss.

The publisher, John Dotson, is no stranger to the complexities of race relations in the workplace. His decades of experience taught him to keep his thoughts and feelings closely guarded to protect himself from all sorts of attacks, he said.

So when asked recently about race relations at the *Beacon Journal*, he was initially stone-faced and defensive, wondering aloud about how much he should say. When he finally did open up, what he revealed was not so much about the newsroom as about the pressures on a black executive in a largely white industry.

"When I came along," Dotson said in slow, measured tones, "I would get up in the morning and I would put on this armor and go to work."

Today it is still his first line of defense, the steely gaze, the tight smile, the terse responses. He slips into that posture as easily as he does his crisp white shirts and banker-blue suits.

"It protects me against all of the assaults that I think I undergo,"

Dotson said. "They are not racial all the time. Some of it is racial. Mostly it is not revealing my inner thoughts because I don't want to make a misstep."

His caution may be one reason staff members have different readings of him.

"I think it's kind of funny how a lot of people in the newsroom, white people in the newsroom, think he bends over backwards to appease and please the black community and black reporters in the newsroom," Chancellor said of Dotson. "When I think if you polled the black people in the newsroom, they'd probably think that it's the other way around."

That is exactly what some blacks in the newsroom concluded after Dotson responded to the petition by backing the editor's decision to reassign Chancellor and later supporting her choice of a white man as a replacement.

To some blacks, the decisions sent the wrong message about racial diversity. "I don't think we have anybody leading us who cares," Yuvonne Bruce said.

But rather than indifference, John Dotson's actions reflect a desire to stay out of day-to-day newsroom affairs, he said. "I try to let the editors run the newsroom," he said.

When he sees fit, though, he does not hesitate to use his power to promote fairness and diversity. Dotson banned publication of the Cleveland Indians' logo, a caricature of an Indian chief, because it offended some readers. He also persuaded a civic group to change the date of an event that the newspaper was supporting after an editor complained that it fell on a Jewish holiday. And he has hired a black general manager who is widely believed to be his heir apparent.

Differences in perceptions of how race affects John Dotson as publisher extend to the upper echelons as well.

Since Janet Leach joined the paper in 1998, she has assumed she carries a burden that Dotson does not. When she speaks in the community, Leach, the first woman to hold the title of *Beacon Journal* editor, is inevitably accused of turning the publication into the *Ladies' Home Journal.*

"It happens every time," Leach said. "I don't think they ever ask John Dotson about being a black publisher because it would be politically incorrect."

Not so, Dotson said, adding: "I just don't talk about it. I mean, when

I appointed Jan as editor, one of the questions to me was, 'What are people going to say, the *Beacon Journal* having a black publisher and now a woman editor?' I mean, that's from within the newspaper."

Dotson even gets regular calls from a reader who points out instances of the newspaper's appearing to pander to blacks.

"That's America," the publisher said. "What am I supposed to do about that?"

The Price of Candor

For now, Carl Chancellor has made peace with his lowered profile at the *Beacon Journal*. Though still a general assignment reporter, he has worked on in-depth projects that he cares about and that Janet Leach says she enthusiastically supports.

He and Bob Dyer say there are no hard feelings lingering between them and that they have grown to respect each other's honesty. The men even talk about someday getting back to the basketball court. (They still lie about who has the better jump shot.)

These days, Chancellor spends his spare time writing a novel about a newsroom and a book of short stories, *Soul Songs*, about coming of age in the sixties. The *Beacon Journal*, he said, will not be his last stop, and he does not spend much time thinking about the race project or the column he lost.

As for Bob Dyer, he still writes a magazine column every Sunday but occasionally questions whether his views have hurt his chances for other opportunities at the *Beacon Journal*, and whether it would be easier to get ahead if he were not a white male.

"I want to make it clear that I don't know in this case, that it's just total speculation, but the thought had crossed my mind," Dyer said.

He has grown more reluctant to write about race these days. He knows he is on safer ground when writing about highway sound barriers or the local soapbox derby. His admirers say he can be witty and touching, whether writing a "letter to heaven" to his mother or a "happy anniversary" column praising his wife as intelligent, loyal and "perfectly comfortable with people of different backgrounds, incomes and colors."

"Sometimes he's writing what he believes is right, sometimes he's just writing what he feels," his wife, Becky, said.

And sometimes he still offends even when not trying to be provocative. Readers and colleagues were sharply critical of one column, meant to be humorous, in which he suggested new mascots for local schools. For a mostly black high school, he offered the name Crackheads—a jab at a member of its basketball team who had been arrested on a drug charge.

"I did not like that one at all," said John Dotson, who characterized Dyer's columns as generally too sarcastic and negative.

Marilyn Miller Roane, a black reporter, confronted Dyer about the column. "I told him, 'You just missed it; this is not funny,'" she said. She has concluded that his column speaks to "crybaby white boys."

Such reactions leave Bob Dyer shaking his head. He argues that the mascot column poked fun at lots of institutions, that he did not single out the black school for ridicule. And he said he was frustrated that people did not remember all he had written to improve race relations. What about the column advocating the hiring of a black news anchor at a local television station? Or the one denouncing harassment of an interracial couple?

Carl Chancellor says he knows about being misunderstood, too. It is a burden he believes he and Bob Dyer share.

"I think the general newsroom perception might be that I'm pretty militant and I'm the 'angry black man,' or something like that," he said, dismissing the notion with a roll of the eyes. "Name-calling is something I'm used to."

Dyer takes it harder.

"Fewer people would think I was racist if I kept my mouth shut," he said. Though tempted to do just that, he says he will not. Remaining silent would mean he had lost all hope of seeing race relations improve.

"If there is a race problem," he said, "it is my problem, too."

In the fall of 2000, Carl Chancellor was thinking about leaving the Beacon Journal; he did not want the paper "to be my last stop," he said. He had written three books—a collection of short stories and two novels, one a mystery based in a newsroom—and was looking for a publisher. At the Beacon Journal, pondering his future, he was still writing features and covering general assignment news.

Bob Dyer also felt that his career was stalled—partly, he said, because he had written so honestly about race. In addition to his column, he was writing features for the paper's Sunday magazine. But his priority, he said, was to raise his two young daughters in a good neighborhood with good schools. And so he planned to stay put for the time being.

The publication of this story in the New York Times *reopened many of the discussions of race relations in Akron and at the newspaper. Carl Chancellor said that, as he had expected, there were no real changes in the newsroom. Bob Dyer said the article had prompted many black colleagues to talk to him about his views on race, and had improved the lines of communication. Both he and Chancellor did agree, though, that they had become closer since the article, which had reinforced a respect for each other's honesty.*

Marcus Jacoby, at bottom center in number 11 shirt, with other members of the Southern University football team, Baton Rouge, Louisiana, when he was quarterback. Southern University

11

The Minority Quarterback

IRA BERKOW

BATON ROUGE, LOUISIANA

A late summer morning and the sun was already harsh on the dusty high school football field. The shirtless blond nineteen-year-old in shorts stained with sweat kept dropping back to pass, his hands at times so wet it was hard to grip the ball. He was throwing to a friend, working "up the ladder," as it is called, starting with short passes and ending long.

But his mind wasn't totally on his receiver. He could feel the eyes of the man in the dark glasses who sat in a car on the other side of a chain-link fence, a hundred yards away.

The boy knew the man was watching. It had been subtly arranged. The National Collegiate Athletic Association does not allow tryouts, but if a college coach happens by a field where kids regularly throw the ball around, well, a coach may argue, where's the harm?

At that time, in July of 1996, Southern University, a football powerhouse among black colleges, desperately needed a quarterback, and the boy, Marcus Jacoby, badly needed a place to play quarterback.

After half an hour, the man in dark glasses, Mark Orlando, Southern's offensive coordinator, had seen enough and drove off.

It had gone well. The boy was invited to the coach's apartment, where after a short visit he was offered a full football scholarship.

The coach explained that the boy had a shot at the starting job, that the intended starter's poor grades had lost him his place on the team and that the two backups did not have the coaches' confidence.

"Sounds good," Jacoby, who had been a star at Catholic High, one of Baton Rouge's schoolboy powers, recalled saying. "But I have to think about it—talk with my parents."

"Practice starts in four days," the coach responded. "We're going to need an answer soon."

Marcus Jacoby was unaware that if he accepted the scholarship, he would be the first white to play quarterback for Southern University. And he would be the first white to start at quarterback in the seventy-six-year history of the black Southwestern Athletic Conference.

Jacoby had grown up in Baton Rouge, and yet he knew practically nothing about Southern, had never even been to the other side of town to see the campus. Until that July day he had spent his life surrounded by whites.

The Business of How to Succeed

Southern's head coach, Pete Richardson, worked out of a modest wood-paneled office lined with trophies. In his three years there, he had turned a laughingstock into a national force. Southern won eleven of twelve games his first year, 1993, and two years later it was the No. 1 black college in the nation.

It is not easy for a black man to become a head coach. Despite his record, Richardson, fifty-four, has never had an offer from one of the 114 Division I-A colleges; only three of them have black head football coaches.

In college he played at the University of Dayton, hardly a football school, and though he had limited natural talent, he reached the professional level, playing three years for the Buffalo Bills. He coached high school ball for a few years, then took the head coach job at Winston-Salem State in North Carolina. Finally, in 1993, he got his big break at Southern, which with its combined campuses is the largest historically black college in the nation.

"I can't get caught up with the thought that, 'Hey, why shouldn't I be at Notre Dame?' " he said in an interview. "I can't get sidetracked or go around with a chip on my shoulder." He is a stoical man and expected stoicism from his players.

That day in his office, the Jacobys said, they were impressed by his quiet intellect, the way he measured his words, his determination. Indeed, the president of Southern, Dr. Dorothy Spikes, often said that she had hired Richardson over better-known candidates not just because his teams had been winners but because of his reputation for integrity, for running a clean program.

Coach Richardson and the Jacobys discussed everything from Southern's rich athletic tradition to the engineering courses that interested Marcus, but for a long while they didn't mention the thing that worried the parents most. The quarterback is team leader. Would a black team accept a white leader? Would the black campus? The night before, at the Jacobys' home in the upper-middle-class white Tara section of Baton Rouge, talk had become heated. "What if they don't like Marcus?" Marian Jacoby had said, tears in her eyes. "What if there's some kind of . . . action?" Marcus had not been able to sleep he was so upset.

Now his father, Glen, an environmental engineer, asked the coach, "How are you going to protect my son?"

The room went silent, Glen Jacoby said later. "I realize that you're concerned," Richardson began, "but I just don't think it will be that big a deal. Sure, there will be some adjustments from all sides. But Marcus will have the backing of the administration as well as the coaching staff."

Coach Richardson pointed out that there were other minorities on campus. He meant that of the 10,500 students, 5 percent were not black, but Marian Jacoby kept thinking about how it would feel to be in a stadium with her husband and 30,000 black fans.

The coach didn't say it to the Jacobys, but no one knew better than he about the strain Marcus would feel being in the minority. As a successful black man Richardson was used to the stares of surprise.

"Walking into a place with a suit and tie on, you're always going to get that second look because you're not supposed to be there." When he coached at Winston-Salem, he had a state government car. "Whites look at you and ask you what you're doing driving the state's car," he said. "You pull over to get some gas and people will address you the wrong way or policemen will look at you funny."

There was something else Richardson didn't say that morning: He was well aware how hostile Southern's fans could be to any newcomer, regardless of creed or color. Many had not wanted him hired. They felt he had come from too small a college; they had wanted a big name in black college football. They had even used race on *him*. Shortly after he arrived, a rumor started that Richardson's wife, who is light-skinned, was white, and that his white offensive coordinator was his wife's brother. None of it was true, but Richardson didn't let it get to him. He knew the best answer was to win, and since he had done so, he was—as Southern's registrar, Marvin Allen, liked to point out—a campus god.

The coach thought he could make this Jacoby thing work. He wasn't sitting there fretting about whether Marcus could learn to be part of the minority. The first game was only six weeks away. As he would say later, he didn't have "ample time to find another black quarterback." Marcus would have to do what all good players did, what the coach himself had done: suck it up.

To reassure the Jacobys, the coach told them about his staff. Of six assistants he had hired when he started in 1993, two were white, one Asian. He was told Southern fans would never stand for that. But after his 11–1 debut season—the year before they had been 6–5—a popular T-shirt on campus featured a photo of the integrated staff, with the phrase "In Living Color."

The parents wanted to think about it overnight, but Marcus did not. He climbed into his Jeep, he said later, and went riding. He was getting his shot, finally. There was nothing he loved like football. As a boy, when he couldn't find a friend, he tossed footballs into garbage-can lids in his yard. His parents held him back in ninth grade, so he would have time to grow, and a better chance to play high school ball. After starring at Catholic, he went to Louisiana Tech, but there, prospects for playing were dim.

Now he envisioned a game night at Southern with a crowd cheering as he threw yet another touchdown pass. When he stopped at a red light, he lifted his head and at the top of his lungs screamed, "Praise God!"

Hard Work, or Privilege?

From the Jacobys' home, Southern was a twenty-minute car trip, literally to the other side of the tracks. On the ride to the first practice, as he drove over the Hump—the small hill that is one of the barriers between Southern and white Baton Rouge—the momentousness of what he had done started sinking in. As he looked around, he began imagining himself playing a game, he recalled. "Would I see a white face?"

Southern's decision to sign a white quarterback made headlines, first locally, then nationally, and the reaction of some whites he knew startled him. When Jacoby called his girlfriend to talk about it, her mother answered. "The niggers over there will kill you," he recalled her saying. "There are bullets flying all over the place. It's a war zone." When his girlfriend got on the phone, she said, "Marcus, I don't want you to call me again." To many on the white side of town, who had never visited this campus bustling with middle-class black students on the bluffs of the Mississippi, it was as if Jacoby had voluntarily moved to the ghetto.

Like many white Americans, he knew there was still prejudice — though, he says, not at home. He had been raised to believe that, after generations of injustice, the country was now a fair place when it came to race, and he had made a few black friends while playing high school ball.

The Jacobys were considered a little eccentric for Baton Rouge, having moved here from California when Marcus was three. His paternal grandfather was Jewish. His mother had attended Berkeley in the 1960s and still had some of the flower child in her. She was a fitness buff, and had even tried putting her family on a vegetarian diet, stocking the refrigerator with so many oat products that Marcus's buddies asked whether they owned a horse. Marcus and his sister at first attended a private school, but their mother felt too many children there were spoiled by wealth. So she taught them at home for five years, until Marcus was a sophomore.

Friends and teachers at Catholic High remember him as hardworking, smart and moralistic, with a strong Christian bent. "We'd make fun of his being so innocent," said John Eric Sullivan, one of his best friends. "By that I mean, he didn't do anything that most normal high school kids are doing. He'd be, 'Watch out, watch yourself,' when guys would be drinking. We'd say, like, 'Marc, relax, man.' " He told them he was waiting until he was twenty-one to drink.

The Southern coaches were impressed with his arm and had never seen a quarterback learn Coach Richardson's complex offense so fast. Jacoby stayed to do extra throwing and often studied game films well past midnight. Southern at times uses a no-huddle offense, meaning the quarterback has to call plays rapidly right at the line, and Coach Richardson felt that of the three candidates, only Marcus Jacoby knew the system well enough to do that. Within days of arriving, he was first string.

That sparked anger among many of his new black teammates. For over a year they had been friendly with the two quarterbacks now relegated to backup, and they resented the newcomer, complaining that he had not earned his stripes. "He was *given* his stripes," said Virgil Smothers, a lineman. "There was a lingering bitterness."

Several felt the decision was racial. "It just became the fact that we were going to have this white quarterback," said Sam George, a quarterback prospect who was academically ineligible that year. "It wasn't about ability no more." Teammates picked at Jacoby's weaknesses — he didn't have "fast feet" and rarely scrambled — and joked that he was the typical bland white athlete, which angered Richardson. "A lot of minorities, they want the flash," the coach said. "We felt we needed a system in order to be successful and a quarterback to operate within the confines of that system."

Except for the coaches, he was isolated. In the locker room, Jacoby recalled, "I would walk around the corner and people would just stop talking."

Even in the huddles there was dissension. Scott Cloman, a Southern receiver, recalled: "The minute Marcus was like, 'Everybody calm down, just shut up,' they were like: 'Who are you talking to? You're not talking to me.' You know, stuff like that. If it was a black person it wouldn't be a problem. They all felt that 'I'm not going to let a white person talk to me like that.' "

His entire time at Southern, Jacoby kept his feelings about all this inside, "sucking it up," repeatedly telling the inquiring reporters what a *great* experience it was being exposed to a new culture. "As soon as I signed and walked onto the campus," he told one interviewer, "I felt like part of the family. I definitely feel at home here."

School and Students in Step

On September 7, 1996, Southern opened at Northwestern State, with Marcus Jacoby at quarterback. Of the 25,000 spectators, half had made the three-hour trip from Southern, not unusual for this football-crazy place. "Fans plan their lives around games," Richardson said. "They fight to get schedules, to see where we're going to play so they can take holidays and go to games."

Southern University families like the Morgans will take more than twenty people to an away game, filling several hotel rooms. Mo Morgan, a supervisor at the local Exxon plant who attended Southern in the 1960s, went so far as to buy a motor home just for Southern football, which made him the object of good-natured ribbing. Friends insisted that "black people don't drive Winnebagos." His wife, Wanda, and about twenty-five of their relatives are Southern graduates, and his youngest son, Jabari, a freshman drummer and cymbals player, was on the field for that same opening game.

For the youngest Morgan, the band was only partly about music. More famous than Southern's football team — having performed at five Super Bowls and three presidential inaugurations — it had real power and importance on campus. The 180-piece Southern band thrived on intimidating lesser rivals on the black college circuit. With its hard-brass sound and its assertive style, the group had a militant edge that old-timers on campus attributed to the influence of the civil rights era, when the band's show was honed.

Robert Gray, who played cymbals with Morgan, said: "When people think about Southern band, they think about a bunch of big, tough-looking, tight-looking dudes with psychotic looks on their faces, ready to go to war. I just think — Southern band — black, all male, just rowdy, loud."

Families like the Morgans were fiercely proud of *their* school and its role in helping generations of blacks into the middle and professional classes — even if the state had long treated it as second-rate. In the early 1900s, legislators planning to create a new campus for Southern considered several locations around Louisiana. But in city after city, white residents rose in protest, and finally the state settled on a site that no one else then coveted. In the 1950s, blacks like Audrey Nabor-Jackson, Wanda Morgan's aunt, were prohibited from attending the big white public campus across town, Louisiana State University. Southern was their only alternative.

Even as late as the 1970s, Louisiana's public higher education system was capable of inflicting deep racial wounds. Wanda Morgan was required to take several courses at LSU as part of a master's program at Southern. In one class, she was one of four blacks, and for every exam, she said, the four were removed by the professor and put in an empty classroom across the hall, one in each corner, while the white students took the exam in their regular seats. The message was missed by no one: black students would cheat.

By the mid-1990s, change was brewing. The year before Marcus Jacoby arrived, Southern and LSU settled a twenty-year-old federal desegregation lawsuit. Both institutions pledged sharp minority increases on their campuses, with 10 percent of enrollment set aside for other races — more whites to Southern, more blacks to LSU.

Alumni like the Morgans were worried. Would Southern soon become just another satellite campus of LSU? Was the white quarterback the beginning of the end?

Mo Morgan and Audrey Nabor-Jackson agreed with an editorial in Southern's student paper saying that a white quarterback did not belong. "There are plenty of young black athletes," it said, "who could benefit from Jacoby's scholarship."

Mo Morgan said, "I didn't like the fact that he was there." About the only Morgan not upset was Jabari. Mo Morgan worried that his eighteen-year-old son was not race-conscious enough. "I came through the movement, I was confronted with things," said the father. "That's one of the things that concerns me—that he hasn't." But Jabari Morgan couldn't have cared less, he was so consumed with the band. Long before starting college, he had begun assembling on his bedroom wall what he called his shrine, a montage about the Southern band that included a picture of the first white band member, in the early 1990s.

Now, in his freshman year, his long-nurtured fantasy was coming true. Standing there that day with cymbals weighing nine pounds each, ready to march into Northwestern State's stadium, he was at the front of the band. The director, Dr. Isaac Greggs, always positioned his tallest and most imposing players—his "towers of terror"—at the front, and Jabari Morgan, at six foot one, was one of them. Football, he said, was about the last thing on his mind.

"It was like winning the lottery."

He wouldn't have cared if Marcus Jacoby were purple, as long as Southern won and people stayed in their seats for the halftime show.

A Mutinous Beginning

Southern lost its first two games. The team was young—ten of eleven offensive starters were new—but what people remembered was the 11–1 record the year before.

For fans, the quarterback, more than any other player, *is* the team—hero or goat. During the second loss, Jacoby recalled, "I heard the entire stadium booing me."

Jean Harrison, the mother of the quarterback prospect Sam George, remembered, "One lady had a megaphone and she was screaming, 'Get that white honky out of there!' "

Chris Williams, an offensive lineman, believed that the other team hit Jacoby harder because he was white: "Teams took cheap shots at him. I really believe that. I mean they hit him sometimes blatantly late after the whistle." Scott Cloman recalled that after one Southern loss, opposing players said, "That's what you all get for bringing white boys on the field."

Jacoby was hit so hard and so often during the first game that he was hospitalized with a concussion. Glen Jacoby, Marcus's father, was sure the blockers were sandbagging their white quarterback, but in interviews at the time, the young man denied it. He still says he believes that it was just the mistakes of an inexperienced line.

After Southern's second loss, an angry fan threatened Jacoby. A coach had to jump between them. For the rest of his career, Jacoby would have a police escort at games. There was a disturbance outside the stadium at another game. Gunshots were fired. Jacoby recalls thinking the shots were aimed at him.

The Tuesday after the second loss, Jacoby rose at 5 A.M., worked out in the weight room, then walked to the cafeteria for the team breakfast. No one was there. He checked his watch. Shortly after he sat down, Coach Orlando came in, took him by the arm and led him through a nearby door.

As Jacoby remembered it, the entire team and coaching staff sat squeezed into a small room. All chairs were taken, so he stood alone against a wall. No one looked at him. Coach Richardson stood. "I think Marcus should know what's going on," he said, adding, "Who wants to say something?"

Smothers, the senior defensive end, rose. The night before, he had talked about staging a strike. Now he mentioned some minor gripes, then added: "We're losing and we feel changes ought to be made. Some guys aren't getting a fair chance."

Someone else said, "Guys are playing who shouldn't."

Orlando walked to the front. As offensive coordinator, he naturally worked closely with the quarterback. But several players felt he favored Jacoby because they were both white. "Let's get this in the open," Orlando said, adding, "This is mostly about Jacoby, isn't it?" Insisting that the quarterback had been chosen fairly, he said: "You have to accept Marcus, he's one of us. We're 0 and 2, but we have to put this behind us."

Lionel Hayes, who had lost the quarterback job to Jacoby, interrupted Orlando. "You're just saying that," Hayes said, "because you're

Jacoby's dad." It got a laugh, though his tone was angry. Jacoby said later: "There was a lot of hate in that room. I felt like I was falling into a hole, and I couldn't grab the sides."

Richardson spoke again: "We win as a team, we lose as a team. Jacoby's doing what he's supposed to be doing, and he'll get better. We all will." He said practice would be at three. "If anyone doesn't want to be on the team with Jacoby as the starting quarterback, don't come."

Richardson remembered: "What I saw was a frustration by some players—mostly seniors—who weren't playing. They weren't playing because they didn't deserve to. And so they needed a scapegoat."

Jacoby remembers feeling like the invisible man. "It was almost as though I weren't there, and they were talking about me," he said. "I wasn't sure where to turn. I felt they didn't want me there— not me personally, but any white quarterback—that I was just another problem."

Three or four players didn't show up for practice, and Richardson cut them. Not long afterward, Virgil Smothers and one of the coaches argued, and Smothers was told, "Clear out your locker."

When the players gathered the next day at practice, before the coaches arrived, Jacoby said, he stood to talk. A few tried to shout him down, but John Williams, a star senior cornerback and devout Christian who would go on to play for the Baltimore Ravens, rose and said, "Man, let the man talk."

"I don't care if you like me or hate me," Jacoby recalled saying. "All I ask is that we can go out and play football together. This is not a popularity contest. I'm trying to win. I'm just trying to be your quarterback."

Winning Works Wonders

Things improved dramatically. Southern won six of its next seven games, beating the two top-ranked black colleges, and was invited to the Heritage Bowl in Atlanta, the black college championship.

"I wasn't getting booed nearly as much," Jacoby said. Some teammates began warming to him. More than anything, they were impressed by his work ethic. During a practice break, players drank from a garden hose. "Sorry, Marcus," one teased, "this is the black water fountain." They called him "Tyrone," and "Rasheed."

"I appreciated it," he recalled. "Things had changed to the extent that some of the players were calling me 'the man.' "

Before games, he and John Williams prayed together. One Sunday the two went to the black church where Williams was a minister.

Occasionally strangers would wish Jacoby well. One day the band's legendary director, Dr. Greggs, greeted him warmly and urged him to persevere.

He felt he was developing real friendships with teammates and Southern students. When Scott Cloman needed a place to stay for a month, Jacoby had him to his parents' home and the two grew close. "Marcus was the first white person I ever really got to know," Cloman said. "I always felt a lot of tension around whites. I'd go into a store and I could just feel the tension. Sometimes you just feel like, 'I can't stand white people.' I didn't understand them. I really didn't want to be near them."

"His parents treated me like a son," added Cloman. Some players now joked when they saw him, "Where's your brother?"

"And some," he said, "called me 'white lover.' Didn't bother me. I had come to understand the Jacobys. A lot of times people fear what they can't understand. Because of being around the Jacobys my attitude toward whites in general changed."

Failure Is Not an Option

At the Heritage Bowl that first year, on national television, Southern took a 24–10 halftime lead against Howard University, then fell behind, 27–24. In the closing minute, Southern drove to Howard's 15-yard line. On third down, with 42 seconds left, Marcus Jacoby dropped back and, under pressure, threw off the wrong foot, floating a pass into the end zone.

"I heard the crowd gasp," he said. "I couldn't believe this was happening." He'd been intercepted. "Their fans must have cheered, but I remember everything being silent." A camera captured Coach Richardson on his knees, hands over his head.

"I dragged myself off the field and sat on a bench and buried my head in my arms," Jacoby said. "A few people, like John Williams, came by and patted me on the back, to be encouraging. But I heard, 'You screwed up real bad this time, whitey,' and, 'You're as dumb as they come.' It was the lowest point of my life."

After the game, Coach Orlando received an anonymous call: "If Jacoby ever plays for Southern again, we'll kill him—and you." The coach said he averaged a threat a week that season. Later, as Orlando and Jacoby headed to their cars, the coach pointed to several trees. In the light of the streetlamps, Jacoby could see a yellow rope hung from each tree. The ropes were tied in nooses.

Eyes of Southern Are upon Him

On campus, Jacoby struggled with all the daily irritations that go with being in the minority. As a white who grew up among whites, he was used to being inconspicuous. Here, he always felt on display. "I hated that," he said, "because it was like I had become just a novelty act."

He found that things he had done unconsciously all his life were suddenly brought to his attention and analyzed. One was the way he dressed. He liked to wear a T-shirt, shorts and flip-flops to class; most students at Southern dressed up for class in slacks.

Another was that the way he spoke, his slang, was different from the black majority's. "Many times I would say something at Southern and they would repeat it and I wouldn't get my point across," he said. "It would get lost in the mocking of how I said it instead of what I said. I might walk into a room and I'd say, 'Hey, how y'all doin'?' " Instead of answering, someone would do an imitation of a white person talking, enunciating slowly. "They'd say 'Hi, guy, how are you doing?' So I just learned to say, 'Hey.' " He believed the classmates were only needling him, but being constantly reminded was exhausting.

"People's eyes were on him," said Chris Williams, a teammate. "He just didn't blend in. I mean, like me, I just blended in wherever I went."

A white with a different personality might have fared better. There was one other white on the seventy-man squad, Matt Bushart. And though as a punter he was at the periphery of the team and little noticed by fans, Bushart had the personality and experience to cope better as a minority. While Marcus had seemed protected and naive even to the middle-class white students at Catholic High, Matt's years at a local public high school where most of his football teammates were black had taught him how to live comfortably among them. While Marcus was more introspective, a loner, a little too sensitive for

some of his coaches' tastes, Matt was noisy, funny, sometimes crude —
so outgoing, his girlfriend said, that he could talk to a wall.

When Bushart's teammates made fun of the country music he liked,
he gave it right back to them about their rap, and kept listening to his
music. "I get kidded about it," he said, "but there's been a song that's
been playing and one of the black guys will come by and say, 'Play
that again, that's actually not too bad.' "

Jacoby loved music, too; playing guitar was an important outlet for
relieving the pressure, but he would not play on campus. As he put it:
"At times the rap just blared from the dorms; I longed for something
that was my own. I couldn't play it on campus because for most of the
time, I was apologizing for who I was. I didn't want to cause any more
turmoil than there was. I didn't want to make myself look like I was
any more separate than I was."

Interracial dating is complicated at Southern. Ryan Lewis, Jacoby's
roommate, says most black men would not openly date a white woman
on campus. "They would keep it low so nobody knew about it but
them," Lewis said. "I've never seen it."

As quarterback, Jacoby often had female students flirting with him.
He felt uneasy, caught between the white and black sides of town.
Among whites, he said, "everybody just assumed the worst, that I was
dating a black girl now because I was at Southern." But even though
there were some "gorgeous light-skinned black girls over there," he
said, and a couple of women from his classes became good friends, he
wasn't attracted. He thinks it was "a cultural thing."

Though college students are confronted with new ideas — sometimes
only partially understood — and encouraged to speak out about them,
Jacoby felt that when he did, he was criticized. At first, in his African-
American history class, when they discussed slavery, he said he tried
to be conciliatory in an oral report. "I would say something like, 'I
can't imagine how terrible it must have been, that people could do
those kinds of things to other people.' And others in the class made
some kind of jokes, but it was like bitter jokes: 'What are you talking
about, Marcus? You're one of those whites.' It was like they were saying
to me, 'Quit Uncle Tomming.' "

Then he worried he wasn't being true to his white roots. "I felt that
I had lost my pride and the respect of friends that I had grown up
with," he said. For his next oral report, he decided to speak his mind
and said that it was unhealthy for blacks to dwell too much on past

racial violence. "There have been tragedies like slavery throughout time," he said. "I don't think one is more important than any other." When he finished, he recalled, "there was an eerie silence and I saw at least three or four people glaring at me."

Increasingly, being in the minority alienated him, made him feel alone. "I learned early on that I was a pioneer in all this and no one else had gone through it and often the best advice I could get was from myself. Because I was the only one who knew the whole situation."

It didn't help that his preoccupied parents were going through a divorce. At one point when he was upset about not fitting in, his mother gave him a copy of *Black Like Me*, the story of a white man in the 1960s who dyes his skin and travels the South to experience being black during segregation. At the time, Jacoby said, "I resented my mother giving me the book. I felt she was almost taking the other side."

One Fits, the Other Doesn't

Blacks, of course, are much better at being in the minority, since they have far more practice and, usually, no choice. When Jabari Morgan was considering colleges, his father told him he was free to pick Southern or a "white" college, but if he picked white, he had better be prepared. Then he gave him the talk about being in the minority that so many black American men give their sons. "You are going to face being called a nigger," Mo Morgan told Jabari. "Now, are you ready to deal with it? If you're not ready to deal with it, don't go."

The Morgans have a family council of elders that meets regularly to guide their young, and one message emphasized is this: "A black person in America has to be smarter and sharper and work harder to achieve the same things as a white person of the same abilities." Mo Morgan says, as a minority, he understands that "the majority is white, and *you* have control and *you* want to keep control."

But Jabari Morgan did not think like his father.

He had always dreamed of attending Southern, but for him its great appeal was not as a racial sanctuary. He considered race simply part of the rough and tumble of life, the cost of doing business in a mostly white world. Southern was the place where he might be able to play in the best marching band in America, as his father had before him.

He determined very early that the best high school marching bands, like the best college bands, were black, and so he fudged his address in order to attend a nearly all-black Baton Rouge school where the band rocked. He figured that that would give him an edge when he tried out at Southern.

As a marketing major who graduated in 2000, Morgan fully expects that he will one day work for a big white-controlled corporation. But as a marching band member at Southern for four years, he was in many ways the ultimate insider in the self-contained black-majority culture of the Yard, as Southern's campus is known.

All the things that Marcus Jacoby found so irritating were second nature to Jabari Morgan—the music, the dress, the vernacular of put-downs and nicknames that is the campus currency. He loved African-American literature class because the poetry and stories reinforced what his family had taught him about black history.

Like all new band members, Morgan went through hazing. But as part of the majority, he never worried that it was about race. Jacoby, on the other hand, felt so unsettled as part of the minority that he often had trouble sleeping.

Morgan eventually joined a fraternity—a support in its own way as strong as the band's.

And, where Marcus Jacoby the minority had no steady girlfriend during his years at Southern, Jabari Morgan the majority began, in his second semester, dating Monique Molizone, an economics major from New Orleans. She had also come to Southern partly for the band—to join the Dancing Dolls, who perform at the band's side.

Comeback and Competition

As much as anything, what got Jacoby through his second year at Southern was a determination to avenge that Heritage Bowl interception, to show everyone he could be a champion. He moved through the 1997 season with a passion, working so hard in the weight room that he could now bench-press 350 pounds; running endless drills to improve his foot speed; and doing so much extra throwing that by day's end it took an hour to ice and treat his arm.

Again, he was first string, but he had competition. Sam George had returned from academic probation. George was a popular figure on campus, known for his hard-partying ways. Though he was only five foot seven, he had a strong arm and terrific speed. His teammates, responding to his take-charge style in huddles, nicknamed him the Little General. "And," Scott Cloman said, "he was black."

Although Jacoby started, Coach Richardson liked bringing in George when the team seemed flat. Both quarterbacks saw race as the true reason behind the coach's substitutions. Jacoby was convinced that Richardson was giving the black quarterback playing time to pander to the black fans; George was convinced that Richardson—influenced by Coach Orlando—was starting the white quarterback because of favoritism.

George wound up playing in five of twelve games. By Southern's third game, against Arkansas-Pine Bluff, both quarterbacks were bitter. After winning its first two games, Southern was losing to Pine Bluff 7–6 at the half. Richardson decided to replace the white quarterback with the black. Jacoby was devastated; he felt he was a proven winner and should not be yanked for one bad half.

Given his chance, George threw a last-ditch thirty-seven-yard pass that tied the game, and threw another touchdown in triple overtime for a 36–33 Southern win.

And yet, come Monday practice, Jacoby was the starter again. Now George was frustrated.

Southern had a 9–1 record going into its two final games. A victory in the next game—the Bayou Classic, against Grambling, its archrival—would assure a return to the Heritage Bowl and a chance for Jacoby to redeem himself. His parents and teammates had never seen him so obsessed. He had trouble sleeping and little appetite. His father called Coach Orlando, worried that Marcus's weight was down.

In a journal account of that period, Marcus Jacoby wrote: "I sat down and wrote out a detailed plan of how I was going to get through these last two games, including my political and motivational moves. My survival as a person depended on these last two games. Nobody, including Coach Orlando, knew the amount of outside forces that were pressing on these last two games. I was at a point where I felt that I was crawling on my knees."

He added, "I dreamed of a time when I could just say that I had accomplished something, instead of fighting for respect, fighting in a classroom full of people who disagreed with everything I stood for, and could have a day of true rest."

Before the big game against Grambling, he pleaded with Coach Orlando. "If you don't pull me," Jacoby said, "I guarantee we'll win our next two games."

"You can't guarantee that," the coach said.

"I just did," Jacoby said. Orlando suggested that if Marcus Jacoby played a little more like Sam George, sometimes scrambling out of the pocket, he might be more effective. Jacoby felt that he was being told to become something he was not, but he was so desperate, so nervous about being yanked, that he followed the advice. He ran, and it worked. In a 30–7 win against Grambling, Jacoby threw three touchdown passes and played the entire game. He was named the Bayou Classic's most valuable player.

A month later he achieved his redemption, throwing the winning pass in a 34–28 Heritage Bowl victory over South Carolina State, capping an 11–1 season that earned Southern the black national championship. "I was happier than I had ever been at Southern," he recalled. On the trip back from that game he slept soundly for the first time in months.

The Going Gets Too Tough

The more you achieve, the more is expected. After that 11–1 season, the talk on campus was that Southern would go undefeated in 1998. But in the opener, with the team trailing 7–0 at the half, Jacoby was pulled for George. Southern lost anyway, 28–7.

In practice on Tuesday, Jacoby overthrew a pass to one of his ends, John Forman, who yelled at him in front of everybody.

Forman would say later that it was just the frustration of having lost the opener, but to Jacoby it was so much more — the final straw. He was sure that Forman was trying to subvert his control of the team to help George, his roommate. "If you have a choice, you choose black first," Jacoby would later say. "I felt that I was all alone again, on an island by myself. It was like I was right back where I had started two years before, with a lot of the same attitudes against me."

He quit football and Southern.

Coach Richardson was surprised and asked Jacoby to stay. But more recently, he said he understood the decision. Because of "the type person he is," the coach said, "it was the best thing for Marcus because it would have killed him." The coach meant that Marcus Jacoby was not emotionally equipped to continue being the solitary white.

When Branch Rickey of the Brooklyn Dodgers wanted to break major league baseball's color line in 1947, he chose Jackie Robinson, not simply because he was a great black ballplayer — there were greater black stars—but because he had experience inside white institutions. Jackie Robinson was twenty-eight that first year in the majors, a mature man who had attended UCLA and served in the Army. He knew what it was like to be in the minority.

When Coach Richardson went after Jacoby, he was just looking for a quarterback.

Reporters hounded Jacoby to find why he had left, but he never spoke openly about it. He never mentioned race. In brief interviews, he told them he was burned out, and in a sense this was true. He had burned out on being in the minority. And as a white, he didn't have to be. In those last months at Southern, he often thought about returning to a white life. "You kind of look over your shoulder and see your old life and you say, 'I could go back.'"

There had been such anguish over the Jacoby-George quarterback battle, and all its racial nuances, but at least on the field, in the end, it didn't seem to make much difference. That year Southern, with Sam George at the helm, finished 9–3, once again winning the Heritage Bowl.

A white quarterback at Southern did make people think. Mo Morgan had been against it, but not after watching Jacoby at practices. "I looked at the three quarterbacks that were there and he was the best at the time. I'm just telling you straight out. It wasn't his ability and I'm not saying he was brighter than the other kids. He just put in the work."

Morgan's son Jabari said he, too, was sorry to see Jacoby go; he liked the idea of a white guy being open to attending a black college.

As a senior, Jabari Morgan reached out to a white freshman tuba player, Grant Milliken, who tried out for the band. He helped him through the hazing. One of Jabari Morgan's friends said he had done it because Milliken was white, but Morgan said no, he had done it because Milliken was really good on tuba.

Morgan even helped Milliken create a dance solo full of shakes and shivers and fancy steps, which was performed at halftimes to wild applause. What the crowd loved, said Morgan, was not just that a white guy could dance.

"The whole point of letting the white guy dance is that we were saying to the world, 'Hey, you can learn our culture just like we can learn yours.'"

Morgan's father continues to be both fearful of his son's more relaxed attitude about race, and a little in awe of it.

"He doesn't think it's something he can't overcome," said Mo Morgan, "and you know, I think he's right. You can get caught up in this, and it will screw up your thinking."

No More Apologies

One weekend in the fall of 1999, at the request of a reporter, Jacoby went to a Southern game for the first time since quitting. This was Homecoming Day, and from his seat in the stands he watched Southern seniors and their families being introduced to the crowd at midfield. It could have been his moment. Ryan Lewis, his old roommate, was there, and so was Matt Bushart, the white punter.

Bushart's name was called, to applause. Jacoby had read in the newspaper Bushart's saying how much he had enjoyed Southern.

The team had won seven straight games at that point, and so Jacoby was surprised during the first quarter when Southern's starting quarterback was replaced after throwing an interception. Jacoby had always been so sure he'd been replaced with Sam George to pander to fans; now Coach Richardson was using the exact same strategy with two black quarterbacks. In the paper the next day, Richardson said he had just been trying to light a spark under the offense.

After the game, outside the stadium, a large black man spotted Jacoby and, extending his hand, said, "Hi, Marcus, how ya doin'?"

"OK, Virgil," Jacoby said. "How you doin'?" The two chatted for a moment outside the stadium—the man said he had left school and was working as an account executive for a drug company—then they went their separate ways.

"That was Virgil Smothers," Jacoby said afterward. It was Smothers who had led the aborted strike against Jacoby. "I guess he figures it's all in the past."

It was not all in Jacoby's past. Though he had moved on—he was now majoring in finance at LSU—his Southern experience still unsettled him. "Just last night I had a dream about it," he said. "Weird dreams. Like some of these people are coming back to haunt me in some way. By these people I mean some of those who I considered friends and who I felt kind of turned on me."

At times he talks about being lucky to have experienced another culture; at others he describes it as "a personal hell." His sister Dana says, "There are some scars that haven't gone away, from the bad things."

After leaving Southern, Jacoby took a while to realize how much pressure he had felt. "I remember one time a few months after I quit—and this was part of the healing process—I said something about country music, that I liked it. And I remember standing around with four white people and thinking, 'Oh, my God, I can't believe I just said that.' And then I caught myself right before I got through that whole thing in my mind and I looked at the people's faces and they were agreeing with me. I went 'Whoa,' I didn't have to apologize for that anymore."

These days, he appreciates walking around anonymously on the mostly white LSU campus. "I got burned out as far as being somebody," he said. "At LSU I've just enjoyed being a part of the crowd."

Marcus Jacoby graduated from Louisiana State in December 2000, and was hoping to find a job in marketing. He still kept in touch with two teammates from his playing days at Southern, Scott Cloman and Ryan Lewis. As for football, he did not play competitively, but occasionally he would head over to a field near his home, send a receiver deep and loft hard, tight spirals into the sky.

After graduating from Southern in May 2000, Jabari Morgan returned as an unpaid "consultant" to the marching band, working with the drum section and helping create new dance routines. He also worked at a local car dealership, and was planning to go to business school. The question was where. His father felt that Louisiana State was the place to go, but the son thought he would probably stay where he felt at home—Southern.

Sections of this story about the Morgan family, Jabari Morgan and life at Southern University were contributed by Kirk Johnson.

Billy Wimsatt, also known as Upski, at a hip-hop party in Seattle following one of his lectures on race at the University of Washington. Nancy Siesel/The New York Times

12

Guarding the Borders of the Hip-Hop Nation

N . R .   K L E I N F I E L D

BROOKLYN, NEW YORK

He waited until the bus was ready to leave before squeezing up front to address the passengers. The Greyhound was going from Chicago to Indiana. It was winter. The sky was suffused with gray.

He surveyed the bunched rows of seats. There were only nineteen passengers, most of them young, most of them black. Billy Wimsatt was white. It was an audience that made him especially comfortable.

He held aloft a slender book. "I wrote this book," he said over the chitter of talk. "It's pretty good. It normally sells for twelve dollars. On this bus, I'll sell it for five dollars, and you can read it along the way free."

It was called *No More Prisons*, and was about incarceration and philanthropy and hip-hop, always hip-hop, for hip-hop was the ever-lasting undertone to his life. He was a writer and activist, and over the years his work had made him something of a minor cult figure in the hip-hop world, a white man with unusual credibility among blacks deeply protective of their culture. He was an unbudgeable optimist, convinced he could better the world by getting whites and people of other races to talk together and work together. He spent most of his time on the road, on a yearlong tour of several dozen college campuses, preaching his message. Now the bus was taking him to Earlham College in eastern Indiana.

Some passengers gave grudging looks of curiosity. What gives with this guy? Six people beckoned for copies. One woman gave hers back after fifteen minutes, opting for sleep. A man behind her bought one. A woman said she'd take one, too. "Cool," Wimsatt said. He gave her a big smile and a hug.

Billy Wimsatt was twenty-seven, still clinging to the hip-hop life. He didn't look terribly hip-hop, and not because he was white. He was balding and brainy-looking, with an average build and an exuberant nature.

He was born as rap music was being invented by blacks and Latinos in the South Bronx. What began as party music became their cry of ghetto pain and ultimately their great hope for a way out. And as hip-hop—not just rap music but fashion, break-dancing, graffiti and the magazines that chronicle it all—blossomed into the radiant center of youth culture, Billy Wimsatt and lots of white kids found in it a way to flee their own orderly world by discovering a sexier, more provocative one.

Like many young hip-hop heads, he regarded hip-hop, with its appeal to whites and blacks, as a bold modern hope to ease some of the abrasiveness between the races. Hip-hop, as he saw it, endowed him with cultural elasticity, allowed him to shed the privilege of whiteness, to be as down with blacks as with whites. For a long time, he felt black in every respect but skin color, he says, which was why he had been able to get away with that much-noticed article seven years ago in *The Source*, a magazine considered one of the bibles of hip-hop.

It was a withering critique of "wiggers," whites who try too hard to be black so they will be accepted. Soon, he argued, "the rap audience may be as white as tables in a jazz club." In the last paragraph, which *The Source* cut from the final version, he warned black artists that the next time they invented something, they had better find a way to control it financially, because whites were going to steal hip-hop.

"And since it's the nineties," he concluded, "you won't even get to hear us say, 'Thanks, niggers.'"

Yes, Billy Wimsatt seemed about as authentically hip-hop as a white guy could get. But as he slid into the complexities of adulthood, he said, he often found himself wondering if that was enough, unsure which culture was truly his. He had drifted a long way from his black hip-hop roots. Now, on these unsettled grounds, he was far from certain he could stay true to his ideas.

A Believer on the Brink

On a clangorous Manhattan sidewalk, Elliott Wilson stopped to study the bootleg rap tapes splayed on a street vendor's blanket. Music emanated from a portable stereo.

"Some dope stuff here," Wilson, a gangly, light-skinned young black man with inquisitive eyes and a contagious laugh, said approvingly. The bargains got him pumped up. He peeled off a five-dollar bill and bought *Opposite of H$_2$O* by Drag-On.

Elliott Wilson had never met Billy Wimsatt, but their lives had traced similar trajectories across the hip-hop landscape. As a writer and editor, he too had spent much of his adult life thinking about hip-hop. And not just hip-hop, but race and hip-hop. Race was unavoidable in hip-hop—what with all those black rappers idolized by white teen-agers—and like Billy Wimsatt, Elliott Wilson was preoccupied with that conjunction and what it meant in his own life.

Which culture was his was not Elliott Wilson's worry. Hip-hop had inspired him to believe that, precisely because he was black, he could achieve what whites simply assumed was theirs by birthright—a gainful life over which he asserted control.

When he read Wimsatt's "wigger" article, he and a black friend were beginning their own hip-hop publication, *Ego Trip*. They saw it as a brash challenge to the established, white-owned magazines like *The Source*. Bubbling with assurance, Wilson had judged the "wigger" article amusing; for all its ridicule of whites, he had still considered it "a white boy's perspective on hip-hop." He certainly hadn't seen it as a prophecy of personal doom.

Now, he sometimes had to wonder. He was closing in on thirty, trying to hold fast to his own idea of the hip-hop life. He had watched with anger and growing pessimism as *Ego Trip* folded and whites asserted ever-greater control over the hip-hop industry. Recently, he had become editor of a promising hip-hop magazine, *XXL*. It was white-owned. And so he wondered if he was selling out, if he would ever become what he wanted on his own terms. Was hip-hop his story, the black man's story, after all? Did hip-hop unite the races or push them further apart?

A White Boy Confined in His Skin

Growing up in Chicago, Billy Wimsatt remembers, he believed the only way he could have a good life was to be black.

His own life felt proscribed. He was an only child. There was rarely music in the house, just the droning news stations. He saw an awful lot of *Nova* on PBS. He was to avoid the unsavory black neighborhoods.

Yet, he recalls, black children seemed to roam freely. They seemed to grow up faster. In fourth grade, his teacher asked if anyone baby-sat. A black girl's hand shot up. Incredible. Black girls were mature enough to baby-sit. He says he longed to live in the projects.

Where he lived was the integrated neighborhood of Hyde Park, in a perfectly diverse six-flat: two white families, two black, two mixed. His father taught philosophy of science at the University of Chicago. His mother was sort of a perpetual student.

At his mostly white private school, he was not especially popular. He imagined becoming a computer programmer, a scientist, an astro-naut. Then, in sixth grade, a black kid told him to listen to a rap song, "Jam on It." "It was like a message from another world," he said.

Increasingly, he disconnected from a white culture that he equated with false desires. He had jumped out of his container, he said, "like spilled milk." After sixth grade, he persuaded his parents to transfer him to a largely black public school. The cool kids, he noticed, wore fat sneaker laces, favored gold jewelry, did graffiti. He began shoplifting fat laces, fake gold jewelry and markers and selling them to hip-hop heads.

He started break-dancing on the streets. And at thirteen, he began sneaking out at night and riding the trains with black and Latino friends, bombing the city with spray paint. Upski was his chosen tag. From then on, little Billy Wimsatt became Upski, one of Chicago's most prolific graffiti artists.

His frazzled mother, dogged by insomnia, would discover him gone at 2 A.M. She barred his graffiti crew from the house (one of them even burglarized the place), sent him to a psychiatrist, threatened military school. When he persisted, his parents plunked him back in private school. But he barely associated with white classmates, he says. Hip-hop had cloaked him in a new identity.

Astonishingly, and much to the dismay of many older people who abhorred its defiant attitude, its frequent misogyny, violence and vul-garity, hip-hop culture was becoming a great sugar rush for young people of all races. Before long, rap would eclipse country and rock to become America's top-selling pop-music format. And whites would be the ones buying most of those rap albums—a full 70 percent.

For many, even most, young whites, hip-hop was ultimately a hobby, to be grown out of in good time. For Upski, it became a cause, espe-cially as the late eighties gave rise to politically conscious rappers like

Public Enemy, with its peppery blend of black nationalism and rebellion. "Once it became a pretty full critique of American life—race, politics and political hypocrisy—that's when it really registered with me," he said.

A Black "Leader of the Nerds"

Elliott Wilson grew up in the Woodside Houses project in Queens, the oldest of three brothers. His mother was of Greek and Ecuadorean roots; his father, a printer from Georgia, was black. Elliott was very light-skinned, and his hair was different from the black kids'. When it came to skin color, he picked up some mixed messages.

He was five when his father told him: "You're going to be judged by who your father is. I'm black. So you're black. Accept it before you get hurt." And he did, he said: "I felt like the black man from the jump."

He also spent a lot of time with his father's mother. She was tough, and she had friends of all races. She called white people crackers, but told Elliott, "Never trust a black person darker than you."

Attending predominantly white schools, self-conscious about his looks, he never really fit in, he says, recalling that time now. The black and white students didn't mix much, and while the black football players were cool, he was no football player. Instead, he befriended the outcasts.

"I wanted to be a cool kid and I wasn't," he said. "But I didn't want to sacrifice who I was to fit into the system. I'd rather create my own system. I wasn't going to be a fake. So I was the leader of the nerds."

His parents sheltered him from the influence of the streets. He watched a lot of television. He loved *Happy Days* and *Good Times*, admired Howard Cosell and imagined becoming a sportscaster. In high school, he says, he increasingly felt himself an outsider. His grades, always good, fell.

But there was hip-hop. Hip-hop was cool, and his growing love of it made him begin to feel cool. His parents bought him a set of Technics 1200 turntables and a mixer. On weekend nights, while classmates were out on dates, he would be home taping the hip-hop shows off the radio.

When he listened to Public Enemy, he began to shake his head knowingly. For young Elliott Wilson, unaware of so much, the group's powerful lyrics of oppression and rage, especially the album *It Takes a Nation of Millions to Hold Us Back*, were an awakening to what it meant to be black in America. He got a Public Enemy jacket, with the group's logo on the back: a black man in the crosshairs of a gun.

He became more aloof. He no longer said hello to white people, even family friends, unless they greeted him first, he now says. They asked his parents, What's gotten into Elliott?

He went to La Guardia Community College — in part because Run of Run-DMC had gone there to major in mortuary science — and then to Queens College. He began writing for hip-hop publications. One day first semester, he had an interview with Kool G. Rap. School felt irrelevant. He walked out of class and never returned. He entrusted his fate to hip-hop, and hip-hop breathed possibility into his life.

"If I came out of school without hip-hop, I wouldn't have thought of owning my own business and having power," he said. "As a person of color, to be legit, you think you have to be a worker for someone. Hip-hop made me believe."

But hip-hop was full of bizarre crosscurrents. When he saw white kids simulating his behavior, he got annoyed. It was one thing if they had grown up in the culture. But those well-to-do young whites who tried to appropriate hip-hop for themselves, he says, were simply insecure "image chameleons."

Right here was the enigma of hip-hop: The black rappers certainly weren't preaching integration, inviting whites into their homes. They were telling their often dismal stories, the pathologies they felt had been visited on them by a racist system they yearned to escape. But so many white kids were turning that on its head. They wanted to live life large, the way the rappers did.

A Reason for Rhymes

The phone rang. Dog got it: "He here. We here. I'll hit you back later. You gonna be in the crib?"

It was afternoon. Like a lot of aspiring rappers, Dog and his friend Trife were living life small, passing time in Dog's rampantly messy apartment in Brooklyn's Clinton Hill section. Passing time was what they did most days. They played games, gossiped, drank Hennessy, chewed over the future. Weekends, they went bowling. They were twenty-three, young black men seeking sanctuary from the streets by rhyming their lives.

With their friends Po and Sinbo, they had formed a rap group, Wanted and Respected. Dog's closet was stuffed with recording equipment; his specialty was creating the beats. He made some slim money doing tapes for kids with their own rap dreams ($100 a tape) and selling shirts on the street. The group had played a few clubs, always gratis. Others shuttled in and out, but life weighed on the composition: members kept getting jailed, and one had been killed.

Dog and Trife had followed a trajectory of intense poverty and outlaw life. Dog's grandmother basically raised him—a dozen relatives packed into a three-bedroom place. Trife grew up with his mother, an R & B singer, and seven others in the nearby projects; he still lived there with her.

They had belonged to a gang called the Raiders, they said, selling drugs and doing other things that landed them in prison. If a white person came into their neighborhood, they said, they robbed him. They all packed guns. "It was bad as Beirut," Dog said. Trife said he still sold drugs, and some of the others did dubious things.

A few years ago, they gravitated to rap, embracing it the way so many poor blacks have long embraced basketball. But it was better. There were more slots. And it seemed to demand less talent. "You don't even have to sing well," Dog said.

"Music is my sanity," Trife said. "If I wasn't doing this, I'd probably be doing twenty-five to life."

Dog laughed. "If it weren't for rap, I'd be dead."

Many older blacks felt rap denigrated their race. They hated the constant use of "nigga" in the songs. Dog and Trife shrugged this off. Rap was raw and ugly, but that was their lives, they said. Rap was a blunter truth.

Dog found it curious that whites—suburban mall rats, college backpackers—bought most rap records. "White people can listen to rap, but I know they can't relate," he said. "I hear rap and I'm saying, 'Here's another guy who's had it unfair.' They're taking, 'This guy is cool, he's a drug dealer, he's got all the girls, he's a big person, he killed people.' That is moronic."

Later, Dog said: "Hip-hop is bringing the races together, but on false pretenses to make money. Look at Trife. He's got two felonies. That means he's finished in society. But he can rap. His two felonies, in rap, man, that's a plus."

"It's messed up," Trife said. "In hip-hop, I'm valid when I'm disrespected."

Trife recited some lyrics he had written:

> *You can't walk in my shoes,*
> *If you ain't lived my life.*
> *Hustling all day, clapping out all night.*

The Cool Rich Kids' Movement

The road to Earlham was speckled with billboards for Tom Raper RVs, the Midwest's largest RV dealer. The trees were sheathed in glass from the freezing rain.

Earlham, a small Quaker college, was predominantly white, marginally into hip-hop. Upski was to give a talk, accompanied by a hip-hop group, Rubberoom.

Upski had dropped out of Oberlin College in his junior year. He had only reluctantly gone to college at all. He spent more time doing graffiti and reading magazines than going to class. He wrote an anonymous column for the black paper that scathingly denounced white people. He had a hip-hop radio show: "Yo, this is live from Chicago." Many people thought he was black.

Even so, he says, he was sporadically queasy about his hip-hop moorings. He knew his infatuation with blacks could be taken different ways. He could be accepted as credible, or taken as exploitative.

"That is the great fear of blacks," he said. " 'Oh, you'll be fascinated with us, and then go back to dominating us and you'll be better at it because you'll have inside information.' " When he had shown drafts of his writings about race to a black classmate at Oberlin, she had slipped them back under his door and stopped talking to him.

He committed himself to journalism and activism. As he put it, "I saw it as my job to get white people to talk about race."

In 1994, a year after his influential "wigger" article, he self-published *Bomb the Suburbs*—part memoir of a white man's life in hip-hop, part interviews with hip-hop figures, part treatise on race and social change. It sold an impressive 23,000 copies. The gangsta rapper Tupac Shakur declared it "the best book I read in prison."

Upski hitchhiked around the country, promoting the book, pushing his views on racial cohesion, further cementing his eccentric renown. "I thought white people would start listening to and liking black people," he said, but ultimately, he was discouraged.

He refocused. He would become a social-change agent, motivating whites to be activists. In the fall of 1999, he published *No More Prisons* and began the "Cool Rich Kids' Movement." He would coax cool rich kids to give money to the cause. He started the Active Element Foundation and, with an ally, a well-to-do white woman, also started a group, Reciprocity, that paid him a modest salary. In 2000, he began his college tour.

At Earlham, before a mostly white audience, Upski said: "The thing that drives me is getting to know people and making relationships across race and class, which doesn't happen so much in America. Some of the stuff I'm going to say is going to sound heavy, and you're going to say, 'Let me go smoke some weed and chill.' "

He bounced around the room, his manner that of the motivational speaker. He said: "My goal today is to encourage you to accept the best and worst things about yourself." He talked about how they were too comfortable in this school, and how he had been "saved" by transferring to a black school after sixth grade. And then Rubberoom performed, and a lot of people left and the remaining ones danced. Upski danced.

Upski had brought along a copy of *Stress*, a small hip-hop magazine published by people of color. Upski told the students to read this, not the white-owned magazines.

He used to write for *XXL*, a fledgling magazine with a white owner and publisher. In 1997, the original black editor and black staff quit after being refused an ownership stake. There were innuendos of racism, but whether it was just business or race depended on the vantage point. Upski, however, swore never to work for *XXL* again.

After all, there were always ways for a smart white guy to make money.

Agonizing at the Monkey Academy

When the editor's job at *XXL* was offered to him in August 1999, Elliott Wilson was put in a delicate spot. He was broke. In college, he accepted a flurry of credit cards and bought all the "fly" clothing. Now he owed $8,000.

He remembers thinking about how blacks needed to think more

like whites. "We have a short expectancy in life," he said. "So we go for the quick buck. That's why kids sell drugs. That's why they rob. We don't feel we can be on a five-year plan to success."

The *XXL* job came with excellent pay—low six figures. But talk of racial tension stained the place. He asked himself, he said, could blacks think he was selling out? First, he had to discuss it with the *Ego Trip* collective. He went over to the Monkey Academy.

Two rooms in a Chelsea basement, the Monkey Academy was a shrine to hip-hop. Roosting on a shelf was a "Talking Master P" doll ("Make 'em say uhhh") and a memento from Puff Daddy's 1998 birthday gala. Rap posters adorned the wall: Snoop Doggy Dogg, RZA, Jungle Brothers.

Ego Trip was five young men of color with ambitions of hip-hop entrepreneurship: Wilson, Sacha Jenkins, Jeff Mao, Gabriel Alvarez and Brent Rollins. They saw race as a depressive undercurrent to everything, and it was the focus of their scabrous humor. "We're always talking about the blacks and the whites," Wilson said. "That's the way me and my boys are."

The very name Monkey Academy reflected their saucy attitude. As Jenkins explained it: "Call me paranoid, but when I meet with white people, I feel that with their eyes they're calling me monkey. So why not wear that proudly? Everyone in hip-hop wants to use the N-word, so why not take it to the next level? Call us monkeys." They especially liked to trace their understanding of society to the *Planet of the Apes* movies, where the light-skinned orangutans controlled the dark gorillas.

Several years ago, the group published *Ego Trip*, which they saw as a magazine about race disguised as a hip-hop magazine. They invented a white owner, one Theodore Aloysius Bawno, who offered a message in each issue, blurting his bigoted views and lust for Angie Dickinson. His son, Galen, was a Princeton-educated liberal who professed common cause with blacks. But in truth, he was an unaware bigot, as Wilson says he feels so many young whites are.

So much of the hip-hop ruling class was white. As Wilson put it, *Ego Trip* wanted "to strike at all the black magazines that are white-owned and act as if they're black." It was a small irony that *Ego Trip's* seed money of $8,000 came from a white man, but at least he was a passive partner.

Though it gained a faithful following, *Ego Trip* stayed financially wobbly. No new investors came forth; the collective suspected the reluctance had to do with skin color. *Ego Trip* gasped and expired.

Now its founders scrambled with day jobs and worked on projects like *Ego Trip's Book of Rap Lists* and a companion album. Hip-hop Web sites were proliferating, and they hoped to start one, too. They said they wanted to hear the roar of money, on their terms. "Black people create, but we don't reap the benefits," Wilson said. "We get punked and pimped. If we were white boys, we'd all be rich by now."

On that August day, he recalls, he sat on the couch, his emotions in an uproar. He had to wonder: was he now going to work for a true-life Ted Bawno? The others, he says, expressed a dim view of the *XXL* offer: "They were feeling I was pimping."

Not long before, he had been music editor of *The Source*. One duty was to rate new albums, on a scale of one to five "microphones." When he gave three microphones to *Corruption* by Corrupt, he says, the white publisher, David Mays, increased it to three and a half without telling him. When he confronted Mays, he concluded that the publisher did not respect him. Mays wouldn't give his side, but as Wilson tells it, he quit over half a microphone.

He felt strongly, he recalls, that he had to help himself. He no longer saw hip-hop as a great equalizer. "Who because of hip-hop now believes, 'I've seen the light, I'm going to save the blacks'?" he would say.

Sure, there was something positive in white kids' idolizing black rappers, but "what's going to happen when these white kids lose their little hip-hop jones and go work for Merrill Lynch?" he said.

What should he do? Months later, he remembers the confusion, the vectors of his life colliding. His throat tightened and he began to cry. He went to the bathroom of the Monkey Academy and composed himself. The message left hanging in the air from the others was, Do what you got to do.

As a black man, how many opportunities would come his way? He had this unslaked desire to prove his mettle. He took the job.

Tapping the Unconscious Biases

Upski went to the Laundromat. Shaking in detergent, he talked about how he was a bundle of contradictions, subject to irrational racist phantasms for which he had no cogent defense. "I have patterns like every other white guy that I'm not very aware of that play out as racist," he admitted. He laughed at racist jokes. Walking down the street at night, he felt threatened if he saw a shabbily dressed black man. "I frequently feel I have more of a level of comfort and trust with white people," he said.

He talked differently to black friends ("Yo . . . That's wack . . . Peace, brother."). It infuriated his white girlfriend, Gita Drury. "I'll say to him, 'Do you know you're talking black now? Can you talk white, because that's what you are,' " she said. "I think it's patronizing." When he got on the phone, she could detect at once the caller's race. When he talked black, she would wave a sign at him: "Why are you talking like that?"

She saw this episodic behavior in other ways: "If we walk down the street and a black person walks by, he will give this nod, raise his chin a bit. He wouldn't do it with a white guy. I'll say, 'Oh, you have to prove to a black person that you're down.' "

Not long ago, Upski recalled, he spoke about race at a prominent college along with a black friend. He was paid twice as much as his friend. He spoke longer, but not twice as long. He never told his friend.

Sometimes, he said, he believed that black people were dumber than whites. Sometimes he felt the opposite. Now, as the washers ended their cycles, he hauled the wet clothes to the dryers. A stout black woman stood beside an empty cart. He asked if she was using it. She stared at him, bewildered. He asked again. Nothing.

Exasperated, he simply grabbed the cart and heaped it with his clothes.

Later on, he said: "When that happened, part of my gut reaction was, 'This is a black woman who has limited brain capacity, and it fits my stereotype of blacks having less cognitive intelligence.' "

Would a white woman have understood?

"It's dangerous for me to even say that," he said. "But that's what I thought."

Embarrassed by Rap's "Babies"

The strip club was scattered with patrons with embalmed looks, solemnly quaffing their beverages. Elliott Wilson pulled up a stool beside a dancer. A fistful of dollars flapped from a rubber band curled around her wrist, the night's rewards.

Strip clubs, in particular this one in Queens, had a powerful hold on him. Though rap was his music, he said, he liked to unwind here rather than at a hip-hop club. There, everyone wanted something. Here, no one wanted anything but his money. "I'm not caught up in me and Puffy having each other's cell phone numbers," he said.

He had conflicted feelings about rap and rappers. "A lot of rappers rap about sex and violence, because people are interested in it," he said. "But it's art. It's poetry. If a rapper says, 'Kill your mother' in a song, it doesn't mean kill your mother. You can't take anything at face value." The real-life violence and arrests of rappers were something else. "Rappers are babies," he said. "They don't know how to balance their success and their street life. When I hear about Jay-Z this and Puffy that, I'm embarrassed to be part of the profession."

Wilson and his friend Gabe Alvarez shared an apartment in Clinton Hill, next to Fort Greene, a gentrifying neighborhood promoted by Spike Lee before he moved to the Upper East Side.

"Part of it's good and part isn't," Alvarez said. "You go a block over and there're the drug dealers."

"It's like the classic black neighborhood," Wilson said. "The liquor store, the bodega. I want good restaurants. I don't want to live in the 'hood. Who wants to live in the 'hood?" He wanted to move to Park Slope.

It was not his thing to go out of his way to patronize black businesses. It was fruitless, he said. He had seen that so much in hip-hop. "There's always a white man somewhere making money," he said. "You can't avoid the white man. My going to a black barber or something doesn't do anything."

Upski Meets Dog and Trife

Upski had gone to get his hair cut at the black-owned Freakin U Creations. He only went to black barbers, and part of his manifesto was to direct at least half his money to minority stores. Fort Greene afforded plenty of possibilities. All in all, though, he found the neighborhood imperfect, already too gentrified. His girlfriend lived there, so he did. He had lived in a black neighborhood in Washington. He said he felt he belonged either in a rich white neighborhood, where he could persuade residents to integrate, or in the true 'hood, where he could organize. He mused about moving to East New York.

Upski chatted with one of the owners, Justice Cephas. Two young black men waited their turn. Cephas was a hip-hop promoter on the side and was working with their group. They were Dog and Trife.

Upski said, "Don't take anything off the top."

Dog studied Upski's pate and said, "What's there to take off?"

Upski laughed. He asked how they felt about whites moving into the neighborhood.

"Five years ago, I would have beaten you up just for sitting in that barber chair," Dog told him.

"Oh," Upski said.

"But I've matured," Dog said.

Later, though, he talked about how he was still deeply bitter toward white people. No white person had ever done anything positive for him, he said. As he remarked of whites: "I've never been with you. Why would I want to be with you now?"

Trife added, "If you're not my people now, you're not my people down the line."

Dog and Trife had told Upski about their group, Wanted and Respected. Trife's older brother had started a record label, Trife-Life Records, and they were working on its first album. They hoped to sell it on the street, create some buzz. All the while, Trife said later, he was thinking, "What is this white guy doing in this barbershop?"

Upski smiled. These young men, he said, reminded him of the black friends he used to run with in Chicago. If he were younger, he mused, he might want to run with them.

The Beatles Parallax

Inside Elliott Wilson's *XXL* cubicle was a computer, a stereo and a table strewn with rap albums. The music was on—loud.

His eyes scanned the screen—copy for the next issue. He fiddled with it. "I'm adding curse words," he said. "Putting in *ain'ts*. Making it more hip-hop."

The publisher, Dennis Page, came in with his beneficent smile. "Hey, man, we doing OK?"

"Yeah."

Page peeked over his shoulder at the screen. He nodded: "That's dope."

They went on like that, bantering.

Wilson called his boss DPG—Dennis Page Gangsta, after Snoop

Doggy Dogg's crew, the Dogg Pound Gangstas. Wilson had given DPG an inscribed copy of *Ego Trip's Book of Rap Lists.* He wrote, "I don't care what people say, I know your favorite color is green."

It was how he felt about the relationship. They were both there for the money, he said.

Dennis Page was forty-six. He had the black walk, the black talk. His father had run a liquor store in Trenton, and Page had hung around with black kids and absorbed their ways. Now, he says, he has no real black friends. He admits he's been called a wigger. "I feel stigmatized by black people in hip-hop who feel I'm exploiting them," he said. "I don't feel I'm exploiting. It's a business. The record companies are white-owned. But I feel I take more heat. Certain black people feel that white people shouldn't even buy hip-hop albums, no less write about it. I'm not saying a black man can't buy a Beatles record."

XXL was just going monthly, and its circulation, which it gave as 175,000, was still far below the leading magazines—*Vibe* sold more than 700,000 copies, *The Source* 425,000. *XXL* had been heavily political, clearly aimed at blacks. To build up the white audience, Page and Wilson agreed to tone it down, focus it almost entirely on the music.

"My magazine isn't some white-boy magazine, though," Wilson said. "It's black, too. I'm not sacrificing what *XXL* stands for." Even so, he added, "it can't be totally black if a white man is signing the check."

"I Preach to Mess Up"

Tuesday dawned muggy. It started badly and got worse. Upski was addressing about 250 students at Evergreen State College in Olympia, Washington. Maybe ten weren't white.

He had gathered a panel of half a dozen students. One, Evelyn Aako, was black. Introducing her, he said: "I don't know her very well, but she's black. And she's going to talk about issues of being black on campus."

Aako gave him an arch look. "That was very weird," she recalled thinking. "Like I was a little dark object."

As Upski began talking, the white audience got defensive. One student said: "Why do we have to talk about race? Why can't we talk about how we're alike?"

Aako was getting disgusted. Finally she told Upski: "I've been sitting here with an uncomfortable feeling in my stomach about how you introduced me. I felt tokenized and on display. This follows a tradition where black people serve as entertainment for white people. That's not what I do."

Upski said: "I screwed up. But what can we do? The world is screwed up."

Some white students were looking irritated. One said: "Can't we hear Upski talk? We can talk about race later."

A black student said: "What do you mean later? We never talk about race."

Some whites left. Virtually all the students of color followed. Before leaving, Aako said, "It's not my job to educate you."

Later, Upski sounded no less confident of his ability to stimulate change. But perhaps, he said, he needed to refine his approach.

"I think the main thing that keeps white people from growing is they're afraid to look bad," he said. "So I preach to mess up. One of my blind spots at Evergreen was that Evelyn wasn't going to trust me, that black people and white people, we're still at war."

Increasingly, he said, he was questioning his own evolution. Here he was intent on helping blacks, and spending most of his time in white culture. He had had a string of black girlfriends, but now he was with a white woman. A few years ago, probably two-thirds of his friends were black and Latino. Now it had flip-flopped.

Hip-hop itself had moved away from political and racial talk and for the most part sold excess and riches, women and violence. So much of hip-hop, he said, was self-denigrating, imitative and shallow. It was candy.

"One of the things I have the least respect for about parts of black culture," he said, "is there's so much pain and insecurity that it gets medicated by aping the worst aspects of white culture."

He talked about how so many of his old black and Latino graffiti friends hadn't survived hip-hop too well. One got locked up for fire-bombing a car. Another fell from a fire escape while trying to rob an apartment. He is now a paraplegic, drinking away his life, Upski said.

And yet, Upski had to admit, he was cruising along. His girlfriend, Drury, had inherited money, though they lived modestly. He didn't earn a lot, but he didn't worry. Until recently, he never took cabs and rarely ate out; he called it flaunting privilege. But now he was traveling more in white circles where everyone took cabs and ate out. So he did, too. And, he acknowledged, he liked it.

"The part of Billy that wanted to be black for a good part of his youth, that's fading," Drury said. "One of the issues in our relationship is he's a chameleon. The thing with Billy, he wants to be liked."

He had always cared so much about how he looked through black eyes, he said. Now his success depended on how he looked through white eyes. He had always dressed poorly and now he owned three suits. Where was he going? he wondered. As you got older, holding on to your hip-hop values seemed a lot harder if you were white.

Traps and Trappings of Success

Elliott Wilson climbed the stairs to the basketball court. The old guys were already there. The doctor had told him he had high blood pressure, a real slap in the face. "I've got the black man's disease," he joked.

Who knew the factors, but he had never eaten properly. He was also feeling the pressure of his job, he said. A friend who had been editor of *The Source* said the same thing had happened to him.

His doctor put him on medication, urged exercise. So he had begun playing full-court basketball three mornings a week. There was an early crowd of young guys, but Wilson wasn't ready for them. He played with a bunch of white guys, some in their fifties and sixties, and one black guy in his seventies. He hit some baskets and missed some. He changed and headed for XXL.

He had now edited four issues. The first one, with DMX on the cover, had outsold any previous issue. He felt he was making a mark, he said. He had his disputes with Dennis Page, but they got along. His *Ego Trip* comrades felt proud of him.

He was making such good money, more than three times what Upski made, but somehow, he said, that wasn't the point. What he really wanted was to "take *The Source* out in a year or two," then expand the reaches of *Ego Trip*. Still, there were always seeds of self-doubt.

"Do I feel secure?" he said. "No. Because I'm black and I have bad credit. Having bad credit in this country is like being a convict. You don't have a prosperity mind-set when you're a person of color. You have something, you always feel someone is going to take it. You're always on edge, wondering what next."

"I Just Want the Money"

Dog twirled the dials and gave Trife the signal to start. In the tiny apartment, Dog and Trife and Sinbo and Po were rehearsing for their album, the one they hoped might be destiny's next chosen one.

Scrizz, Trife's brother and the CEO of Trife-Life Records, was listening like a jittery father. With no product yet, Trife-Life was not a paying job for him. His background, like that of the others, was drugs and crime. At the moment, he was out on bail while fighting an assault charge.

Wanted and Respected started in on its song "All the Time." Golden bars of light streaked through the windows. Scrizz tapped his foot. He, too, had a got-to-happen mentality. He didn't much care who bought the album, white or black, but he knew where the money was. "I just want them to eat it up," he said. "I just want the money."

It came down to that. A group of young black guys in Brooklyn rhyming their lives, betting on a brighter tomorrow sponsored by white kids' money.

Dog turned up the music. They cleared their throats and kept rapping.

Through the fall of 2000, Billy Wimsatt continued to pursue his causes and seek support for his foundations, and Elliott Wilson continued to serve as editor of XXL *magazine and remained part of* Ego Trip. *In late October 2000, Dog and Trife and their rap group, Wanted and Respected, released their first single, "Fix Ya Face," on the Trife-Life label created by Trife's brother. The song managed to get some radio time, and the group members were selling copies themselves on the streets of New York. From the proceeds, they intended to produce a second single and their first album.*

Sergeant Maria Brogli (right) going over tactical plans for warrants to be served with undercover narcotics agents and Detective Johnny Gonzalez (left), who was formerly an undercover agent. Angel Franco/The New York Times

13

Why Harlem Drug Cops Don't Discuss Race

MICHAEL WINERIP

NEW YORK, NEW YORK

Friday, February 25, 2000, at 5 P.M., there wasn't a single narcotics officer on the streets of Harlem. Everyone was being held inside on standby in case of a race riot. The Diallo verdict was about to come down.

On East 107th Street, at the police headquarters for Harlem narcotics, cops gathered around several televisions to watch the verdict, a couple of hundred plainclothes officers in two big rooms, maybe a third of them black and Hispanic. They appeared from interviews to be split racially, much as people had been by the O. J. Simpson case. The whites — officers like Sergeant Maria Brogli and Detectives Lee Macklowe and John Montes — hoped the four Diallo officers would be found not guilty. The blacks — detectives like Johnny Gonzalez and the undercovers Derrick and Rob — felt they should be found guilty on at least some counts. "Forty-one shots," said Derrick. "That's excessive."

Feelings ran deep. No case in recent years has hit the police closer to home. As Brogli said, "There but for the grace of God. . . ." Every officer with any sense, white or black, fears mistakenly shooting an unarmed man like Amadou Diallo. Talk about jamming up a career.

All eight members of Sergeant Brogli's narcotics team have stories about almost squeezing the trigger. In Detective Gonzalez's case, he remembers running after a drug dealer, Earl Thomas, on 143rd Street, and as he got close, the man dropped to the ground and with his back to Gonzalez, reached into his waistband. "MAN WITH A GUN!" is what flashed through Gonzalez's mind. In a split second, the detective had to decide: shoot, or jump him and risk being shot. He risked it. This time, Earl Thomas was reaching in to dump his drugs before being arrested.

"I almost shot an unarmed man in the back," said Gonzalez. "It would've been the end of my career. I would have been like the Diallo cops."

But dark-skinned plainclothes officers have a second, more chilling fear: that someday, a white officer will accidentally shoot them. And that, they said, made them view the Diallo case differently.

Several years ago, before going undercover, Derrick recalls being in street clothes, on his way to work at the 63rd Precinct in Brooklyn, when he saw an elderly woman being robbed by two teenagers. He managed to get the woman into his car, subdue the attackers (though he had no handcuffs) and persuade a passerby to call 911—an effort that would win him a hero's medal. But as he waited for backup, he was scared. Most officers at the 63rd were away at a funeral that day. He feared that the officers who showed up would not know him, and that he would be in danger—a black man in street clothes with a gun. Seeing a patrol car approach, he waved his police ID over his head and kept screaming: "I'm a cop! I'm a cop!"

Race colors everything for Harlem narcotics detectives. It lies beneath the surface in a dispute over tactics between a white sergeant and a black undercover detective. Race is out there in the neighborhood where Brogli's team pits African-American informers against Dominican drug dealers. Race is in the police radio descriptions ("suspect is a dark-skinned Dominican, mid-twenties . . ."), and race amplifies the anger on the street when the police drive up and arrest yet another dark-skinned man.

The biggest police race case in New York City in years, Diallo—the 1998 killing of a black man standing in the doorway of his Bronx building by four panicky white policemen—touched every Harlem narcotics officer in the room that day to the core. And yet Brogli's team had never discussed it. Cops do not discuss race. It's too risky. They need to get along.

As the Diallo verdict was read charge by charge that rainy February evening and it became evident that the four officers would be cleared on every count, Brogli was so delighted she felt almost as if she had been personally exonerated, and Derrick was so bitter he could not stop pacing. But despite the enormous emotion of the moment, the whites did not cheer or whoop; the blacks showed no outrage. There was barely a sound in the room.

Working a Brown Neighborhood

When Sergeant Brogli sees a dozen brown-skinned Dominican men standing on the corner of 141st Street and Broadway in Harlem, she thinks, "Drug dealers."

"Most are involved in drugs, probably," she says. "That's the best assumption I can make."

And even though she is a five-foot-tall woman dressed in everyday clothes and driving an ordinary van, the moment they see her, they give the warning whistle that means "cops on the block, five-oh, policia."

"*La Terrible*," they whisper as she approaches. "*La Bruja*" ("the Witch").

The very visible, white Brogli could not do her work without her undercover detectives, whose dark skin renders them invisible on these streets.

For five years Detective Johnny Gonzalez, himself Dominican-American, was an undercover for Brogli, posing as a drug user, a brown man disappearing into a brown neighborhood. He'd buy the drugs, leave the scene, radio in a description of the dealer, and then Brogli and her team of mainly white investigators would speed their vans up the street and grab that one man from the dozen on the corner.

So deft is the whole thing when done properly that dealers don't have a clue which person they sold to was the undercover cop. Often they don't figure it out until months later, when they go to trial and the undercover is there on the stand.

"Can I ask what you're taking me in for?" a surprised Victor Figueroa said when arrested during a buy-and-bust one evening in May 2000 as he stood at 141st Street and Hamilton Place with $2,650 in his pockets.

Brogli always has the same answer: "You really don't know what you did? You'll find out."

Smart cops like Brogli and Gonzalez know how to use race wisely, how to turn race to their advantage to enforce the law.

For five years, Detective Gonzalez—nicknamed Johnny G.—returned over and over to the same five blocks, 140th to 145th Streets, sometimes making $5 "nick" buys, sometimes buying thousands of dollars in cocaine, and never was he found out. Among Harlem drug cops he is a legend, an easygoing, jokey, charming, streetwise man who, occasionally, when things went wrong, got in fistfights with dealers but took pride in never having used his gun. Dealers loved Johnny G. They invited him into their apartments, they kidded with him, their mothers fed him, their girlfriends flirted with him and most important, they trusted him, enough to sell him their drugs, more than five hundred buys, hundreds of arrests, hundreds of guilty pleas and convictions.

On the streets, Johnny G. used whatever he could to get an edge. Usually he pretended to be African-American, acting as if he knew only English. Then the Spanish-speaking dealers would talk openly in front of him, sometimes spilling their secrets. But other times he bought from Dominican dealers who hated blacks, who would make blacks wait for their drugs, who would tell their steerers in Spanish, "Have all the monkeys stand over there."

"Then I'd be Dominican," said Gonzalez. "To get done faster."

He was so smooth at switching it on and off, from Dominican to African-American, from cop to cokehead, that at times his wife, Sonia, would catch him slipping into a street character as he played with their two little sons and would gently remind him, "Johnny, you're home now, you're not working."

The Perils of Going In Cold

Gonzalez may be Dominican, but when he sees those young Dominican men on that corner, he has the same reaction as Brogli: "Ninety percent are working in drugs."

Still, he insists, he does not stoop to racial profiling. He would not go cold into a corner full of black and brown men and try to make a buy, he says, unless his investigators had gathered evidence that a specific dealer was operating there. They should be able to tell him whether the dealer is selling in grams or ounces, crack, coke or heroin, whether it's shiny "fish scale" or powdery, whether the brand name is New World Order or Bazooka, so he knows what to ask for.

That is where Gonzalez draws the line between good police work and racial profiling. "It's insulting to walk up to a guy just because he's black or Dominican standing on a corner and say, 'Who's working?' " That is the distinction he makes between using race fairly and misusing race.

At times, he says, white sergeants have told him, "Go over to that group of Domos and see who's working."

"You can't say no to a direct order," Gonzalez said. "You just go up, walk past and tell the sergeant nothing's going on." A dozen black and Hispanic undercovers working with him in Harlem said in interviews that they had defied a sergeant's orders in the same way.

Among these undercovers, Brogli is a favorite, the rare white sergeant with a reputation for listening to undercovers and speaking up for them. "Maria has a mouth on her," says Rob, one of her undercovers. In May, 2000 as the team put together a list of buy-and-bust locations, a white investigator, Lee Macklowe, said he had a tip that cocaine was being sold from a street-level window on 140th near Hamilton.

"Just bang on the window," he said. But Brogli was upset. She made him call his informer. "Find out if they're selling nicks, grams, dimes," she said.

Later, the undercover making that buy, Nelson, quietly thanked her. "Way to go, Sarge," he said.

Going in cold increases the risk. Some narcotics officers, including Brogli, suspect that is what went wrong earlier this year when Patrick Dorismond, an unarmed black man, was killed during a buy-and-bust by an undercover near Times Square. It may have been a case, they say, of a narcotics team working late, one body short of the nightly quota of five arrests, approaching a group of black men cold and having it blow up in their faces.

Dark-skinned undercovers are touchy about racial profiling because most, including Gonzalez, say that when off duty, in their neighborhoods or out driving, they have been targets of white officers. One undercover, Tyrone, says that while driving home from work to Brooklyn he gets stopped an average of one night a week. Two of Brogli's black undercovers, Derrick and Rob, describe standing outside Rob's home in Brooklyn after work, having a beer, and being approached by a man who asked, "Who's working?"

Derrick and Rob didn't bother explaining to that plainclothes cop that they, too, were cops. They just shook their heads and waited until he left. "You know it's because we're black," Derrick said.

"You develop thick skin," Gonzalez said. Besides, working with Brogli for seven years—first as an undercover and for the last two years as an investigator—he has learned there are harder things than being a black policeman. "Females on the job have it worse," he said.

He thinks it is what makes Brogli a fairer boss than most whites; a female officer knows what it's like being in the minority.

Lately, he has been worried that she may be leaving narcotics and he may be assigned a new sergeant. And in an office where the top boss, the captain, changes every few months, where conditions are so cheesy that officers have to bring in their own toilet paper and lock it in their desks, your sergeant is often your only protection.

A Trained Eye Sees Blue

Maria Brogli is no bleeding heart. She is an aggressive Italian-American cop who has tackled men resisting arrest and slammed others against walls, who has been kicked and punched, had her nose broken and a flowerpot dropped on her head, and still got the collar. She thinks race is overblown as a police problem, but will not watch *The Sopranos*, the television series on the Mafia, because she feels it is biased against Italian-Americans.

Going up cold to blacks on a corner doesn't bother her because it's racial profiling. It bothers her because it's lazy and risky.

And she cannot abide laziness. In recent years, her team has ranked first or second, among the forty-five units working northern Manhattan, for felony arrests, search warrants, drugs confiscated. While most sergeants are satisfied doing buy-and-busts, twice she has undertaken complex yearlong investigations that involved extensive wiretaps.

When asked about dealing with race on the job, she says, "I don't see black and white, I see blue." But she is not blind about blue. In the mid-1990s, during a scandal at the 30th Precinct, two informers fed her tips on corrupt officers. She drove the informers to the internal affairs office in Harlem, contributing to the convictions of Officers George Nova and Alphonso Compres.

She is a short, stocky, unglamorous thirty-eight-year-old woman who has attained respect in a department dominated by white men. Her lieutenant, James Byrne, likes to smoke a cigar in the van and offer comments on young female passersby. ("Wouldn't you like to spoil that one?" is a favorite.)

She never expected to be a cop. After attending racially mixed Bronx public schools and scoring 1400 on her SATs, she was premed at New York University. But her father, a commercial photographer, suffered a stroke, and she needed a job to support the family. She applied in 1983. A requirement then was clearing a five-foot wall—no easy task for a woman who *claims* to be five feet tall. She practiced, she prayed to St. Anthony, but on the first of two tries she failed. "There was a tall black instructor," she recalled. "He says: 'What's the matter, munchkin? You can get over the wall. When you're running, don't look at the wall, look beyond the wall.' "

That is a pretty fair metaphor for her rise in the department. As a rookie, she was repeatedly given the complaint room, traditional duty for women, typing forms. Whenever possible, she traded for patrol, working her way onto the streets. In 1990, after passing the sergeant's test, she was sent to the 28th Precinct in Harlem, hard duty for any white, let alone the first female supervisor assigned there. As is the rule on the force, a separate supervisor's locker room was provided, by moving a wall of lockers to partition off a corner of the women's room for her. "You could hear them laughing on the other side of the lockers and you're alone," she recalled. She learned to bang her locker when she entered, so cops on the other side knew she was no snoop.

In narcotics she gets impressive numbers, in part because no one puts in longer hours. A single woman living with her widowed mother, she often stays past midnight.

But her success also comes from pushing hard on the street. It is because of officers like Brogli that men in this neighborhood learn always to carry identification. Though there is no law saying they must, they know if they don't, and are stopped, they can be hauled into the precinct for a few hours, their names run through the computer for outstanding warrants.

On May 9, her team did a buy-and-bust at 141st and Amsterdam, arresting Pedro Pereira and confiscating $1,374. Standing on the same corner was Juan Payano, thirty. He didn't have drugs or much money. Nor did he have identification; he said he couldn't remember his address.

"He don't know where he lives?" Brogli asked. "He's got no ID?"

"He says he's only been here fifteen days and he's legal," said her senior detective, Felix Berrios, interpreting the Spanish.

"Does he know he can be arrested for no ID?" said Brogli, who kept him standing there about ten minutes. "Ask him if he wants to go to jail." He didn't. "Ask him where he lives again."

"Riverside between 136 and 137."

"Is he going to learn the building number now?" Brogli asked.

"He says he'll never forget."

Later the sergeant said: "I wanted to see if he changed his story and got nervous and blurted anything out. I think he's lying through his teeth."

A Racial Chameleon

It is as if Johnny Gonzalez was raised to be an undercover. He grew up in a working-class Dominican family (his father was a welder, his mother a beautician), in Brownsville, a tough African-American section of Brooklyn where he would see Mike Tyson and Riddick Bowe on the streets. He attended P.S. 41, a black school, then went to I.S. 302, a Puerto Rican school, where his Spanish helped. "If you met me when I was in elementary school, you'd assume I was black," he says. "But with Puerto Rican kids I became Puerto Rican."

When he began dating Sonia, a Puerto Rican, her dad was nice until he realized this boyfriend was Dominican. "Dad would not answer the door," she said. "My father used to say, 'He's a Dominican man, they don't know how to treat Spanish women.' "

Sonia, who is also a cop, says her co-workers assume that Johnny is black. Sometimes even she teases him, "Johnny, what are you, anyway?"

He applied to the department in 1987, but failed the psychological test. At the time, the test was being challenged in court as biased against minorities; under an appeals procedure, he was allowed to see a nondepartmental psychologist, and was approved after a two-year delay.

The first whites he and his wife knew well were cops. A few years ago, he moved to Long Island for the schools; it took the family time to adjust. "There was a blond boy, Jimmy, across the street," Gonzalez recalled. "When my son Mark saw him, he said: 'Dad, what's wrong with him? He doesn't have any color.' "

More Risks, More of the Time

When Sergeant Brogli needed a new undercover, she looked at photos of two black officers she had never met and picked one.

"It's like the NBA draft," said Rob, a black undercover, who has been traded among narcotics teams a few times. "They say, 'Grab him, he's a big black body.' " There is a logic to it—the poorest neighborhoods tend to be black or Hispanic and often have the biggest street narcotics problems. A minority undercover is less conspicuous.

But it means that from Day 1, when a team is assembled, race enters the room. Narcotics headquarters looks as racially divided as a school cafeteria. The undercovers sit together. In their free time they play backgammon. They tend to be younger and city-bred; many own motorcycles.

The jobs they do are different, and that sets them apart, too. Most police work can be dangerous, but day in and day out, undercovers take more risks. Detective Gonzalez has been locked in a dealer's apartment with a gun to his head; he has had his jaw broken; he has been accused of being a cop several times by dealers and has had to lie his way out of booby-trapped apartments. Often, he has worked without a gun.

On the other hand, to protect their identities, undercovers are excused from the daily duties that make police work miserable. They do not have to transport sick, angry or foul-smelling prisoners ("stinkies") to jail; execute search warrants; or do crowd control at events like the Diallo protests. They are not allowed to have their full names or photographs used in the press.

While other cops do grunt jobs, undercovers play backgammon. Resentment builds. Race isn't mentioned, but it's there. Returning from executing a tedious search warrant, Detective Macklowe noticed an undercover's car parked in the lot. "How do these kids afford BMWs?" he asked.

Gonzalez would not let the comment pass. "They live at home," he said. "They're not carrying a big mortgage." Indeed, it is a constant gripe among undercovers that they get pushed for more buys by white bosses seeking more overtime to pay off their heavily mortgaged houses out by Exit 68 on the Long Island Expressway.

The two groups of officers do not always communicate well.

"OK, this is how it's going to work," Sergeant Joe Simonetti said one day in the summer of 1999, outlining a series of buy-and-busts. He told Nelson, who had been working as an undercover less than a year, to make two buys: a $10 crack buy and a $300 cocaine buy. Several veteran undercovers winced. To do a $10 buy, you dress down, like a crackhead; for the other buy you need to look groomed, moneyed. You can't be both at once.

When Simonetti had finished giving orders, several from Brogli's team working backup, including Gonzalez, put on bulletproof vests, then piled into the elevator to head out. Just before the door closed Nelson rushed up. Gonzalez could see fear in the young undercover's eyes. "He wants me to do both," Nelson said.

"That's crazy," said Gonzalez. "It's your call. You have to know what's safe and watch out for yourself." As the elevator door shut, Nelson knew what to do.

Same Show, Nth Performance

Narcotics enforcement is a frustrating cat-and-mouse game between officers and dealers who, after years of crackdowns, are savvy about dividing and concealing each step of the operation. Rarely do the police get the drugs, the money and the dealer together. Repeatedly Brogli's team arrests dealers, and the next day, standing in that very spot, there is someone else — or even the same person.

In November 1999, they executed a search warrant at the basement apartments at 605 West 141st Street, where some tenants are so poor they live in luggage storage bins. In the room of Ramon Ortiz, the superintendent, Detective Rob Arbuiso found drug paraphernalia, including a scale; a hundred plastic sandwich bags commonly used to package cocaine; and $132,750 in cash. The money was confiscated as drug profits. Ortiz was notified that he could reclaim it if he proved he had earned it legitimately; he never has. But they found no drugs, and Ortiz was quickly back on the street. His misdemeanor charge on paraphernalia possession is still pending.

Weeks later, they searched in the same building, hitting Apartment 21, which was leased to an elderly woman who had recently had a liver transplant.

"We're going to knock instead of banging down the door," Simonetti said. "We don't want to give her a heart attack."

Inside, near a painting of the Virgin Mary, were two bedrooms that she sublet, both equipped with locks. In one room was a sleeping Dominican, who was forced into the hall in his underwear, cuffed and questioned. He told Gonzalez he had no idea who lived in the other bedroom, had never seen anyone going or coming. In that second bedroom officers found a plastic bag containing about $60,000 worth of cocaine. The old woman with the new liver said that she had never seen anyone go in or out of that room. And neither she nor the man in his underpants had a key for it.

As Lieutenant Byrne mulled over whom to arrest, a man rushed up the stairs. He said that his name was Alberto Rivera Jr., and that he was the old woman's son.

At first he said he lived there; when he heard why the police were there, he said he didn't. Gonzalez asked if Rivera had an ID, and before he knew it, Rivera was reaching into his pants.

"Don't do that until I tell . . ." began Gonzalez, but it was too late. Rivera was pointing a dark brown wallet at the detective, who started, then relaxed. "Don't be making any fast moves like that," the officer sighed.

In the end the lieutenant compromised. He said he doubted that charges against the old woman would stick and didn't want her dropping dead in the prisoner van; he was suspicious of the son but had nothing. So he decided on the man in underpants. "We don't want to be embarrassed going into the neighborhood and coming out with no one," the lieutenant said. "This sends a message." They would take him to the precinct, check for outstanding warrants, and then, if he was clean, let him go. All of which they did.

To cops, who often feel they're in a losing battle against the dealers, it's a way to apply some leverage, maybe persuade someone to inform; in the neighborhoods, it smacks of racial profiling.

On these streets, dark-skinned men are often stopped, questioned, then let go. In May 2000, Simonetti's team searched 601 West 141st Street, Apartment 41. As several officers entered the apartment, others detained fifteen men standing on the nearby corner of 141st and Broadway. Inside the apartment, the cops reported a rare trifecta: they seized 1.5 kilos of cocaine and about $3,000, and arrested eighteen-year-old Jorge Rodriguez (who subsequently fled and was being sought on a bench warrant).

Outside on the street, the police lined up the detained men against a wall to see if any had keys to Apartment 41. Sometimes this works; a few weeks before, on the same block, they caught two dealers this way. This time no one had a matching key. One man had a small amount of coke and was arrested; a second had $2,000 in cash and a Kenwood two-way radio. There was another Kenwood inside the apartment, but the frequency didn't match. He and the other fourteen were let go after half an hour.

As the police searched the men, a mainly Dominican crowd gathered, joking with the cops. Pointing at the men on the corner, a young woman called out, "Why are you bothering them? They're just working," and the crowd and cops shared a laugh.

But just as often, the crowd turns nasty. The previous year, Flor Blum was arrested for buying $35 of crack. When she realized she would be handcuffed and put in the prisoner van, she began screaming. In the back of the van, she hurled herself against the walls, slamming her body against Gonzalez and his partner, Detective Scott Signorelli. "Please let me go, let me get out of here!" she screamed. "I'm phobic!"

They tried to calm her, but she kept screaming. "I need water! I have AIDS, sir! I swear, I don't want to do this! It's only a job to you. What do you care?" She began hacking up phlegm, spitting all over the back of the van. Gonzalez could not tell: Was she high? Having an anxiety attack? Faking it? Might she go into cardiac arrest? That could end a cop's career fast. They stopped and bought her a bottle of Poland Spring, but she continued to scream and thrash so much, the van rocked. "My T-cells are going down! Please let me go, sir!" When they parked on 135th Street to try to calm her, a crowd gathered outside the rocking van. "What are they doing?" a woman asked. "Are they beating her?"

"They're beating her?" yelled a second woman. Suddenly there was a bang on top of the van; someone had hurled an egg off a roof at the police. Gonzalez drove off. Blum screamed the whole way to the precinct. Later she apologized, saying, "I just get phobic." She was given a desk appearance ticket and took a taxi home. Ultimately, charges were dismissed.

All of this makes narcotics officers feel bitter, as if it were the 1920s and they were reliving Prohibition. "Everyone sees this is a joke," said Jason, an undercover. "They know we ain't putting no dent in drugs."

Lieutenant Byrne, who oversees Sergeant Brogli's team, says the only answer is legalizing drugs. "In my humble opinion, we're doing nothing up here," he said after another long day of buy-and-busts.

There Goes the Neighborhood

It's supposedly common knowledge: black New Yorkers distrust the police. But on the streets where Brogli works, the biggest supporters of the police are African-American. In the last fifteen years, this neighborhood may have changed from primarily African-American to Dominican, but the citizens council that meets monthly at the local precinct, the 30th, is headed by an African-American, Hazel O'Reilly, and dominated by African-Americans. At council meetings it is mainly black residents who attend to ask for *more* police enforcement, *more* drug arrests, who want *more* people jailed for loitering and trespassing.

Detective John Montes, a Hispanic cop who walked a beat for two years before joining Sergeant Brogli's team, says his best informers here were black. On these streets, the African-Americans are frequently the older, better-established families who moved here in the 1950s. Many are middle-class government workers, small-business owners and professionals, and often they are resentful that Spanish is now the primary language spoken in the Broadway shops; that able-bodied Dominican men line the sidewalks all hours of the day; and that the police consider the neighborhood drug trade, controlled by Dominicans, the worst in the city.

At a 30th Precinct meeting, an African-American homeowner asked that the police do loitering sweeps, calling in the National Guard if necessary. The woman, a single professional with a master's degree, complained in an interview about the Dominicans: "They hang out on the corners—they have so many children. When I go into one of their stores, I try to line up to buy something the American way, but it's all chaos, the Dominican customers all milling, they don't know how to go in order."

In a dozen interviews in their homes, African-Americans complained about Dominicans ruining the neighborhood, sounding very much like the Jews and Italians who once dominated this area and began leaving forty years ago, complaining about the blacks moving in.

Citing fear of retribution from dealers, all but one refused to be cited by name. The one who allowed her last name to be used, Mrs. Roper, ran a beauty shop but moved "when the neighborhood started going down because of the Dominicans."

"We had a nice building, until we got a Dominican superintendent and every time an apartment came available, he'd put in some of them, and each one looked like a drug dealer," said Mrs. Roper, a great-grandmother and a member of the scholarship committee at her Baptist church. "They'd play their music so loud, and this one time, a Dominican boy ran into our place and stole the money for the electric and a gold chain. I tell you the Dominicans destroy everything."

Dominicans Take the Rap

Everyone at headquarters has a racial or ethnic identity and gets needled about it. Lee Macklowe, a Jew, is introduced to a Jewish reporter as "a fellow member of the tribe." When Sergeant Simonetti treats his team to bagels, he lifts up a dark brown one and yells to Detective Luis Nieves-Diaz, a black-skinned Puerto Rican: "The pumpernickel's for you, Lou! Heh-heh!"

The one slur rarely spoken is "nigger." In a year's time, a reporter did not hear it. Whether that was because, as Sergeant Brogli says, this generation has been conditioned against it, or because, as Derrick, a black undercover, says, racial animosity still runs too deep to joke about the word, it seemed off-limits.

On the other hand, in these streets where most arrested for drugs are Dominican, it's open season on "Domos." Many are from poor, rural parts of their Caribbean island, where record-keeping isn't precise, and officers making arrests jokingly wonder if the Domo will know his birth date.

Sergeant Neil Nappi, who is white, was trying to help Brogli's team persuade an arrested Dominican to give up information about a drug ring. In the midst of questioning him, Nappi started talking about Dominican women. "They're beautiful, but big trouble," he said to another officer. "You don't want to knock 'em up. There's a couple of little redheaded Dominican kids running around, belong to guys at the 30th. Cops get their checks garnished, it breaks up marriages— they're dangerous." As the cop spoke the Dominican man stared at the floor; he provided no useful information that day.

But there are times when the stereotype is true—that the able-bodied dark-skinned man standing on the corner day after day is up to something—and playing all the obvious hunches may pay off for the police.

In September 1999, Brogli's team bought drugs on 141st Street. Soon the van pulled up, and while Hector Espinal stood among a group of Dominican men, Detectives Gonzalez and Montes quietly arrested and cuffed him.

"Why'm I getting locked up?" he asked. A woman with a baby said, "He's just standing here." In Espinal's pocket was a Progressive Labor Party flier, headlined "Racist Cops Kill Workers in Cold Blood."

Back at the 30th, doing the paperwork, two detectives could not agree on whether Espinal's eyes were hazel or brown. "Hector, look at me," said Brogli, getting so close you could barely squeeze a dime between them. "Light brown," she said, and while she had his attention, she mentioned that he might be able to knock some prison time off by cooperating. She did not tell him that based on an investigation, they believed he belonged to a ring run by a dealer with the street name D.B.

"I'm not a drug dealer," Espinal said.

"We'll go upstairs and talk," Detective Berrios said.

They took him to a windowless interrogation room, where he sat at a table, one hand cuffed to the wall, and sipped a Poland Spring they had bought him. "I go up on that block, but I mind my business," Espinal said. "I'm not out there with anybody else. All I do is hang out there and smoke weed."

"We're telling you, you sold drugs," Brogli said.

"Hector, I'm going to treat you like a man, not a boy," Montes said.

"I don't work for anybody," Espinal repeated.

"One-shot offer," Brogli said. "Talk now or the offer's gone."

"I don't know about sales," Espinal said. "I'm just trying to get it in my mouth."

"You have kids?" Berrios asked. Espinal said he wasn't married.

"Yeah," Berrios said, "but you got a kid, right?"

"Saturday he turned one," Espinal said.

"You don't think about the kid now," Berrios said, adding that Espinal could face fifteen years. "You won't see him until he turns seventeen possibly, and by that time he could have him another daddy." They all stared while Espinal swigged Poland Spring. "What are you thinking about?" Brogli asked.

"You doubt if we are telling you the truth," Berrios said.

"I don't work with nobody," Espinal repeated.

"You have exactly one minute," Brogli said.

Espinal mumbled something. The cinder-block room went dead as a tomb. Next time he said it loud and clear: He got his stuff from "some cat named D.B."

"So you get it from D.B.," Montes said.

"D.B.'s that chubby kid," Espinal said. "I'm not big like you think. I just got a lot of years in the stuff."

They said they knew he had to be a seller, an able-bodied man, with no steady job, hanging on the street.

"I don't got a lot of expenses," he said. "I stay with my mother, plus I had a legal job—back in '96."

"So you only make a couple of bucks," Brogli said.

"Just to feed my child and my mother and my girlfriend and me," Espinal said. "Not to bring no guns, or no kilos."

"How you get in contact with him?" Montes asked.

"On the block," Espinal said. "D.B. used to live with his girlfriend, but don't anymore."

"To feed you, your mother, your baby and your girl, he's got to be around a lot," Montes said.

"Even his ex don't know where D.B. lives," Espinal said.

Montes asked if D.B. lived with his mother.

"I don't be talking to that crackhead bitch," said Espinal (who was indicted on drug-selling charges and faced trial).

Looking Out for Each Other

Members of a police team spend enormous amounts of time together. They discuss all forms of personal minutiae, including their dental work, their sleeping problems, whether they're having regular bowel movements and which relatives they're not getting along with.

They do not discuss race. They did not discuss Diallo.

And yet when the verdict came down, from interviewing them separately it was clear that each group knew how the other felt. Neither could afford to offend the other; light and dark, they needed each other to get home safely at day's end.

And so, the eerie silence after the verdict.

Despite the racial divides in that room, at some point, most had helped out when others were jammed up. When Pete, one of the few white undercovers, was new, he had a terrible time making buys. His first month he did only two, well short of the five quota. Johnny Gonzalez took him aside and gave him tips about blending in, like finding a group of druggies to stand in line with and taking care to hand over the money in the same wrist motion as the guy before you. But more than that, he leveled with Pete. He told him that as a white, he wouldn't be able to act like a brown Spanish guy. It helped Pete create his own character. Pete changed, from jivey white dude to homeless crackhead. His record is now thirteen buys in a month.

On the other hand, Gonzalez, a gifted street cop, is weak on writing skills and awful about finishing his paperwork. At one point Lieutenant Byrne threatened to dock him a few days, for work that was months overdue, and told Brogli to stay out of it. ("I want to put the fear of God in him," the lieutenant said.) Even so, the sergeant called Gonzalez at home late at night and gave him tips on writing the forms in his own words.

In the two years between Amadou Diallo's death and the announcement of the verdict, Brogli spent perhaps 5,000 hours with Derrick and Gonzalez. They may never have discussed the case, but she knew their hearts. "Derrick's thinking it could have been him standing in that doorway," Brogli said after the verdict.

Those were the very words Derrick used when asked later. "It could have been us," he said. "It could've been an undercover."

Up the Ladder

In May 2000, the new civil service list for lieutenants came out. Sergeant Brogli has friends all over the department, and one who got an early peek called her at home: "Is this *Lieutenant* Brogli?"

"Ma!" she called out. "I made the list!"

The police bureaucracy moves in inscrutable ways, and it could be months before the promotion takes effect and she is transferred. Fearing her departure, Gonzalez has been looking around. He is not a good test taker, did poorly on the sergeant's exam. Like a lot of blacks and Hispanics, he took the undercover job because it put him on a fast track for a detective's shield and higher pay. It is a common avenue for minorities who either aren't good test takers or don't want the responsibility of being a sergeant.

But at thirty-five, after doing five years as an undercover and two years as an investigator, he says he feels too old to return to that life, and now the options are less glamorous. Ideally he would like to stay with Brogli until she changes jobs, and he said to her, "Maria, if you just tell me to stay, I will."

That's what she wanted, too. She's crazy about Johnny G., even if his paperwork is a nightmare. But she knew he had a couple of offers pending and it would be unfair to ask. "The door that opens now may not be open later," she said, and they laughed because she sounded like one of those fortune cookies that come with the Chinese takeout they order on the overnight tour.

Out with Prejudice

Years ago, when Gonzalez was on uniformed housing patrol in Red Hook, Brooklyn, white officers couldn't tell what he was by looking at him and were guarded until reading his name tag. "Then they'd say, 'Oh, you're Gonzalez—these blacks, aren't they like animals with all their kids?' "

"Now I'm in a Dominican neighborhood," he said. "I'll hear some sergeant, not knowing I'm around, talking about Domos this, Domos that."

"I had a white cop ask me, 'How many in your family are drug dealers?' " said Gonzalez, who doesn't drink alcohol. "I told him, in my family, nobody."

If the police can be too quick to label, Gonzalez says, they are only reflecting society.

On a warm afternoon, dressed as usual in plain clothes, he met downtown with a prosecutor about a case, then stopped in a deli near Chinatown for an iced tea. One sip and he nearly spit it out. He knew immediately it was the extra-sweet tea that heroin addicts on methadone often crave. "Sorry," said the Asian woman behind the counter, exchanging the drink. "This is junkie iced tea." An honest mistake? Or had she assumed he was a junkie from a nearby methadone clinic because he is brown-skinned?

You could go crazy trying to get to the bottom of every slight, says Gonzalez, and he doesn't bother. He is an upbeat family man. His view of the narcotics officers he deals with each day: "There's not that much prejudice in the room."

A Poor Homeland

Making assumptions about Dominicans and drugs is not wholly an act of racism. Federal officials consider the Dominican Republic a major drug depot. In part that is because it is halfway between Colombia, where the cocaine is grown, and the United States, where it is snorted. And unlike Haiti on the other side of the island, the Dominican Republic shares a language with Colombia. But the most common reason that Dominicans join the drug trade, Gonzalez says, is that most are very, very poor. He visits the island a few times a year to see his mother, who has retired there, and tells this story:

He is driving on the island with his two-year-old son, Mark, when the car breaks down. There is a shack nearby, and he walks to it carrying Mark. Inside there is a single lightbulb dangling from a cord. He asks the woman living there to use a phone. She takes down the number, and before he knows it he sees a boy running through the fields; the woman has sent her son to the nearest phone, a few miles away. Then she disappears out back and kills a chicken. She pulls plantains from a tree and makes the New York City detective and his boy a meal. A lost afternoon turns festive. Finally a mechanic arrives with the detective's mother, but when they try to give the woman money, she will not take it. She says it would be an insult.

Now every time he visits the island, he stops by her shack to drop off some small gift, like clothes his children have outgrown, and is greeted like a rich man.

"You drive around the D.R.," he said, "and in the middle of rows of shacks, you see one big house, a big car, a satellite dish, and you know it's drug money. These Dominican kids see it, too, and they have no other way and they take a chance. Most are not bad people. They come up humble, country people. It's a choice of living in a shack or getting something better for their families."

When Johnny Gonzalez sees the brown men lined up on 140th Street, he thinks drug dealers, he says. But he also thinks of the bare lightbulb and the boy running miles through the fields to the nearest phone.

Sergeant Maria Brogli and Detective Johnny Gonzalez continued to work together through the fall of 2000. Brogli's promotion to lieutenant hadn't come through yet — she had advanced from No. 450 to No. 200 on the civil service list and expected to hear something in the beginning of 2001. "You know the department," she said. Gonzalez was offered a position training new undercovers and investigators in Brooklyn, but said no so he could stay on the street and continue working with Brogli.

Several of those arrested are now in jail, including Hector Espinal, who pleaded guilty to drug sale and was sentenced in October 2000 to one to three years.

Brian G. Smith, Rick G. Castañeda, and Richard W. Lewis (left to right)
in Tranquility Park, Houston, Texas.
Monica Almeida/The New York Times

14

Bricks, Mortar and Coalition Building

MIREYA NAVARRO

HOUSTON, TEXAS

It was an anonymous woman in the balcony who started the song, in a small voice, and as the notes drifted over the auditorium, heads turned and a hush fell.

Soon those around her joined in, hesitantly at first, then more boldly, until the triumphant words of the hymn widely known as the Negro National Anthem seemed to be cascading to the floor of the hall.

There, more of the political faithful filling the Wortham Center picked up the tune as they rose from their seats, and now hundreds were singing in a tide of jubilation that swept over the stage, as if to embrace Lee P. Brown, who had stood along with them, visibly moved. He had become Houston's first black mayor that inaugural day in 1998, and to many in the audience he was a symbol of newfound strength.

"Lift every voice and sing," the people sang, "till earth and heaven ring. Ring with the harmonies of liberty!"

For all their joy, though, the day had been more than a celebration of victory for blacks. It had also been a testament to how racial and ethnic groups in Houston had put aside their suspicions and rivalries and come together largely out of self-interest to achieve power.

In the audience were faces from that winning coalition. There was Richard G. Castañeda, fifty-four, a Mexican-American who owned an engineering firm in metropolitan Houston. He had cast his lot with Lee Brown and become active in his campaign because he had trusted the candidate when he said he would be fair to Latinos. And as a businessman who got 70 percent of his work through a Houston affirmative action program, Castañeda needed an open door at City Hall.

He had had doubts about supporting a black candidate, he said. There were distant, bruising memories of being harassed by blacks. But he had recognized that in Houston, where blacks, Anglos and Hispanics each made up roughly a third of the population, the twenty-first century would require interracial alliances in both politics and business if any one group's interests were to be served. Hispanics, he said, might even act as a swing group, allying themselves with Anglos or blacks when it served their interests.

But watching Brown bask in his moment of triumph, Castañeda said, he also felt apprehensive. "I wanted to see who he would surround himself with," he remembers thinking. "Who is he going to turn the power over to?"

It was a question that had come up during Brown's campaign. One cold morning at Velia's Cafe, about one hundred prominent Latinos gathered to meet the candidate over breakfast. There was one thing everybody wanted to know, Castañeda recalled, and the question was finally asked: "One person got up and said, 'Look, we're concerned you're going to screw us over and give everything to the blacks.' "

Only rows away from Richard Castañeda at the Wortham Center sat Richard W. Lewis, fifty-one, a white man with a large stake in Brown's victory. It was Lewis who had nudged Castañeda, a business associate, to help the campaign and to bring other Latinos on board.

Lewis was no friend of affirmative action. In backing Lee Brown, who was, he had risked alienating the people he worked with when he broke ranks with his own Houston Contractors Association, of which he was a past president. The group, most of whose members were white, had supported the white Republican front-runner largely because he opposed affirmative action.

Lewis, who describes himself as a "Republican from the womb," had fallen in behind Brown, a Democrat, on the basis of a simple calculation: Brown would win. And as the owner of a local construction company, Lewis, too, depended on a friendly City Hall. Ninety percent of his business came from municipal contracts. Backing the man he presumed would be the next mayor seemed only prudent.

"I wanted to be in a position of influence," he said, "and you can't influence a loser."

But when he heard the Negro hymn swelling up from the crowd, he said, he suddenly felt unwelcome.

"It turned me off," he recalled. Imagine the Republican had won, he said, "and we had started singing the Confederate song. It would have been equally out of place. It alienated you, and that was the specific purpose of it, I'm sure."

Brian G. Smith, who is black, also had a lot riding on Lee Brown's victory. Smith, a forty-one-year-old architect who runs his own construction inspection company in Houston, had worked, like Richard Lewis, as a Brown fund-raiser and with both Lewis and Castañeda on the new mayor's transition team. He was counting on Brown's election to provide opportunities for blacks like him who do business with the city.

"The feeling had been that whites would stay in control of Houston," Smith said. Now, "it was like, 'Wow! Our day has come.' It felt like, at this time, it was good to be black."

More than anything, Brian Smith had wanted a mayor friendly to affirmative action. He remembered the affront of being denied work because he was black. Like Castañeda, he owed most of his business, 95 percent, to the city law that sets aside about 18 percent of city contracts for companies owned by minorities and women. And for Smith, public projects like water systems, stadiums and rails were where the money was.

So his support for Lee Brown, like that of the other men, had largely been bound up with his business interests. Which was nothing new for him. From the day Smith started his company, in 1987, business had driven his political involvement, no matter the candidate's color.

"For selfish reasons," he said. "Trying to get work." This time, with a black mayor, he said, "I hoped for access."

Smith was away on Inauguration Day and sent his mother to attend the ceremony in his place. She told him about how glorious it had been when everyone stood in a great wave and sang the hymn. He remembers how he felt on hearing about it.

"Electrified," he said.

Reaffirming Affirmative Action

Access, influence, money: all had been part of the political calculus for Richard Castañeda, Brian Smith and Richard Lewis. In the end, all three had put practical considerations ahead of racial ones. Much as he yearned for a black mayor, Smith said, he would have opposed Brown if he had not supported affirmative action.

Lewis, for his part, swallowed any misgivings because, he said, Lee Brown was "a sincerely decent man" whom the white community could do business with.

"What you worry about is getting a radical," he said. "I don't want a Klan member as mayor, or a black militant."

Lee Brown was no radical. He had been Houston's police chief in the 1980s. In 1990, David N. Dinkins, New York's only black mayor, lured Brown to the city to be its police commissioner, a job in which he took some heat for the roundly criticized police response to racial violence in the Crown Heights section of Brooklyn. He had also been President Clinton's director of national drug control policy.

When the polls closed in a runoff election in 1997, Brown had vindicated the men who had gambled on him, defeating the Republican Rob Mosbacher, a businessman and son of a former commerce secretary in the Bush White House, by 6 percentage points. Though Anglos made up slightly more than half the turnout, Brown had won with 97 percent of the black vote, 66 percent of the Hispanic and 23 percent of the Anglo, according to an exit poll by Robert M. Stein of Rice University.

For Smith and Castañeda, the election of Lee Brown was reassuring. They could be confident of continued business with the city under its affirmative action program, especially now that it had just dodged a bullet.

A conservative initiative to scrap the city's program had been on the ballot that election year. The measure reflected a national mood against programs intended specifically to benefit minorities. But thanks to a record turnout by minority voters, and despite a 2-to-1 Anglo vote to scuttle the program, the law was preserved. That gave Houston the distinction of being the only major city in the country to retain affirmative action in a challenge at the polls.

To Lewis, affirmative action was just another form of welfare that in effect robbed him of profits. In his ample business with the city, he had been required to subcontract to minority-owned firms even when it was not to his financial advantage.

It was thus a measure of his pragmatism that he could still back Brown despite their polar differences on a critical campaign issue. Lewis had decided that it was only one issue.

As he analyzed the mayoral race in 1997, he said, he could see that Anglos in Houston were outnumbered in the aggregate by blacks, Latinos and Asians from Vietnam, China and India. Demographic trends were also suggesting that Anglos would dwindle in numbers even more. The days of conservative Republican mayors—his own choice, he acknowledged, if he had had his druthers—were pretty much gone.

So his city, the nation's fourth largest, had been transformed. "I feel like I can't do anything about it," Richard Lewis said. Except work with it.

In the two and a half years since Lee Brown's inauguration, the pragmatism that drew the three men together has begun to bear fruit in the form of new business and political alliances and an opportunity to collaborate on a major city water project.

But to Castañeda, the new order is less about Brown than about the larger demographic forces. "Regardless of who is mayor now, that mayor has to be accountable to a lot of people," he said. "I don't think there's any way that in the future anybody can screw us over. We've just learned too much about the political system for that to happen."

He and others have also learned what can be gained through a system of "racial coalitions," he said.

"If you measure it in terms of dollars," he said, "we've never made as much money as we're making."

The Middle Plays Both Ends

In the tug of war between blacks and Anglos, Hispanics can pull on either end of the rope. Richard Castañeda began to demonstrate this shortly after the election.

He was raising money to pay off the mayor's campaign debt and calling Anglo engineers he knew, many of whom belonged to the trade group that had supported Brown's opponent. They would be wise, he told them, to deal with the Brown administration outside of the trade group—and to be associated with the allies of the mayor.

"I told them, 'We can help you,' " he said.

In exchange, the bigger Anglo-owned firms would help smaller Hispanic ones land work, at least as subcontractors. And they would pool money to donate to political candidates, to make them pay attention.

His case was persuasive. An informal Hispanic-Anglo alliance christened the Dirty Dozen was born, and it raised more than $100,000. Hispanic engineers had not only won points with the mayor by helping to retire his debt; with City Hall as the lure, they had reeled in Anglos for common gain.

Today, the Dirty Dozen—there are actually fifteen, and ten of them are Anglo—chase projects together, send work one another's way and meet with city officials as a group.

Richard Castañeda and his partner at Omega Engineers, Edelmiro Castillo, who is also in the Dirty Dozen, have a second power base: the Houston Hispanic Architects and Engineers, a fifty-member association that tries to cultivate good relations both with big companies and with politicians.

In May 2000, Castillo, the president of the Hispanic group, got a call from his counterpart with a group of Asian-Americans. Minorities should unite, the Asian architect said. Castillo agreed. The timing was right. They had a fair-minded black mayor. A bustling economy had turned Houston into a boomtown for the construction industry. There were lawsuits testing affirmative action.

"We're going to say we're the coalition of the minority groups," Castillo said, "and whenever there are any decisions made, we want to be a part of it."

A glue binding Houston's minority groups was the city's affirmative action program, which set goals, not quotas, for minority participation. The program ensured minority-owned companies that they would have a shot at getting a piece of city contracts. The companies' political connections at City Hall ensured that they would have an edge on the minority competition.

Castañeda used to think affirmative action was for losers. He called it "white-collar welfare," he said.

But that was before he went into business for himself in the 1980s just as Texas's oil and construction industries were going bust, and he went through half his savings in six months to support his family. Affirmative action saved his business, he said.

Not all opportunity should be predicated on skin color, Castañeda said; a person's ability and determination are still the primary ingredients for success. But before the affirmative action law passed, in 1984, about 1 percent of city contracts went to firms owned by minority group members and women; now about 18 percent do. He said he wondered if the number would not go back to single digits if the law disappeared.

"My conscience tells me that affirmative action is a good way to give people opportunities without social upheaval," he said.

Teaming with Anglos on one hand and nonwhites on the other, Houston's Hispanics display a kind of cross-racial dexterity that blacks and whites appear to manage less easily. Castañeda has a theory about why. "There's still big mistrust between the whites and the blacks," he said, "and I think it's still much easier for each group to get together with Hispanics than each other."

Yet Richard Castañeda suspects there is a limit to how close blacks want to be to Hispanics. When a Mexican-American friend ran for county judge, Castañeda called four black business friends to solicit money and got no answer. "I don't know if they don't trust me, or they're just cheap, or they don't have any interest," he said, "but I've never been able to break through that barrier."

At least among Anglos, he said, he can find a few who will give money, and sometimes one who will tell it to him straight. In the case of the judge's race, he called Richard Lewis to find out why his contractors' group was not returning calls.

"Hey, partner," he remembers Lewis saying, "let me tell you what the problem is. That boy doesn't know how to talk. He sounds like he just came from Mexico. There's no way he's going to win."

Castañeda had understood, he said. He had even advised the candidate to take a diction class, to lose the accent. The man refused, saying voters would see beyond that. He lost.

Richard Lewis agrees that Anglos and Latinos get along better. Latinos are less confrontational than blacks, less "hardheaded," he said.

He prides himself on working with people of different races. His foreman of ten years, Leroy Robinson, is black. His crews are mostly Latino. He is a mentor to minority business owners. And he defends his trade group, saying it welcomes everybody. It is the minorities who shun it, he said.

"You can't separate yourself and then holler integration," he said.

For Lewis, affirmative action was all downside. By making him give minority-owned firms almost a fifth of the construction work he gets from the city, he said, the law forces him either to subcontract work that his company could do itself or to pass up Anglo subcontractors who charge less.

"Affirmative action is unconstitutional," he said. "Why don't we just call it Anybody but Whites?"

His main argument against the program is that it is no longer needed.

"When I first got into construction, it was a bunch of cowboys," he said. "They were drinking and chasing women. Now, by and large, they are business people. They take Metamucil at eight o'clock and go to bed at nine.

"That changes the way everybody looks at each other. When I hire a man, I could care less what color you are. If you're dependable, if you don't steal, we embrace you."

If someone like Castañeda needs affirmative action after sixteen years in business, he said, maybe he should not be in business.

The notion that affirmative action is a crutch, to be accepted with shame, angers Smith. "I don't cease being black, or being discriminated against," he said, an edge in his voice. "That doesn't change, so I'm not trying to graduate out of this."

He added: "If there's nothing to force majority firms to contract minority firms, they wouldn't do it. Why split the pie if you can have all of it? It is a race issue, but it has more to do with money."

There was not much pie for blacks when Brian Smith began looking for a job in 1984 after he received his degree in architecture from Southern University in Baton Rouge, Louisana.

"I would lay out my nice portfolio and people would hardly look at my work," he said. "They'd look at me and say, 'No, we're not hiring.' "

Black firms were hiring, and Smith found work. But in 1987 he decided to take advantage of the affirmative action law and opened his own firm, Brian Smith Construction Inspection Inc., providing not architecture but construction management.

Today, even with thirty-four employees and a good track record, Smith finds his dealings with white-owned companies to be "really something." He is asked absurd questions, he said, like whether he offers employee benefits. "They think you work out of your house," he said, "or it's just you in a room and you're pulling their leg."

But he says he does not feel threatened when he walks into a meeting with white men. "I don't bite my tongue," he said. "I don't view this as a white man's world." He added, "I'm there because I'm fighting for the money that's on the table."

Smith said a pilgrimage to Africa in 1992 did more than anything to equip him to deal with racial indignities. In Ghana, where he believes his ancestors were from, he toured a castle where slaves had been held for transatlantic passage. In the dungeon, he said, he saw the "door of no return" through which slaves were pulled onto an auction block and then onto ships. Above the auction block he found a church.

The slave sellers, he said, "would auction off slaves downstairs, and then they would go upstairs in their own chapel and pray to the same God I pray to, and they call themselves Christians."

It only confirmed for him, he said, that if white people were capable of that, they could not be superior to him.

From the outset, Smith felt more at ease shopping his services among Hispanic firms. With their lighter skin, Latinos may be more acceptable to whites than blacks, he said, but he nonetheless feels a kinship with Latinos as members of a minority group. On an issue like affirmative action, he said, they are on one side and whites like Lewis are on the other.

"There's no hope for us as minorities if he can't acknowledge that it's wrong that less than 40 percent of the population gets 90 percent of the work," Smith said.

Affirmative action, he added, has been "the only thing in the last two hundred years that has excluded whites.

"So I can't feel sorry for them."

With Each His Own

About forty boys and their relatives were gathered in Hermann Park on a Saturday in the spring of 2000 for a Cub Scout rite of passage. While his father snapped pictures and his mother looked on proudly, Brian Nelson Stewart Smith, age seven, stepped out of a cluster of boys when his name was called, a shy smile under his big round glasses, and received a yellow neckerchief, a symbol of his rise in rank. Everyone applauded. Everyone was black.

The parents had set up tables of food and drink under the pitched roof of an open-air pavilion. The elder Brian Smith had provided the inspectors while the city was building the pavilion. So in some ways the setting carried symbolic weight of its own. It was a testament to how far Smith had come, starting from the low-income housing he had lived in until he was nine.

Yet the occasion also attested to how much Smith wanted Brian and his other son, twenty-three-month-old Micah, to relive parts of his own childhood. The younger Brian belongs to the same scout pack that his father had. It meets in the same black church, Wheeler Avenue Baptist, that Smith has belonged to since age six and where he is a deacon. As a boy, Brian Smith, whose parents were college graduates, attended a predominantly black public school. His son goes to a predominantly black private school.

Smith says he is giving his sons a racial grounding before they are "tainted" by the world. He himself remains anchored in a black world. He is on the board of a black-owned bank. His best friends are black. He takes family vacations to Africa.

Smith and his wife, Elizabeth, forty-three, a NASA engineer, live in an upper-middle-class, racially mixed neighborhood. They planned to move into a mostly black area nearby, where they bought a four-bedroom house with a pool and a tennis court.

"It is a conscious choice," Smith said of the effort to furnish his sons with a black identity. "Once you know who you are," he said, then "go learn about other cultures."

If Brian Smith's world is largely segregated, so are those of Richard Castañeda and Richard Lewis. The three men may run into one another at a political fund-raiser or at the Department of Public Works and Engineering. Two of them may even get together for the rare social occasion. Once, Lewis and his wife dropped by the Castañedas' to pick up some plants; the couples live in the same suburb, Katy. Once, the Castañedas went to a ballgame at the Astrodome at the invitation of Smith, who had rented a box.

But generally, so separate are their private and professional lives that both Castañeda and Smith were stunned to learn that Lewis was an ordained minister who sang every Sunday at a little church in Matagorda, a small town on the Gulf of Mexico where the Lewises have a weekend home. Indeed, the blunt, wisecracking businessman who wears jeans and black leather boots and carries a concealed handgun barely resembles the Richard Lewis who spoke with teary eyes one Sunday. The pastor, C. J. Molmen, was retiring from the Community Baptist Church after nine years, and this was his last service.

The church has fifty members, but on this day the pews held only seventeen, including two black women and a Hispanic family of four. Molmen was the one who ordained him the previous December, Lewis told the congregation. The pastor was also the one who had encouraged Lewis's wife of fifteen years, Betty, a forty-four-year-old former hairdresser, to play the piano. She had never touched a keyboard, she said, but one day, at the pastor's prodding, she sat down and played.

"It was a miracle," she said.

The son of an electrician who was also a Baptist deacon, Richard Lewis grew up in Port Arthur, a refinery town on the Gulf. In 1970, after college, he took a job with an engineering company that transferred him to Houston. But he grew restless quickly and decided to start a construction firm with two partners.

Eighteen years later, RWL Construction Inc., which specializes in utility projects like water mains, has fifty employees and enough profits to easily pay for a grand new Southern Colonial home for Richard and Betty Lewis. They are planning to move in soon, their three children — two from his first marriage, one from hers — having grown.

The new home, in Eagle Lake, a small town west of the city, came with white pillars, a guest house and a black-face porch figure. Lewis said he was getting rid of the figure, though, just as he was getting rid of the many other artifacts — "Southern folk art," he calls them — depicting blacks that decorate his home in Katy. "I don't want to offend anybody needlessly," he said wearily. "It means nothing to us. Now everybody has gotten so darned sensitive."

While Smith and Lewis each retreat to one world, Richard Castañeda has his feet in two. He reared his son and daughter in the mostly Anglo environment of Katy, where he and his wife, Christina, fifty-three, an accounting assistant with ExxonMobil Chemical, moved twenty-five years earlier.

Yet he has always regarded San Antonio as home. That is where his mother's homemade tortillas await. That is where Spanish is spoken. It is also where the Castañedas go on many holidays and weekends.

Richard and Christina Castañeda grew up poor in San Antonio but in the comfort of their own kind, they said. "The best enchiladas are made with welfare cheese," Mr. Castañeda said. He remembers his childhood world as giving him little sense that he was part of a minority.

Where he grew up in San Antonio, in the 1950s and 1960s, everybody around him was like him, he said. The barber and the butcher were Mexican-American. So were the sales clerks downtown. There were Mexican-American elected officials all over the place, even a congressman, Henry B. Gonzalez. Castañeda says he even thought as a child that because there were so many Mexican-Americans, they must be above both blacks and Anglos at least a notch.

That view had to change with time, but he remembers thinking that if Anglos really were the dominant group in the city, Mexican-Americans definitely came in second. A pool in a public park had been open to whites and Mexicans, but not to blacks. The fanciest movie theater in town, the Majestic, had a back entrance for the "colored." That meant blacks, not Mexicans.

Still, there was the occasional incident to remind him of Anglo attitudes toward Mexicans. Once, in tenth grade, when he and the only black student in his class were talking, the teacher snapped, "I don't want to hear any comments from the colored gallery."

Castañeda remembers wondering, "What are you talking about?"

It wasn't until he had left home, though, that he felt the full force of prejudice, he said. When he was in the Navy for two years, in the late 1960s, blacks had been as bad as whites in making his life miserable, he said. They called him spic, half-breed, pancho. They harassed him when he spoke Spanish. He had expected to be a radio man. Instead, he said, "I washed dishes for eight months" on a ship carrying five hundred men.

"They had a perception of me like the lazy Mexican," he said.

Such treatment only fed his resolve that his children would never endure the same. Unlike Smith, Castañeda was determined that his son and daughter would live in the Anglo mainstream. They could have a sense of their Mexican heritage, he said, but first they were American. He did not want them to be harassed for speaking Spanish. "I thought the opportunities were better if my kids were raised completely American," he said.

Castañeda said he resented being asked whether he considered himself Mexican or American. "People keep trying to put me in a situation where I have to choose between one culture and the other," he said.

And it grates on him when people assume he is from Mexico — when he is asked about soccer and even flamenco. He said he had ancestors who were born in Texas when much of it belonged to Mexico, in the early nineteenth century. Yet people will ask him, "When did your family come to this country?"

"And then you start talking to them and you find out their grandfather came here in 1910. But they consider themselves real Americans because they're white."

Richard Castañeda finds little in common with Mexican immigrants or foreign-born Hispanics. He recalls his father saying, "Trust only your own kind." But a City Council election five years ago underscored for him the fallacy of wearing ethnic blinders. Most Latino Democratic voters supported the Cuban-American candidate, Orlando Sanchez, against a white Democrat, even though Sanchez was a conservative Republican.

Orlando Sanchez turned out to oppose affirmative action. Born in Cuba and raised in Houston, Sanchez, forty-two, said Latinos should not be expected to behave as one. "I see Hispanics getting together on global issues — if the police are singling us out, if banking institutions are denying us home loans," he said. "But we won't be a cohesive force like African-Americans."

Sometimes the priorities of the American- and foreign-born Hispanics are starkly different. Once, Castañeda said, a Nicaraguan acquaintance asked him to make a donation to buy a bulletproof car for the new president of Nicaragua. He chose not to.

"Let them shoot him," Castañeda said, "I don't care."

And he laments that the image of Mexican-Americans has become tied to that of the penniless immigrant crossing the border illegally. "That's what keeps the image of the Mexican-American down," Castañeda said. He said he finds more in common with black and Anglo native Texans than the "wetbacks," a term that sometimes slips into his conversation.

Still, he has begun to have second thoughts about his decision to Americanize his children so completely that neither ever learned to speak Spanish. Now that the country has become increasingly multicultural, he said, "it's an advantage" to be bilingual. "I've actually done them a disservice," he said.

His children came to recognize a need to embrace their heritage. As adults they both migrated to San Antonio, back to where their cousins and grandparents live and where they spent summers as children. Last year, Castañeda's daughter, Denise Ramirez, twenty-seven, married a Mexican-American, Gerardo Ramirez—and not only for love, she said, but for their shared Hispanic values.

"I feel I have a pretty good grasp on my culture," said Ramirez, a public school social worker. "I'm really proud of it. So was my brother."

Her brother, Ricardo Cristian, known as Cris, was killed in December 1999 at the age of twenty-four. He had been driving home after a hockey game when his new red pickup truck went off the road and into an embankment.

The previous May he had earned a bachelor's degree in technology from his father's alma mater, the University of Houston, and had taken a construction management job with a San Antonio firm.

While packing up his belongings after the death, his family found a Spanish-language instructional tape in the stereo. In his wallet, his mother said, they found a list of things he was looking for in a wife.

"Hispanic," he had written at the top.

A Calculated Move Pays Off

After Lee Brown was elected, Richard Lewis attended a meeting of the Houston Contractors Association, the mostly white group he had led some years back. He was confident that he had done the right thing by supporting Lee Brown, he remembers, but he was also feeling betrayed.

Through his support for Brown, Lewis had wanted his contractors' group to benefit, he said. He had wanted them at least to hedge their bets by staying neutral and giving money to both candidates. But when the association's political action committee decided to endorse Mosbacher and Lewis stood his ground, the committee stripped him of the chairmanship.

"He couldn't eat or sleep for days," Betty Lewis said.

Lewis did not resign from the association; he was still dead set against affirmative action, and the group carried that banner. It had even filed a lawsuit against it. He also knew, he said, that his ties with the Brown administration would be fleeting. Brown is now in his second two-year term and by law can serve only one more.

But for the moment Lewis was in and his fellow contractors were out, and he did not want them to forget it.

At the association's meeting that day, Lewis waited for someone to acknowledge the results of the vote. Finally, he recalls, someone said: " 'Well, Richard, I guess you were right. I know that you won't have a grudge and that if we need your help, you'll be there for us.' "

Without a word, Lewis stood up and unbuttoned his shirt to reveal a T-shirt. It showed a cartoon character with a lipstick mark on its buttocks.

"That," he said, "was my answer."

More than two years later, Richard Lewis is no less confident that he did the right thing. Indeed, Lewis, Castañeda and Smith all say they have no complaints about how the mayor has treated them.

In part because of their connections to the Brown administration, ties that were forged during the 1997 campaign, the three were selected to join a team of industry professionals competing for a $100 million contract to build the Northeast Water Purification Project. The team is led by a group of private companies that also chose the men because they brought racial diversity to the table. Though the project is not subject to affirmative action regulations because it is being built with private money, it will still need to obtain approval from the city, the plant's client, and the City Council is made up of blacks, whites, Latinos and one Asian-American. In this case, Castañeda says, political realities have dictated the need for diversity, with or without the law.

"In Utopia, this is how it should work," Castañeda said.

But whatever promise of equal opportunity is embodied in that team, it is not a reason to scrap affirmative action, he said. Even with a mixed population and a multihued council to represent it, he said, there would be no guarantee that minority companies would be given a fair shake in an industry still dominated by Anglo-owned companies. And in politics, he said, even a minority leader could be bought or could enter into an alliance out of self-interest.

"I don't think you can leave it up to people's judgment," he said.

Lewis, Smith and Castañeda all agree that one of Mayor Brown's legacies will be the way he has led minorities, not just blacks, into government. But a looming question is how well the minority alliances that got him elected will survive the big demographic changes that are expected. Brown came to power in a city in which the Anglo, black and Hispanic populations had reached a rough parity. But Texas demographers say that he happened to catch the moment when these three groups, moving at different speeds or in different directions, were passing one another on the population charts.

As recently as 1960, whites made up 70 percent of the city's population, blacks 23 percent and Hispanics 7 percent. By 1997, whites were 35 percent, blacks 28 and Hispanics 31. By 2030, it is projected, Latinos will account for more than 50 percent of the population of Harris County, which includes Houston. Whites, meanwhile, will dip to 21 percent and blacks to 11 percent.

Whether the growing Hispanic numbers will translate into power at the polls is uncertain. In the 1997 election, only 13 percent of the turnout was Latino, compared with 32 percent black and 52 percent Anglo.

But whatever movement there is toward greater Hispanic power, Lewis is not troubled by it. He said he did not know many whites who fretted about their shrinking numbers.

"They're not concerned about it as long as green controls," he said. "They're the establishment. That's the establishment you have to blend with, and if you're not going to blend, you're not going to be accepted."

If one prospect is a kind of assimilation, as Lewis envisions, and another is continued ethnic divisions, as others predict, yet another is long-term coalitions, which Castañeda said he hoped for.

"If the blacks and Hispanics made a coalition, they could do a lot," he said.

To Smith, blacks may have achieved power at City Hall just in time to hand it over to Latinos. "At some point, we are not going to be able to get a black mayor," he said. "I hope we'll have a Hispanic mayor that we can trust to be inclusive."

A more immediate issue is the fate of affirmative action. Some city officials see it as a stabilizing force, but with lawsuits pending, opponents like Lewis expect a court to strike down the city law. Already, the Brown administration has endorsed two new race- and gender-neutral contracting programs.

Smith said he was more afraid of an economic downturn than the demise of affirmative action. With the numbers of people in minority groups increasing, he said, demands for parity are likely to increase, and "we'll be more and more protected."

Still, he said, he is exploring investing in a restaurant chain. And he said he was in talks with African entrepreneurs in Chad for what would be his first international construction management contract.

Lewis and Castañeda see a different picture, one without affirmative action. But while Lewis is pleased by that prospect, Castañeda is resigned to it. He said it would force him to reassess his options.

"Doing business without it would be too uncertain," he said. "I still don't see the private work out there."

He said he would probably close his doors without the government work and do something else: go back to school, maybe study environmental law, or move his business to San Antonio.

When the time comes for the men to cash in or retire, they plan to retreat to their separate worlds. The Castañedas think of moving permanently to a lakeside home near San Antonio and their son's grave. Lewis plans to live at least part of the time in Matagorda. Only Smith feels rooted in Houston.

The three have made a living in the same arena, sometimes helping each other get jobs, sometimes coming together out of mutual interest. But outside that arena, they said, they were not sure whether they would have any reason to see one another again.

Most relationships outside the family are superficial anyway, Castañeda said.

And though Houston has made him feel "95 percent comfortable" around other ethnic groups, he said, there is that remaining 5 percent, which he calls distrust.

"I know they're watching what they say," Castañeda said of Lewis and Smith, "because under normal circumstances, they could be saying something insensitive towards me."

Smith, who views opposition to affirmative action as racist, said he had nothing in common with Lewis except their support for a mayoral candidate. He said he felt closer to Castañeda.

But Lewis says friendship is not the point; tolerance is — "where we don't have this open hostility toward one another."

"You work together well; we treat each other civilly," he said. "We send each other work.

"How close are we supposed to be?"

In the fall of 2000, with the fate of affirmative action in Houston still undecided, business was booming for Rick G. Castañeda, Richard W. Lewis and Brian G. Smith. The three men teamed up on a couple of new government contracts — Lewis and Smith on a city sewer rehabilitation project, Castañeda and Smith on the construction of a new county building. But Smith in particular made it a point to reach out to the others.

"We really are very different, particularly Richard Lewis and I," he said. "I thought it'd be good, because the more he knows about me the more comfortable he'd feel about black people and about doing business with black people. When we see each other we speak now."

Lewis was receptive. "We have a camaraderie now that we didn't have before," he said.

Castañeda said he had become more active in his role as the Hispanic man in the middle. People like Lewis and Smith, he knew, often felt more comfortable with him than with each other.

"There's good people in any race, and I need to be more trusting and more friendly to those people rather than stay in my circle of people with Spanish last names," he said. "I'm starting to do more of that."

Don Terry watches as his mother, Jeanne Terry, attends a twenty-fifth anniversary reunion of Congress of Racial Equality (CORE) members outside of Chicago, Illinois. Michelle V. Agins/The New York Times

15

Getting under My Skin

DON TERRY

When I was a kid growing up in Chicago, I used to do anything I could to put off going to bed. One of my favorite delaying tactics was to engage my mother in a discussion about the important questions of the day, questions my friends and I had debated in the backyards of our neighborhood that afternoon — like Who did God root for, the Cubs or the White Sox? (The correct answer was, and still is, the White Sox.)

Then one night I remember asking my mother something I had been wondering for a long time. "Mom," I asked, "What am I?"

"You're my darling Donny," she said.

"I know. But what else am I?"

"You're a precious little boy who someday will grow up to be a wonderful, handsome man."

"What I mean is, you're white and Dad's black, so what does that make me?"

"Oh, I see," she said. "Well, you're half black and you're half white, so you're the best of both worlds."

The next day, I told my friends that I was neither black nor white. "I'm the best of both worlds," I announced proudly.

"Man, you're crazy," one of the backyard boys said. "You're not even the best of your family. Your sister is. That girl is fine."

For much of my life, I've tried to believe my mother. Having grown up in a family of blacks and whites, I'd long thought I saw race more clearly than most people. I appreciated being able to get close to both worlds, something few ever do. It was like having a secret knowledge.

And yet I've also known from an early age that things were more complicated than my mother made them out to be. Our country, from its very beginnings, has been obsessed with determining who is white and who is black. Our history has been shaped by that disheartening question. To be both black and white, then, is to do nothing less than confound national consciousness.

My mother denies it, but it has also sometimes confounded our family. For as my mother was answering my bedtime question, my brothers, David and Robert, her children from an earlier marriage, were going to sleep in a house fifteen miles away. My father was black. David and Robert's was white. They lived with my grandmother in an all-white neighborhood. I lived with my mother and my younger sister, Diane, in Hyde Park, a mixed neighborhood on the South Side of Chicago. We shared a loving parent, but we lived in separate Americas. We have spent most of our lives trying to come together.

My father, Bill Terry, was born in Covington, Kentucky, in 1921, the grandson of slaves. In his youth, he was a professional boxer. Later, he went to work as a bodyguard for the unions in Chicago, cracking scab heads. He was one black man who was not at all shy about standing up to authority. In his late thirties, he became an actor. He was good at it, too. My mother told me years later that when my father walked onto a stage to deliver his lines in *The Death of Bessie Smith*, the audience gasped. "He had presence," my mother said. "Incredible presence."

He was a lifelong integrationist, but the nonviolent civil rights movement was not for him. He could not understand how protesters could allow themselves to be roughed up and spat on at sit-ins and not defend themselves. Bill Terry didn't turn the other cheek; he threw the other fist.

My mother, Jeanne Katherine Ober, was born in 1918 and was reared on a dairy farm outside the village of Greenwood, Illinois. She was sent to high school in Chicago and then, at twenty-five, she returned home to marry the son of a wealthy farmer. It was a rocky union: her husband drank too much, and after eight years of marriage, my mother left, taking her two sons to Chicago—David was eight, Robert was two. There, she opened a nursery school and became involved in civil rights work through her Unitarian church. Until then, she had never personally known a black person.

My parents met in 1956, at a party of racially mixed hipsters. He was thirty-five; she was thirty-eight. As my mother tells it, she had been eyeing my father for much of the evening. He was the center of attention, with his boxer's grace and a smile that could light up the darkest corners of the room. Before long, my father asked my mother to dance.

At six feet, two inches, he towered over her. Soon, my parents were living together—along with David and Robert—in my mother's four-bedroom Colonial in Evanston, a Chicago suburb. Ten months after they met, I was born.

I was six months old when my father decided he wanted to sell the house and move to California. When my mother's mother heard about the plan, she had a fit. My grandmother said the boys needed stability and insisted they live with her and her second husband, Gerhard Raven.

My staying with Grandpa Raven was not an option. On the day Grandpa Raven found out my mother was carrying a black man's baby, he got uncharacteristically drunk. My grandmother told him about the pregnancy at a restaurant because she felt that perhaps if she explained it in a public place, he might not explode. When they got home, Gerhard poured himself a drink and took it outside to the front porch. He sat on the cement steps muttering about the "goddamn niggers."

When we left for California, the plan was for my parents to send for my brothers once we got settled. But "instead of getting settled," my mother said, "we got poor." We quickly ran out of money. My father lost his landscaping job and stopped looking for work. Less than a year after arriving in L.A., he hopped into our car and disappeared without saying good-bye.

My mother was desperate. She used her last few dollars to buy a plane ticket to get the two of us back to Chicago, where she knew my father was headed. We arrived around Christmas with nowhere to go. My grandmother made it clear that we were not welcome at her house. We spent the holiday sleeping in the home of a black friend of my mother's. "I was disowned," my mother said recently, when I asked her about those days.

"Was it because of me?" I asked, sounding to myself like a little boy again. "Was it because I was black?"

"No," my mother said. "No, it had nothing to do with you. My mother was mad at me for going through the money."

I was surprised at how relieved I felt. I wasn't sure that I believed her, though I desperately wanted to. One of the nightmares of race is that it's sometimes hard to distinguish between cruelties—hard to know what is racism and what is the simple human infliction of pain.

A white friend of my mother's from the civil rights movement allowed us to move into his roach-infested tenement on the edge of Hyde Park. A few weeks after we got settled, my father reappeared and my parents reconciled. We were a family again—except that my brothers continued to live with my grandmother and Gerhard.

A year later, in 1959, my parents had a daughter, Diane. I remember how happy I was that we were all together. It was especially great to have my father around. If I bugged him enough, he would put down his paper and, like his hero, Paul Robeson, sing "Ol' Man River" for me. On hot summer evenings, when it seemed the whole neighborhood was out, my father would scoop me up in his arms and run with me through the warm evening air. I was home. My dad was with me; it was heaven.

Hyde Park itself played a major role in my happiness. The neighborhood, which is home to the University of Chicago, had been integrated since the late 1940s, despite the early resistance of the university. By the time I came along, having a black father and a white mother was common in Hyde Park. In fact, there were so many biracial children running around the neighborhood when I was a kid that it was almost hip to be "mixed," as we called ourselves then. It was so hip that some people who weren't pretended that they were. Sophia, for example, was white, but she told everyone that her father, who was from the Soviet Union, was a "black Russian"—"You know, like the drink," she said. Since she was only trying to fit in, we forgave her her lies.

Most of the mixed kids in Hyde Park were pure-blooded mulattos, so to speak. There were Bob, Michael, Rebecca, Cindy, the Twins and many others. All of them had black fathers and white mothers. With so many kids who looked like me and with so many parents who looked like mine, it was easy to feel completely comfortable saying I was simply half and half. My memory is one of togetherness.

That's not to say that even in this utopia the power of race was entirely absent from our lives. When I was a boy, my father would perform a ritual. He'd plop his long brown arm down on a tabletop and ask me if I could see the red tint in his skin. "See there," he'd say. "That's the Indian blood in me. You have it, too. All the Terrys do. We're a quarter Cherokee."

I'd carefully inspect his arm, turning it over in the light, but all I could ever see was the brown skin of a black man. I thought it was a strange game. He did not look like an Indian. His skin was brown. There was nothing red about him.

There was nothing red about me either. My complexion is the color of sand. The texture of my hair is somewhere between kinky and curly. I have my father's full lips, and my nose and thick eyebrows come from my mother. When I look in the mirror, it is easy for me to see Europe and Africa dancing across my face like lovers.

Other people, however, aren't sure what they see. When they ask, "What's your nationality?" I often suspect that they really mean: are you on our side or their side? Can we trust you, brother? Are you dangerous, nigger? I'm not sure my answer can ever really change the interaction. These questions, these loyalty oaths, have followed me most of my life.

In 1962, our world changed. My parents got into a vicious argument. My father had been out carousing and my mother was fed up with him drinking up what little money we had. In a flash, my father had his big hands wrapped around my mother's throat, squeezing as hard as he could, banging her head against the wall. It sounded like a thunderstorm. I was terrified. I had heard my father yell before, but he had never picked my mother up by her throat and screamed into her face, "Bitch!"

I had no idea what to do, so I threw myself at his tree trunk of a leg and tried to bite him. Whenever I think of that night, my father transforms, in my child's memory, into one of those scary talking trees in *The Wizard of Oz.* "Daddy!" I screamed. "Please stop hurting Mama. Please, Daddy. Please."

He would not stop. I bit him again. He banged her head some more. My cousin Junior, who was a grown man, but not nearly as grown as my father, somehow persuaded him to stop, and my mother slumped to the floor, holding her throat and looking almost as scared as I was.

In a few minutes, the police seemed to fill up the apartment with their rough voices and the sound of their clubs slapping against their leather gun belts and holsters. They yelled at my father to turn around and to put his hands behind his back so they could put the handcuffs on. I was confused. I didn't know what was happening. After all, the only time I really saw my father with his hands behind his back was when he brought me candy from the corner store. He would make me guess which hand held the sweets.

Then the police took him down the stairs, and I remember being scared all over again. I begged them not to take my father away, but they never turned back.

After that, my parents separated for good. My father moved to New

York City to pursue his acting career. My mother was left with two children in a crumbling apartment. Sometimes my mother had to choose between buying food for us or paying the utility bills. Once, when the electricity was cut off, my sister and I snaked an extension cord under our front door and plugged it into a socket in the building's hall so we could have a lamp to do homework. We went on public assistance.

The only salvation was that, bit by bit, we started to see my grandmother and brothers again. Of course, we could only visit my grandmother's yellow brick bungalow on the far North Side of Chicago when Grandpa Raven was at work or out of town on one of his fishing trips. Grandpa Raven had a bad heart. My grandmother was afraid that the stress of seeing his stepdaughter and her black children would kill him. So we made sneak visits.

To me, my brothers seemed rich. There was a push-button television console in the living room, a new Dodge in the garage and a freezer stuffed with ice cream bars in the basement. My grandmother, whom we called Nana, would also sneak my brothers down to Hyde Park, reminding them, "Don't tell Grandpa Raven."

Gerhard Raven died when I was eight. His heart finally gave out. But I can sleep easy that the sight of a black child in his family was not what killed him. He died never having laid eyes on me.

As far I was concerned, Grandpa Raven was an unrepentant racist; to my brothers, however, the man who took them fishing couldn't have been a better surrogate grandfather. "He was better than a father," David said. "He was a great guy. He was not a man motivated by prejudice." My brother even had an explanation for the drunken rantings on the steps that day: "Rather than blame Mother," he said, "he blamed 'the niggers.' "

In my view, David is just as blinded by his love for Grandpa Raven as I am by my hate. I tell myself that Gerhard is racist evil incarnate. In my heart, though, I know there is more to it than that. The truth is a child's truth: I had wanted Gerhard to be my grandfather, too.

After Gerhard's death, we visited my grandmother every other weekend, making up for lost years. One night, I stayed over at Nana's. When it came time for my bath, I hopped into the tub, pretending to re-create the moon landing, which had just taken place. I had one foot in when Nana called from the living room, "Remember, Donny, just because your skin is darker doesn't mean I can't see the dirt, so scrub hard."

Nana didn't mean to hurt my feelings, but she did. Yet I never thought of her as prejudiced. She was an elderly white woman, trying to make her way in a changing world. She never said "nigger." She said "Negro." She tried to treat everyone fairly. She called me "darling" and "honey bunch." She made sure there were always plenty of big chocolate chips in the pantry. I loved her dearly and she loved me. Without her, we would have sunk completely into poverty.

Biracial though I was, my first real memory of being called "nigger" was the same cruel rite of passage it has been for black children the country over. I was seven, and I was playing football with a group of white kids in a suburb twenty-five long miles from Hyde Park. A boy, about my age, saw me in a neighbor's yard and started jumping up and down. He pointed at me excitedly as he chanted: "Nigger. Nigger. Nigger."

I was shocked. I wasn't a nigger. My mother was white. Couldn't he see her standing there, a few feet away? He had heard me call her mom at least a half-dozen times: "Mom, I'm having too much fun. Mom, please can we stay a little longer so I can play with my new friends?" Couldn't he tell I was only half black? He could have easily called me whitey, honky or cracker. Why didn't he do that? I had just as much white blood in me as black. And even if I was all black, why was he calling me names?

I tried to go after the boy, but my mother pulled me back. Then she did something that shocked me—and filled me with joy. From ten feet away, she threw a plastic cup at the kid, hitting him in the head and sending him running down the street, calling for his mother.

A few years after the football game, I was walking down the street with a white friend. A well-dressed member of the Nation of Islam asked me if I wanted to buy a copy of *Muhammad Speaks*, the group's newspaper. "No thanks," I said.

"Come on, brother, help your people out."

"No thanks."

"Man, you just want to be with Europeans," the Muslim said bitterly, pointing his paper at my friend.

"My mother is a European," I said.

"Brother, I'm sorry for you," the Muslim shot back.

Other moments also made it clear that a mixed family seemed foreign to the eyes of America. In the summer of 1972, when I was fifteen, my brother David, who collects old Packards, took me to Nebraska to pick up a 1956 Patrician. I was excited—it was my first out-of-town trip with one of my brothers. At the car owner's house, David introduced me to a white man in white shoes. He leaned against a white picket fence.

"This is my little brother, Donny," he said. The man and I shook hands. Then he stared at me. I had a huge Afro; David's straight brown hair was cut Young Republican short. The man winked at David. "You mean you work together?" he asked.

"No," David said. "I mean this is my brother."

"Oh, I get what you're saying," the man said. "The Bible says we are all brothers under the skin. It's good to see people taking the word of God to heart."

What a fool, I thought to myself then. Today I know: as a person of mixed race, it's the norm to have your closest relationships questioned at every turn.

Until I went to college, racial difference stood out for me precisely because it was the exception to the rule. In college, it became a defining force in my life.

It didn't start that way. In 1975, when I discovered Oberlin College, I was confident I had found a place where I could be my mixed-race self. As a stop on the underground railroad, Oberlin had a special reputation for enlightened race relations. It was the school's brochure that sold me, though. Featured prominently was a picture of two baseball players conferring on the mound. One player was white with a long ponytail, the other black with an Afro. It looked like home.

But at the start of freshman year, I was startled to see a very different picture. When I walked into the dining room, black students were sitting together at a group of tables in the middle of the room; white students were eating together at tables along the windows. At football and basketball games, black fans usually sat with blacks, whites with whites. The intramural sports teams were rarely mixed.

For a while, I tried to re-create Hyde Park at Oberlin. I hung out with a mixed group of friends and my intramural teams always included white guys and black guys—and slow guys of every color. I decided not to join the African Heritage dorm. But even on this supposedly liberal campus, trying to live integrated was an uphill battle.

A black student asked me once, "My man, where's the mail room?"

"See that brother over there?" I said, pointing across the nearly empty room.

"What brother?"

"That one," I said. "That blond dude."

"Man, that's no brother," he said. "That's a white boy. What's wrong with you?"

What was wrong with me? I wasn't split in two—the world was. And yet I was the one expected to adjust. Being away from Hyde Park was a shock to my racial system. I felt even more out of step with most white students. For the first time, I was exposed to white people who had not known black people as friends, neighbors or even classmates.

One night, I was visiting a white girl and her white roommate in their dorm. The door was open and we were just talking. Another black student was also there, flirting with the roommate. I was just about to leave when a white girl walking down the hall passed the open door and stuck her head in. She looked disgusted. "What's this," she asked, "a soul-brother session?" I was stunned. What did race have to do with anything? We were just two guys rapping to two girls and not getting anywhere. The girl I was visiting looked embarrassed. I wasn't sure if she was embarrassed about her rude neighbor—or that her rude neighbor had "caught" a couple of brothers in her room.

Fed up, I embraced blackness—as a shield and a cause. I signed up for a course on black nationalism. The decision was one of the most important developments of my life. Black studies saved me. It gave me a sense of discovery both academically and personally. Black studies helped me find an identity. As important, it helped me for the first time to understand my father's anger.

The more I learned the more I began to realize the struggles a black person born in 1921 had to go through just to survive. Once, after reading about the brutality of the race riots following the First World War, I had to walk around the library to cool off. That was my father's welcome to life. I didn't want to run into any of my white friends that afternoon. I didn't know what I might say to them.

At last, I felt in touch with my rage that race, even at my "progressive" college, mattered so much; that I could not completely be who I was, Don Terry, an integrated man, with a white mother and a black father; that I would repeatedly be lumped in a broad racial category— black—and treated like a caricature instead of the complicated individual I knew myself to be.

It was exhausting and maddening, being constantly judged by people who thought they knew so much about me solely because of the color of my skin when in fact they knew nothing at all. I seemed to be the only one to understand that the Don Terry who went to campus rallies to protest the school's investments in South Africa could, at the end of the day, relax to the Rolling Stones. Disgusted by the world's refusal to see me as mixed and individual, I chose "blackness."

My decision, I've come to believe, had as much to do with anger as anything else. I started using the term "white boy," something I had never done in my life. It felt liberating at first, like standing up to a bully. But I felt guilt when I went home to Hyde Park and spent time with my family and old friends. I was afraid I was becoming a racist.

One afternoon, I was driving my mother's tiny Volkswagen. She was sitting in the passenger seat. One of my best friends, Danny Gnatz, a white guy with hair down past his shoulders, was in back. We were talking and laughing when a fat white man, driving a big American car, suddenly cut in front of me. We nearly collided. I slammed on the brakes, glared out the window and shouted, "You stupid white son of a bitch."

As soon as I said it, I felt like jumping out of the car and running away in shame. At first, my mother and Danny pretended that they had not heard. What was going on with me? What did race have to do with it? "I'm sorry, you guys," I said. "That's OK, Donny," my mother said, patting my arm. Danny slapped me on the back of the head, signaling that everything was all right. But we drove a long way in silence.

The incident in the car caused me to question my behavior, but not my identity. When I returned to Oberlin, I enrolled in more black studies courses and became even more involved in the anti-apartheid movement. I left Oberlin a thoroughly black man.

After college, I went into journalism, hoping to do good in the world as my parents had tried to do. My first job was at the *Chicago Defender*, a small and struggling but historically significant black newspaper. I then went on to work for a number of larger papers in the Midwest before coming to the *New York Times* in 1988.

In just about every one of these jobs, my reputation was built as much around my race as my journalism; I was the black man with a big mouth, ready to get loud at the slightest racial slight—the brother with a boulder on his shoulder. An editor at the *Chicago Tribune*, where I used to work, called me the most contentious young reporter he'd ever met.

Once, at the *Times*, as I was finishing a crime piece, an editor came up to me and asked whether the arrested man, whom the police had roughed up, had a criminal record. I put it right back to him: how come you're not asking me if the cop has a record of brutality complaints? In short, I was the one who could always be counted on to ask the editors why our stories on welfare seemed to focus on black people when more whites received public assistance.

And yet. And yet even as a "black man," I remained confusing to the world around me, including the black world. One weekend, after I had joined the *Times*, I brought home a girlfriend—a talented black woman, a poet and fellow journalist. I took her to meet my brother David. His young daughter, Julie, was wild that afternoon, running around the house, jumping on the furniture and singing "Heartbreak Hotel" over and over.

Afterward my girlfriend, rubbing her temples with both hands, told me, "That Julie is a white brat." I was startled by how much those words hurt. Why couldn't Julie just be a brat? She was a little kid. I used to shoot arrows down the hall of our apartment; my brother Robert loved to run barefoot through the snow. In my family the kids, black and white, are wild. Not long after that, my girlfriend and I broke up. Julie may have been a brat, but not a white brat.

I like to joke that my mother had four children, if you don't count any of the men in her life. David is a successful stockbroker. Robert is an artist and boat captain. My sister, Diane, has spent the past twenty-two years battling schizophrenia. Diane has a daughter, Wakara, who was reared mostly by my mother and me and who graduated from Oberlin in May. When she accepted her diploma, David was there, just as he has been for every one of her graduations—and every one of mine.

Still, though we are adults now in a more enlightened time, race can appear like a ghost, disrupting the life of our family. A few years ago, I was at David's house. It was a cold Chicago night, yet inside, with flames crackling, we felt wonderfully warm. David was mixing drinks. Julie, then twelve, announced to us that she had received an A on her seventh-grade social studies assignment. "Would you like to see my project, Uncle Donny?" she asked me.

Using old photographs, Julie had laid out one hundred years of the family's history, culminating in the well-kept suburb where she and her family now lived. She handed me the three-ring notebook. Under a photograph of my mother on a pony, the caption read, "This is a picture of my Grandma Jeanne when she was twelve years old on the family farm in Greenwood, Illinois." A few pages and decades later the text reported: "This is a picture of my Uncle Robert in the '6os. As you can see, he was a hippie." There were pictures and words about almost everyone in the family, including Julie's dog, Buddy, and her cat, Clipper. There were pictures of everyone, except for Aunt Diane, Cousin Wakara and Uncle Donny, the black members of the family.

I could not believe that we had been left out. Then I figured I must have gone through the pictures too fast. Or maybe, I thought, putting down my glass, it was the drink. So I went through the book a second time, searching for our pictures, or at least a few words about us. "I'm not in this," I said, closing the book and handing it back to Julie. "What's up with that?" There was only awkward silence.

Though I tried to let the incident go, I found myself one day raising it with David's son, Noah, who had just returned from the Navy. Noah listened to the story, and then told me one of his own. He was showing his photo album to a black shipmate. When the sailor turned to pictures of Wakara and me, Noah said: "The guy was happy. He patted me on the back. He said, 'We don't have to worry about Noah. He's part black.' "

My nephew paused. "I told him I'm not part black," he said. "It didn't matter to him. He was still happy." And so was I.

My brother Robert lives in a small city in Washington state, largely isolated from the rest of the family. It is clear, too, that he has isolated himself from memories of our childhood. His distance—both geographic and emotional—is understandable, for he bears the wounds of an eight-year-old who was left behind by his mother. When I asked Robert questions about the past, he repeatedly said he did not remember and that I should ask David. But one afternoon, as we drove through his town, he slowly began to open up.

Robert does not think he harbors any ill will toward black people because of Bill Terry's role in dividing our family. But I'm not so sure. "You could say," Robert said, "that a black person came in and tore up the family." He didn't say, "You could say another man came in and. . . ."

"You could blame Bill for destroying the family," he went on, negotiating the road's curves. "But I don't think that has rubbed off on me as being a racist. I don't think it's affected me in a negative way. You can see it affecting someone like Grandpa Raven, though," he continued. "He had a little bit about him that was kind of Aryan.

People build up these barriers and it's hard for them to climb over them."

We headed toward the town's waterfront, and the more Robert talked, the more I worked to hide my anger and my hurt—and to remember his. "Mother," he said, "seemed to develop a propensity for black men."

I simmered. What did it matter that Mom had black boyfriends? She lived on the South Side of Chicago and was involved in the civil rights movement. There were a lot of black men around. If she had white boyfriends instead, would Robert say that she had developed a propensity for white men?

It began to rain and we passed a couple of young Latino men standing on a corner. Robert glanced at them and said his town wasn't the same anymore. More and more people who looked like gang members seemed to be showing up, many of them Latino. "I get upset with the country changing so much," he said.

Jesus, I thought to myself. What the hell does that mean? If Robert had been any other white man talking about the "good ol' days" and the changing country, if I had been interviewing Robert as a reporter on assignment, I would have been convinced I'd found a racist. But even in the midst of my anger, I kept forcing myself to try to believe that Robert was not a racist. He was my big brother, a star athlete, the guy I wanted to impress when I was a kid.

No matter what, I was willing to give him the benefit of the doubt, something I realized I do not often do for most white people. "I don't think I'm a racist," Robert said, making me think he had read my mind. "But maybe I am. I hope not."

If Robert and I were struggling with race—after all, in heavy traffic, I occasionally mumble about bad-driving white boys—his eight-year-old son, Henry, was not. One day, Robert, Henry and I drove up to Vancouver, Canada. We spent a wonderful afternoon going to museums and eating fish and chips. In the evening, we headed home, with Robert driving and Henry and me sitting in the back. At the border, Robert pulled into the line of cars waiting to go into the United States. From the backseat, I could see the American border guard, a young black man, wave several cars through with hardly a word. When it was our turn, however, he walked slowly around our car, peering into the windows. Something was suspicious about us. "Where are you going?" he asked Robert.

"We're going home," Robert said.

"Who's that in the backseat?" the guard asked, pointing at me.

"That's my brother."

"Your brother?"

"Yeah," Robert said. "We're half brothers." I cringed at the word "half." The guard looked at me again. He was on the verge of asking another question, when Henry leaned across my lap and, poking his head out the window, said, "He's my Uncle Donny and we love him."

The young American still looked suspicious, but he stepped aside and waved us on our way home.

Perhaps, I thought, that's the best we can hope to do — to insist upon our allegiance to one another, our brotherhood across the divide — and try to go home.

And my parents? My mother went back to college when she was in her forties and has been a schoolteacher ever since. At eighty-two, she teaches history and conflict resolution at an alternative school, Sullivan House, on the South Side of Chicago.

Not long ago, I tried to ask her why she didn't bring David and Robert with us to California. It was a gentle summer day and we were in a small Catholic cemetery near her hometown. My mother sat in the grass next to her mother's grave. She was hugging her knees to her chest. Her back was turned to me. She was crying.

We had been to the cemetery many times over the years, but I could not remember my mother crying before. The tears were my fault. I was asking her questions. The child in me wanted to know what she was thinking when she left my brothers behind. Didn't she see the harm it would do to us all? But all she answered was: "I was at my wits' end in those days. Everything was falling apart."

She paused. "We had no money. I guess I just thought the boys were living with Nana and Gerhard and they were better off."

Leave her be, I told myself, as I looked out over the graves of my ancestors. What good can come from dredging up painful memories?

My father died of cancer in 1998 in New York City at age seventy-six. I hadn't seen him for two years, though I had kept track of his acting career, which included a role in *Forrest Gump*. A group of my father's friends arranged a memorial to be held in his apartment building — though I finally could not bear to go to the service, all those years late. My grief and anger over his abandonment was still strong. A friend brought me a videotape of the service.

I was pleased to see a parade of mourners of all colors walk to the front of the room and say kind things about my father. They said he had stopped drinking, that he had found peace with God, that he had become like a grandfather to some of the children in the building. It was the kind of integrated gathering he had fought for and loved.

One speaker was a stylishly dressed white man in his late sixties. He said he and my father had spent a lot of time talking about my father's childhood. The man started choking up and walked away.

The man, it turned out, was a psychologist my father had started seeing when he was seventy. A few months after watching the tape, I called him. We talked about the fact that Bill had fathered seven children with four different women—three white, one black. With the obvious exception of my sister, I barely know any of them. "He was repeatedly touching on the issue of white women as if he were trying to make rational in somebody else's eyes how he had lived his life," the therapist said. "He couldn't see it as accidental that he had a succession of nonblack women in his life who gave birth to his children."

The therapist said that my father wanted to have racially mixed children in part to prove himself to his mother. As a boy he had been passed from relative to relative and was never really sure of who his father was. Bill also told the therapist that his mother had been disappointed that his skin was a dark shade. By having lighter, mixed-race children, he was saying, the therapist concluded: " 'Look at these beautiful children I've produced.' It was a search for approval."

I believe that chasing white women was more than that for my father. It was about fighting back against pre–civil rights America. One thing that my father liked about white women, he told his therapist, was the fact that seeing them on his thick brown arm drove white men crazy. It reminded me of something my father had told me once: "I took my wife anywhere I wanted to go. I'm a man."

The day after my father died, I wandered through his apartment. I ran my hands over his books, his saxophone and the photograph on the wall of his hero, Paul Robeson, dressed as Othello. My father's love for Robeson was one of the few uncomplicated joys we shared. After my father died, all I wanted was that picture.

I took the picture down and hugged it. Then I peeked into my father's closet and slipped on his too-big-for-me leather jacket, knotting the belt tightly like a little boy playing Daddy. I took a series of deep breaths and inhaled the aroma of his pipes, lifting them to my nose from the carousel on the coffee table.

Then, from under his bed, I pulled a small strongbox with a broken lock. It was full of documents. One was a copy of my birth certificate. I was surprised and touched that he had it. Then I noticed what he had done to it. On lines 8 and 13 of the document, the clerk's office for Cook County, Illinois, had recorded that my father was "Negro" and my mother "Caucasian." My father, however, had a different idea. Using dark blue ink, he had crossed out the references to race on my birth certificate, leaving just "father" and "mother."

On paper, at least, he tried to give me a gift that could not be fully realized in his life: the gift of family that transcends divisions of race.

On paper, it was that simple.

Disgusted by the world's refusal to see me as mixed and individual, I chose "blackness."

Part II

The
Conversations

16

Removing the Filter:
Unmediated Conversations about Race

A white man sings in an all-black gospel choir, for fun and spiritual connection. A group of Mexican immigrants learns to make sushi Korean-style. A black corporate lawyer fights with her sister because, now middle class, she is no longer black enough. A redheaded teenager finds himself by becoming Chinese. Decades into the experiment of integration, race still infuses our quotidian interactions, remaining a source of misunderstanding and enlightenment, alienation and togetherness. Unmediated and without the journalistic filter, public figures and private citizens talk about how race affects their lives. In the very tangle of experiences—rendered in these individual voices—lies the most naked picture of ourselves.

FIRST IMPRESSIONS
Derryck Adu-Gyamfi and Sean Donahue
MT. VERNON, NEW YORK
———

DERRYCK ADU-GYAMFI: Sean and I were playing. He didn't want to wrestle anymore, because he thought I was going to punch him in the stomach, but I wasn't going to punch him in the stomach. Black and white kids can be friends with each other, if you're in the same class. But they can't get married, because they don't match. They can't have a kid together. But they can be boyfriend and girlfriend. Like, my friend James likes Lauren. He's black and she's white.

SEAN DONAHUE: People are black and white because God chose them that way, because he just wanted to. I don't know why. Yes, black and white people can get married. If they have a kid, it could be either black or white. Someone in my class said James wanted to marry Lauren. But I like Bianca, because her drawings are pretty.

Growing up, did your parents talk to you about race? What did they say? What did you take away from the conversation?

"We looked beyond the skin—always—and everyone had that 'aloha' spirit."   —Asian woman

"I decided that race was not going to be how I lived my life."
                                                                             —Black woman

"I just remember feeling, 'What is it about me that everyone hates so much?' "   —Black woman

"What epitomized their obvious sentiments, to this day, was their fear of cities and getting lost in the 'bad parts of town.' Granted, there are many 'bad parts of town' that can be found everywhere, but the only defining aspect I can remember is that they were always predominantly African-American neighborhoods."   —White woman

"I would never give my daughter an African name—not that that's bad, but people equate your name with what type of race you are."
                                                                             —Black woman

"They told us that while American culture may allow us to move and function in society, we would never be fully allowed to join society. American society (particularly the white sector) will always frown upon us and will try to hold us back if they feel that we are moving ahead too quickly."
                                                                               —Asian man

"You had to pick the whitest guy, didn't you?"   —Black woman

"I got older and realized the ignorance of whites and how some whites react to people when they preconceive them before they get to know them."   —Black man

"When I asked her, she responded, 'Because you are Negro and Negro children are not allowed to be on the *Mickey Mouse Club.*' I was stunned because I knew very well that I was Negro and that there was a difference between Negro and white people but I had always been told that with hard work, nothing can stand in your way."   —Black woman

"My grandmother once told me that God wanted the races to be separate and that's why he created Africa." — White woman

MIXED DOUBLES
Shane Vavera, Amily Mak, NouDeng Sy and Chris Colvin
OKLAHOMA CITY, OKLAHOMA
—

SHANE VAVERA: Amily's got a good personality, she's fun to be around. Race doesn't matter to me. It's no concern. I mean, I'm half Iranian. But yeah, Asian women, I think they're more exotic. Really, what concerns me about the girl is the eyes, and the Asian women have beautiful eyes, the form and the shape of them. It's a plus for me. I had another Asian girlfriend before. And I like their skin color: tannish, not just white, white, white. A girl with color. It's just different; it's more sexual. It's not just like Plain Jane.

AMILY MAK: I'd never really dated a white guy. My parents encouraged me to date who I wanted, but I was just hanging out with the Asian community, so I dated Asian guys, who are more traditional. They expect you to clean house and stuff. I think it's hard for them to see a girl who wants to go out and do stuff, not just start a family. Asian guys say rude things to make me feel bad about dating a white guy. They're just jealous. One night I was going to be with Shane, and someone said, "Oh, she's turned white." There are definitely people who think Asian girls are hot. It's flattering. Why is it offensive? They're not saying we're ugly.

NOUDENG SY: My mom loves the fact that I'm dating a white guy. I guess it's because I dated three Asian guys, and only one of them lasted over a year. White guys are more laid-back. Asian guys are so scared about impressing people and being responsible that they're stressed out. I'm not saying I would never date an Asian guy, but if I did, it would mean I would be willing to be more homey—to give up a little side of myself for him. The first time I dated a white guy, a lot of Asian guys looked at me like I was stuck up: "She's too good to date an Asian guy." You know, I used to think guys wouldn't want to date Asian girls. But nowadays, Asian women are in. I hear all this stuff about how Asian women are more exotic-looking, and a lot of guys want that. We all saw *Road Trip*, and when that guy said "I have a thing for Asian women," Shane and Matt were like, "Hell, yeah!" And Amily and I were like, "Oh, my God."

CHRIS COLVIN: What do I like about Asian women? I guess their complexion, their skin tone and stuff like that. Just a real golden color. And I like that Nou's petite, she fits right in my arms. Asian women are more attractive to an extent, but I really like to find out the personality. A few generations ago, it would've been awkward, but now there are lots of multicultural kids.

How are interracial families and relationships perceived by families, friends, co-workers and strangers in the street?

"I still find it odd that when people look at [my husband and me] together, they do not see a loving married couple. They see a white woman with a black man. And there have been people who are not shy about voicing their racist opinions."   —White woman

"I was never followed in a shopping mall or had my bags checked by a clerk until I went shopping with my [black] husband." —White woman

"As a fifty-six-year-old woman, possessed of prejudices originating from white, middle-class Southern culture, I am certain that I am not unique when I proclaim that I will never marry or date outside of my race."
—White woman

"Sometimes I look at my husband and wish he were black so he could understand instantly where I'm coming from, that I didn't have to work to communicate my frustration, anger, hopelessness and sadness with the racial situation in this country."   —Black woman

"I turn off my eyes and ears now mostly, to avoid the fury I feel when noticing whispers and glares from disapproving folks when I am with my interracial family. I know what places locally to avoid." —White woman

THE TELLTALE HEART
Charles Cooper Barefield and Olga Rodriguez
NEWPORT NEWS, VIRGINIA

—

CHARLES COOPER BAREFIELD: I got a heart transplant in 1999. I wanted to write the donor family, but I did not want to open old wounds. Then I got a letter from Olga, the donor's daughter. She wanted to meet. That day, I walked over, handed her flowers and held out my arms. She gave me a great big hug and next thing I knew, she was crying. She just kind of slid down and said, "I want to listen to my dad's heartbeat." I was just holding her, comforting her. It felt natural. It was rather teary for me as well. He died and I lived. Every day I pray for him. I told one of her brothers that we should plan an extended family reunion. I was surprised that Olga's father was Latino. It doesn't matter, but you don't normally think about that. Now I sign my name as Carlos Cooper Barefield instead of Charles.

OLGA RODRIGUEZ: I had this desire to hold Charles's hand, but I did not want to scare the guy. My dad wouldn't like me saying this, but we Hispanic people, we show our emotions, but American people, they like to plan everything. Even in love, they're that way. But when Charles held my hand, my dad's spirit embraced me. My dad was from the Dominican Republic, and he died waiting for his citizenship. Every time he talked about this country, his eyes got watery. When he died, I put a little American flag in his hand with a rosary. I don't have words to describe the emptiness that he left. But just knowing that his heart is beating, part of him is alive out there — it's mystical, no question about it.

SMALL-SCREEN REALNESS
Mhagony and Shawana Clark
NEW YORK, NEW YORK

—

MHAGONY: I think it's great how everyone is listening to rap, you know, Spanish and white people and all. I don't think that black people should keep rap to themselves. But even if I wasn't pregnant, I would never wear a thong or show off my body like a lot of black women in rap videos. And I don't rap about things that people expect me to. So many black rappers who live in the suburbs, they feel like they have to seem like they're from the ghetto to sell records. At the same time, rappers from the projects only want to be around the new rich people they meet. It makes us look negative, either way. There are so many stereotypes about black people that still live on. I don't know why that is, because it's white kids that are going around shooting each other in schools.

SHAWANA CLARK: I'm lucky because people can't tell if I'm really black, and they always ask me if I'm Puerto Rican, Dominican or Indian. Today I wanted to look Indian, because I always get more attention if people don't think I'm black. I didn't want to look too thug anyway, like I was from the projects. I want people to take me seriously. Sometimes I get mad when people ask me what I am, though. When I say I'm black, they often tell me I must be lying: "You can't be black, because no black girl can ever look that pretty." It's funny, because it's black people who say that.

LONGTIME NEIGHBORS, NEWFOUND FRIENDS
Gladys West and Betsy Harper
GRIFTON, NORTH CAROLINA

—

GLADYS WEST: I like to visit Ms. Harper every week. I've known her my whole life, but we've just only become friends seven years ago. We had no connection to each other growing up, because I couldn't talk to whites unless I worked for them, and I never worked for Ms. Harper. I'd see her on the street in Grifton, though. She was the best-looking white woman I ever saw, better-looking than any movie star. She was built nice and had large blue eyes. I never wanted to look like her, though, because when I looked in the mirror I knew I was something myself, well built, with long hair. I knew I was just as good as her, even if no one else thought so. I thought we could be friends one day, because she was just so calm-looking, never stuck up. Many years later, I bought oil from her husband, who was an oilman. I heard he liked collards, so I made some for him. That's when I first started visiting them. Ms. Harper invited me right in and we found out we had a lot in common. Now we get together and talk about recipes, and I've told her how to make collards and molasses pudding. I have other white friends, too, and you know what? I never worked for any of them. I'd like to think that racism in Grifton is a thing of the past, but it isn't. It will never go away. And it's not just in whites. There's hate on both sides. Young black kids grow up here now and hear how we weren't allowed to mix with whites when I was growing up, and they'll get so angry and let the devil in. Me, I don't look at the news, because I don't want to see anything that will get me mad at whites. I just try to get closer to God and visit people like Ms. Harper and be nice to them and hope they will be nice back to me.

BETSY HARPER: Today Gladys came by, unannounced. She often just stops by. We just sit around like two friends, talking about flowers and food. That I'm white and she's black doesn't play a factor in our relationship. Except when we go to church. She stays with her congregation, and I stay with mine. I've always made a special effort to treat black people like people. I think it's because Grifton was so small when I was growing up. The population was only five hundred. So my daddy taught me that if we treated the black people as if they were like us, there would be no trouble. Even though blacks and whites are supposed to get along better now, I feel there's more tension because there are now twenty-five hundred people living here. Everybody can't know everybody else anymore.

FRIENDS AND ALLIES ACROSS THE DIVIDE
Barney Frank and Maxine Waters
U.S. HOUSE OF REPRESENTATIVES, WASHINGTON, D.C.

—

BARNEY FRANK: If one of us has an amendment, the other one may jump in and help out.

MAXINE WATERS: And we come by and talk to each other about an amendment, and we hit the room and we're on the same track.

FRANK: There's like a window of communication with us, a look, a nod.

WATERS: That's right.

FRANK: I got here ten years before Maxine, and when I got in, it was still tough for a woman. The first generation of women in Congress were the older generation of widows that came. And the men didn't treat them fairly. But there's this whole generation like Maxine who came here and said, "Wait a minute, we're here just the same as you."

WATERS: When I hit the Legislature in California, everybody started talking about how *aggressive* I was. And I said, "*I am?*" I had this one legislator. He told me, I'll never forget. I had been working on

What was your most painful or uncomfortable moment having to do with race?

"My wife called for beauty treatment . . . they said, 'We suggest you go to somewhere else.' "   —Asian man

"I was not served, yet I was in uniform."   —Black man

"Having my intelligence questioned because of the color of my skin."
                                                                        —Black man

"The first time a childhood friend leaned over the back fence and called me a nigger."   —Black woman

"And she said, 'Oh my God, you're black! You never told me he was black.' "   —Black man

"The neighbors would not be happy if we rented to you."
                                                                      —Black woman

"Affirmative action is obviously a good thing, so how did I feel being an exact target of it?"   —White man

"There was a sign on the boardwalk with a line down the middle. One side said 'Whites only' and the other side said 'Colored only.' It was as if there was an invisible boundary drawn in the sand because the white side of the beach was spotlessly clean and the colored side was absolutely covered with dragonflies."   —Black woman

an issue, and I went down on the floor, and it was perfectly within the rules to amend his education bill [*laughs*]. But I didn't have his permission. And he told me: "I don't like your style. And you have this kind of in-your-face thing." I was shocked. And I said, "Well, that's *who I am*."

FRANK: That's a gender thing, and one thing that goes together: being gender-stereotyped. Both women and gay men are not supposed to be tough.

WATERS: We're supposed to be apologetic.

FRANK: Exactly right: thank you for letting us be here. And neither one of us for a minute ever thought that was appropriate.

WATERS: You know what? Something about the black experience has caused blacks in general to know how to support what they think is right and what needs to be supported.

FRANK: *The* demographic group that has by far the best record on gay and lesbian issues is the Congressional Black Caucus. They have a better record than the gay caucus. Not the *openly* gay caucus. There's a couple of closet cases that don't vote with us.

WATERS: Unfairness in the black community is something that's dealt with in a lot of different ways, but dealt with. And you see this support for Clinton on impeachment—

FRANK: This is a key point.

WATERS: And a big outpouring from blacks, it was because that prosecutor—they knew him. They understood what that was *aaalll* about.

FRANK: They were treating this straight white guy like he was black or gay.

STANDING OUT AT WORK

DR. MAE C. JEMISON
General Practitioner
HOUSTON, TEXAS
—

MAE JEMISON: Majoring in engineering, I would have been one of maybe two or three African-American students in my classes. Some professors would just pretend I wasn't there. I would ask a question and a professor would act as if it was just so dumb, the dumbest question he had ever heard. Then, when a white guy would ask the same question, the professor would say, "That's a very astute observation." As a medical student, sometimes I needed to hear the criticism in order to become a good doctor. Also as an engineer, and as an astronaut. But many times what's lacking is the praise. Race is always an issue in the United States. You always run into people who aren't comfortable with you. But we all—the way people look, whether or not they're heavyset, for example, influences us. Anyone who says he isn't influenced by race is lying.

WERNER SOLLORS
*Professor, Department of Afro-American Studies, Harvard
University*
CAMBRIDGE, MASSACHUSETTS
—

WERNER SOLLORS: Most African-American studies departments are really integrated, so I'm in a minority, but rarely the only white. Non-Americans and Americans who are not of black African ancestry have always been present in the field. It's fascinating—the extent to which the students trust each other. There's more openness in the academic world. The term "race" is a European coinage that became popular in Spain during the Inquisition. It has largely been abandoned by twentieth-century scientists. There's no biological concept of race that any scientist believes in. There's only racism. But the term is surprisingly alive in the U.S. It was startling, coming to the United States from Germany. The fact that the black-white divide still seems to carry so much *meaning* in the U.S. is something that I had to adjust to, something I still have difficulties adjusting to. The ethnic fault lines run in different directions in different countries. Many black American writers have viewed France as a haven from racism—but North Africans tend to disagree. The black-white divide here is not as deep as the ethnic divide is among what would look like blacks in Rwanda and Burundi, or as the ethnic divide is among whites in Northern Ireland or in the Balkans. As academics, since we're specializing in the decoding of stereotypes, it would be hard for us to believe in them. But sometimes I'm expected to be superorganized since I was raised in Germany. That turns out not to be true.

REBECCA LOBO
Forward, New York Liberty
NEW YORK, NEW YORK
—

REBECCA LOBO: In the locker room, people might make jokes about "the white girls," but it's always in fun. When I was in college, the basketball players would sit together in the cafeteria, and since some were African-American, it was natural that their African-American friends would come sit with us. So I probably met more African-Americans than I would have otherwise. We sometimes joked about race. I remember one person saying, "We get perms to straighten our hair, and you get perms to do the opposite." Sometimes, it's not until you hear it from the outside that you think about it. I hear my teammates saying, "A taxi's not going to pick me up, it's going to pick up the white lady five feet away," but they laugh about it. I was sunbathing once and an African-American teammate said, "Rebecca, you better not spend any more time in the sun or you won't be able to get a cab." My attorney is a black gentleman, and sometimes in a restaurant he'll say, "People are glaring at us." I'll look up, and there might be a couple at another table looking at us disapprovingly. I'm hopeful about race, but I think there's a long way to go.

CHARLEY PRIDE
Country Singer
NASHVILLE, TENNESSEE

—

CHARLEY PRIDE: The reason there aren't more [black] country singers is probably that in our culture nobody has been individual enough to pursue it, and there was a systematic way of being kept out. Just like being the first senator or the first congressman. But from early childhood, I have been what I am, which is a country singer who happens to have a permanent tan. I was taught to work hard, to be fair, to protect myself, the whole nine yards. I listened to country music, and I sang it in spite of being laughed at. My own sister laughed at me and said, "What are you doing singing *their* music?" This permeates the whole country, this "us, y'all and them." I didn't want to capitulate to it. I feel people in this country experience racism every day. There's "y'all" and there's "us." A lot of people will come up and say, "How does it feel to be the first colored, Negro, Afro-American, African-American country singer?" I say, "It feels the same way it did when I was the first colored country singer." I started at an early age. I've been called the "N" word. I remember the first time, and it sticks in my mind. We were putting down butane tanks, out in the country. And the fellow I was working for — I should have been in school, I was about fifteen — sent me to get a wrench. Well, I didn't know what a Stillson wrench was. I went over to the flatbed and brought the wrong one back. He said, "Nigger, don't you know what a Stillson is?" I thought about what to do. He was down on the ground, and my first instinct was to stomp him

Think about the casual derogatory remarks people make about people of other races. How often would you say you hear such derogatory comments from people you know?

"I hear derogatory remarks from people that I know probably every single day . . . and it always makes me uncomfortable."   —White woman

"I call all my friends niggers and stuff like that and nobody pays attention. I call all my white friends, all my Asian friends, my latin friends. I just call everybody niggers."   —Black man

"I can remember being on the bus one day and people making fun of my eyes, and it was so hurtful."   —Asian woman

"I hear something derogatory at least once a day and it's usually directed at me. Granted, people don't think they are being rude when they get in your face and say 'What are you,' and when you tell them they argue with you."   —Multiracial woman

"Blacks seem to use a lot of derogatory language about themselves, such as 'ho' and 'bitch' to describe women and 'nigger' to describe each other. I grew up learning that it was a bad and painful word for blacks."   —White man

on the face. But my mother's upbringing told me, Don't do that. I said: "My name's not Nigger. My name is Charley." He was disarmed and treated me differently after that. I don't mind being a role model, but if the news media and other people tell me to go out and save your people, that's just more "them and us." You want as many fans as you can get, but to go out and specifically try to win someone over, I don't think anybody should do that. Ninety-nine percent of my fans are white. All I did was sing the music I love. My sister who laughed at me for singing "their" music is glad now. I just bought her a new van.

ELIEZER BROOKS
Rabbi, Congregation B'Nai Y'rushalaim
NEW YORK, NEW YORK
—

ELIEZER BROOKS: I'm descended from Orthodox Moroccan Jews. My great-grandfather was a leader in the Jewish community in Brazil. My parents were in the West Indies, then Panama. I didn't meet many white folks in Panama. I came to the States in 1945 after I worked on an Army transport ship during the Second World War, and then went to yeshiva in 1960. I was the only black person. In my own life I lived Jewish. Didn't eat pig, went to synagogue. I married a Puerto Rican woman in 1967. Her parents didn't practice any religion, but they were probably Jews. Her name was Miriam Martinez. Our daughter is a Lubavitch. I also studied at the Lubavitch. It was very difficult. I had more difficulty in Brooklyn from the non-Jews than from the Jews. The Hispanic people wrote "Jew" on my door in crayon. Everything turned out all right because I moved away. When it comes to the way we worship, at one time complexion didn't matter. Now, if you are "white," the other white people might tell you you shouldn't love a black person. Even in the Jewish community. In the Bible it says, "Remember you were slaves in Egypt." So they should remember not to be oppressive. But the oppressed usually becomes the oppressor, that's true everywhere you go. For me, as long as my daughter is married to a Jew, I don't care whom she marries, Chinese, Japanese, whatever. I have the idea of trying to build a Hebrew school for minorities. Separate, because it doesn't work the other way. On the surface, it may seem like society's changed, but you know and I know it remains the same.

MARCUS SAMUELSSON
Chef, Aquavit
NEW YORK, NEW YORK
—

MARCUS SAMUELSSON: I've had a million opportunities to turn my life into a bitter, sour experience. If I picked a fight every time I experienced racism, it would take up my whole day. In the restaurant, I have people eating out of my hand. There are forty or fifty nationalities represented on the staff, and I don't think I've ever seen a racial incident there. I'm black and I'm the boss, so you don't make race an issue. But then I go outside at eleven at night and I struggle to get a cab. It's a reality check. I laugh, because 90 percent of the cabdrivers are Pakistani and Indian. They've bought into this whole "black is bad" concept. And they look so much like me, if you put a hat on them, they wouldn't get picked up either. I was born in Ethiopia and adopted by Swedish parents. My Swedish grandmother cooked in rich people's homes, and she really inspired me. Everything was like a professional kitchen. As a black person living in Sweden, you knew about the black stars in America—Carl Lewis, Mike Tyson, Michael Jackson—not the ordinary people. I wanted to be in New York, in a place where there would be an Indian doctor, a Chinese lawyer, all different types, all integrated, where I'd see all different cultures just taking the subway. Racism, in a way, prepares you for real life. When I was a kid in Sweden, stuff happened. People would call you "nigger." But it didn't put me down. I'm extremely driven, partly because I'm going to show people. But if I had been fat, they would have teased me for that.

Judging from your own personal experiences, would you say race relations have gotten better, gotten worse or stayed about the same over the last ten years?

"Race relations have improved. The laws that have been passed to protect minorities have really helped minorities. By no means is it perfect, but I think it has improved."   —White man

"My car has been vandalized about every month, and my tires get cut, my car gets scratched and I get all kinds of notes in my mailbox. So I would say [race relations] got worse."   —Black man

"You're always going to have people who are racist or prejudiced about something. You're never going to have it perfect."   —White woman

"When you look at the high-tech fields, you don't see a lot of African-Americans or women."   —Black man

"I say that [race relations] are worse only because we tend to hide it more than we would normally do . . . It just sits there and boils until you reach that exploding point."   —Black woman

"Until white Americans are willing to recognize the institutionalized racism in this country, I believe blacks and whites will go on living in somewhat separate (and therefore diminished) worlds." —White woman

"Worse! As we become more multicultural, people are beginning to really divide themselves based upon face."   —Black man

"I can't drive across the U.S. in a rented car without getting stopped."
                                                                  —Latino man

"Rare these days is no-holds-barred, in-your-face, outright hatred exhibited in work and social settings. Most people, black and white, have the good grace to be embarrassed about such negative public displays. Racism is private now."   —Black woman

"I have had more racial incidents in the last ten to fifteen years than I have had all of my life. If I had to guess, I would say that it has to do with the current situation in America, and the fact that I work in the corporate world and for the most part live in a predominately white, upper-middle-class neighborhood."   —Black man

Interviews by Catherine Saint Louis, Emily Nussbaum, Joshua Green, Reena Jana, Robert Mackey, Andy Young and Chris Mitchell. Selected responses collected by Earprint Productions, Naila Robinson, Apryl Bailey and Aimee Pomerleau or volunteered by readers of the *New York Times on the Web* (nytimes.com).

17

Writing about Race (and Trying to Talk about It)

A generation ago, after riots in several major cities, the Kerner Commission warned that the United States was in danger of becoming two nations, one black and one white. That has not happened.

America is now an inescapably multiracial society from which there is no turning back for whites or blacks — in its schools, its workplaces, its churches, its military and its cultural institutions. Yet divisions and frustrations persist on both sides, in minds and hearts if not in the laws of the land.

For various reasons, however, most Americans, especially white Americans, do not like to share their personal feelings on race. In 1997, President Clinton proposed a national "conversation" about race. A committee was appointed and town meetings were duly organized across the country. Most of those who showed up were civic activists interested in public policy. Almost no one dared to discuss private attitudes, a more subtle and potentially divisive subject. Yet these attitudes lie at the heart of the racial question because it is attitudes and feelings that determine how we actually interact with one another, and whether we get along.

The reporters who wrote these fifteen chronicles spent as much as a year on their projects, returning again and again to the people who eventually came to inhabit their narratives, learning a bit more each time about their fears and frustrations and hopes.

In nearly every case, African-Americans were far more willing to talk about race, in large part because they have endured America's long history of discrimination and live with its consequences every single day. Yet in the end whites began to open up as well, sharing their thoughts about a subject that many would just as soon avoid and others do not think about at all. The fact that whites and blacks, as well as

Latinos and Asian-Americans, were eventually able to address painful issues with great candor is a great reportorial accomplishment.

Whether they chronicle success, failure or just plain inertia, these are stories that report race relations as they actually exist on a human scale in America. In a way, without deliberately trying to, the people who populate these stories provide the uncomfortably candid conversation about race that Clinton sought but never got. The stories hardly depict a perfect world, but they do depict a country in which citizens bring strong feelings, deep thought and, in a heartening number of cases, resilient spirits to one of the abiding issues of American life.

Eight *New York Times* editors and reporters were asked to talk about working on the "How Race Is Lived in America" project, looking specifically at how their own attitudes about race were affected by the experience. The conversation, held on June 19, 2000, was moderated by Sam Roberts, a *Times* editor. The panel consisted of two editors, Gerald Boyd and Soma Golden Behr, and six reporters: Dana Canedy, Steven Holmes, Mirta Ojito, Janny Scott, Ginger Thompson and Michael Winerip. Canedy, Holmes and Winerip also acted as editors on the project. The following are excerpts from the conversation.

SAM ROBERTS: Why is race a more sensitive subject than sex or sexual orientation or ethnicity?

STEVEN HOLMES: Labels get affixed to people for saying "the wrong thing." It may be unfair but it's true. If a guy says something about women he can jokingly say, "Well, I'm just a chauvinist, I'm just a chauvinist pig," and make a joke out of it. I don't think you run across anybody who would jokingly refer to himself as a racist. It's such a radioactive subject because these labels are so explosive. I mean, you know — bigot, Uncle Tom, sell out — you name it.

ROBERTS: A number of the people who worked on this series, particularly some of the white reporters and editors, said that they felt a certain inadequacy in dealing with race.

GERALD BOYD: The dirty little secret is that a lot of the black reporters and editors felt inadequate as well.

DANA CANEDY: Plus, ordinarily if you feel inadequate about a story, within two days of reporting you no longer do. It's not the same with race. With race, you can report month after month after month and come to no final conclusion. I can do a business story or a science story or a legal story and figure out right from wrong, up from down. With a race story it's tougher because there are no absolute rights and wrongs.

JANNY SCOTT: What was different for me was that these stories called for a degree of nakedness that you don't normally experience as a reporter—it started at the very beginning, when we met all day at Soma's house and we were asked to reveal ourselves in a way that's not normally asked of us. And to reveal ourselves on this incredibly rocky terrain.

GINGER THOMPSON: Most times when we go into stories, even stories about race, we are able to identify good guy/bad guy, good agency/ bad agency. With these stories, there wasn't a conclusion. There wasn't an "aha moment."

CANEDY: Or a villain or a hero.

THE DIFFICULTY OF TALKING ABOUT RACE

MIRTA OJITO: I was having lunch, as I often did, with the black subject in my story, Joel, and I was trying to understand exactly what it was that he felt about white Cuban-Americans. And he said, "I just wish they were all like you [Ojito is a white Cuban-American], that they could be here having lunch with me normally, like you are." That was very nice, but I immediately thought, I'm here having lunch with you because I'm writing about you. The truth is that living in Miami I probably would have never met Joel. But after I met him, I liked him.

BOYD: But that sounds like what people would say about race thirty years ago. That—

ROBERTS: What do you mean?

BOYD: That whites would say, "Boy, I don't know any blacks." But then if they really met a black for some reason, they would say, "Hey, that black is pretty nice, you know." "One of my best friends is a black boy." "John Doe is a nice black. He is a good man." And "If only—I didn't know that because I'd never come in contact with him."

THOMPSON: My landlord said that to me just two weeks ago. So don't think. . . . It's not just thirty years ago.

BOYD: But the difference today is that any well-meaning white or any well-meaning black who wants to be involved, exposed, who wants to deal with somebody of the other race has opportunities.

OJITO: But I wasn't really referring to the fact that he was black. It's the fact that his world is so different from mine. It's differences in socioeconomic status more than anything else. I mean we wouldn't have met. I wouldn't go to Liberty City normally. That's not where my friends live in Miami. So our worlds would not have come together.

SCOTT: These reporting experiences are not like real life. Because in these situations you have the license—because of what you're doing—to go like some superconducting supercollider immediately to the heart of the matter. And all of a sudden you can ask the kinds of questions that you would never normally be able to ask. There's this instant intimacy about it. That to me was the most exhilarating thing. You could ask all these taboo questions.

HOLMES: It was exhilarating to try and get people to talk about it. And it makes you wonder, or yearn—doesn't it make you wonder why more people don't? It makes me yearn for more people to be able to do this.

BOYD: I don't know why it takes a yearlong *New York Times* project on how race is lived in America to get a white reporter or a black reporter to have serious conversations with a person of the other race about race.

CANEDY: Well, one of the things our series showed us is that people still live in very segregated worlds.

SOMA GOLDEN BEHR: But why don't we even talk to the people at work? What about just turning to the person near you who's of a different race and saying: "Why are you reacting that way? Why are you so angry?"

HOLMES: Soma, I think you're being naïve. I think most of the time when people allow themselves to do that the person either calls them a racist or something else or withdraws.

GOLDEN BEHR: You have to be willing to slip up every once in a while.

BOYD: I don't understand why it is such an overpowering, difficult, awkward, impossible situation. That day in and day out whites will go home and talk about situations that they disagree with or don't understand but can't confront blacks about. And blacks will go home and basically have the same conversation with their loved ones. I don't understand what it is about race that makes this so—I mean, I understand people want to be PC, I understand people don't want to be misconstrued. I understand all those things. But I don't understand what it is about race that makes people unwilling to try, especially given what has gone on in this country over the last ten years or fifteen years.

ROBERTS: Has anyone found the answer in the past year?

GOLDEN BEHR: Well, Steve offered an answer. That you get labeled fast. You've got to be careful or somebody will take it wrong. And you have to know somebody pretty well before you take that risk.

WHOSE ISSUE IS IT?

HOLMES: For better or worse, race is seen as a black thing. Mike, did you find that there was a sense among the white cops that you were dealing with a black subject here?

MICHAEL WINERIP: Yeah, I think the cops, the black cops and the dark-skinned cops, the Latino cops, were much more comfortable talking about race than the white cops. The white cops kept feeling that they would be misconstrued, taken out of context. That they were going to sound as if they belonged on the Abner Louima case or the Diallo case.

BOYD: But there's talking and there's talking. I mean, I think if you played back our conversation here today you'd probably find that blacks, myself included, have been doing the most talking. I don't think we've been saying anything, frankly. And I think that's often the case, myself included. I think, Sure, you can get blacks to talk about race because it is certainly our world and we live in it and we see it constantly every day. But to what degree do we really allow blacks to say what is truly on their minds, what race does to them, what race means to them, how race makes it impossible for them or how race drives them crazy one way or another. Blacks don't have that conversation. That's not the conversation.

ROBERTS: With whites.

BOYD: With whites. And many of them don't have it with other blacks.

HOLMES: Oh, I think we do.

OJITO: Isn't part of the problem that whites don't have many black people to have that conversation with? Soma asked why we don't have this conversation in the newsroom. Turn around and talk to

your colleague. Well, I don't have a lot of black people to do that
with in the newsroom. I have no idea what it was like fifteen years
ago.

BOYD: Well, we've got a few more.

OJITO: But you know what I'm saying. You have to go out of your way
to have that conversation.

RACE OR SOMETHING ELSE?

ROBERTS: Mike, you've said that you and Gerald disagreed about the
hip-hop piece. How much of that was race and how much of it was
Gerald's own perspective or lack of interest or sense of humor or
whatever?

BOYD: I'm very interested in hip-hop.

WINERIP: Gerald is very interested in hip-hop. It's just that he didn't
know it was funny. That's what we argued about.

ROBERTS: O.K., but in arguing about that with a black editor, how
did that affect the argument?

WINERIP: N. R. "Sonny" Kleinfield had this white hip-hop character
who was essentially, I thought, hilarious. One of the phenomena of
hip-hop is that white young people sort of adopt this black urban
culture. And this guy was that to the ten-thousandth degree. He was
so extreme, he was a cartoon. I found it funny but Gerald kept
saying, "I don't get this guy." It was one of the few times when we
were doing this that I really felt as if race might be in the room.
Gerald and I screamed at each other the whole series. But a lot of
it was about how you do narrative journalism: Is this story too edgy?
Is this story mainstream enough? But this was a moment when I
felt, I trust my sense of humor. I think it's funny. He doesn't think
it's funny. Is it that he doesn't have a sense of humor? Is it that he's
black and I'm white?

ROBERTS: Gerald, did you see race in that conversation?

BOYD: To be honest, no. I thought it was his lack of judgment, faulty
judgment. But I think the larger issue, which hip-hop certainly represented, was, To what degree is race funny? You're dealing with an
issue that has enormous economic, social and even political costs to
younger blacks and middle-aged blacks, as well as younger whites.
And you're trying to explain it to an audience that is not so young,
to make sense out of it. Is it funny? I don't think it is.

HOLMES: What happens when race is involved is that there's always this thought in the back of your mind, as there was in this case. How much does it have to do with taste? And how much does it have to do with race?

SCOTT: We have no facility for addressing the subject. We have the facility to say, "You're from St. Louis. I know it's why you have this St. Louis bias." But we're just not comfortable with saying, "Along with the fact that you're from St. Louis and you're a girl, you're also black."

HOLMES: Right. I think *comfort* is the operative word.

SCOTT: Getting back to this question of why it's so hard to actually have these conversations, we're just out of practice. Or we've never been in practice. Everybody backs off. I hope in the future I will be less inclined to back off.

ROBERTS: Would the stories themselves have come out different if they were written by a white reporter instead of a black, or a black instead of a white?

THOMPSON: I certainly think that there would have been different things considered if Mike had written my story.

WINERIP: But if you had ten white males all doing Ginger's story at the *New York Times*, you would have had ten different stories.

CANEDY: Or if you had ten black reporters, you know, or if Ginger had done my story or if Mike had done my story, the same dynamics would have played out. I mean it has to do with class issues, socio-economic backgrounds, all those things.

THOMPSON: But that doesn't mean race isn't an issue.

ROBERTS: So race is one prism but not the only prism.

THE QUESTIONNAIRE

SCOTT: I saw that questionnaire [a list of race-related questions that some reporters asked their subjects and that some also answered themselves] and I thought, Ugh, how much do I want to reveal? Then we also had to ask the same questions of our subjects, and I called up Charles Dutton, and I went through the questionnaire with him, and it was fun. When I came to the point, "Did you have white friends as a child?" he said: "No, of course I had no white friends. You know I grew up in a black public housing project. There were a couple of white people there, and I played with them

maybe in the daytime. But no white person ever came to my house."
And he was completely frank about it. I hung up the phone and I
thought, If he can do it, I ought to, too. I should say, Of course
there were no black people in my childhood. And then I thought,
You can't, as a white person, do that as easily. Even though as a
child it's not your decision that you're living in a totally white suburb
and going to a totally white school. But that's where the issue of the
moral failing comes in. You feel as if it's a failing.

ROBERTS: So what did you say on the questionnaire?

SCOTT: Well, I didn't answer that question accurately, actually. The
question was: Who was the first person of another race who left a
meaningful impression upon you? What happened was the honest
answer was one thing, which I'll tell you. And I went to my husband
and I said, "Should I give this answer, because I know it's embarrassing." And he said: "It will be used against you. It will be used
to judge the quality of your story." So I gave an answer that was not
untrue, but it happened later on. The answer that I didn't give was:
I grew up in a totally white suburb; I went to very white schools
until I was fourteen. I lived in a very white world. And the first black
person to leave a meaningful impression upon me was a woman
who sat on a stool at the entrance to the farmers' market where my
mother would shop every Saturday—with a tambourine in her lap,
in a long dress, raising money for her church in a part of the town
where I lived that we never saw. And every Saturday when we would
go to the farmers' market, we were told to go over and give a quarter
to Sister Jackson. Now, that was the first person. And that's a terribly
painfully revealing fact about my past, and I didn't put it in the
questionnaire.

HOLMES: Excuse me. What's so painful?

SCOTT: Because it shows how benighted my childhood was. And, obviously, Charles Dutton was perfectly comfortable saying the same
thing about his own childhood. But he could be comfortable with
it, and you tell me why I'm not.

HOLMES: But it wasn't . . . As you said before, it wasn't your fault.

SCOTT: Mike, you seem to understand what I'm saying even though
Steve and Dana profess not to. Do you think that they're being
honest in saying that it wouldn't be held against me?

WINERIP: I know what you mean. I mean, it's kind of you're less
experienced, you're more protected, you grew up in an ivory tower,

those kinds of things. And I think we all like to think of ourselves as worldly and urban and having this variety of experiences.

HOLMES: But if you were to say that you didn't know any plumbers or carpenters, nobody would hold that against you. You wouldn't think that would be held against you. But if you didn't know any black people, that would be—

SCOTT: Plumbers are not subject to persistent discrimination.

YOU HAVE TO FIGURE OUT HOW WHITES WANT YOU TO BE

BOYD: What is major to me, because I've seen it time and time again, is the weight blacks give to race. Blacks give race so much weight that you can't be yourself, you have to try to figure out how whites want you to be. And it doesn't change based on how much success you have. That was one of the things that came through in some of our stories. Race is out there, time and time again. And if you're not careful, it's going to reach out and slap you and knock you down in some way and you'll never be able to get up from it. Now, there's some truth in that. I'm not minimizing that. But to give whites and race so much power is to me incredibly destructive and counterproductive and hurts. And yet it happened and it still happens.

GOLDEN BEHR: In our editing discussions we shocked reporters by what we asked them to reflect on and come back at us with. And sometimes we got some fights with reporters who didn't want to go there. There were tears, there was emotion. But there were breakthroughs afterward.

HOLMES: Yeah, but Soma, I'm curious: Did you feel that race was the reason, that they were afraid of a particular racial aspect of—

GOLDEN BEHR: I think sometimes it was and sometimes it wasn't. I think sometimes people are being protective of something that they didn't want to really write about.

LOOKING AT OURSELVES

ROBERTS: Dana, you looked at another newsroom. You looked at Akron. What did looking at that—the experience of looking at that newsroom—teach you about our newsroom?

CANEDY: Well, I think one of the things it taught us is that whether you're talking about the *New York Times* or a bank or a factory or a retail store, institutions struggle with the same kinds of issues of diversity.

ROBERTS: Gerald is looking skeptical.

BOYD: Oh, no, no, no. I think everybody struggles with diversity. What this taught me about the *Times* and race are a couple of things: that I think it is out there in the thick of our newsroom; it is all over the place; and that we seldom engage it, for whatever reason.

HOLMES: Another thought, which is less about the institution. Dana, you were dealing with this white columnist, who I considered an absolute jerk. I was curious about how you were able to deal with this guy who reveled in his ability to say things that would put black people on edge.

ROBERTS: As a black reporter?

HOLMES: As a black reporter.

CANEDY: I don't think he sees himself that way, number one. Also, I think the beauty of having time to do these stories is you see people as full, complex characters and not one-dimensional figures. And so in spending a lot of time with him I got to see him as a father, I got to see him as a journalist, I got to see him as a friend, I got to see him in his role as a husband, as someone involved in that community. So it was easier for me to see him not just as someone who'd written some columns that black people used to label him as racist. I had, I think, as tough a time understanding the black columnist just because he, for example, is very shy and was a very reserved person.

WHAT WE TALK ABOUT WHEN WE GO HOME

BOYD: When I started out in the early 1970s, it was very popular to be black. Every white had to have one. And so you'd go to dinner parties and you'd sit around the table and you could tell lies for days and nobody would challenge you. And the assumption was if you were a black professional you could speak for 12, 14 million black people: all black people think this. And then something happened in this country as more and more blacks got into the workplace and became professional; it became clear blacks disagreed and we didn't see things all the time alike. But that was fifteen, twenty years ago. What has happened since then, I think, can basically be described as racial fatigue. I think whites have, in their view, tried to reach out and accept and understand and they feel, for the most part, that blacks have not been responsive. I think blacks feel they have tried to be heard and understood and that whites haven't heard them, haven't been responsive. And so what you have is just indifference. And what I've always wondered is how much whites and blacks actually do talk about race in the privacy of their own bedrooms.

GOLDEN BEHR: Whites don't have to think about race very much. I've just grown convinced that blacks think about race all the time because they're the minority in the room all the time and that that just raises a lot of issues for them. And that whites have the luxury, if that's what it is, of cruising along.

BOYD: We struggled with race, we struggled with -isms a lot in the late 1960s and early 1970s, whether it was racism or sexism or—this was the generation that was going to change the world. We were trying to deal with them as well as we could, day in and day out and week in and week out.

GOLDEN BEHR: So do you have racial fatigue?

BOYD: Oh, yes. Especially after this project.

WINERIP: Well, as a white person I got racial fatigue from this project. I found myself mad sometimes having to think about all this stuff. I didn't want to. It's like what you say, Gerald, I don't think whites have to think about it as much. And this project made me fatigued. I was angry about how much I had to think about it. And I was tired of thinking about it.

HOLMES: What angered you about it?

WINERIP: Trying to get to the bottom of it. Was this moment racial or wasn't it racial?

ROBERTS: Janny, that's something you had with Charles Dutton. Is he just kind of a bombastic, aggressive, larger-than-life character or was he acting this way, on some level, because he's black?

SCOTT: This is a person who is intensely conscious of race, says he sees race in absolutely every interaction. Months into the process I emboldened myself to ask the question, "So if race is a factor in everything, how is it a factor in our conversations?" And he, with characteristic bluntness, said it's a factor in that I distrust you. And he said, "I'm going to say a lot of things to you that you just won't understand." At the time, you know, it was painful to hear. In retrospect, it was absolutely true.

ROBERTS: Why did he talk to you?

SCOTT: I asked him that question and he said, "Well, I haven't seen any black reporters around here."

IS THIS RACE?

THOMPSON: Well, I guess what I was thinking is that blacks all the time are thinking: Is this race? Am I being perceived some way because I'm black? I think that black people are constantly filtering race in the way that we are thinking about how we are being perceived in a conversation.

CANEDY: I wanted to give an example of that. As a black business reporter at the *New York Times*, I have to interview CEO's of Fortune 500 companies all the time. Sources I've made over the phone and have talked to for months and have never met, a lot of times they really don't know that I'm black. I can't tell you the number of times I've shown up at companies. I mean, I could be the only one in the lobby, and the executive assistant for the CEO will walk right past me two or three times, just not even seeing me because they weren't expecting a black person. There have been plenty of times when I'm going to an interview with a source who has given me good information but has never met me. And I have to think, Oh, boy, when this person discovers I'm black—what I call "black surprise"—is the dynamic of the relationship going to change?

THE TAKEAWAY

ROBERTS: What did you want readers to come away with? What do you want them to walk away with that they didn't have before?

CANEDY: I hope they don't walk away at all. I mean really, I hope that conversations are going on now and that there's a momentum that continues for a while.

BOYD: I think people assume an awful lot when it comes to race. That if they explored it or put it out there or challenged it or threw it up, it would probably not hold up. Maybe truth is a bit more complicated than they believe.

ROBERTS: Has working on this series changed you?

GOLDEN BEHR: It has changed how I think of some of my friends. A couple of them admitted that they didn't see, they didn't understand, the drama of this. Which really shocks me. We showed what's going on in a silent world where people don't go, and I thought that was an enormous contribution. I hope people will understand that there is a lot of unfinished work to do to understand each other. I found it pretty shocking to find people who said, "Well, isn't that just another story about race?"

THOMPSON: It's what race is in America. It's not Diallo. It's working in the same office every day. Someone described it as a low-grade fever. Something you go home with every day and it gnaws at you, it nags at you and you're irritable over it.

SCOTT: It just gets down to what we've been talking about, that every-thing seems to be seen differently by different people. You can never get your hands around what exactly it is that you're talking about. And then to be entrusted with so much of two people's lives and to try to get within that at this elusive thing. . . . I feel humbled by it.

18

Knowing Your Subject, Knowing Yourself: Journals from the Writers and Photographers

"SHARED PRAYERS, MIXED BLESSINGS"
Kevin Sack, Writer

—

I have Pat Buchanan to thank for leading me to the Tabernacle. Four years ago, while covering Buchanan's presidential campaign, I accompanied him one Wednesday night to midweek services at several Pentecostal churches in Lake Charles, Louisiana. Each church, to my amazement, was somewhat integrated, and by the end of the evening I found myself far more interested in the racial dynamics of the churches than in Buchanan's declaration that he would wage a "cultural war for the soul of this country."

I made a mental note: something was happening in these churches that was worth exploring. Unfortunately, the demands of daily journalism kept me from turning that thought into a story until my editors tapped me for the *Times's* project on race. I felt instinctively that an integrated church, particularly a conservative Southern church, would provide a rich case study in the mechanics of integration. Given time to really examine such a place in Atlanta, where I am the Southern bureau chief, I felt confident that I would find something revealing about the state of race relations and the viability of integration.

I was a boy of eight in Jacksonville, Florida, when the Reverend Dr. Martin Luther King Jr. was killed, and my greatest professional regret is being born twenty-five years too late to cover the civil rights movement. But as a native Southerner, I have always had an abiding interest in race. And as a reporter who has spent most of his career in the South, I have come to conclude that today's racial stories, the subtle stories of how blacks and whites negotiate their way through a more equitable world, are just as interesting as the ones I missed. I also see the integration of the Tabernacle as one of many signs of incremental progress in the South, often found in unlikely alcoves.

When I first arrived at the Tabernacle, I expected to find a church where integration had taken hold in the pews but had not extended beyond the church walls. I could not have been more mistaken. Before long, I was being welcomed into people's homes for Sunday dinners, potluck suppers and fish fries. (Pentecostals frown on drinking and smoking, so food is their guilty pleasure.) Each occasion was thoroughly integrated, and in a strikingly natural way. It often occurred to me that the gatherings might be the only ones in Atlanta in which the races were mingling so authentically at that moment.

It took a while to become accustomed to Pentecostal worship. But it took no time to be moved by the unity on display in a choir practice, or in an ushers' prayer circle. At a potluck dinner one Friday night, I felt myself choking up while watching prayerful congregants, black and white, lay their hands together on D. K. Fraser, a beloved elder of the church who was in poor health.

From my first visit, I found the people of the Tabernacle to be the warmest and most welcoming I had ever encountered. They greeted me with hugs, asked after my family and included me in outings. If I missed a Sunday or two, they lightheartedly accused me of backsliding. When I sat in for several weeks on a men's class that was modeled on Promise Keepers, they invited me to their banquet and awarded me a certificate along with the others. The pastor and I joked that I was probably the first Jew ever to receive one.

Above all, the members of the Tabernacle openly shared their stories of race, stories that were often painful and perplexing. Blacks described the wounds of their childhood. A white mother spoke of her angst about her daughter's relationship with a black man. Another white woman struggled to understand the scornful attitude she always sensed in a black store clerk. They told their stories honestly and forthrightly, despite the sensitive subject matter. For that, I owe them my gratitude, and offer my sincere wish that their experiment will thrive and prosper.

James Estrin, Photographer
—

The first time I went to the Assembly of God Tabernacle church in Decatur, Georgia, it was for the 1999 Christmas pageant. I started photographing that week because, for the first time at the church, the baby Jesus was being portrayed by a nonwhite child.

During the services, I watched as the black churchgoers and the white churchgoers prayed fervently together, sharing a deeply personal moment. After the pageant, I left Atlanta so that I would be home in time for my own Christmas ritual — dinner with my best friend at his mother's house. I am a modestly observant Jew who is passionate about his religion. My friend Alex Blackwood is a devout Christian of Jamaican descent and a pediatrician who leads a medical research laboratory. He lives in Ann Arbor, Michigan, is a single father and has been my best friend since I was four years old. As far back as I can remember, I have spent Christmas with him and his mother, Lucille, at her home in New Rochelle, New York.

As I entered the house with my wife, Randy, and our children, Elizabeth, six, and Marshall, four, I felt enveloped in the warmth of childhood memories. My parents are gone, and there are few places now where I can feel unconditional love. This house is one.

For this dinner, the guests included people from the Caribbean, Africa, America and China; black, white and Asian; Jewish and Christian. They included Lucille's four children, her four grandchildren and various other nonrelatives who have become family during her seventy-eight years.

As my kids raced around with Lucille's grandchildren, I talked about the race project and the Tabernacle church. The conversation turned to why race was such a difficult issue. "What's so complicated?" Alex asked. "Look around. This should be normal."

As several of us talked, we were confronted with the bitter truth that race is always a presence in this country, particularly if your skin is not white. "When you leave this house," Alex continued, "race is everywhere."

As we prayed (a nondenominational prayer) over the Christmas dinner, I thought about the fragility of the Tabernacle members' struggle. And I wondered about what it was that I had really observed. Was this congregation of blacks and whites the foundation for a true multiracial community? Or had I simply arrived during a moment of transition, from a white church to a mostly black church? I said a quiet prayer for them.

"BEST OF FRIENDS, WORLDS APART"
Mirta Ojito, Writer

—

I found out I was pregnant the day I met Joel Ruiz. It was a Friday, August 6, 1999, about a month and a half into the search for two subjects—one black, one white—who would help me illustrate the complexity of race relations among Cubans in Miami.

Both events—finding out I was pregnant while I was miles away from home and locating the right black person for the article so early on in my quest—took me by surprise. The news of my pregnancy came as I visited a dear friend, a gynecologist, and casually mentioned that I was not feeling well. He gave me a quick pregnancy test. "Congratulations!" he said, and hugged me. I said I was late for my next appointment and rushed off, crying tears of happiness all the way to my first meeting with Joel at the black-owned bar where he works.

I had arranged to meet Joel the week before. He was a distant relative of a black Miami Cuban whom I had called while looking for a guide in Liberty City, one of the oldest black neighborhoods in South Florida. He suggested his wife's cousin, Joel, who was young and connected and had lived in Liberty City. I called, and Joel was willing to help, so I decided to drop by for a chat.

In the end, Joel and my pregnancy proved to be good for each other. He loved to eat. I was always hungry.

In five months of almost weekly visits to Miami, Joel and I conducted a gastronomic tour of the city. We had fresh grouper by the Miami River, shrimp in garlic sauce in a Cuban restaurant, stuffed rabbit in a Spanish restaurant in Little Havana, and a wonderful avocado salad in a Dominican cafeteria. It was a fair bargain. He got to know some of the city's best restaurants. I got to know him. The *Times* picked up the tab.

There was an added bonus to our lunches and dinners: they gave me a firsthand opportunity to understand what Joel feels when people see him only for his color. Because I am a woman, people assumed we were a couple. Because I am white and he is black and this was Miami—an extraordinarily segregated city with few interracial couples—people stared everywhere we went. At first the stares didn't bother me; I hardly noticed them, in fact. But Joel did, and he did not like it. As I got to know him, I could tell when he had detected what I began to call "the stare." He would become guarded in his answers, antsy, eager to get the check. When my pregnancy started to show, the stares became more intense, and they began to bother me. Once, in a Spanish restaurant in Calle Ocho, the heart of Cuban Miami, an older blond woman with dark glasses fixed her eyes on us during the entire lunch. I had never discussed "the stare" with Joel. That day, I decided to bring it up.

"She must think I am your wife," I said.

"Or my parole officer," he said.

I didn't know whether to laugh or cry. We left.

Toward the end of my pregnancy, during my last trip to Miami, I took Joel to Joe's, perhaps Miami's best-known restaurant. It is famous not only for its delicious stone-crab dishes but also for its long lines. The restaurant does not accept reservations. It is not uncommon to wait three hours for a table. I was hoping we would get lucky on a weeknight and avoid the crowds. I was wrong.

About a hundred people waited for tables that night. I was about to suggest we go someplace else when a maître d' approached Joel and warmly shook his hand. The man was a regular at the bar where Joel worked. He made a fuss over my huge belly. "Let me get a chair for your wife," he told Joel in front of the hungry crowd, then led me to the front of the line. I pretended to be weaker than I really was, but in truth I was euphoric. Joel, who had never been to Joe's, could not understand how lucky we had been.

"The stare" was so intense, I kept my own eyes on the floor. For the first time, though, I was sure nobody cared that I was possibly the pregnant wife of a much younger black man—the only black patron in the restaurant that night. I think they stared, intently and coldly, because they knew we were going to eat Joe's stone crabs before them. And we did.

Librado Romero, Photographer
———

When I first laid eyes on Joel Ruiz, he was playing basketball with friends in a local Miami high school gymnasium. I didn't take pictures of him at first because we hadn't been formally introduced, and I had been told he was reluctant to be photographed. The same was true with Achmed Valdés when, a few days later, I saw him in a park where he met with his friends each weekend to play soccer.

With both men there wasn't much that set them apart from all the other weekend athletes across the country, sweating out the frustrations of jobs, families and life in general. They were skilled in their chosen sports, aggressive, committed to helping their teams win. But no more so than a lot of regular guys shooting hoops or kicking a ball around a nice green field.

It wasn't until a few months later in Cuba that I understood the courage and desperation that these two young men had exhibited when they fled to America for opportunities that didn't exist in their homeland. I stood, first with Joel's father and later with Achmed's, on the same beaches south of Havana where each had watched his son leave on a separate makeshift raft and disappear beyond the horizon. We looked out over a calm ocean together, and I couldn't imagine what it would take to get me to climb aboard and set sail for Florida, ninety miles away.

When I was a boy, my friends and I would sometimes hitch rides on slow-moving boxcars, jumping off as the train picked up speed. Once, a train got to moving too fast and a desperate decision had to be made: jump now and risk injury, or travel to a distant place and force your father to come pick you up. The greater the distance, we knew, the greater the punishment. So we jumped. But what we felt in those harrowing moments was nowhere near what Joel and Achmed must have experienced as they set out onto a treacherous sea.

When I returned to Miami and saw Joel and Achmed again, I had a new respect for what they had accomplished. I told them as much in separate encounters. I said that most people could never realize what it must have been like out there on a tiny raft with no land in sight and with no idea of what to expect. Each, in turn, reacted identically. A slow single nod, their eyes acknowledging that what I said was true.

I thought back to a village in Cuba, where we had a late-afternoon meal in an open-air cafe with Joel's sister and father. The father talked at length about his son's departure, and when we had finished eating and drinking, our driver asked Joel's father where he would like to be taken. I thoughtlessly chimed in, "How about Miami?"

He didn't smile, but he looked at me and said, "Don't play with our emotions."

"WHICH MAN'S ARMY"
Steven A. Holmes, Writer
—

It wasn't exactly a breakthrough, but I remember it as the day that gave me hope that I would be able to get close to some of the drill sergeants of Bravo Company.

I had been at Fort Knox only a short time, and I was worried. Like many people my age and of my class, I had had almost no contact with men and women in the military throughout my life. In my younger days, in the late 1960s and early 1970s, the Army was something to be avoided lest one end up slogging through a rice paddy in Vietnam. After the draft ended and the military became more blue collar, I knew fewer and fewer people who served in the Army. As a reporter, I had covered politics, foreign policy, the courts and race. I had never covered military affairs to any great extent.

So here I was covering an institution that I hardly knew and dealing with race, a potentially embarrassing and explosive subject. I worried how I would connect with these soldiers.

My first experiences at Fort Knox hardly gave me any cause for hope. Fort Knox officials suggested that I concentrate on one of two companies. The first one, Delta Company of the 281 Tank Battalion, was a disaster. The company commander was wary. He wanted to keep me under tight control. Every time I showed up, I was to be escorted around either by him, his second in command or the company's first sergeant. Several times, drill sergeants would grab young recruits, march them over to me, stand them at parade rest and bark at them, "Tell this reporter about race relations here!"

Bravo Company was completely different: warm, welcoming, relaxed. I was allowed to come and go as I pleased, and to talk with anyone in public or in private without the company brass hovering over me.

Still, access was one thing; making the connection was something else altogether.

It happened on a sweltering day in July. The privates were attending a class, and most of Bravo Company's drill sergeants were bored. I had wandered into an office and plopped down on a couch to chat with Sgt. First Class Rogelio Gomez, who was reading a newspaper and chewing a plug of tobacco.

Gomez, an eighteen-year veteran, started complaining loudly about low Army pay. The conversation echoed through the cinder-block hall-ways of the barracks, and other people wandered in. First came Lt. Paul Bergson, the second in command, then Sergeants Luis Perez, Robert Boler and Earnest Williams. Williams would wind up as one of two main subjects of my article.

Soon the gathering became spirited. Talk moved from military pay to other issues—politics, the state of Army standards, women serving in combat, gays serving at all. Though these men held, for the most part, deeply conservative views on most subjects, not everyone agreed, and everyone wanted to get his opinion in.

Soon we moved the conversation from the office to outside the classroom, where the recruits were hearing a lecture. Other drill ser-geants joined us, and the arguments continued at high intensity. Sud-denly one of the drill sergeants turned to me and said in amazement, "You know, you're a real catalyst for conversation."

During a lull, Williams told me he had to move the company's truck to another spot and asked if I would like to ride along. Inside the cab, he began speaking about his frustration at not getting a promotion and how he felt he was not getting ahead because he was black. For the moment, he asked that his comments be off the record, that I not use them. I agreed.

As I listened to Williams and thought about the lively talk I had just had with the other drill sergeants, a thought came to me. These were men who were pleased that a reporter for the *New York Times* wanted to know what they thought. At a time when so much of the news media seems fixated on the lives of politicians, celebrities and dot-com millionaires, they couldn't believe that a major newspaper was inter-ested in them. I heard it time and again during my time at Fort Knox. I heard them explaining to incredulous friends and spouses that the *New York Times* was doing a story on how they felt. Yeah, they said, the *New York Times*, no kidding.

Except for the time when Williams spoke of it in the cab of the truck, race hardly came up that day. And that wasn't disappointing at all, because I knew it would. It would be hard. The men would be reluctant to discuss their feelings about race. Anybody would be. But I knew I was on my way toward gaining their trust. There was no rush.

Driving back to my hotel room that night, the thought kept coming into my head: "This is going to work out just fine."

Ozier Muhammad, Photographer
—

I went to Fort Knox with reporter Steven Holmes to see whether the United States Army was as racially harmonious as it was reputed to be. But I already had the answer. I was sure it wasn't.

I had never served in the military. Though I was eligible during the Vietnam War, I was not drafted. And if I had been, I would have chosen prison. I did not believe in the war. I did not believe the Viet Cong were the enemy.

Protesting our country's involvement in wars was a tradition with my family. My grandfather, my father and all my uncles except one were sent to prison for refusing to serve in the armed forces. Race was at the heart of their refusal. To the older men of my family, drafted during World War II, the military's racial policies mirrored those of the Jim Crow South.

Under the leadership of my grandfather Elijah Muhammad, members of my family founded the Nation of Islam. The nation was a community of black nationalists that embraced a philosophy of self-determination and a set of religious teachings slightly resembling those of Islam. Elijah Muhammad defined our—black folks'—enemies. During World War II and throughout the wars in Korea and Vietnam, the Nation of Islam understood that there was no distinction between the evils of racism on our shores, of Nazism in Europe or of Communism in much of the world. Thus it was the Nation of Islam's policy that Muslim men would not serve in our armed forces.

That policy began to change after the death of Elijah Muhammad, who was succeeded by my uncle Wallace Muhammad. My uncle believed that it was up to the individual Muslim whether to serve in the military. He saw it as a matter of conscience. Although he had gone to prison for refusing military service, he recognized that after Vietnam the military had begun to evolve, for the better. Today, many African-American Muslims accept joining the armed forces as their patriotic duty.

Steve Holmes and I discovered signs of this evolution at Fort Knox. Most of the sergeants in charge of Bravo Company, the unit we were examining for the race series, were black. But we also found evidence that much had not changed between the races. There were unmistakable racial tensions between the company's white and black sergeants.

Steve and I decided that on our first morning together at the base we would join the company on bivouac — a field exercise that involved a ten-kilometer march. The average age of the sergeants was twenty-eight; that of the privates, eighteen, but we middle-aged journalists managed to keep pace. On bivouac the men were less guarded, more emotionally exposed. And I found that things were not much different in the Army than in the outside world. I heard young black privates, for example, bandying the "N" word about.

Now, I am old enough to remember when black folks would put their lives on the line to challenge the use of that epithet, so I asked a black drill sergeant about the Army's policy on it. He told me that the "N" word was not to be tolerated. I heard the word used several more times during my three visits to Fort Knox — each time by a black private.

At another point a tempest arose when a white drill sergeant used the epithet in a training exercise. He defended his use of it, saying he had been demonstrating to the black recruits how the enemy might use the word to demoralize them if they were captured. Some black privates and sergeants were unpersuaded, however, and successfully demanded an inquiry.

The "N" word offends me. Even so, I found it odd that the black privates would get so incensed over a white sergeant's using the word. Some privates used the word as commonly as the pronoun "you" — and in earshot of the offending white sergeant.

In many ways, the anxieties and concerns troubling some of the military men we encountered reflect those of the larger world. It was plain, for example, that some of these white and black boys, becoming men in a hurry, had come from poverty. For them, the army was clearly a step up in life, and unfortunately one of the few avenues available to them to escape poverty. It was also clear to me that white soldiers were needlessly wary of their black counterparts' getting a leg-up, just as in the civilian world whites often feel threatened by affirmative action. To me, Fort Knox encapsulated where we are as a nation of whites and blacks. There were signs of progress, there were signs of the old divisions.

And yet I left there with some optimism. After viewing the military up close, and imagining what it must have been like when my grandfather took a stand against it, I am certain it is becoming a better institution, just as I believe we Americans are striving to be a better people.

"WHO GETS TO TELL A BLACK STORY?"
Janny Scott, Writer
—

The idea was simple: Find a couple of writers of different races working together on a television show, attach myself to them and watch how race made itself felt in their work. But finding people willing to co-operate was not simple, since television shows are mostly written by white people and the entertainment industry seems willing to indulge reporters only insofar as they can be counted on to write nice things.

It took months to find them, but I finally inflicted myself upon David Simon and David Mills, two journalists turned television writers working on an HBO miniseries based on Simon's book about an inner-city drug corner. They had been friends for twenty years and had worked together in the past. Mills warned me when we first spoke that their relationship was "almost beyond any sort of feeling each other out about race."

Then HBO hired Charles (Roc) Dutton to direct their series. Dutton was a product of the very world that Simon had captured as a reporter, and he had as much authority as anyone to represent that world. "The real issue now is not between David Mills and David Simon," Mills told me that July, after Dutton had been hired. "It's that Roc is taking the material and putting his stamp on it. That will be the power issue now."

Over the following eight months, I followed the three of them. By temperament, Dutton was the most inclined to unwrap his feelings, no matter how contradictory they might seem. The first time we sat down to talk at length, he spoke for four and a half hours. In an unlit office, the twilight outside dwindling until the room was engulfed in darkness, he talked about his experience of race with an unfamiliar and liberating bluntness.

The challenge, we reporters had all been told, would be getting our white subjects to speak honestly, white people having figured out long ago that the most profitable course was to keep their mouths shut when it came to race. Simon was far more comfortable with race than most white people. But he was an uncommonly shrewd subject, a journalist who had used the same stand-around-and-watch style of reporting on two successful books with intimidating results.

If he sensed Dutton's ambivalence toward him during those months shooting in Baltimore, he did not let on. Only when the filming was almost all over, and we began to replay the experience, did he ask if he had been the only one who had been discreet. Even then, he revealed no anger. He always seemed to give Dutton the benefit of the doubt. He had assumed, he said, that Dutton would never trust a white reporter enough to be indiscreet himself.

Not that Dutton did trust me. He said many times that for him, race was a factor in everything. So one day in October 1999, in a church basement in East Baltimore where the cast and crew were eating dinner, I asked him: If race was a factor in everything, how was it a factor in our conversations? How did it affect what he chose to say and not say?

"First of all, distrust," he said without hesitation. "A basic distrust. So when I tell you things that you write about, you're going to look at it from the perspective of a white woman journalist talking to a black guy about a black story, and you'll interpret it that way and it will come out that way." What was more, he said, "A lot of this you probably won't understand."

Then why bother to talk to a white reporter at all? I asked him, stung. "Well, they don't have a black one here, do they?" he said, laughing.

Andrea Mohin, Photographer

The HBO miniseries *The Corner* was in its final week of shooting when I arrived on location. My first impression was that the crew had created an island in the middle of the worst neighborhood in Baltimore. The streets were cordoned off, and I had to walk several blocks with my camera equipment. The crew seemed tired and cranky and unhappy about my presence. Who was this outsider with a camera? Why was she lurking about?

I made a point to shoot from a distance in the beginning, assuring the crew that I wouldn't interfere with their work. Much of the miniseries was shot indoors, where, it turned out, there wasn't enough room for another body. Besides, I apparently couldn't be trusted to keep my shutters silent during the takes. I therefore spent much of my time observing the mingling of urban reality and the made-for-TV version of it as people in the neighborhood watched the action from their steps.

I was allowed access during some outdoor scenes, but they often occurred at night and were difficult to document. Even on the last day of shooting, as I zoomed in on a crucial moment, a crew member deliberately sneaked into the frame and made a face.

On past assignments, whenever I felt unwelcome, I have looked for an ally. In Baltimore I soon realized it would be the director himself, Charles Dutton. He was one of the few people who made me comfortable on the set. He seemed to understand what I was trying to do. And perhaps he could empathize with an outsider who was not being accepted. I realize now that what I had experienced was a subtle, although minor, form of discrimination.

But as the tacit support from Dutton became apparent to others on the set, I was allowed, finally, to slip into the background so that I could document the dynamics of the story.

"A LIMITED PARTNERSHIP"
Amy Harmon, Writer
—

By the September morning of my first meeting with Tim Cobb, one of the founders of RelevantKnowledge, I was in a bad mood. I had spent two months approaching black executives in various industries, from investment banking to hair care, asking them to talk candidly with me about how race enters into their business lives, and to let me observe it myself over several months. Every one of them, often through a company spokesman, congratulated the *Times* for tackling this subject. Then, every one of them declined to participate.

I knew I was asking for a lot. All of my colleagues on the race series had found it difficult to get people to talk about race, whether the context was a school or a church or a factory. And business types, ever mindful of their company's stock performance, are more wary than most about talking without a script, on any subject.

The idea was to find two executives at senior levels, one white and one black, and to explore their relationship. Because the pool of African-Americans in senior business positions was small, I had decided to first find a black executive willing to cooperate and then go from there.

Most of the other reporters for the series had found that blacks were relatively forthcoming about their feelings on race. The opposite was true with me. Eventually I began to realize that the number of rejections I was receiving, and the reasons that were given—usually off the record—said a lot in itself about race in American business.

The list of those who said no includes many of the highest-ranking blacks in corporate America: Kenneth Chenault, soon to become chief executive of American Express; Richard Parsons, president of Time Warner; Lloyd Ward, chief executive of Maytag and one of two blacks to hold the top job at a Fortune 500 company. They were joined by about three dozen others. A letter describing the project that was circulated on my behalf among the more than two hundred members of the Executive Leadership Council, an association of senior black business executives, elicited no response.

"Many of our members have not found that it is advantageous to participate in articles like this," a representative of the group told me. A managing director of a Wall Street brokerage firm put it more bluntly. "There's no upside," he said.

Some did see an upside—a platform to give advice to other blacks climbing the corporate ladder, an opportunity to expose the subtle kinds of racism that some said they had experienced not infrequently. But then they would have to go to work with their white colleagues the day after the article ran, and where would that leave them?

The black executives I spoke to in person, sometimes in multiple sittings as they considered the idea, offered several kinds of objections. Some did not want to draw attention to their race, preferring to be recognized solely on the basis of how good they were at their jobs. Others worried that their white colleagues would see them as egotistical, or as using the *Times*'s attention as a power play.

In many cases an executive said he wanted to avoid being seen as having a chip on his shoulder about race. And some said they just had to work too hard—particularly as African-Americans in an environment in which blacks still held less than 1 percent of senior executive positions—to take the time to talk to a reporter at such extraordinary length.

In some cases a company's public relations apparatus seemed to thwart an executive who might otherwise have been willing to cooperate. Arnold Donald, who was the president of Monsanto Corporation, told me that he saw the *Times* article as a vehicle to enable others to benefit from his experience. Then his public relations people sent me the following guidelines:

1. Monsanto will arrange ALL interviews in advance with both Monsanto and non-Monsanto people who are speaking on behalf of Arnold Donald and Monsanto.
2. Amy Harmon is not permitted to speak to anyone without prior approval from Monsanto.
3. Public Affairs person will accompany all interviews.
4. Monsanto is prohibited from giving reporter diversity statistics that are not already publicly available.
5. Amy Harmon is not permitted to interview former Monsanto people without approval of Monsanto.
6. All background research must be approved by Monsanto.

Having become accustomed to such responses, I sat down that morning with Tim Cobb to explain in more detail the article I had outlined on the phone. "This would be one in a multipart series that the *Times* is working on about race relations in America," I recited wearily. He interrupted. He had thought about it already, he said, and, in what I came to learn was a characteristically impulsive decision-making process, he had decided to do it.

He told me he wanted to do it for his father, who had marched for civil rights, and for his young sons. And, he added jokingly, "I've done well enough that if I can never do business again after this, it doesn't matter."

In the end, Cobb and his partner, Jeff Levy, were not the only ones to agree to let me view their business world through a racial prism. But their unusual willingness to be introspective about race drew me to them.

In the days before the article went to print, however, Cobb demonstrated that even a brash Internet entrepreneur with abnormal risk tolerance could be subject to misgivings. I had called him to check the spelling of a name and the age of a child. That done, there was a pause. Then he wanted to know: "Am I going to be able to do business again?"

Richard Perry, Photographer

On the night before my first visit to Atlanta and my first meeting with Jeff Levy, I did what most photographers do before an important trip.

I packed too much stuff. Maybe I'd have only ten minutes with this guy. Maybe he wouldn't understand what I wanted to do over the many months to come. What if he just said: "OK, where do you want me to stand? You done yet?" Did he know what he was getting into? When a photographer doesn't know what to expect, there is comfort in having too much stuff.

I wore a jacket and tie for our first meeting. Anyone who knows me, particularly my superiors at the *Times*, would have been amused. I tend to wear jeans and a shirt (no tie), no matter the occasion—even when I was meeting with top editors during a stint as the paper's page-one picture editor. With Jeff and Tim, though, I started off trying to be someone I'm not.

Jeff was as comfortable and casual in our first meeting as I wish I could have been. He moved through his office with grace, whether answering the phone, using his computer or dealing with the demands of various people. Not a moment was left unfilled; not a moment was unproductive.

I am fascinated by what makes people like Jeff Levy and Tim Cobb different from most of us. Despite their different backgrounds and races, the same entrepreneurial heart seemed to beat within them, the same focus and demand for efficiency of time and energy. They seemed to have the ability to squeeze more out of a day than the rest of us.

One afternoon, while giving us a tour of his new house, Tim took particular delight in showing us the entertainment center he had designed, complete with a wide-screen high-definition television set and a sound system that made you duck for cover. He started up *The Thomas Crown Affair*, with its suave, risk-taking hero, saying it was important for us to see the movie if we wanted to understand him. Then, while we sat and watched, he ran out and picked up his boys, took them to dinner, did some shopping for the house, ordered Thai food and walked back in with the whole bundle a short time later.

On another day Jeff found himself with just a few minutes between appointments in Manhattan. He had just finished a live CNN interview and had a board meeting later downtown, in SoHo. So where did he go, dragging me along? Uptown, to Barney's, in my *New York Times* automobile. Once there, he attracted a sales clerk in a heartbeat. Now, I'm not a Barney's guy, but I was feeling left out. So as Jeff walked out moments later with his substantial provisions, I, too, had acquired a Barney's bag.

I tried on my expensive shirt later that night for a friend. The verdict: too big, bad color, just not you. The shirt still sits in its Barney's bag in my closet. I can't quite bring myself to return it.

"AT A SLAUGHTERHOUSE, SOME THINGS NEVER DIE"
Charlie LeDuff, Writer

___

It rained for weeks. There were dead, bloated hogs floating along the North Carolina coast. Whole towns destroyed. Lumberton, where I had rented a small house, got soaked but escaped without much damage.

I had gone to Durham for a weekend. When I returned to Lumberton, my neighbor, in her Southern way, came over to welcome me back. I opened my door. The place was filled with water. Lizards and mice and insects had taken shelter inside. A rodent crawled out of my boot. When I had rented the house, the landlord told me it sometimes got a little wet. He didn't say anything about a swamp.

"No way, baby," my neighbor said. "You couldn't get me to stay in there even if I didn't have no legs." Her ankles and knees were knotted and swollen like tree branches, and she was taking medicine for them. It was funny, what she said. I wrote it down.

The swamp didn't matter much. There was nothing of value inside. My desk was a closet door laid across some old tires. The bed was a board and mattress. The heat came from the oven, and the floor was cement. I had a clock radio, a lamp, some books, paper and pens on the desk. That stuff stayed dry.

I had rented the little house because I didn't want to live way off in the country in a trailer, as so many do. This place was only twenty miles from the Smithfield Packing Co., where I worked cutting meat from shoulder bones with a knife so sharp it could go through your arm.

I went to North Carolina to write about work. Race and work. The story, I felt, was important, and I was committed to living simply and working hard.

Up at a quarter to 4 in the morning, home by 6 P.M. When you work like that, the one thing you have to look forward to is break time. The thought of break time gets you through the day. You think about it even before you start your day. So when the boss starts nibbling away at your rest period, you get angry. Even a reporter who earns a good salary from a big company gets angry.

The shoulder line was supposed to be staffed with twenty-four people, a crew leader told me. But the job was so grueling, people avoided it, and at any one time we had only eighteen people working there. So, to make production, the people who control the pace bled the work time over into our precious half-hour break time, leaving us just nineteen minutes to take off our gear, run upstairs to the cafeteria for a cup of coffee and a cigarette, and back downstairs to put on our gear before the shoulders started rolling down the belt and falling on the floor.

The factory floor always got giddy around recess. Nearly all the workers wore a watch on their chests. We knew when it was time for break. Invariably, the boss would tell us that our watches were fast. Everybody's. By the time the boss let us off the line, our watches read 8:41. The boss said it was 8:30.

There was only one clock in the work area—up in the cafeteria— and by the time we got there our watches read 8:45. The cafeteria clock said 8:50. Suddenly, our clocks were slow.

We had time for one cigarette and maybe half a cup of coffee, although some people had learned to eat their food as quickly as a hound. When we returned to the production line at the top of the hour, the meat would already be moving. As if by magic, our watches now showed the correct time.

One of the prisoners I worked with was very tall. He was able to see a clock in the superintendent's office above the conveyor belts on the factory floor. The Americans—mostly black inmates—began to complain loudly that their time was being stolen. They pointed out the clock to the line supervisor. Surely the superintendent kept the right time? The supervisor told us to keep working. The inmates told him something else and walked off the line. They knew their rights. I went with them. The Mexicans stared in amazement at our mutiny. They kept on working.

We came back from break after having two cigarettes and a full eight-ounce cup of coffee. We had won! Or so we thought. When the midday break came around, a man to my right asked me what time it was and I asked the tall man on my left. He looked up and turned to me wide-eyed. The clock was gone.

Victory had been snatched away. The tall man said the place reminded him of his life behind the cinder blocks and steel bars. I thought about my swamp and my mice and my wife back home.

Edward Keating, Photographer
—

I was nearly killed nine years ago while covering the racial violence in Crown Heights, Brooklyn, for the *New York Times*. Chased down by an angry mob of about a hundred people of color, stripped of my cameras and beaten with fists, feet, metal pipes and baseball bats, I was finally knocked unconscious when I was struck in the back of the head with a brick. Two transit cops, one white and one black, on their way to McDonald's for dinner, appeared miraculously and risked their lives by breaking through the crowd to rescue me.

I regained consciousness to see the two cops looking over me and trying to decide what to do while they fought back the pressing crowd. "Kill the white cop!" the mob chanted. "Leave the brother alone!" The cops finally dragged me into the subway to safety.

The violence had been set off the previous night when a black boy was struck and killed by a car in a caravan carrying the spiritual leader of a community of Orthodox Jews. The next three nights were hell, and they began a critical period in the history of race relations in New York. Most people, including me, would be forced to confront a problem that was tearing their city apart.

I grew up in an affluent Connecticut suburb in the 1960s. Secure behind old stone walls and trimmed hedges, safeguarded by burglar alarms, this was a world far removed from any discussion of race. It was a world of good schools, safe streets and perfect teeth; a world of mothers who had the time and the luxury to get their kids off to school, meet with other ladies to play bridge and squeeze in a tennis lesson before arriving home to meet the school bus and prepare dinner. Their husbands were corporate bigwigs who headed out for the city in the morning and returned on the train at night just in time for dinner, a little pumped up from the ride home in the bar car.

In this world, people of color were the ones who came to your house to work, and they worked hard. They dug the ditches for new septic systems, served the guests at parties, laid blacktop for new driveways. When one of the workers came inside to use the bathroom, you appeared to be busy in the next room, out of sight.

The better jobs went to the plumbers, the electricians, the painters: people from the ethnic white working class of the town, most of them Italians, the descendants of laborers and the stonemasons who had immigrated here earlier in the century to build the summer and weekend houses for the rich gentry from New York. These were the people you left alone in your home if you went out to do an errand or to go to the club. A nice smile with the expectation of one in return made our dealings civil, Christian and right. We talked about the work that was to be done, and that was it. Where they lived was unclear, unimportant. At the end of the day, they simply pulled away; they disappeared.

A few blacks lived in our town, and the town managed from time to time to come up with money to build housing for what few people of need there were. But you heard that these people drank a lot, that there might even have been a prostitute or two. There were a few black kids at the country club: the children of a woman who worked at the local country day school. As part of her job benefits, she was given an honorary club membership—excluding use of the golf course—for as long as the school employed her. This was the same club that had for years denied membership to one of the town's finest, a physician to many of the club's members, simply because he was Jewish. There were also a few black kids at the school, but almost no one knew them. They never seemed to have boyfriends or girlfriends but always managed to maintain that sense of humor and that great smile. Everyone liked them, wondered how they did it, but most thanked God every day that they had been born white.

Once, when I was fourteen, as I was riding home from school, the car I was traveling in passed a black man running down the road in the opposite direction, toward town. He was in street clothes; he looked like someone you might find sitting at a counter in a diner having a cup of coffee. He was in a full run—in a hurry, it seemed; nervous, I thought; suspect. Arriving home a few minutes later, I went straight to the telephone and called the police.

An hour later I called the police again to check up on things. I was told that, yes, the police had picked up the man. His car, it seemed, had run out of gas about a mile up the road. I hung up and just stood there, ashamed of myself, wondering why I had assumed the worst about a man simply because he was black. I realized right then that that must be a big part of what it was like to be a black man in America: if you're black, you're suspect, and if you run down a country road in a white town, some fourteen-year-old kid might just sic the cops on you. I knew I had been unjust and wondered, How many men had been convicted of crimes and had spent their lives in jail or even been lynched for doing no more than being in the wrong place at the wrong time, or running down the wrong road at the wrong time?

And yet a part of me was angry at this black man for running, for inciting my fear, for bringing out the worst in me. He should have known better than to run, I thought. This only confused me, and only made me angrier with myself. I was certain of my prejudice, though; I knew I had hurt this man in a way he did not deserve. I wished more than anything that I could tell him how sorry I was.

More than twenty years passed, and there I was, beaten in a race riot in Crown Heights, given refuge in a subway station, my head bleeding, waiting for an ambulance as the roar of the crowd drifted down through the grates. Not done with me, the crowd surged around the station for nearly forty-five minutes, preventing an ambulance from getting through. They resembled a modern-day lynch mob: they were after me because I was white. After a full detachment of cops arrived, the paramedics were able to get to me and, protected by a wall of blue uniforms in riot gear, I was led out of the subway and into an ambulance. A convoy of police cars escorted me to the hospital. Afterward, I was asked by the police if I would be able to identify any of my attackers from mugshots. I probably could have; I had a clear picture in my head of many of their faces. But I was tired of fighting. I decided to end it right there.

You have to let go at some point. The conflict goes on forever if you wait for a tactical advantage, or for the score to somehow even itself. In the end, the only violence and hate we can really control is our own. I let my attackers go, along with my anger and my guilt. A bit lighter now, I got back to dealing with the only person I could change: myself.

"WHEN TO CAMPAIGN WITH COLOR"
Timothy Egan, Writer
—

More than ten years ago, an earnest-looking man knocked on the door of our old house in Seattle and said he wanted to talk about politics. Oh, thrill: it was a warm afternoon, the sun bouncing off Lake Washington, and the last thing I wanted to do was chat with a policy wonk who couldn't find anything better to do on a Saturday in September. He introduced himself as Gary Locke, my state representative, a former

Boy Scout, Yale graduate, Seattle native. Hey, fine. How about those Washington Huskies? No, seriously, he wanted my vote. (He also knew what kind of stain to use on my cedar deck so it wouldn't gray.) When he left, I said to my wife: that guy could be governor someday. It wasn't that he had any particular charm, magnetism or vision. He just seemed so devoid of cynicism—a rare commodity for a politician.

Gary Locke became someone who filled one of history's small niches: America's first Chinese-American governor. And when I began to look at how nonwhites govern in a state that is 89 percent white, he became my primary subject.

About the same time that I met Locke, I heard about another man whose life would figure prominently in this story, Ron Sims. I had signed up to coach Little League baseball, and the person whose influence loomed largest over the pee-wee diamonds in our neighborhood was Sims. He was a coach and motivator, of the "visualize a base hit" school, a powerful, funny speaker. Our teams were made up of whites with stiff mitts, orthodox Jews who couldn't play on Saturdays, Samoans with power swings, African-Americans trying to mimic Ken Griffey Jr.'s home-run trot, and everybody in between. Sims, who became one of the highest-ranking black politicians in the West, saw youth sports in South Seattle as the future hope of America. A meritocracy—with positive role models.

When I set out to try to see the world as Ron Sims and Gary Locke did, I thought I knew both men. As it turned out, I knew very little about either of them. Oh, sure, I was familiar with the public faces, the surface. What I did not know—and still can only partly understand—was the kind of calculations these men had to make in order to govern in a state where most people did not look like them.

I came to believe that Gary Locke, the Chinese immigrant's son, had the easier task. I was determined not to see him as a typical product of the "model minority" mold so often assigned to Asian-Americans. He professed to have no racial scars, even when he became governor and the local conservative talk-radio station took to calling him "Chairman Locke," as if he were a traitor to the nation of his birth.

A hundred years ago, Asian-Americans were marched out of their homes at gunpoint and told to get out of town. They were viewed as a threat. Now Asian-Americans were telling me that, for whatever reason, the present stereotypes about them—hardworking, honest, efficient—were helping them. One politician, born in Taiwan, even said he played up his accent because it was such a plus among white voters.

Something much different was at work in public attitudes toward black politicians. It is the rare African-American who tries to play up his race to win the votes of whites, at least in the State of Washington. Ron Sims was a complex man who was generous and bighearted in letting me follow him around and try to get at his soul. His racial scars were deep, and he had to go out of his way to distance himself from stereotypes. As one of his friends said: "His race precedes him in every room he walks into." Some days I thought Sims was going to collapse amid this balancing act. But he had a happy warrior quality as well, and it seemed to sustain him.

I started out thinking that I would write about the fastest-growing minority in the nation, Asian-Americans, and about how the rise of Gary Locke was evidence of a new society emerging on the West Coast in the post–civil rights era, one in which blacks, Latinos, Asians and whites would share power. In the end, I wrote a different story. In the midst of my reporting, a friend of mine who thinks Ron Sims could one day be president said that my story was going to ruin Sims's career—that he would forever be known as "the black guy" who let a *New York Times* reporter into his life. No one said the same thing about Gary Locke. Indirectly, my friend made the point that I initially did not want to believe: that all is not level in a part of the country that likes to think it has shaken off the encumbrances of the past.

Andrea Mohin, Photographer

I first saw Ron Sims, the King County executive, in a quintessential Seattle setting. He was buying a caffe latte on board the ferry to Bainbridge Island in Puget Sound on a rainy January morning. We hadn't yet been introduced, but I presumed that this man must be in the public eye. He had that aura about him, the gloss of a real communicator. He was heading to the island to speak to students about Martin Luther King Jr. on the eve of the holiday honoring King's birthday.

As he later addressed the students—almost all of them white, first at a middle school, then at a high school—my initial impression of him was proved right. He was a deft speaker, drawing insightful parallels between the personal and the historical. And he was a powerful speaker: his recollections of how racism had scarred him were riveting, and many in his audiences were moved to tears. At one moment I had the rare experience of wanting to put my camera down and simply listen.

Later, I felt compelled to tell him how much I had admired his speeches. I told him how strange it had felt for me, a white person from multiracial New York City, to be surrounded by so many white people. He seemed to immediately understand my comment; he moves in an almost all-white environment every day. The Seattle metropolitan area he represents is about 85 percent white.

As we left the island, Sims gave me one of his trademark bear hugs, the first of many.

That same weekend I met Governor Gary Locke at a reception, noticing immediately his broad smile, which made him stand out as he worked the crowd. But I was uncertain. Would I be able to get a close, personal view of this man? Would I be allowed to play the fly on the wall as he went about his business in the capital, Olympia? I had tried to make arrangements to spend time with him but had been frustrated.

But in the end my concerns proved unfounded. Locke included me in every moment of his day and made sure I felt at ease. Often his two small children — Emily, three, and Dylan, one — came to visit the governor's office. Emily even accompanied her father to closed-door meetings with her crayons in hand. Yet Locke always struck me as the consummate leader, and his staff clearly admired him.

On my last day in Washington state, I was scheduled to spend a half hour photographing a private Locke family dinner at the home of the governor's brother, Jeff, in a Seattle suburb. It was a rare opportunity. But as I arrived in town I discovered that there were several streets with the same name, with only the designations of "Street," "Road," "Court" and the like to distinguish them; the address I was carrying, of course, didn't say which.

As my scheduled half hour came and went, I drove round and round in a frenzy of street signs and cell phone calls hoping for a chance to salvage the day before I left for New York the next morning. Then the car phone rang.

"Andrea?" came the voice on the other end. "This is Gary. Where are you?"

I stuttered. "Gar—, uh, Governor, thank goodness. You found me."

The governor himself had come to the rescue. I not only made the dinner, but he even asked me to stay longer after I had excused myself. The next day, as I dropped off my rental car at Sea-Tac Airport on my way home to New York, the Washington State Legislature was at an impasse over the budget. Noticing my *New York Times* corporate credit card, the rental agent asked what sort of news I was there to cover. When I explained that we were examining why a predominantly white state had elected minority representatives, she exclaimed: "We don't care if they're green! We just want the budget passed!" Maybe, I thought, politics could be color-blind after all.

"REAPING WHAT WAS SOWN ON THE OLD PLANTATION"
Ginger Thompson, Writer

—

The terrifying experiences of Bill Gwaltney as the first African-American superintendent at the Fort Laramie National Historical Site did not make it into my article about the Cane River plantation. He was the person, however, who most convinced me to pursue history as a topic for our series on race. (And it was Gwaltney who had recruited one of the main subjects in my article, Carla Cowles, into the National Park Service).

If the Confederate flag demonstrations in South Carolina were not enough proof of the volatility of history in relationships between people of different races, then consider what happened to Bill Gwaltney and his wife in Wyoming.

The assignment at Fort Laramie was Gwaltney's dream job. The fort, established in 1834, had been a major fur-trading post that later became the staging area for the American takeover of Indian lands, some of them held sacred, in the Great Plains. Gwaltney had been a lifelong student of African-American military history. As a child he spent Saturdays at the library with his grandfather reading about the exploits of the black unit known as the Buffalo Soldiers in the Indian Wars; he later staged numerous Civil War battle reenactments for the National Park Service and worked as a consultant on the Civil War movie *Glory*.

A tall linebacker of a man with a face full of freckles, Gwaltney arrived at Fort Laramie in 1994 steeped in the valiant and tragic history of the struggle for control of the American frontier. But only one side of that story was being told at the park—a side that portrayed the bravery of the whites who had been stationed there. The most popular attraction was a daily demonstration of the old bakery, which once produced some seven hundred loaves of bread a day.

"I did not want us to be devoted to nostalgia," Gwaltney recalled. "That bread was delicious, but it once was fed to a bunch of men who went out and did a pretty ugly and dangerous job.

"They nearly wiped out entire Native American villages. And the history of that conflict is not dead, especially to the ancestors of those who were slaughtered.

"Cookies and knitting do not make good history."

Gwaltney began visiting local Native American leaders to ask for advice on developing programs that would allow the park to portray their versions of historical events. And he required the park's interpreters to wear more authentic costumes and to make sure that their staged gun battles were based on actual events. "I wanted a program that would be just as fair to the descendants of Indians as it is to the white settlers and soldiers," he said.

It was not long before park staff members began receiving complaints; some reported being questioned about Gwaltney's white wife. Gwaltney was called to respond to local elected officials who had questions about the direction of his programs.

Unmarked vehicles began to park in Gwaltney's driveway some nights, headlights on, engines running. Gwaltney began keeping a flak jacket and night-vision goggles in the trunk of his car. No one was ever arrested. Eventually his bosses in Washington came to town to negotiate peace. But worried about his wife's safety, Gwaltney abandoned his job by the end of his first year. In the summer of 2000, he was chief of interpretation—a lesser job than that of superintendent—at the Rocky Mountain National Park in Colorado.

Gwaltney later speculated that his troubles at Fort Laramie had been driven as much by money and power as by his programs.

The overwhelmingly white community, he believed, could not stand having a black man in such a high-profile position. As the head of a federal agency, Gwaltney said, he controlled some of the best-paying jobs in the area, and a significant portion of the local economy depended on the tourism.

"It only looks like the twentieth century," he said in 1999. "But I have seen things that say it just ain't so."

Fred R. Conrad, Photographer

—

I like Leslie Vercher's face. He cannot hide his feelings or his thoughts. This man should never play poker.

I began to get to know Leslie when I asked him to pose for a photograph in the doorway of one of the slave cabins on the grounds of Magnolia Plantation, in Natchitoches, Louisiana. The plantation had been home to his grandparents and father, who were sharecroppers. It was where some of his brothers and sisters were born. He had strong feelings about the cabins, and most were not happy.

The quarters were being preserved by the National Parks Department and were to be part of the Cane River Creole National Park. The fences and porches and windows were all gone. The only thing that remained were the shells of buildings, filled with the spirits and memories of those who had lived there during slavery and afterward, in the days of sharecropping. I needed a connection to those spirits' past. I needed Leslie.

Leslie was no fool, and there was no way that a *New York Times* photographer was going to take advantage of him. He had lots of questions about me, the photograph that I wanted to take, and why he was in the story. We talked a lot. I could not have deceived Leslie even if I had wanted to; it is impossible for me to hide my feelings. Finally, he allowed me to take his photograph.

Weeks later, after I had shot the last pictures for the story, Leslie and I visited a few juke joints with my assistant, Michael Nemeth. We had a great time listening to Lou Pride on the jukebox, drinking Budweiser and playing pool. I told Leslie about my grandfather, who for many years was a professional poker player. I had begged my grandfather to teach me how to play poker. He refused, saying, "Why should I teach you how to play poker when your face gives everything away?" Leslie responded, "You shouldn't play pool for money, either."

"GROWING UP, GROWING APART"

Tamar Lewin, Writer

—

The South Orange–Maplewood schools in New Jersey stood out right from the start as I shopped around for a racially mixed school district where I could observe a friendship between a black student and a white.

Partly it was the numbers: there just weren't many districts with such a mix of black and white as this one. And in some districts where the numbers looked promising, the income differences between the black and white kids cut so deep that there wasn't much social mixing.

But what really made South Orange–Maplewood unique among all the districts I contacted was the number of people there who were interested in talking about race. I would describe the project over and over, and the response would be something along the lines of: "How fascinating. I can't wait to see what you find."

LuElla Peniston and Sarah Gold, two thoughtful guidance counselors at the high school, helped me find the first round of potential subjects for my article. They gave me lists of names of students and set up discussion groups in which teenagers talked with stunning candor about racial slights they had experienced, and about how their friendships had changed.

I talked to dozens of students and parents. Only a few declined interviews.

It took me a while to notice that even in this very mixed district, most of the parents led quite segregated lives—and no one seemed to know of a single long-standing friendship between a black student and a white one that had endured into high school. But everyone could suggest other people whom I might talk with.

The meandering path that led me to Kelly and Johanna and Aqeelah was typical of the process: Peniston put me in touch with Malika Oglesby. Malika suggested her boyfriend, Jamie. Jamie told me his younger brother, Jared, was dating a white girl, Kelly. And when I went out to lunch with Jared and his mother—my first visit to Arturo's Pizza in Maplewood Village—they mentioned Kelly's friendship with Johanna and Aqeelah.

I was dubious. Too complicated, I thought, to take on a mixed threesome, when I'm looking simply for a black-white pair.

But I arranged to meet them at Arturo's, too, first Kelly, with her mother and big sister, and then, a couple of days later, Johanna and Aqeelah. We talked a little about their relationship, but I mostly kept pestering them: Come on, who are the black-white best friends in your class? Lord knows, they tried to help, racking their brains for candidates. Their friends were always wandering in and out of Arturo's, and at one point Johanna got up, went to a group of boys by the counter and started interviewing them herself: Did they know any really close black-white friendships? But nobody did.

Over the summer, as I came to realize how unusual these three girls' friendship was, I got more and more interested in how it would weather high school.

When I first visited Sierre's house, to tell her and her mother about the project, I said I'd probably be around school a lot.

"That's so cool," Sierre said, "kind of like that movie where Drew Barrymore goes back to high school."

But it wasn't like that at all. I'm a middle-aged mom, not a movie star, so I didn't adopt teenage fashion, I didn't get a new boyfriend, and I remain as hopelessly uncool as ever. And it was as hard to find ways to be with these kids as it would be to hang out with my own kids' friends. (My son, the same age as Johanna, Kelly and Aqeelah, loved hearing about them, wanted to visit their school and kept saying how awful it must be for them to have me around asking all these questions.)

In the fall, I went to a lot of classes, where I was surprisingly interested in what the teachers had to say about Hammurabi and the Universal Declaration of Human Rights and owl-pellet dissection. The kids chewed gum and passed notes, but I was riveted.

The classroom is not the best place to watch kids interact. Or talk to them. So I cut back on classes and concentrated on the volleyball games, the basketball games, the ninth-grade dance, the pep rally, the Martin Luther King Fashion Show, the eighth-grade sleepover.

I didn't much talk to the kids at these events, but later, away from school, I could ask them how things had gone for them, what they had noticed, what they thought of what I had noticed. Sometimes we were all surprised. At the ninth-grade election assembly, the black candidate for class president, Stephanie, got the largest and loudest response by far. Everyone thought she was a sure bet. But when the results were announced, it was the white candidate, Jeremy, who had won. Everyone was baffled. But it turned out that less than a quarter of the class had voted, and that more whites had voted than blacks. That prompted some interesting conversations about who really "owned" the school.

I took kids out to eat. Starbucks. The Blue Moon Diner. The Bagel Chateau. And most of all, Arturo's—where Kelly said they would never

have been allowed to stay so long without a grown-up. After one mar-
athon session, the guy behind the counter came over to say that he
and his co-workers had a bet going about whether I was from the
school board or a newspaper. Reporter, I said. "That's what I thought,"
he said. "The school board wouldn't be asking so many questions."

What never stopped impressing me was that so many kids stayed so
interested in the questions, in thinking about race in their lives. For
some, the conversations seemed to fill a need, helping them think
through issues they rarely discuss across race lines.

I'm hoping their stories will encourage a lot more conversations.

Suzanne DeChillo, Photographer
—

The reporter Tamar Lewin spent over a year in Maplewood and South
Orange, New Jersey, before I was assigned to take photographs for this
article. I was warned that I must be careful not to destroy the trust that
she had built with the students and parents she was writing about. One
parent had already pulled her child out of the story. Another was on
the verge of doing so. Barred from one middle school, Tamar was one
nervous reporter.

Make no mistake, although Maplewood and South Orange are models of interracial harmony, people there were uneasy about the prospect
of someone sticking a camera in their children's faces to document
the state of race relations in America. Would I get thrown out of
school? It wouldn't be the first time. One of my fondest memories is
being asked to leave DeWitt Clinton High School in the Bronx while
working on a story. Sitting in a principal's office when you're over forty
can be funny, but you don't take pictures that way.

For me, this race story was not easy; I had no epiphanies. In the
end, I feel I failed: I did not capture how race was lived in these
communities. I think I got lost at the racial divide. The divide was too
complex; people kept crossing it all the time. They crossed it for food,
friendship, love, sports, concert tickets, jokes, music and answers to the
questions on the biology-lab exam.

Once, at a segregated table in the lunchroom at Columbia High
School, I thought I had found the great divide. Five minutes later, a
white student who needed help with a math problem stopped by the
table of the black brain trust, pulled up a chair and destroyed that

image of self-segregation. This was a fluid social situation. Kids separated and came together again over and over.

On my first day in Maplewood, I loved it. It looked like the little
village that comes with the Lionel train set. Best of all, blacks and
whites mixed easily, eating pizza, standing in line at Baskin Robbins,
taking the train to New York. I watched two eight-year-old girls, one
black and one white, eagerly sharing the books they checked out of
the library. Integration works. Isn't this what we wanted in the 1960s
and 1970s, a place where we marry one another, and where we live
together? I felt safe here. But some teenagers told me it's a boring
place where nothing happens.

While working on this project, I viewed a show at the New-York
Historical Society in Manhattan called "Without Sanctuary: Lynching
Photography in America." I wondered how any black people in America could ever trust a white person. In this race story, a black student
says the same thing. I went back to school and for over a month I
struggled with race, togetherness and separateness; I traveled to South
Mountain Elementary School, Columbia High School and Howard
University. Then I traveled to my childhood. I grappled with prejudice
and race in my family, school and work.

Over the course of a month, Tamar and I talked often on the phone,
but we were never together in Maplewood. She had finished her reporting. The story was in the bag before I started taking pictures. When
I had one last picture to take, I became the nervous one, and Tamar
and Nancy Weinstock, the photo editor on the project, talked me
through it.

In the end, I did not get thrown out of school, and only one person
refused to be photographed. In the end, this story was good for me.

"THE HURT BETWEEN THE LINES"
Dana Canedy, Writer
—

"I probably shouldn't say that. Do you have to use my name?"

When I set out to report on race relations in the *Akron Beacon
Journal* newsroom, that is how some of the staff members initially
responded when asked how African-American and white colleagues get
along there.

Over lunches, dinners and drinks, I slowly developed a rapport with the people who would eventually shape the story. By the second month of reporting, most had agreed to on-the-record interviews, allowing me to use their names and titles.

As a reporter, I'm used to dealing with people who are reluctant to be quoted in the newspaper. But I was surprised that other journalists would be just as hesitant. They seemed hypocritical, I thought. But then I asked myself if I would want to talk to a reporter probing my thoughts on race relations. The truth, I had to admit, was that I would be hesitant, too.

It's not that my views on race are particularly controversial. But who knows better than a journalist the consequences of unintentionally saying the wrong thing?

No matter your occupation—construction worker, police officer, bank president, teacher or, yes, journalist—for most of us, openly discussing race with anyone other than your most trusted confidants can seem risky.

Say that you're tired of white people asking if you think you got the job because of affirmative action, and someone might take offense. Say that African-Americans focus on race too much, as one *Beacon Journal* staff member did, and you risk being branded a racist.

Soon, you're thinking: Did I just commit career suicide? Will my co-workers still ask me to lunch? Will some African-Americans think I'm not black enough for even wondering if what I say might hurt my career or rub some people the wrong way?

It is enough to make anyone want to say, "No comment."

And so I respected the good folks at the *Beacon Journal* for their bravery and their contributions to a *New York Times* project that they came to believe was important. Even so, I felt a knot in my stomach when I wondered what life would be like for them if the publisher and editor did not appreciate their honesty.

As I "peeled the layers" of the story, which was my mandate, an interesting dynamic unfolded. African-Americans—perhaps assuming we shared an unspoken understanding because I am African-American, too—opened up sooner and were far more negative about the state of race relations in the newsroom than many of their white colleagues. I could not help wondering whether the white reporters and editors would have been more revealing to a white reporter.

As a journalist I am trained to get at the truth. So I felt as if I were on shaky new ground when during the reporting of my article I realized that beyond the obvious there is no one truth when it comes to race relations.

And in writing down these reflections, I found myself doing what journalists do every day. I sketched out an interesting beginning, crafted a logical body of the essay and edited my thoughts as I went. But I have had trouble doing here what usually comes quite naturally in writing an article—coming up with a pithy ending, known as a kicker.

Maybe that's because there is no easy conclusion. You might call that one of the few truths there are about race relations in America.

Stephen Crowley, Photographer

—

Waiting in the newsroom of the *Akron Beacon Journal* to take a picture that might say something meaningful about race relations, I fell into a reverie about my own history.

My views on race as an obstacle in American life are filtered through the prism of my father's experience. Paralyzed from the age of two by polio, he spent his life in a world filled with obstacles, both internal and external. Early on, he learned that he would be set apart for the rest of his life. As I watched him struggle against physical barriers as well as misconceptions about his abilities, I learned not to judge a person by where he is in life but by how far he has come.

My father's obstacles were not racial, of course, but I was able to apply the same lessons to my developing attitudes about race. Racial harmony may be an unattainable ideal, but if it is ever to come, it will take patience, a willingness to forgive (sometimes a trespass is rooted in naïveté) and a respect for the obstacles we all face.

"THE MINORITY QUARTERBACK"
Ira Berkow, Writer

—

My involvement in this story really began in December 1996, when I went to Baton Rouge, Louisiana, to write about Marcus Jacoby, the white freshman quarterback at historically black Southern University— the first starting white quarterback in the Southwestern Athletic Conference. It was just before the Heritage Bowl, the annual showcase for two of the best black college football teams in the country. That year, Southern was to play Howard University.

It was a good story, and a mostly happy one for Marcus—up to that point. He had led the team to the big bowl game, and though he had received a few threats and had experienced some uncomfortable moments as one of the few whites at Southern, things seemed to be working out for him. He had largely succeeded, he felt, in establishing his right to be at the school and in winning the acceptance of his black schoolmates.

But then came the crushing loss in the Heritage Bowl. Southern lost by three points when, in the final seconds, Marcus threw an interception, ending his team's last chance for victory.

Neither the outcome of the game nor what happened afterward were mentioned in my original article, and a lot of it hadn't been told until I wrote this story in 2000: how some blacks at Southern reacted to the loss with sudden hostility toward Marcus, seeing him now as an interloper; and how some whites expressed prejudices and fears of their own.

The beauty, of course, lay on the other side of the story: how blacks and whites alike, including his family, understood and accepted and encouraged Marcus; how Marcus himself developed a mental and physical toughness as he progressed at Southern.

In his sophomore season, Marcus led his team to the black national championship. But after the first game of the next season, he quit the team, saying there were tensions and pressures he could no longer deal with. Later he transferred out of Southern altogether. His views on race relations as he experienced them, often as a minority of one, were both surprising and gratifying to me, in that they were both thoughtful and generous. Despite his youth—he was twenty-three at the time— and the little time he had had after leaving Southern in which to gain perspective, his views were clear and considered, I thought.

Like anyone who might have been in his shoes, Marcus was reluctant at first to talk to a reporter. The attitude was either "let sleeping dogs lie" or "it's none of your business." Even after he agreed to participate in the *Times* project, he was cautious.

But being around someone—in this case, a reporter—for almost nine months can break down barriers. This was equally true of coaches, classmates, teammates and family members. Marcus's story did not come out in one gush. It came out over a long time. But, I'd like to think, it did come out.

Kirk Johnson, Contributor

—

I was sitting in the kitchen of a Baton Rouge barbecue joint one spring afternoon, talking with the owner, Don Dillon, as he turned and basted his slabs of ribs. I'd come to talk with him about the Southern University marching band. People on campus had told me that the band was the school's heart and soul, and that if anyone could say why that was so and what made the band tick, it was Dillon. He had played for it, then helped lead it for many years as an assistant band director.

Musicians are just different, Dillon said, poking at his ribs. They love what they do, and that changes everything. The words struck home. I'd spent enough time by then with various band members, especially Jabari Morgan, the lead cymbals player, and his father, Mo, a former baritone horn player, to feel that the band had some kind of special power. But I hadn't been able to put my finger on what it was. I suddenly saw that it was the most obvious thing of all: the music itself.

The marching band is by all accounts the most purely distilled expression of what Southern University represents, the clearest statement on campus of the black cultural experience. But it was also the most instantly welcoming place to a white reporter who wandered in one day on a whim to hear the band rehearse.

The music was brassy and jazzy and hard and lean and loud, and all of its 180 members but for one freshman on tuba were black. But I came to think that the language of that music, communicated through the musicians, was deeper than the colors of our skin. The music was about joy, not black or white. And it roared from the horns and thundered off the drumheads in a way that changes everything, just as Dillon had said. Maybe, I began to think, the music reached beyond race because it was older than race: it blasted through the things that divide us to reach somewhere down inside where the old human tribe still lives. Or maybe it's just a great show that you can't help loving no matter what color you are.

I ultimately left Baton Rouge a bit more hopeful that racial divisions in America could be bridged, not perhaps by talking about them, though that's a start, but by getting ourselves all together in a room with a big brass band, locking the doors and telling the musicians to play for all they're worth.

Nicole Bengiveno, Photographer

My mission as a photojournalist is to capture the very moment that tells the story. The job becomes a greater challenge when the subject is of a sensitive nature, or the people involved are self-conscious, as Marcus Jacoby was. The pressures he had felt as the white quarterback for an almost all-black team at a historically black university had clearly been painful for him. And so had quitting the team and leaving the school. I saw him as a perfectionist who didn't want to fail.

When I first called Marcus, we had to work through some of his concerns. Although he wanted to tell his story, he said, he was wary of making too big a deal of it. My impression was that he was trying to get over his hurt and get on with his life. When I suggested that we shoot a few photographs back on Southern's campus, he could not bring himself to return, so we decided to stick to the present: I photographed him at Louisiana State University, to which he had transferred. There, he no longer played football and seemed to keep pretty much to himself. He appeared to be a young man trying to make up for lost time.

Jabari Morgan, on the other hand, the Southern marching band member, was not only Marcus's counterpart in the article but an emotional counterweight. Where Marcus was self-conscious, Jabari was so involved with his marching band and his social life, surrounded by friends and family, that he would forget I was there, hovering with my camera.

I take my job very seriously. Inherent in it is a responsibility to be respectful and true to the subject. Most of the time, that happens naturally: people go about their business and I snap away. There are other times, though, when I'm overwhelmed by the vulnerability of my subjects and the trust they show me when I point my camera in their direction. A picture can be excruciatingly personal in those moments, and so final and so visible to the world.

"GUARDING THE BORDERS OF THE HIP-HOP NATION"
N. R. Kleinfield, Writer

"So do you want a wigger or just a regular white guy?"

That was one of the early questions I got from a hip-hop head when I started casting about for subjects for an article set in hip-hop culture.

I had no idea what the answer was. "Wigger?" It was a while before I even understood clearly what the word meant.

But I quickly appreciated that it was going to be a lot more complicated settling on a white subject than on a black one. With a white, I had to fumble with concepts of authenticity and credibility and, yes, wiggerdom. It was a lot more straightforward narrowing down the roster of potential black subjects.

All whites in hip-hop seemed to be viewed with varying degrees of suspicion or derision, even by other whites in the culture. Whites talked a lot about whether they were "legitimate" and "authentic," blurry concepts at best. But those qualities were so important if you were white, because your skin color alone guaranteed that many would view you as an interloper. And the worst thing to be was a wigger.

"Wigger" was a term that whites who disliked hip-hop constructed to deride whites who liked hip-hop. It got defined in different ways. Generally it was applied to someone who tried too hard with too much effrontery to behave as if he were black so that he would be accepted by blacks in hip-hop. The word had to do with not being genuine, not being yourself, but being some bizarre caricature. It was not entirely clear to me when you stepped over the bounds of trying too hard. When were you a near-wigger as opposed to a full-fledged one? One black hip-hop head, being sardonic, elaborated this way: "It could be a white guy who not only talked and acted like us in some phony way, but actually went and discriminated against other white people to try to prove how black he was."

I read one article that tried to take matters a step further and draw a distinction between a "wigger" and a "wigga." By the author's reckoning, a "wigga" was someone who tried too hard to be down. A "wigger" was someone who genuinely understood and appreciated black culture and was a legitimate participant in it. But I didn't hear anyone else go along with that.

A lot of people would tell me that the word doesn't even get used much, except by the media when they write broad-based stories about hip-hop culture. But when I tried to avoid using it and inquired of hip-hop heads about a particular white person who interested me, I'd get comments like, "Ah, he's kind of a wigger." Or, "Why do you want some wigger in your story? What can a wigger tell you?"

Upski, the white subject I settled on to accompany my main black subject, Elliott Wilson, had actually been one of the first journalists to write about wiggers. He was accused afterward of helping to popularize the term. In his article on the subject, Upski was not kind to wiggers, and he told me that he had never thought of himself as one. But I couldn't help wondering to what extent he tiptoed on the edge of wiggerdom, especially in his early days of immersion in black culture.

Hip-hop is a world much invested in slang and fresh identities. Almost everyone went by an invented name, the wackier the better, it seemed. In the long run, though, appellations like "wigger" didn't seem to serve much purpose. People couldn't be pigeonholed so neatly.

Did I wind up with a wigger or just a regular white guy? All I know is, the guy is white. Either that's dope or it's not.

Nancy Siesel, Photographer

I admit I was skeptical when I first heard about the person I would be following for an article about hip-hop. In a few days, I was told, I would fly to Indiana to photograph Billy Wimsatt, aka Upski, a white journalist and champion of hip-hop who lectured at college campuses. He would be speaking at Earlham College, in Richmond, Indiana. Hmm, a white guy named Upski, a Quaker college in the heavily white Midwest, to examine racial issues in hip-hop culture. OK, clearly this would be a challenge.

I had envisioned something different when I was teamed with Sonny Kleinfield for the article. My only two assignments having to do with hip-hop culture had been far removed from Indiana. One was a wedding, a grand, lavishly choreographed event uniting Sandra (Pepa) Denton of Salt-n-Pepa and Anthony (Treach) Criss of Naughty by Nature. The other was the funeral for Christopher Wallace, known as Notorious B.I.G., the Brooklyn rap star who was killed in a drive-by shooting in Los Angeles. The most striking part of that scene was the almost palpable tension between the largely white police force and the crowd of black fans who had waited for hours to catch of a glimpse of their hero's white hearse. There was a sense in the air that something was going to happen, and it did. After the motorcade passed, a group of teenagers began dancing on some parked cars. The police responded with nightsticks and clouds of pepper spray. A peaceful, mournful day had ended in chaos.

Arriving at the Earlham campus, my destination was its coffee shop, a large two-tiered room where the event was to be held. But when I got there, the shop was deserted, and there were no posters advertising Upski's appearance. I started to panic. Nobody's going to show up for this thing, and I had braved a two-lane rural road in a near-blizzard to get there. Just then Upski strolled in. He looked more like a banker in baggy pants than an activist. As if reading my mind (or maybe my face), he assured me that the word was out and that students would be there.

He was right. By the time Upski took the microphone, the place was packed. The crowd reflected the racial makeup of the college: almost entirely white. They had turned out to hear a lecture improbably titled "Why Earlham College Is America's Best Hope to Save Ourselves in the 21st Century." As Upski spoke, darting across the stage to connect with people, I realized my limitations as a photographer. At that moment it seemed nearly impossible through a still and silent image to express the ideas Upski was attempting to convey.

The students were riveted as he recounted his own fears: "I'm afraid that if I followed my heart, blacks wouldn't like me anymore and I wouldn't like them"; "I'm afraid if black people had the privileges I had, they'd take my job." I wondered how the students felt about what they were hearing, for here was Upski, saying things about race that would make most people profoundly uncomfortable, things that are rarely uttered in a public forum. And it occurred to me that some of these students had no doubt gone through school without ever having had real contact with a black person.

As I drove back to the motel, I thought about how different my own education had been: attending a mostly white elementary school in the Bronx and later a racially mixed high school in Westchester County, in a suburban district that had adopted busing to achieve desegregation. But more than having black classmates, it was having black teachers as role models that probably affected me more than anything—people like Ainsley Adams, a science teacher from Trinidad.

As a photographer, I have become intimately acquainted with neighborhoods that many white people would not visit alone. Often I am the only white person to be seen. It was in one of those neighborhoods that I met Dog, Trife and Po, the members of the Brooklyn hip-hop group who appear in the article. As we drove around Brooklyn one day in my shiny gold rented car discussing interracial relationships, Dog told me to take the back streets; he couldn't be seen with a white woman, he explained. Bad for the image. He told me he would never be with a white woman because black men had been killed for even looking at white women.

From the backseat, however, Trife said he didn't have a problem being seen with a white woman. They asked me if I had ever had relationships with black men. I told them I'd had several.

Later, I photographed them at a rehearsal in a Manhattan studio, where I listened to them sing "Fix Your Face," "Talking in Eternal Sleep" and "Rock and a Hard Place." The last one I found disturbing because of its repeated use of denigrating terms for a female character. Dog told me I was misinterpreting the song—that it is about the pressures of being a performer and attracting women while trying to remain loyal to your girlfriend.

At the end of the session, Trife told me that I must have had a great-grandfather who was black, because, as he put it: "You're black on the inside. Yeah, you're mad cool."

"WHY HARLEM DRUG COPS DON'T DISCUSS RACE"
Michael Winerip, Writer

—

We knew if we were going to write about race in America we had to write about the police. And we knew, as a New York newspaper, we'd better do our damndest to write about New York City's police. And we knew the only way to get access was to go right to the top, since the police department's public information office under Mayor Rudolph Giuliani was famous for not returning a reporter's first several hundred phone calls. So Joe Lelyveld, the executive editor of the *Times*, asked the mayor for an audience, and we explained the series to him one day in May 1999. After forty-five minutes, right there on the spot, the mayor said yes. (This was the new, more open Mayor Giuliani, a year before the press recognized him as that).

It was the police commissioner, Howard Safir, who suggested a narcotics unit, since they work in racially mixed teams of about eight: mainly black and Latino undercovers, backed up by white investigators and a sergeant.

As a magazine writer, I've done a lot of immersion journalism, but always the subjects had agreed to having me along. This time, it wasn't the working cops who had agreed; it was their superiors, and the cops were the ones stuck with the race reporter. Sergeant Maria Brogli was welcoming from Day 1, but for a while it was uncomfortable for everyone. As one cop told me early on, "Everyone makes their names on the backs of cops—prosecutors, politicians . . ." He stopped there, but the message was clear: reporters, too.

At first, every time I took out my notebook, I'd get asked, "Why're you taking notes on that? Did I say something racist?" But what I was really trying to figure out those first few months was all the difficulties of being a cop; before I could write about race, I had to understand all the nonracial things that can make being a cop a miserable job. Like the working conditions, which are crowded, dirty, depressing. One of the first things that struck me was that cops in narcotics, a supposedly elite unit, have to bring their own toilet paper from home and lock it in their desks for safekeeping.

One sweltering night in May 1999, Brogli took the dealers she had arrested to be processed at the 30th Precinct. The station house was oppressively hot and dark. The city budget didn't allow for the air-conditioning to be turned on until June, and most lights were switched off to keep the room as cool as possible. The cops, their skin slick with sweat, sat in a dark room with the drug money seized that night, squinting as they stacked it into piles by a dim light from the other side of the room.

Daily I'd put on a bullet-proof vest and go out with the team when it did buy-and-busts. Sometimes the cops sat for hours, doing nothing, waiting for the undercover to finally call in a description of a dealer. I sat beside the handcuffed prisoners in the p-van, as the vehicle for transporting the arrested is known—just a big empty Dodge Caravan with a metal floor and no seats. I stood beside cops armed with a search warrant as they smashed a battering ram into a door, not knowing who would be on the other side when the lock finally gave and the door popped open. I felt the mix of boredom, fear and anger that goes with being a cop.

I saw close up the anger, fear and boredom of the people arrested by the cops.

It was months and months before I started asking the first tentative questions about race. And it was a full year before I sat with Brogli and finally asked her the question I had known I would have to ask from the first day I met her: "When you see a group of dark-skinned men standing at the corner of 141st and Broadway, do you think they're drug dealers?"

After we'd spent a year together, she answered me honestly. Yes, she thinks they're drug dealers. But by then she knew that I knew what she meant.

Angel Franco, Photographer

I am Ana Rivera's first-born in North America, and my son, Osvaldo, is my first-born in America—or, as we call him, the real American. He feels totally at home here. His Spanish isn't great, and that doesn't bother him.

But I fear for him as he walks the streets of America, feeling confident that he is protected by all of the privileges of being an American. I fear that this same false sense of security might one day bring disaster crashing down on him, because of the color of his skin.

I worry because he feels at home in a place where I hear names yelled at me—names like "almost black," "half-bake," "spic" or "rag-head." I fear for him as he ventures out. I worry he'll face the insult of being stopped and questioned by the police because he doesn't look to them like an American. I fear he'll know the anger at being treated like a third-class citizen in the America he loves so much, the America his grandfather fought for in World War II. I fear that in his comfort with the system, someday he will reach for his wallet and get shot, tortured or dragged to death for being a black Latino in his America full of dreams and hopes.

At the same time, these dreams and hopes are what I pray for him to have.

So it comes as a surprise when I hear that the paper I work for is doing a major examination of how people live with issues of race in America, and that the photo editor for the project chose me to live with a narcotics unit based out of El Barrio. This is where I learned to fight, play stickball and dance. This is where I learned the rules of injustice. This is where I heard my mother sing songs of loves gone sour as she mopped the floor of our one-room apartment. This is where she lectured me and my brother on how Puerto Ricans should act around Americans: move fast when you work for them and don't look at their faces. This is where she warned us that if we were stopped by "la hara," slang for the police, we must not run, because they'll beat you, kill you and plant a zip gun on you.

So at forty-nine, here I go with all the survival wisdom a mother can give her sons. Fearing the police and yet, like my son, believing in justice and the American way, I am introduced to Sergeant Maria Brogli, a short woman, like my mother, and her narcotics team. I will be living with them for a year, good or bad. I am armed with four Leica cameras, a bullet-proof vest and my mother's words: don't look at their faces.

I begin my sojourn with the narcotics cops in the aftermath of the Amadou Diallo shooting. I quickly learn about some sore issues in the police department: the second-guessing of officers; gender discrimination; racial tension—brown or black versus the Americanos (whites) who run the show. I learn how Maria protects her team. I learn from her how to watch the edges even more as I take up the camera. I learn police procedure. I learn about a door take-down and the sound of bodies rushing into an apartment, yelling "Police! Policia!" I learn how officers come to an instant halt when they find children in the apartment. Maria ribs them about it. "I just find it amazing that when you guys see children, you become soft," she says.

I also feel the anger of brown and black cops who can't tell their white male bosses how stupid and racist they are just by being ignorant of others around them. I also see the eye-speech between people of color, when in their hearts they know something is wrong but cannot speak for fear of being branded too sensitive or rebellious.

I experience the tactics of white police officers as they arrest a young Dominican man, telling him that he had better talk because there is a cell for a pretty boy like him with a tougher guy waiting to make him his wife. I overhear them talk about poor people. "Why do these people like to live like this?" they ask.

As I see officers ramming down doors, I wonder what it is like to be the white ones, knowing that their lives depend on fellow officers of color yet feeling secure that at this moment they all are blue.

Lots of times as an arrest goes down in El Barrio, I think that if it were me cuffing the suspect, and Ana Rivera was watching, she'd wear me like a shoe. The disgust in her eyes would kill my soul. The shame I feel just by thinking about it is reflected on Detective Johnny Gonzalez's face when he has to arrest a fellow Dominican.

I realize that Gonzalez's life is not so different from mine. He is an expert at a job that requires him to go into the Dominican and black communities and relate to the people who live there, then come back and report to the Americanos what he has uncovered.

So what's changed about race in America? People of color are still doing the dirty work—reporting on ourselves and then being second-guessed. I hope that one day my son's America really does become a place we all truly share, a place where differences are respected and even embraced.

"BRICKS, MORTAR AND COALITION BUILDING"
Mireya Navarro, Writer
—

The first thing you notice on your first visit to Houston is the friend-liness. Strangers say hello on the street. Drivers stop to let you in. People—not only black, white and Latino but Chinese, Indian and all the other nationalities represented in this diverse city—seem comfort-able in their skin.

City officials often point out that though Houston is the nation's fourth-largest city, it has none of the racial problems of other big cities like New York and Los Angeles, none of the open hostilities. And that is true. But in reporting my story about three men in the construction industry, I was surprised to find that the city is as self-segregated as any other.

Rick Castañeda, Richard Lewis and Brian Smith are all successful company owners and college-educated men, yet each had his reasons for not associating with people of other races or ethnic groups after the workday. For all three, personal life revolved around family. For Lewis, a Baptist minister in a mostly white church, and Smith, a Baptist deacon in an all-black church, religion took up much of their free time.

As Lewis told me, there are important people in his life he has not talked to in years. He just does not find the time.

Still, I could not help noticing the seating arrangement of a con-gregation of seventeen during a service one Sunday at Lewis's tiny country church in Matagorda, Texas. Two black women chose to sit in the back, a Latino family of four filed into a middle pew, and all the whites sat in two clusters in front. A few weeks later, at a meeting of white and Latino engineers that I attended with Castañeda, a similar pattern emerged. With one exception, the white engineers sat together in two groups. The exception was the lone woman at the meeting. She sat with the Latinos.

This seemingly instinctive self-segregation both saddened me and made me feel fortunate. In the twenty years since I left Puerto Rico for the United States, I have lived in richly diverse cities—Washington, San Francisco, New York, Miami—where I did not have to go out of my way to befriend people of other races or ethnic groups. In college, I had friends from Nigeria and Iran. In San Francisco, my best friends were white, Asian and Hispanic. In New York and Miami, they were Hispanic, white and black.

What has mattered most in these friendships is what we have had in common: education, career, everyday interests. My friends have been friends because they are journalists like me, or single like me, or night owls like me.

I had been a bit surprised to find that business friends of many years like Castañeda and Lewis did not necessarily see a need to go further in their relationship, to get to know each other better. They were perfectly satisfied with what they had.

But in evaluating my own relationships, I also found evidence of self-segregation. I belong to a Latina women's group. The only organization I pay dues to is also Hispanic. And outside my family, I have very few true friends, and most of them belong to minorities.

Do I restrict relationships based on color? I still think I do not, but since my involvement in the race project, it has been something I cannot help but watch out for.

Monica Almeida, Photographer

—

How do you photograph race and cultural identity? That was the challenge I faced while working on this story about three businessmen in Houston, one black, one white and one Latino. As a photojournalist, truthfulness and fairness are as important as exposure and composition. And as a Latina, my awareness of stereotyping and visual cliché was particularly acute.

I was allowed to meet the challenge and do my job thanks to the generosity of these three men. They welcomed me into their lives. Photographing people as they are takes a great deal of time and patience, especially for those being photographed. There I was, a stranger with a camera, clicking away at what must have seemed to be the oddest moments. Even so, they invited me to photograph them with their families, in their churches and in private business meetings.

I observed personal moments: Brian Smith's beaming smile while watching his son at a Cub Scout ceremony and his quiet intensity during an investment meeting; Richard Lewis's soulful singing at the small Southern Baptist church he attends with his wife, Betty; Rick Castañeda's joking with colleagues while waiting for an engineers' association meeting to begin and his quiet prayers after lighting a candle in memory of his son, who died recently in an automobile accident.

After three trips to Houston and two to San Antonio, I grew to appreciate the strengths these men shared. They were hard workers, strivers who had built their companies from the ground up. And they were dedicated family men, each proud of his roots, with a firm sense of history and of who they were, as individuals and as Americans.

So how do you photograph race and cultural identity in America? I'm not sure that you can in an obvious way. Our lives are much more subtle and complex than what a single frame may be able to capture.

"GETTING UNDER MY SKIN"
Michelle V. Agins, Photographer
—

A few days after finishing my work on Don Terry's story, I was driving in the East Village of Manhattan when suddenly Jeanne Terry, Don's mother, crossed my mind. I had spent a good part of six weeks photographing her and the Terry family, and now I found I missed her. So I picked up my cell phone, which I had programmed with the numbers I had been using most frequently, and punched in the number 12. When she answered, I was nearly speechless with embarrassment.

"Jeanne, hi, this is Michelle."

"I know," she said.

"This might sound silly," I began, "but you were on my mind, and I miss you. Is that silly?"

"No-ooo," she said, "I miss you too! By the way, Donnie's on the line."

I blanched, wondering what Don was thinking—me, calling his mother. I apologized and said: "I might want to call you sometimes. Is that OK?"

"Of course," she replied. "I hoped you would stay in touch."

My reaching out to Jeanne like that startled me. As the photographer in this story, it was sometimes hard to establish a direct relationship with members of Don's family. I felt a bit like an outsider. Unconsciously, perhaps, I believed Don had tried to keep me from seeing his story while he was reporting it. And, understandably, at times he kept me at arm's length from his family. At one point, I begged my editor to replace me. The assignment wasn't working out for me, I told her. She reminded me of how hard this was for Don. She told me to be patient. For Don, these weren't just subjects for an article; this was his family, and he was about to reveal to the world, and to his family, his innermost thoughts about them.

My own mother's father was white, and she passed for white at her place of employment on Chicago's North Side. She gave me to my grandmother when I was two weeks old because I was too dark. My grandmother and grandfather were the only family who loved me for being me. When my mother came to visit my grandmother, my friends would say: "Is that really your Momma? Because her hair is good." To add insult to injury, she wouldn't let me call her Momma in public. Most members of my family are light-skinned, and they would mock my dark skin.

I grew up a half mile from where Don grew up in Hyde Park, our homes separated by Washington Park. But my neighborhood, Grand Boulevard, was completely different from his. Hyde Park was that rare thing in those days: an interracial community. My neighborhood was poorer and not integrated. All my friends were black. Most were from working-class homes. As an adolescent, I loved taking the bus west on 51st Street past Cottage Grove, just to imagine what it would be like to live there, in such a perfect place, where all colors were accepted.

When I was fourteen, I left my grandmother's church, Pilgrim Baptist, on the South Side, and joined Good Shepherd Congregational, because the majority of the congregation lived in Hyde Park, in upper-middle-class homes. I wanted to be like the children there. I wanted to be exposed to the things they were exposed to. I wanted to prove to my family that my dark skin wasn't a handicap.

Jeanne Terry touched my soul because throughout her life she remained the same. She was a mother to all her children, regardless of their color—unlike my own mother. I respect Jeanne Terry for that. Maybe if my Momma hadn't died at twenty-eight she would be proud of her dark-skinned daughter now.

The *New York Times* Poll on Race: Optimistic Outlook But Enduring Racial Division

KEVIN SACK WITH JANET ELDER

Thirty-five years after the dismantling of legalized segregation, a majority of Americans maintain that race relations in the United States are generally good, but blacks and whites continue to have starkly divergent perceptions of many racial issues and they remain largely isolated from each other in their everyday lives.

The *New York Times* poll on race reflected some of the same complex tensions that surfaced in the *Times's* examinations of contemporary race relations in America. The poll—like the stories of individual communities living across a stubbornly enduring racial divide—suggested that even as the rawest forms of bigotry have receded they have often been replaced by remoteness and distrust in places of work, learning and worship.

The poll, which surveyed 2,165 adults, detected some signs that both blacks and whites believe race relations are improving. The proportion of those surveyed who said race relations in the country were generally good—57 percent—was at its highest mark in ten years, a full 16 percentage points higher than in 1990. Large majorities of both races—63 percent of whites and 79 percent of blacks—said they approved of interracial marriage, compared with only 44 percent of whites and 70 percent of blacks who said so in a 1991 poll.

And the percentage who said the country had made real progress in reducing racial discrimination—74 percent, including 78 percent of whites and 58 percent of blacks—was about 25 percentage points higher for each group than in May 1992, just after the deadly rioting that followed the acquittal of four white Los Angeles police officers in the beating of a black motorist, Rodney G. King. The percentage of blacks who see progress has doubled in that period.

But in question after question the poll also revealed a core of blacks—about four in ten, many of them college-educated—who find little to celebrate even today. Those blacks, for instance, said they thought that race relations in the country were generally bad and that there had been no real progress in eliminating racial discrimination since the 1960s.

On many questions, particularly those related to whether blacks are treated equitably and whether race plays too large a role in the national discourse, blacks and whites seemed to be living on different planets. Blacks were roughly four times more likely than whites to say they thought blacks were treated less fairly in the workplace, in neighborhood shops, in shopping malls and in restaurants, theaters, bars and other entertainment venues.

Indeed, one of the few areas where blacks and whites were most in agreement was in their perceptions of racial hostility. Similar percentages—39 percent of whites and 45 percent of blacks—said they thought that many or almost all white people disliked blacks. And 45 percent of whites and the same percentage of blacks said they thought that many or almost all black people disliked whites.

The continuing complexity of racial attitudes, and the awkwardness of discussing them forthrightly, came through clearly in the poll results. Taken as a whole, the respondents' answers offered a far more nuanced view of race than was apparent during the height of the civil rights struggle, when battle lines were more clearly drawn and bigotry was more clearly expressed.

Befitting the subject matter, the poll was rife with seeming contradictions. Most striking, perhaps, was a telescopic pattern in which people of both races depicted themselves as far more sanguine about race relations in their own communities, and far more sensitive in their own views, than they believed to be the case elsewhere. Susceptible perhaps to the pressures of political correctness, they seemed to strive to depict themselves and their neighbors as open-minded and accepting while projecting less enlightened views on the rest of the country. And the farther from home, the worse things seemed.

For instance, 88 percent of whites and 82 percent of blacks said race relations were generally good in their neighborhoods. Similarly large majorities of whites and blacks said race relations were generally good where they worked and at their children's schools.

But the numbers dropped when people were asked to characterize race relations in their communities, and they dropped more precipitously when they were asked about race relations in the country. Fifty-eight percent of whites and 51 percent of blacks said race relations in the country were generally good, while 30 percent of whites and 40 percent of blacks said they were generally bad.

Similarly, nearly all respondents — 93 percent of whites and 95 percent of blacks — said they would vote for a qualified black presidential candidate if one was nominated by their political party. And yet, most of those surveyed — 55 percent of whites and 62 percent of blacks — agreed that the country was not ready to elect a black president.

In another example, 85 percent of whites said they did not care whether they lived in an area where most of their neighbors were white or where most were black. But two-thirds of the whites said they thought most white people preferred to live in white areas. And perhaps most telling, 85 percent said they actually live in areas where they have no or few black neighbors, the same percentage that said they had no preference.

The poll, which was conducted in June 2000, surveyed 1,107 people who said they were white and 934 who said they were black. It has a margin of sampling error of plus or minus 3 percentage points for each racial group.

To determine the views of the country as a whole, the responses of blacks were weighted to equal 11 percent of the total, the proportion used by the Census Bureau. According to the Current Population Survey, 11 percent of Americans are black and 89 percent are nonblack. With the exception of the prevailing pessimism expressed by college-educated blacks, the poll turned up few variations in responses based on geography, education, age or income among blacks.

All in all, blacks and whites seem to feel that these times of relative peace and prosperity are good ones. Seventy-three percent of those questioned, including 73 percent of whites and 80 percent of blacks, said their opportunities for success in life were better than those of their parents. And 40 percent, including 39 percent of whites and 44 percent of blacks, said they thought the next generation of Americans would have a better future than their own. The proportion who said they believed things would get worse — 31 percent, including 30 percent of whites and 35 percent of blacks — was substantially lower than in past polls by the *New York Times*.

But when questions focused more specifically on racial issues, a schism quickly emerged. Asked whether whites or blacks had a better chance of getting ahead, for example, 58 percent of whites said the playing field was now level, a view shared by only 39 percent of blacks. Fifty-seven percent of blacks said whites still had advantages, compared with only 32 percent of whites.

There were similar gaps in black and white perceptions of how blacks are treated in various circumstances.

Two-thirds of blacks, for example, said blacks were treated less equitably by the police, a view shared by only a quarter of whites. Forty-two percent of blacks said they felt they had been stopped by the police simply because of their race, compared with only 3 percent of whites.

"Blacks are still having the same problems," said a seventy-nine-year-old retired black woman from Long Beach, California, who responded to poll questions and a follow-up interview but did not want her name published. "Being black, you're discriminated against when you try to buy something you want unless you assert yourself. If the store is crowded, you're pushed aside because the sales clerks would rather wait on someone else. Progress means being considered on the same level with any other race."

Predictably, the variation in attitudes about equal opportunity and treatment gave rise to differing views about programs that make special efforts to help minorities get ahead. Blacks favored such programs 76 percent to 11 percent, while whites were ambivalent, with 46 percent saying they favored them and 44 percent saying they opposed them.

The poll detected a surprising degree of social interaction between blacks and whites. Large proportions of both races said they had close friends of another race, 76 percent of whites and 84 percent of blacks. Similarly large numbers—69 percent of whites and 84 percent of blacks—said they had socialized with someone of another race outside their homes in the last month. Forty-three percent of whites and 58 percent of blacks said people of another race had visited their homes socially in the last month.

George Norris, forty-four, a black man from Baltimore, said he gets together every other month or so with colleagues from the moving company where he works. "We shoot pool, have some drinks, have a cookout or watch some movies," Norris said. "It's basically the same group of folks, white and black. They come over to my house or I go to theirs."

And yet the poll made it clear that most Americans do not live, work or worship with those of other races. Eighty-three percent of whites said they worked with only a few blacks or none at all. Ninety percent of whites who attended religious services at least once a month said that none or only a few of their fellow congregants were black, while 73 percent of blacks said that almost all of their fellow congregants were black.

In general, whites expressed a certain fatigue with racial issues. More than half—54 percent—said the news media devoted too much time to race. But 44 percent of blacks, by contrast, said that the media talked too little about race, while 28 percent said the media talked too much about it and 23 percent said the media devoted an appropriate amount of attention to it.

Two-thirds of blacks also said that politicians talked too little about race, and the same number of blacks said that improving race relations was one of the most important challenges facing the country. Only one-fourth of whites said it was one of the most important challenges, while 65 percent said it was important, but so were other issues. And whites were more than three times as likely as blacks—33 percent to 10 percent—to say that too much has been made in recent years of the problems facing black people.

The Complete Poll Results

The *New York Times* poll is based on telephone interviews conducted June 21–29, 2000, with 2,165 adults from throughout the United States.

Black Americans were sampled at a higher rate than normal to permit analysis of black attitudes in greater depth. From all national polls completed by the *Times* and CBS News since October 1998, every household in which a black respondent had been interviewed was recalled for the poll, as well as one-twelfth of the households in which a nonblack respondent had been interviewed earlier.

Of the total in the new poll, 1,107 said they were white and 934 said they were black. There were too few respondents of other races to show their results separately. The original samples of telephone exchanges had been randomly selected by a computer from a complete list of more than 42,000 active residential exchanges across the country. Within each exchange, random digits had been added to form a complete telephone number, thus permitting access to both listed and unlisted numbers.

Within each household, both in the original polls and the new poll, one adult was designated by a random procedure to be the respondent for the survey.

The results of the new poll have been weighted to account for household size and number of telephone lines into the residence and to adjust for variations in the sample relating to geographic region, sex, age, marital status and education. Blacks and nonblacks were then weighted back to their proper proportion of the overall population. In theory, in 19 cases out of 20, the results based on such samples will differ by no more than three percentage points in either direction— for blacks or whites—from what would have been obtained by seeking out all American adults. For smaller subgroups, the margin of sampling error is larger.

In addition to sampling error, the practical difficulties of conducting any survey of public opinion may introduce other sources of error into the poll. Variations in the wording and order of questions, for example, may lead to somewhat different results.

1. Compared to your parents' generation, do you think in general your opportunities to succeed in life are better than theirs, about the same as theirs, or worse than theirs?

	Better	Same	Worse	DK/NA
2/2000 CBS Total	72	22	5	1
2/2000 CBS White	71	23	6	—
2/2000 CBS Black	78	18	3	1
6/2000 Total	73	16	10	1
6/2000 White	73	17	9	1
6/2000 Black	80	10	8	2

2. Do you think the future of the next generation of Americans will be better, worse or about the same as life today?

	Better	Worse	Same	DK/NA
6/1990 Total	28	36	31	4
6/1990 White	28	36	32	4
6/1990 Black	31	37	29	3
11/1991 Total	26	43	28	4
11/1991 White	25	43	30	3
11/1991 Black	34	41	20	5

	Better	Worse	Same	DK/NA
12/1992 Total	25	40	31	5
12/1992 White	25	38	32	4
12/1992 Black	23	49	22	6
2/1993 Total	22	49	22	7
2/1993 White	19	52	22	7
2/1993 Black	37	35	23	5
11/1994 Total	18	57	21	3
11/1994 White	16	59	22	3
11/1994 Black	28	52	18	2
3/1995 Total	16	58	20	6
3/1995 White	15	57	21	6
3/1995 Black	20	63	12	5
2/2000 CBS Total	44	27	27	2
2/2000 CBS White	41	27	29	3
2/2000 CBS Black	50	27	20	3
6/2000 Total	40	31	26	3
6/2000 White	39	30	28	3
6/2000 Black	44	35	17	4

Note: Before December 1992, the question was stated: "Do you think the future for the next generation of Americans will be better, or worse, or about the same as people today?"

Note: A June 1989 CBS/TBS poll found total responses as: Better— 25%; Worse—52%; Same—18%; DK/NA—5%.

3. What do you think is the single most important problem for the next generation of Americans to solve?

	Total	White	Black
Environment	12	12	2
Racism	3	2	7
Education	8	6	10
Social Security	1	2	—
Healthcare	3	3	2
War	1	2	1
Moral issues	4	5	3
Family values	3	4	2

	Total	White	Black
Economy	2	2	1
Jobs	3	3	3
Crime	9	9	13
Drugs	7	7	14
Youth crime	2	2	2
Parenting	2	2	4
Other			
DK/NA	13	13	13

4. In general, who do you think has a better chance of getting ahead in today's society—white people, black people, or do white people and black people have about an equal chance of getting ahead?

	White people	Black people	Equal	DK/NA
12/1997 Total	43	5	46	6
12/1997 Whites	39	7	49	6
12/1997 Blacks	63	1	30	7
2/2000 CBS Total	33	5	59	3
2/2000 CBS White	29	7	62	2
2/2000 CBS Black	57	—	38	5
6/2000 Total	36	6	55	4
6/2000 White	32	6	58	3
6/2000 Black	57	1	39	3

5. In order to make up for past discrimination, do you favor or oppose programs which make special efforts to help minorities get ahead?

	Favor	Oppose	DK/NA
12/1997 Total	55	39	7
12/1997 White	50	44	6
12/1997 Black	80	11	9
2/2000 CBS Total	59	32	9
2/2000 CBS White	54	36	10
2/2000 CBS Black	85	10	5
6/2000 Total	50	39	11
6/2000 White	46	44	10
6/2000 Black	76	11	12

6. Do you think race relations in the United States are generally good or generally bad?

	Generally good	Generally bad	DK/NA
5/1990 Total	41	50	8
5/1990 White	43	50	7
5/1990 Black	33	57	10
5/1992 Total	25	68	7
5/1992 White	25	67	7
5/1992 Black	20	75	·5
6/1997 Total CBS	38	52	10
6/1997 White CBS	37	53	10
6/1997 Black CBS	27	66	7
2/2000 Total CBS	52	38	10
2/2000 White CBS	56	34	10
2/2000 Black CBS	31	57	12
6/2000 Total	57	30	13
6/2000 White	58	30	12
6/2000 Black	51	40	9

7. Do you think race relations in your community are generally good or generally bad?

	Generally good	Generally bad	DK/NA
6/1997 Total CBS	72	23	5
6/1997 White CBS	72	23	5
6/1997 Black CBS	74	20	6
2/2000 Total CBS	79	17	4
2/2000 White CBS	82	14	4
2/2000 Black CBS	62	31	7
6/2000 Total	80	15	5
6/2000 White	81	14	5
6/2000 Black	72	22	6

8. Do you think race relations in your neighborhood are generally good or generally bad?

	Generally good	Generally bad	DK/NA
6/2000 Total	88	8	4
6/2000 White	88	7	4
6/2000 Black	82	14	4

9. Do you work for pay full time, work for pay part time, are you retired, or are you not working just now?

	Full-time	Part-time	Not working	Retired (vol.)	DK/NA
6/2000 Total	56	11	21	12	—
6/2000 White	55	11	23	11	—
6/2000 Black	59	10	15	16	—

10. If work either full-time or part-time: How about where you work— do you think race relations where you work are generally good or generally bad?

	Generally good	Generally bad	DK/NA
6/2000 Total	87	9	3
6/2000 White	90	6	3
6/2000 Black	71	24	5

11. Do you have any children who are school age?

	Yes	No	DK/NA
6/2000 Total	34	66	—
6/2000 White	32	68	—
6/2000 Black	45	55	—

12. If school-age children: How about where your oldest child goes to school—do you think race relations at your child's school are generally good or generally bad?

	Generally good	Generally bad	DK/NA
6/2000 Total	85	7	8
6/2000 White	87	6	7
6/2000 Black	79	9	11

13. Some people say that since the 1960s there has been a lot of real progress in getting rid of racial discrimination against blacks. Others say that there hasn't been much real progress for blacks over that time. Which do you agree with more? Would you say there's been a lot of real progress getting rid of racial discrimination or hasn't there been much real progress?

	Progress	No real progress	DK/NA
5/1992 Total	50	46	4
5/1992 White	53	43	· 4
5/1992 Black	29	68	3
6/1997 Total CBS	61	34	5
6/1997 White CBS	62	31	7
6/1997 Black CBS	52	46	2
2/2000 Total CBS	71	26	3
2/2000 White CBS	74	23	3
2/2000 Black CBS	55	43	2
6/2000 Total	74	22	4
6/2000 White	78	18	4
6/2000 Black	58	39	3

14. What about for other minority groups? Would you say there's been a lot of real progress getting rid of discrimination or hasn't there been much real progress?

	Progress	No real progress	DK/NA
6/2000 Total	57	33	10
6/2000 White	58	32	10
6/2000 Black	48	40	12

15. How important do you think improving race relations is to the future of the United States—do you think it's one of the most important things we need to do for the future; or it is important, but so are other issues; or it's not that important to the future of the U.S.?

	One of most important	Important but so are other issues	Not important	DK/NA
6/1997 Total CBS	38	55	5	2
6/1997 White CBS	32	62	5	1
6/1997 Black CBS	71	26	2	1

	One of most important	Important but so are other issues	Not important	DK/NA
2/2000 Total CBS	36	58	4	2
2/2000 White CBS	29	65	4	2
2/2000 Black CBS	64	30	4	2
6/2000 Total	31	60	7	2
6/2000 White	26	65	7	2
6/2000 Black	66	29	2	2

16. These days, do you think the media talks too much about issues of race, talks too little, or talks about the right amount about issues of race?

	Too much	Too little	Right amount	DK/NA
6/2000 Total	49	15	30	6
6/2000 White	54	10	31	6
6/0000 Black	28	44	23	5

17. These days, do you think politicians talk too much about race, talk too little about race or talk about the right amount about race?

	Too much	Too little	Right amount	DK/NA
6/2000 Total	30	31	30	9
6/2000 White	33	26	32	9
6/2000 Black	11	64	19	5

18. If answer, ask: Do you think that in the long run that is good for America, bad for America, or don't you think it makes much difference one way or another?

	Good	Bad	Doesn't make difference	DK/NA
6/2000 Total	23	40	25	4
6/2000 White	24	38	25	4
6/2000 Black	20	53	18	3

19. These days, do you think ordinary people talk too much about race, too little about race, or about the right amount about race?

	Too much	Too little	Right amount	DK/NA
6/2000 Total	16	32	45	7
6/2000 White	16	29	48	7
6/2000 Black	18	49	29	3

20. If answer, ask: Do you think that in the long run that is good for America, bad for America, or don't you think it makes much difference one way or another?

	Good	Bad	Doesn't make difference	DK/NA
6/2000 Total	30	33	28	2
6/2000 White	31	31	28	2
6/2000 Black	24	48	24	1

21. How comfortable do you think most people feel when they do have conversations about race with someone of another race—very comfortable, somewhat comfortable, somewhat uncomfortable or very uncomfortable?

	Very comfortable	Somewhat comfortable	Somewhat uncomfortable	Very uncomfortable	DK/NA
6/2000 Total	8	30	44	11	7
6/2000 White	8	32	44	10	7
6/2000 Black	6	25	43	18	8

22. What about you? How comfortable do you personally feel when you have a conversation about race with someone of another race—very comfortable, somewhat comfortable, somewhat uncomfortable or very uncomfortable?

	Very comfortable	Somewhat comfortable	Somewhat uncomfortable	Very uncomfortable	DK/NA
6/2000 Total	47	33	14	4	3
6/2000 White	45	34	15	4	3
6/2000 Black	54	24	12	7	3

23. How much do you feel you know about the history of blacks in America—a lot, some, not much, or nothing at all?

	A lot	Some	Not much	Nothing at all	DK/NA
2/2000 CBS Total	27	58	13	1	1
2/2000 CBS White	24	61	14	1	—
2/2000 CBS Black	52	38	8	1	1
6/2000 Total	30	52	16	1	1
6/2000 White	28	54	16	1	—
6/2000 Black	49	40	10	1	—

24. How much black history do you think public schools in this country teach—do they teach too much, too little or about the right amount of black history?

	Too much	Too little	Right amount	DK/NA
2/2000 CBS Total	4	46	34	16
2/2000 CBS White	5	39	39	17
2/2000 CBS Black	1	85	9	5
6/2000 Total	7	44	31	18
6/2000 White	7	39	34	20
6/2000 Black	2	81	13	4

25. If school age children in q. 10: What about the school your oldest child attends? Do they teach too much, too little or about the right amount of black history?

	Too much	Too little	Right amount	DK/NA
6/2000 Total	3	40	40	15
6/2000 White	4	33	45	17
6/2000 Black	—	72	19	9

26. About how many of the people who live in the immediate area around your home are black—none, a few, about half or almost all?

	None	A few	About half	Almost all	DK/NA
2/2000 CBS Total	21	55	14	8	2
2/2000 CBS White	23	62	13	2	—
2/2000 CBS Black	1	22	26	51	—
6/2000 Total	23	54	15	7	1
6/2000 White	25	60	12	2	1
6/2000 Black	3	21	31	45	—

27. If employed either full- or part-time: About how many of the people you work with are black—none, a few, about half or almost all?

	None	A few	About half	Almost all	DK/NA
6/2000 Total	29	51	14	5	1
6/2000 White	31	52	13	4	1
6/2000 Black	5	48	29	17	—

28. Would you say you attend religious services every week, almost every week, once or twice a month, a few times a year, or never?

	Weekly	Almost weekly	Monthly	Few times a year	Never	DK/NA
6/2000 Total	31	9	15	24	20	1
6/2000 White	32	8	14	24	20	1
6/2000 Black	32	13	26	17	12	—

29. If attend religious services once a month or more: About how many of the people at your church or synagogue are black—none, a few, about half or almost all?

	None	A few	About half	Almost all	DK/NA
6/2000 Total	29	49	9	12	1
6/2000 White	34	56	7	1	2
6/2000 Black	1	8	17	73	—

30. Is the spiritual leader of your church or synagogue black or white?

	Black	White	Other (vol)	DK/NA
6/2000 Total	13	79	4	3
6/2000 White	3	91	3	4
6/2000 Black	84	12	3	2

31. If white in q. 30: How do you think most of the members of your congregation would feel about having a black spiritual leader of your church? Generally, do you think they would think of it as a good thing or a bad thing?

	Good thing	Bad thing	DK/NA
6/2000 Total	49	21	30
6/2000 White	49	22	29
6/2000 Black	71	9	20

32. If white in q. 30: And what about you? How would you feel about having a black spiritual leader of your church? Generally, do you think it would be a good thing or a bad thing?

	Good thing	Bad thing	DK/NA
6/2000 Total	73	5	22
6/2000 White	73	6	21
6/2000 Black	81	—	19

33. If black in q. 30: How do you think most of the members of your congregation would feel about having a white spiritual leader of your church? Generally, do you think they would think of it as a good thing or a bad thing?

	Good thing	Bad thing	DK/NA
6/2000 Total	54	12	34
6/2000 White	60	3	38
6/2000 Black	51	21	29

34. If black in q. 30: And what about you? How would you feel about having a white spiritual leader of your church? Generally, do you think it would be a good thing or a bad thing?

	Good thing	Bad thing	DK/NA
6/2000 Total	69	7	24
6/2000 White	70	1	30
6/2000 Black	68	12	20

35. About how many of the other customers at the places you usually go shopping, such as grocery stores or pharmacies, are black — none, a few, about half or almost all?

	None	A few	About half	Almost all	DK/NA
2/2000 Total CBS	5	58	33	4	—
2/2000 White CBS	6	61	31	2	—
2/2000 Black CBS	3	31	47	17	2
6/2000 Total	6	53	35	3	3
6/2000 White	7	56	32	2	3
6/2000 Black	3	32	52	12	1

36. Do you think most white people prefer to live in areas where most of their neighbors are white, most of their neighbors are black or don't you think most white people have a preference?

	Most white	Most black	No preference	DK/NA
6/2000 Total	69	—	19	12
6/2000 White	67	—	21	11
6/2000 Black	82	—	11	6

37. What about most white people you know personally. Do you think most of the white people you know prefer to live in areas where most of their neighbors are white, most of their neighbors are black or don't you think most of the white people you know have a preference?

	Most white	Most black	No preference	DK/NA
6/2000 Total	49	—	45	6
6/2000 White	49	—	45	6
6/2000 Black	56	1	36	7

38. What about you? Do you prefer to live in an area where most of your neighbors are white, most are black or don't you have a preference?

	Most white	Most black	No preference	DK/NA
6/2000 Total	20	1	74	4
6/2000 White	24	—	72	3
6/2000 Black	3	10	85	2

39. Do you think that no white people dislike blacks, only a few white people dislike blacks, many white people dislike blacks, or almost all white people dislike blacks?

	None	A few	About half	Almost all	DK/NA
5/1992 Total Gallup*	—	58	35	3	4
10/1995 Total Gallup*	—	58	33	3	6
6/1996 Total Gallup*	—	51	43	3	3
7/1996 Total Gallup*	—	52	40	4	4
4/1998 Total Gallup*	1	56	37	3	3
2/2000 CBS Total		68	25	2	4
2/2000 CBS White	1	71	24	2	2
2/2000 CBS Black	1	57	30	4	8
6/2000 Total	1	53	37	2	7
6/2000 White	1	52	38	1	7
6/2000 Black	—	49	39	6	6

*Note: Gallup recorded "none" as a voluntary response.

40. Do you personally know any white people who dislike blacks?

	Yes	No	DK/NA
2/2000 Total CBS	56	43	1
2/2000 White CBS	57	43	—
2/2000 Black CBS	53	43	4
6/2000 Total	56	42	1
6/2000 White	57	42	1
6/2000 Black	55	43	2

41. Do you think that no black people dislike whites, only a few black people dislike whites, many black people dislike whites, or almost all black people dislike whites?

	None	A few	About half	Almost all	DK/NA
5/1992 Total Gallup*	—	39	46	10	5
10/1995 Total Gallup*	—	39	44	10	7
6/1996 Total Gallup*	—	46	43	6	5
7/1996 Total Gallup*	—	47	40	6	7
4/1998 Total Gallup*	1	47	40	8	4
2/2000 CBS Total		55	37	3	5
2/2000 CBS White		56	36	3	5
2/2000 CBS Black		52	38	3	7
6/2000 Total		46	42	4	8
6/2000 White		46	42	3	8
6/2000 Black	1	49	43	2	5

*Note: Gallup recorded "none" as a voluntary response.

42. Do you personally know any black people who dislike whites?

	Yes	No	DK/NA
2/2000 Total CBS	41	58	1
2/2000 White CBS	36	63	1
2/2000 Black CBS	68	30	2
6/2000 Total	36	63	1
6/2000 White	31	68	1
6/2000 Black	67	32	1

43. Do you think most people have close friends of another race?

	Yes	No	DK/NA
6/2000 Total	65	29	6
6/2000 White	62	32	6
6/2000 Black	76	21	3

44. What about you? Do you have any close friends of another race?

	Yes	No	DK/NA
6/2000 Total	79	21	1
6/2000 White	76	23	1
6/2000 Black	84	16	—

Note: In 1981, a poll conducted by Yankelovich asked, "Have you ever had a close friend who was black?" The responses were: White—yes 44%; no—56%. A 1994 poll conducted by NBC News asked, "Do you have a close friend whose race is different from yours?" The responses were: Total—yes 74%; no 26%.

45. Think about the people you have socialized with outside of your home in the last month. Have you socialized in the last month with someone of another race?

	Yes	No	DK/NA
6/2000 Total	72	27	—
6/2000 White	69	31	—
6/2000 Black	84	15	—

46. Think about the people who have visited your home in the last month for social reasons. Have any of those people been of another race?

	Yes	No	DK/NA
6/2000 Total	48	50	1
6/2000 White	43	55	2
6/2000 Black	58	41	1

47. Think about the homes you have visited in the past month for social reasons. In the past month, have you visited the home of someone of another race?

	Yes	No	DK/NA
6/2000 Total	42	58	—
6/2000 White	36	64	—
6/2000 Black	56	44	—

48. In recent years, do you think too much has been made of the problems facing black people, too little has been made, or is it about right?

	Too Much	Too little	Just right	DK/NA
6/2000 Total	30	22	42	7
6/2000 White	33	18	42	7
6/2000 Black	10	51	34	6

Questions 49–53 are about the treatment of blacks in various settings in the respondent's community. The questions are based on a Gallup question asked in 1965 which read: In your opinion, how well do you think Negroes are treated in this community—the same as whites, not very well, or badly? 1965: Same 56%; Not very well 21%; Badly 3%; DK 20%.

49. Just your impression, are blacks in your community treated less fairly than whites on the job or at work?

	Yes, less fairly	No	DK/NA
2/1997 Gallup Total	18	70	12
2/1997 White Gallup	14	74	12
2/1997 Black Gallup	45	46	9
8/1998 Total Gallup	13	79	8
8/1998 White Gallup	9	83	8
8/1998 Black Gallup	42	50	8
6/2000 Total	15	69	16
6/2000 White	11	73	16
6/2000 Black	40	44	16

50. Just your impression, are blacks in your community treated less fairly than whites in neighborhood shops?

	Yes, less fairly	No	DK/NA
2/1997 Gallup Total	21	74	6
2/1997 White Gallup	18	76	6
2/1997 Black Gallup	42	53	5
8/1998 Total Gallup	14	83	3
8/1998 White Gallup	11	86	3
8/1998 Black Gallup	31	64	5
6/2000 Total	13	78	10
6/2000 White	9	82	9
6/2000 Black	34	56	10

51. Just your impression, are blacks in your community treated less fairly than whites in stores or in the shopping mall?

	Yes, less fairly	No	DK/NA
2/1997 Total Gallup	22	72	6
2/1997 White Gallup	19	76	5
2/1997 Black Gallup	46	49	5
8/1998 Total Gallup	19	77	4
8/1998 White Gallup	16	81	3
8/1998 Black Gallup	41	54	5
6/2000 Total	15	78	7
6/2000 White	10	83	7
6/2000 Black	46	48	7

52. Just your impression, are blacks in your community treated less fairly than whites in restaurants, bars, theaters, or other entertainment places?

	Yes, less fairly	No	DK/NA
2/1997 Total Gallup	20	75	5
2/1997 White Gallup	16	79	5
2/1997 Black Gallup	42	52	6
8/1998 Total Gallup	13	83	4
8/1998 White Gallup	10	86	4
8/1998 Black Gallup	34	60	6
6/2000 Total	15	78	8
6/2000 White	10	83	7
6/2000 Black	45	48	8

53. Just your impression, are blacks in your community treated less fairly than whites in dealings with the police, such as traffic accidents?

	Yes, less fairly	No	DK/NA
2/1997 Total Gallup	34	51	15
2/1997 White Gallup	30	54	16
2/1997 Black Gallup	60	33	7
8/1998 Total Gallup	33	57	10
8/1998 White Gallup	29	61	10
8/1998 Black Gallup	55	38	7
6/2000 Total	31	53	16
6/2000 White	25	58	17
6/2000 Black	66	24	9

54. Do you approve or disapprove of marriage between people of different races?

	Approve	Disapprove	DK/NA
6/2000 Total	65	26	9
6/2000 White	63	29	9
6/2000 Black	79	15	7

Note: A 1972 Gallup poll asked, "Do you approve or disapprove of marriage between whites and non-whites?" The responses were: Total—Approve 29%, Disapprove 60%, DK 11%; White—Approve 25%, Black—Approve 61%. The responses to the same question in a 1978 Gallup poll were: Total—Approve 36%, Disapprove 54%, DK 10%. In 1991, Gallup changed the wording of the question to "Do you approve or disapprove of marriage between blacks and whites?" The responses were: Total—Approve 48%, Disapprove 42%, DK 10%.

55. If your political party nominated a black for president, would you vote for that person if he or she were qualified for the job?

	Yes	No	No party (vol.)	DK/NA
1994 Gen. Soc. Survey	88	9	—	3
2/2000 Total CBS	94	3	—	3
2/2000 White CBS	94	4	—	2
2/2000 Black CBS	96	2	—	2
6/2000 Total	93	3	—	4
6/2000 White	93	3	—	4
6/2000 Black	95	2	—	2

56. Do you think America is ready to elect a black president, or not?

	Yes	No	Depends (vol.)	DK/NA
10/1996E	46	43	5	6
2/2000 Total CBS	37	52	4	7
2/2000 White CBS	36	53	4	7
2/2000 Black CBS	27	66	2	5
6/2000 Total	33	56	4	7
6/2000 White	34	55	4	7
6/2000 Black	32	62	1	6

57. Thinking about black teachers, would you say that there should be more, should be fewer, or is the number about right?

	More	Fewer	About right	DK/NA
2/2000 Total CBS	48	1	28	23
2/2000 White CBS	44	1	29	26
2/2000 Black CBS	67	1	21	11
6/2000 Total	46	1	33	21
6/2000 White	42	1	34	23
6/2000 Black	67	1	26	7

58. Thinking about black professional sports players, would you say that there should be more, should be fewer, or is the number about right?

	More	Fewer	About right	DK/NA
2/2000 Total CBS	5	14	69	12
2/2000 White CBS	2	16	67	15
2/2000 Black CBS	18	4	69	9
6/2000 Total	5	15	67	13
6/2000 White	3	17	65	15
6/2000 Black	14	7	73	6

59. Thinking about black businesspeople who head large companies, would you say that there should be more, should be fewer, or is the number about right?

	More	Fewer	About right	DK/NA
2/2000 Total CBS	54	1	27	18
2/2000 White CBS	47	1	31	21
2/2000 Black CBS	90	—	6	4
6/2000 Total	50	1	31	17
6/2000 White	44	1	35	20
6/2000 Black	89	1	8	3

6o. Thinking about black medical doctors, would you say that there should be more, should be fewer, or is the number about right?

	More	Fewer	About right	DK/NA
2/2000 Total CBS	59	—	24	17
2/2000 White CBS	53	—	26	21
2/2000 Black CBS	84	1	11	4
6/2000 Total	54	—	29	17
6/2000 White	49	—	32	19
6/2000 Black	87	—	10	3

61. Thinking about black sports coaches and team executives, would you say that there should be more, should be fewer, or is the number about right?

	More	Fewer	About right	DK/NA
2/2000 Total CBS	43	1	37	19
2/2000 White CBS	35	1	42	22
2/2000 Black CBS	76	1	16	7
6/2000 Total	42	1	39	18
6/2000 White	37	1	43	19
6/2000 Black	74	1	20	6

62. On another subject, if you had some trouble with the police—a traffic violation maybe, or being accused of a minor offense—do you think that most likely you would be given a harder time than other people, would be treated about the same as anyone else, or would be treated a little better than most people?

	Harder	Same	Better	DK/NA
4/1991 Total	9	77	10	4
4/1991 White	6	80	11	4
4/1991 Black	28	62	4	6
9/1995 Total CBS	10	78	9	3
9/1995 White CBS	5	82	10	2
9/1995 Black CBS	28	57	7	9
2/2000 Total CBS	12	76	8	4
2/2000 White CBS	4	84	9	3
2/2000 Black CBS	52	37	3	8
6/2000 Total	10	74	12	4
6/2000 White	5	78	14	3
6/2000 Black	45	43	4	7

63. Some people say the police don't show respect for people, or they use insulting language. Has this ever happened to you?

	Yes	No	DK/NA
4/1991 Total	18	82	1
4/1991 White	16	83	1
4/1991 Black	28	72	—
9/1995 Total CBS	18	82	—
9/1995 White CBS	17	83	—
9/1995 Black CBS	24	76	—
2/2000 Total CBS	24	76	—
2/2000 White CBS	21	79	—
2/2000 Black CBS	36	64	—
6/2000 Total	22	78	1
6/2000 White	18	81	1
6/2000 Black	32	68	—

64. Do you generally think of the police as friends, more as enemies, or don't you think of them in either of these ways?

	Friends	Enemies	Neither	DK/NA
4/1991 Total	56	3	38	3
4/1991 White	60	2	36	2
4/1991 Black	37	10	45	7
9/1995 Total CBS	50	4	43	3
9/1995 White CBS	55	3	38	3
9/1995 Black CBS	30	7	57	6
2/2000 Total CBS	50	7	41	2
2/2000 White CBS	54	6	38	2
2/2000 Black CBS	29	15	50	6
6/2000 Total	47	8	41	4
6/2000 White	52	6	39	3
6/2000 Black	27	16	51	5

65. Do you think the police in most big cities are generally tougher on whites than on blacks, or tougher on blacks than on whites, or do the police treat them both the same?

	Tougher on whites	Tougher on blacks	Same	DK/NA
4/1991	—	51	34	15
9/1995 CBS	2	56	30	12
2/2000 Total CBS	—	56	31	13
2/2000 White CBS	—	53	33	14
2/2000 Black CBS	—	78	13	9
6/2000 Total	1	56	27	16
6/2000 White	1	53	29	17
6/2000 Black	1	76	12	11

66. It has been reported that some police officers stop motorists of certain racial or ethnic groups because the officers believe that these groups are more likely than others to commit certain types of crimes. Do you believe that this practice, known as racial profiling, is widespread or not?

	Widespread	Not widespread	DK/NA
2/2000 Total CBS	58	31	11
2/2000 White CBS	54	34	12
2/2000 Black CBS	84	11	5
6/2000 Total	60	27	13
6/2000 White	55	30	15
6/2000 Black	84	9	8

67. Have you ever felt you were stopped by the police just because of your race or ethnic background?

	Yes	No	DK/NA
2/2000 Total CBS	10	89	1
2/2000 White CBS	4	96	—
2/2000 Black CBS	38	61	1
6/2000 Total	8	91	1
6/2000 White	3	96	1
6/2000 Black	42	57	1

68. Was there ever a specific instance when you felt discriminated against because of your race?

	Yes	No	DK/NA
2/2000 Black CBS	38	61	1
6/2000 Total	24	75	1
6/2000 White	17	83	—
6/2000 Black	62	38	—

69. If yes in q. 68 What happened?

	2/2000 Black CBS	6/2000 Total	6/2000 White	6/2000 Black
Denied employment	17	3	2	9
Refused service	15	2	1	6
General	13	3	2	5
Treated suspiciously	13	1	—	7
Falsely accused by police	8	1	—	8
Racist comments/jokes	5	1	1	1
Financial discrimination	4	1		1
Racial profiling	4	3	1	13
Discrimination in school admission	3	2	1	4
Segregated on bus/restaurant	3			
Reverse discrimination	5	6	—	
Other	7		2	6
DK/NA	8	2	1	4